TEXAS MERCHANT

Number Eleven:
Kenneth E. Montague
Series in Oil and Business History

TEXAS MERCHANT

Marvin Leonard & Fort Worth

VICTORIA BUENGER
WALTER L. BUENGER

TEXAS A&M UNIVERSITY PRESS
COLLEGE STATION

Copyright © 1998 by Victoria Buenger and Walter L. Buenger
Manufactured in the United States of America
All rights reserved

Second printing, 2008

The paper used in this book meets the minimum requirements
of the American National Standard for Permanence
of Paper for Printed Library Materials, Z39.48-1984.
Binding materials have been chosen for durability.
∞

All photographs courtesy of Martha V. Leonard unless otherwise noted.

For a complete list of books in print in this series,
see the back of the book.

Library of Congress Cataloging-in-Publication Data

Buenger, Victoria L.
    Texas merchant : Marvin Leonard and Fort Worth / Victoria Buenger,
Walter L. Buenger.
        p. cm. — (Kenneth E. Montague series in oil and business
history ; 11)
    Includes bibliographical references and index.
    ISBN 0-89096-844-6
    1. Leonard, Marvin. 2. Leonards Department Stores—History.
3. Department stores—United States—History. 4. Businesspeople—
United States—Biography. 5. Fort Worth (Tex.)—History.
I. Buenger, Walter L. (Walter Louis), 1951–   . II. Title.
III. Series.
HF5465.U6L463   1998
381'. 141'092—dc21
[b]   98-27607
   ISBN 13: 978-1-60344-054-7 (pbk.)   CIP
   ISBN 10: 1-60344-054-2 (pbk.)

FOR OUR MOTHERS,
JANICE THOMPSON BUENGER
AND
MADGE LUQUETTE

Contents

List of Illustrations	ix
Acknowledgments	xi
Introduction: Advancing Conditions and Satisfied Patrons	3

CHAPTERS

1. Patches	15
2. "Razors and Cheese," 1918–27	32
3. "Not Content to Drift," 1920s–38	61
4. My Price or No Price, 1938–48	88
5. Greater Leonards and Greater Fort Worth, 1948–60	119
6. Suburbs, the Subway, and Security, 1960–69	157
Epilogue: "His Part in Our Times"	190
Notes	199
Bibliographic Essay	229
Index	239

Illustrations

Marvin breaks ground.	*page* 5
Photo Essay: Change over Time	*beginning page* 9
Family portrait, 1901	*page* 18
Marvin with high school class	26
Produce display	44
Obie in Leonards, 1920s	48
Crowds before the big move	76
Marvin's characteristic swing	81
Marvin and Mary	84
Everybody's, late 1940s	96
E. Henderson, Obie, J. F. Norris, and Marvin	102
Marvin with Ben Hogan at Colonial	111
Children at Grand Opening	121
Escalator	125
Family portrait, 1952	147
Marvin and others at Shady Oaks	149
Subway construction	168
Aerial view of the city	176
Marvin in 1970 portrait	191

MAPS

Northeast Texas	*page* 17
Downtown Fort Worth, 1918–30	36
Colonial, 1936	80
Greater Fort Worth, 1940 and 1960	120
Shady Oaks, 1958	148
Northwest Fort Worth, 1970	181

FIGURES

Nongrocery Openings and Closings, Fort Worth, 1919–28	*page* 57
Net Profits After Bonuses	163

TABLE

The Many Faces of Leonards in the 1920s	*page* 45

Acknowledgments

We owe thanks to many people for their help and support in completing this book. Jenkins Garrett tracked down and scheduled interviews with dozens of former employees and friends of Marvin Leonard. His recollection of the store and of Marvin was deeper and broader than anyone else we talked with, and he often went to great extremes to find information we requested. Marty Leonard, Miranda Leonard, and Madelon Leonard Bradshaw talked freely with us and supported the project in many ways. Marty, in particular, gave us open access to her collection of Leonards memorabilia, family photographs, and company archival material. She graciously answered our many questions and searched for answers not readily at her fingertips. Like Jenkins she insisted that this be an accurate and complete history. Marty and Jenkins enriched this book.

Early in the project our friends Larry Hill, Bob Calvert, and Tom Born helped with the oral interviewing process. Later, Born, S. M. Duffy, and John Impson indexed many of the interviews. Duffy also helped prepare the questionnaires and spent hours on the phone encouraging folks during the follow-up process. He also thoughtfully critiqued early drafts of various chapters of the manuscript.

Several others deserve our thanks for commenting on the manuscript. John Maddux not only read and corrected the manuscript, he gave us access to numerous documents and aerial photographs in his office files. Without his help the sections on Everybody's in the 1950s and real estate in the 1960s would have been much less complete. Comments from the two anonymous readers for the Press also improved the manuscript.

Brian Linn carefully read the entire manuscript and never shied from showing us where we could improve. He helped keep our sense of humor intact while going through the long process of revising and polishing. For all that and his friendship we are grateful.

Mike Campbell, Diana Campbell, and Don Chipman offered us unfailing hospitality on our many stays in the Fort Worth area. They listened patiently to our stories of Leonards and encouraged us to keep going.

Researchers always owe a debt to the librarians who help them. We especially appreciate Ken Hopkins and his staff in the Local History division of Fort Worth Public Library. We also depended on librarians at the University of Texas at Arlington and at Texas A&M University.

Close to two hundred other people contributed to the project by participating in oral interviews or by responding to our questionnaire. Their comments and explanations added nuances to the book that we could never have gained from only using written sources.

Our family and friends have borne the ups and downs of a five-year project. They were unfailingly supportive and understanding. We appreciate and love them all the more for it. In particular, Katherine Luquette always listened with interest to new Leonards stories and patiently endured our complaints about our workload and the frustrations of completing a long project. She spent hours with our children so that we could meet various deadlines. Valeri Noles Prusha, whom we hired as a babysitter, but who became much more than that to our family also contributed greatly to our ability to complete this project. Finally, although we have received a great deal of help in writing this book, the mistakes you find are all ours.

TEXAS MERCHANT

LEONARD BROTHERS CREED

TO build a business that will never know completion, but that will progress continually to meet advancing conditions.

TO evince a knowledge of merchandise that will be authoritative to a notable degree.

TO create a personality that will be known for its strength and friendliness.

TO arrange and co-ordinate activities to the end of winning confidence by meriting it.

TO strive always to secure and maintain the satisfaction of every patron.

–The Whisper, 1929

Introduction
Advancing Conditions and Satisfied Patrons

Beginning in 1918, John Marvin Leonard, later joined by his brother Obadiah Paul "Obie" Leonard, built "one of the largest and most diversified merchandising establishments in the South." Marvin Leonard did more than sell wares. He brought the National Open Golf Tournament to Fort Worth in 1941 and devoted much time and energy to promoting and improving golf in the Southwest. Colonial Country Club, Shady Oaks Country Club, and the residential communities around them stand as testimony to Marvin's ability to bring ideas to fruition. Investments in oil, banking, insurance, and commercial real estate added to his fortune and his reputation for shrewdness. "The store," however, made all else possible for Marvin and etched the greatest mark on Fort Worth. The history of Leonards underscores the close association between downtown retailing, urban identity, and urban growth in twentieth-century America.[1]

The store went by many names. In its early years the name usually included "Leonard Brothers" and then a phrase that described the merchandise offered. By 1930, customers increasingly called it "Leonard's" or "Leonards" and eventually those names appeared in their advertising. Apparently, the apostrophe came and went according to the whims of the ad designer. "Greater Leonard's" was introduced in grand-opening advertisements for the newly enlarged store in 1948. Even though the name fit a store that covered several blocks of downtown and offered a wide range of merchandise, the public never took to it. Soon customers and the ad department reverted to "Leonards."[2]

More than twenty years after its closing, customers still fondly recall Leonards. Recollections of Toyland at Christmas, amazing bargains, theatrical promotions, and novel new product demonstrations all bring smiles. Leonards was not just their store, but the town square where they met their friends. Customers bought groceries and left them at the package stand while they shopped for farm implements, sporting goods, hardware, or clothes. Afterwards, they pulled their cars to the curb and exchanged their claim checks for their groceries. In a type of ritual, these customers now pull out shopping bags, cups, and book covers with the Leonards logo. They point to furniture purchased at Leonards, still giving good service. They brag about the only store in the world with its own private subway whisking shoppers from off-site parking, under city streets, to Leonards Downstairs Store. With tears in their eyes, they wish Leonards still existed.[3]

For some, wistfulness and tears also come when they talk of Marvin Leonard. They describe a father figure, a friend they could always count on. They remember his kindness and generosity—the time Joe Cano, the greenskeeper at his golf courses, could not afford to send his sick wife to the doctor. "Mr. Marvin" sent her to Dr. Alden Coffee's clinic and paid the bill.[4]

Others remember a man difficult to know who kept a part of himself hidden. Never gregarious, but a skilled conversationalist, he talked to men and women, rich and poor, black and white, with equal ease. After inquiring about their family, he shared a quip, a self-effacing shrug of his shoulders, and a wry smile. Yet he seldom shared his thoughts, hopes, fears, and anxieties even with his own family. Instead, he strove to protect them and secure their future. He was in control—the relaxed, efficient problem solver. He wore the best suits, ate the best food, and owned the most exclusive country club. "Mr. Marvin" liked to go first class.[5]

That phrase "Mr. Marvin" may strike a sour note with those raised outside the South of the 1890s to the 1950s, but it offers a first step toward understanding a complex personality and what that personality meant to his store and his community. "Mister" combined with the name that friends and family used had a well-understood meaning. It meant familiarity and respect, kinship and hierarchy. The Mr. Marvin or Mr. Sam [Rayburn] of countless southern towns controlled access to power, wealth, and education. They were not called "Uncle," the term children used for their family's oldest and closest male friends, white or black. Nor were they cold, impersonal centers of authority.[6]

When friends and customers referred to Leonard as "Mr. Marvin" or to his brother as "Mr. Obie" they implied more than respect. The brothers *were* the store. They created and embodied Leonards, making it familiar and personal. Customers believed they could walk in and see Mr. Marvin and Mr. Obie anytime. Employees knew that every Christmas Eve Mr. Marvin and Mr. Obie waited at the store until it closed so that they could personally thank each employee. Yet familiarity had its limits. The "mister" indicated the power and influence of the brothers and the centrality of the store in the lives of Fort Worth's citizens.[7]

Building Leonards required more than personality. It required mastering a complex industry often neglected by management scholars and historians: retailing. Continuous, incremental change defined the industry. Each day, thousands of merchants across the country sought fresh means to appeal to fickle customers. They scoured the trade journals for ideas and turned to their suppliers for alluring

Marvin Leonard supported a wide range of charities. Here, with his typical smile, he breaks ground for the new Lena Pope Home in 1950.

merchandise and news of trends. Most importantly, they watched their competitors closely. In this fishbowl atmosphere, promotions, layout, merchandising techniques, and lines of merchandise that worked in one store soon appeared elsewhere.[8]

Success in retailing, particularly outside the largest metropolitan areas, required imitation and continuous adaptation. Even the most innovative stores followed more than they led, and Leonards frequently adopted ideas pioneered by other stores. It did not add a self-service option to its grocery department until more than a decade after Piggly Wiggly brought the practice to Fort Worth. It first used mannequins to display clothing and installed escalators in 1946, fifty years after their introduction in major department stores in New York, Chicago, Boston, and Philadelphia. Even Leonards' well-publicized policy of accepting all returns without question was standard procedure among retailers when Leonards began the practice in 1918.[9]

Yet, as Marvin Leonard's career demonstrated, emulating effective techniques was not enough. Profits also grew from evaluating each new opportunity and adopting practices that best suited the store's situation and its customers. Not every innovation was right for every store at every time. Marvin's sense of the correct fit between his store and his customer base was proven time and again as the enterprise grew from a twenty-five-foot storefront in 1918 to a massive store sprawling over six and one-half blocks of downtown and boasting its own subway in 1963. Within the open-air atmosphere of retailing, Marvin and Obie created not only a store appropriate to their city and their customers, but a unique place to shop—a place that by 1948 offered a stunning assortment of goods. Where else could you buy a fur coat and a can of tuna, a piano and a tractor?

This one-stop shopping center succeeded in part because the brothers mastered complementary spheres of activity. Marvin knew what would sell and possessed an instinct for the spectacular and memorable. Grand fireworks displays and Leonards scrip issued in 1933 when currency was scarce fixed the image of Leonards as the friend of the working folk in the public mind. Obie supplied mastery of the physical layout of the store—the ability to propel goods and people through the store. Moving delicious-smelling bread from the top-floor bakery to the grocery with an ingenious conveyor system lowered the cost of bread and added to Leonards' image as a fun place to shop.[10]

Marvin, in particular, gave the store its focus—an enduring commitment to large volume, low markup, quick turnover, and the everyday people of Fort Worth. He evaluated every potential new method or new department with that focus in mind. By remaining true to this center, he guaranteed the store a broad and loyal customer base. Like dime store magnates F. W. Woolworth and S. S. Kress, Marvin Leonard gave common folk entry into the world of consumption that glittered around them. He offered less-affluent customers the thrill of hunting for a bargain and buying small luxuries.[11]

Low prices were the foundation of Leonards' mass appeal. From the first years when he primarily dealt in railroad salvage and bankrupt grocery stock, Marvin built close ties between suppliers and his store. He worked for the best possible price by paying quickly and buying in large quantities, and he taught his brother and his buyers to do the same. He avoided the cost of storage by pricing goods attractively. Profit came from high volume, not high markups. Marvin told his managers, "Better a fast nickel than a slow dime." He went on to explain how to make a profit from thread: "You don't make much per item, but you sell a lot of it."[12]

Low prices, a unique combination of goods, a clear focus, an efficient division of responsibility, and intelligent emulation of competitors were not enough to bring success over the long history of Leonards. Marvin also adjusted and experimented with the management, structure, and image of his business. In the process, Marvin, with the help of his brother, made and remade the store.

From its founding in 1918 until about 1938, Leonards resembled a cash-only general store, an ever-larger version of the progressive stores Marvin observed in Northeast Texas on the eve of World War I. Fort Worth served one of the largest trade areas in the United States, and the general store's familiarity appealed to rural customers. As Leonards grew in the 1920s and 1930s, however, Marvin and Obie adopted many management practices typical of large department stores.

After 1938, the store, even with its emphasis on groceries and hard goods, increasingly resembled a modern department store. While Leonards retained some flavor of an old-time general store that stressed price and looked familiar to rural folk, by the 1948 expansion Leonards' managerial system and emphasis on fashion and selection mirrored mid-priced department stores across the country. Leonards, however, was far larger than its competitors and offered a much more diverse product line.

After 1948, the store rambled over and under the streets of Fort Worth, and each area of the store took on a more distinct personality. By the early 1950s, greater scale made controlling diverse divisions and an increased number of employees difficult. As he had in the past, Marvin took a pragmatic look at how other retailers handled these problems. He hired top-level managers with experience at Montgomery Wards and other chain stores. The regimented structure they brought with them increasingly determined strategy.[13]

Chain store structure required a larger bureaucracy to control costs, and that bureaucracy eventually reduced Leonards' flexibility and inflated its traditionally low expenses. As costs and then prices edged up, a new merchandising strategy emerged. "You Can Find It at Leonards" joined "More Merchandise for Less Money" in store advertisements in the 1950s. By 1960, selection replaced price as the store's greatest strength.[14]

The necessary balance between maintaining low prices and adjusting to new conditions would have ended decades earlier except that Marvin achieved "hands on management without touching." He gave department and division managers great autonomy, but he also instilled loyalty and commitment. Managers learned to think like him and sought to make a profit for him. At the same time chain store methods brought greater bureaucracy, Marvin and Obie's advancing age, their growing interests in other businesses, and their desire to pass the reins of management on to the next generation of Leonards reduced their daily involvement in the store. Committees and memos gradually replaced the highly personal managerial techniques of the past. Obie's construction in 1963 of a subway that connected the store with off-site parking was the brothers' last grand gesture.[15]

The close identification between the institution and its owners makes a history of the store a biography of the Leonard brothers. In particular, it is a biography of Marvin Leonard, the majority stockholder and founder who defined the store and always reserved the right to have the last say. Yet you cannot separate Marvin, his store, and other businesses from Fort Worth's history. In Leonards' first two years of business the city's population and economy grew at staggering rates. That boom hid mistakes and allowed Marvin time to build up a business. In the years that followed, meeting advancing conditions meant more than adapting to business trends. It meant reacting to Fort Worth's evolving competitive conditions, economic ups and downs, and growing suburbs. In the 1920s and again in the 1950s, Fort Worth's growth drew large-scale grocery chains and other national retailers to town. Suburban growth in the 1950s and the construction of suburban shopping malls in the 1960s threatened all downtown retailers. For a time, Leonards and its subway postponed the decay of downtown by supplying easy access for shoppers. But in the 1970s, like so many other downtown department stores, Leonards vanished.

Before vanishing, Marvin Leonard and his store played major roles in adapting Fort Worth retailing to the city's changing human landscape and helped create a unique identity for the city. In that sense, Marvin was a creative pioneer. In 1918, the city was an overgrown country town and Leonards was easily overlooked. By the late 1920s, farm folk came to Leonards first on Saturday. Oil, construction, railroading, and meat packing added a large working class to the city, and Leonards became the blue-collar store of a hard-working city. During the Great Depression, Leonards offered low prices for everyone, solutions to the problems brought by economic collapse, and a colorful diversion. Fort Worth and Leonards were still fun. From the beginning, both blacks and whites shopped at the store, but the black population in the city's center increased dramatically after the start of World War II. Thanks in part to the leadership of Leonards, Fort Worth desegregated faster and was a little less scarred by its Jim Crow past than many other southern cities. In these and numerous other ways, Marvin and his store earned customer loyalty while defining the nature of the community.

Fort Worth shaped Marvin and Leonards. He ran his business to make a profit, not to lift up the masses. Yet customers do not keep a shopping bag from a long-dead store without reason. Marvin Leonard and his store gave something to the community that went beyond more merchandise for less money. They gave opportunity and identity.

Change over Time

Leonards interior, 1918. Marvin, with his sleeves rolled up and wearing his apron, poses in the middle of his few employees.

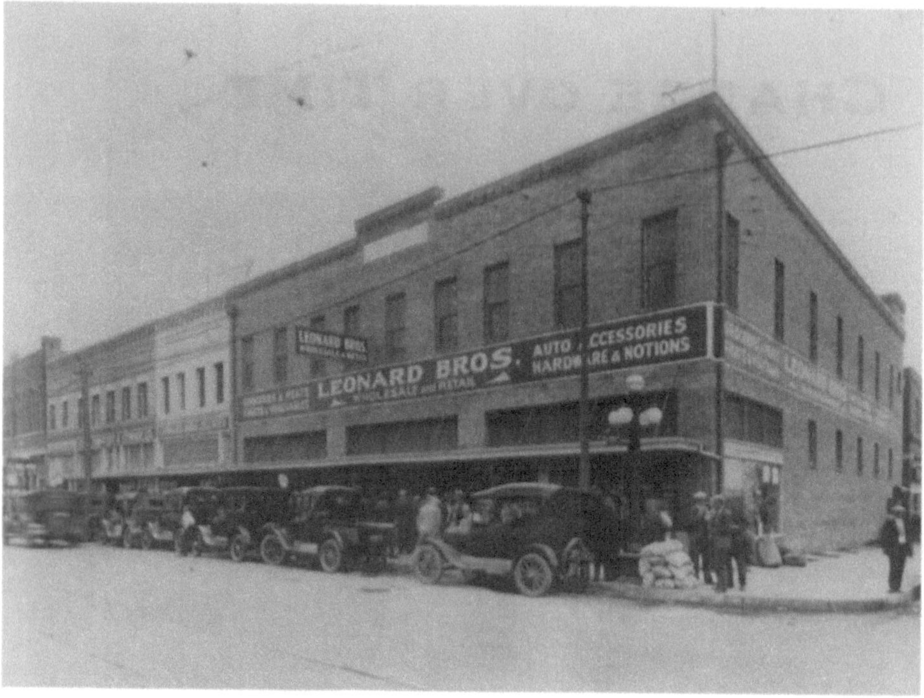
LEONARD BROS.
HARDWARE & NOTIONS

1934
Santa Claus

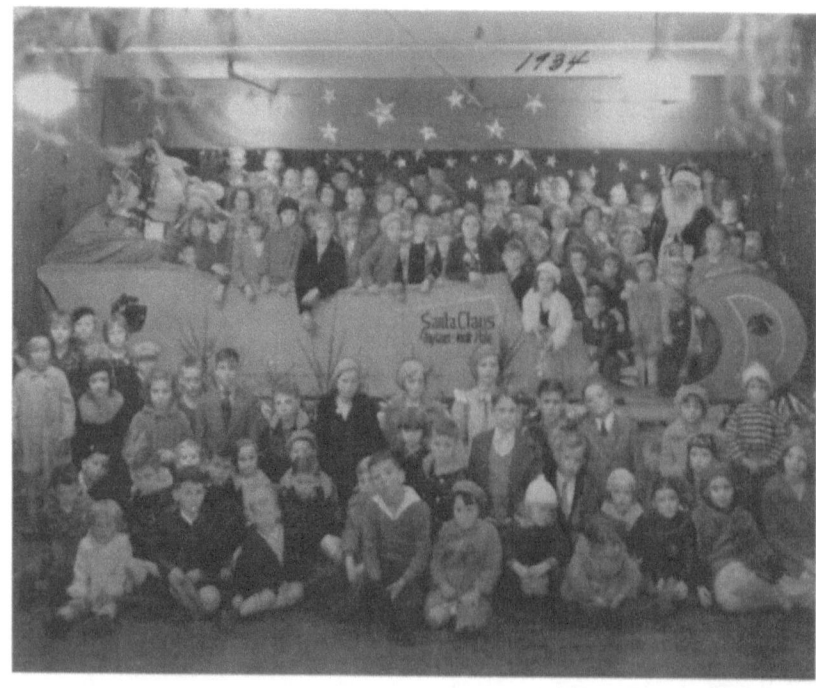

Leonards interior, 1940. New air-conditioning ducts and vents, added during the expansion in the late 1930s, can be seen above the busy meat counter.

(opposite, above) Leonards exterior, 1926. By 1926 Leonards filled about half of the block, and customers pulled their cars up to the curb to haul off their purchases.

(opposite, below) Toyland, 1934. By the time Leonards moved to a new building in 1930, Toyland had become a Christmas institution in Fort Worth.

Leonards exterior, 1948. This shot shows how the 1930 building was connected to the new five-story Food Store above First Street.

Leonards interior, 1950s. During the 1950s Leonards drew large crowds to its special promotions, as at this Fall Sale.

Leonards interior, 1963. During the grand opening of the subway and the new Home Store, invited guests exit from their first subway ride.

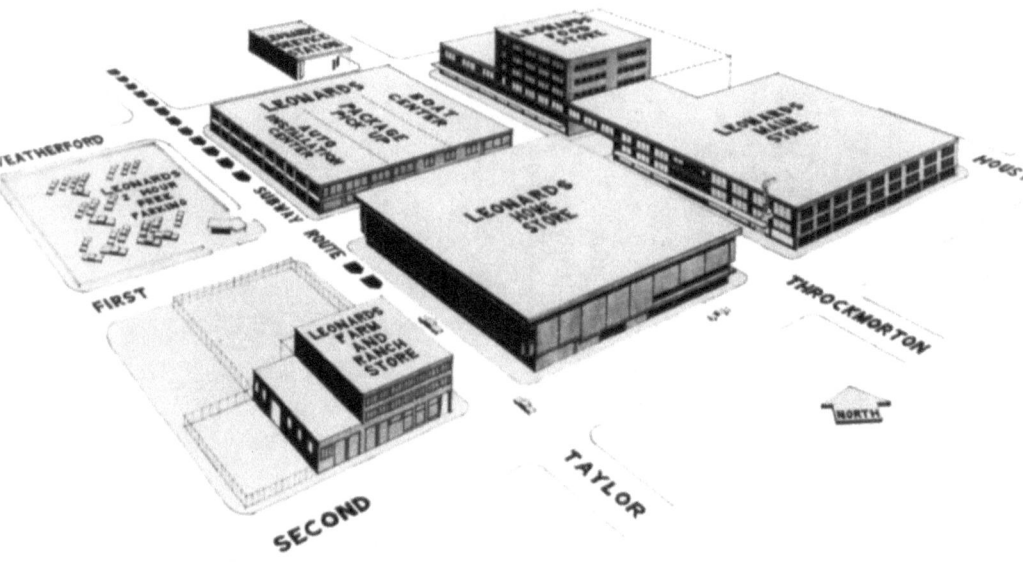

Subway and full store layout, 1963. By 1963 Leonards sprawled over and under parts of seven blocks of downtown Fort Worth.

Patches

When Marvin Leonard died on August 26, 1970, Fort Worth lost one of its most respected citizens. Praised for his marketing genius, his common touch, and his vision, Marvin Leonard appeared larger than life. As he told the story, his childhood schoolmates called him "Patches" because his frugal mother patched his clothes so many times. For admirers, these humble roots that he shared with his brother and long-time partner Obie were the start of a rags-to-riches story. Two poor farm boys moved to the city and achieved success through hard work, native cleverness, and perseverance. As was said of him a few years before his death, "Starting with little more than vision and faith in the American dream, Marvin Leonard rose from farm boy to prominence in many business enterprises including oil, insurance, banking, real estate, building and retailing." At his death, an editorial in the *Fort Worth Press* summed up the popular opinion of Leonard: "His was the true Horatio Alger story, the hard-working rugged individualist who made his mark despite any and all obstacles."[1]

Yet the "patches"-to-riches myth was more myth than reality. Certainly a grain of truth flavors the Leonard legend. Marvin came to Fort Worth, a young outsider from rural Northeast Texas, and quickly rose in affluence and power. Few would select Linden, Texas, as an incubator of such success. There, on a farm just outside town, John Marvin Leonard was born February 10, 1895.[2]

Marvin's family, however, was not poor by local standards. They did not fit William Humphrey's description of his paternal grandfather in nearby Red River County who "would contract with a landowner to farm on shares, fifty-fifty, by the year. When his disappointing crop was gathered, they would pack their few belongings in the wagon and hitch the team to it and move." In contrast to a life that robbed children of hope, Linden and his family gave Marvin stability, a decent education, and the belief that he could and should be a success. His clothes were neatly mended, not tattered. Those cloth patches did not translate into patches on his ambition. Instead, they were symbols of a stubborn insistence that he and his family could rise in the world if they could just save enough money.[3]

LINDEN

Marvin was born in hard times. Despite being the county seat of Cass County, Linden's population slipped from 444 in 1890 to 316 in 1900. Buffeted by a nationwide depression and afflicted with stagnant cotton prices, tenant farming increased dramatically. By 1900, 40 percent of Cass County farmers grew their crops on someone else's land.[4]

Located in Northeast Texas, the eastern border of Cass County touches both Arkansas and Louisiana, and the county was as typical of those states as of Texas. Before 1900 virgin stands of shortleaf pine covered the uplands. In lower-lying areas, oak, hickory, walnut, ash, and sweetgum grew so tall that they blocked out the sun. Where water stood, cypress and black gum dominated the landscape. Much of the upland was moderately fertile sandy loam with a clay sub-soil. Near the creeks, bayous, and rivers, more-fertile alluvial soils predominated. As in the neighboring states, about 40 percent of the people on the land were black. The other 60 percent were almost entirely white, native-born southerners. In 1910, when the county's population reached 27,587, fewer than a hundred residents were foreign-born or had foreign-born parents.[5]

Ties to the South extended beyond the land and the people. Marvin and Obie Leonard's childhood was spent in a world where, as the *Texas Almanac* put it in 1904, "Cotton is almost as necessary to the human family as bread."[6] Production soared as the expansion of railroads opened new regions for the crop. When prices were good and the volume of the crop high, prosperity and optimism reigned. From the end of the Civil War to 1900, however, the price seldom remained high for long. Those who had expanded production of cotton in good times found it difficult to repay their loans in bad times and were often forced to sell their land. Even those who kept their land had trouble helping their children acquire farmland. Much of Northeast Texas filled with southerners trying to escape the fall into tenancy by moving to a new region where land was generally less expensive and more productive. Some succeeded. Many failed.[7]

Prosperity did not elude all southerners. In the 1880s, small towns like Linden grew as control of the cotton trade shifted from distant cotton factors in Memphis, New Orleans, and Galveston to small-town merchants. Much of this change derived from the expansion of railroads and a credit system into the southern countryside. Staples came in over the railroads. Cotton purchased from farmers went out the same way. Taking advantage of this transformation, merchants lent cotton farmers capital to expand production and supplied staple goods on credit until the fall harvest. In return, most customers sold or traded their cotton to these merchants.[8]

Marvin and Obie's father, Obadiah John Thomas Leonard, aspired to be one of these merchants. John Leonard, born in Georgia in 1853, and his wife, Emma

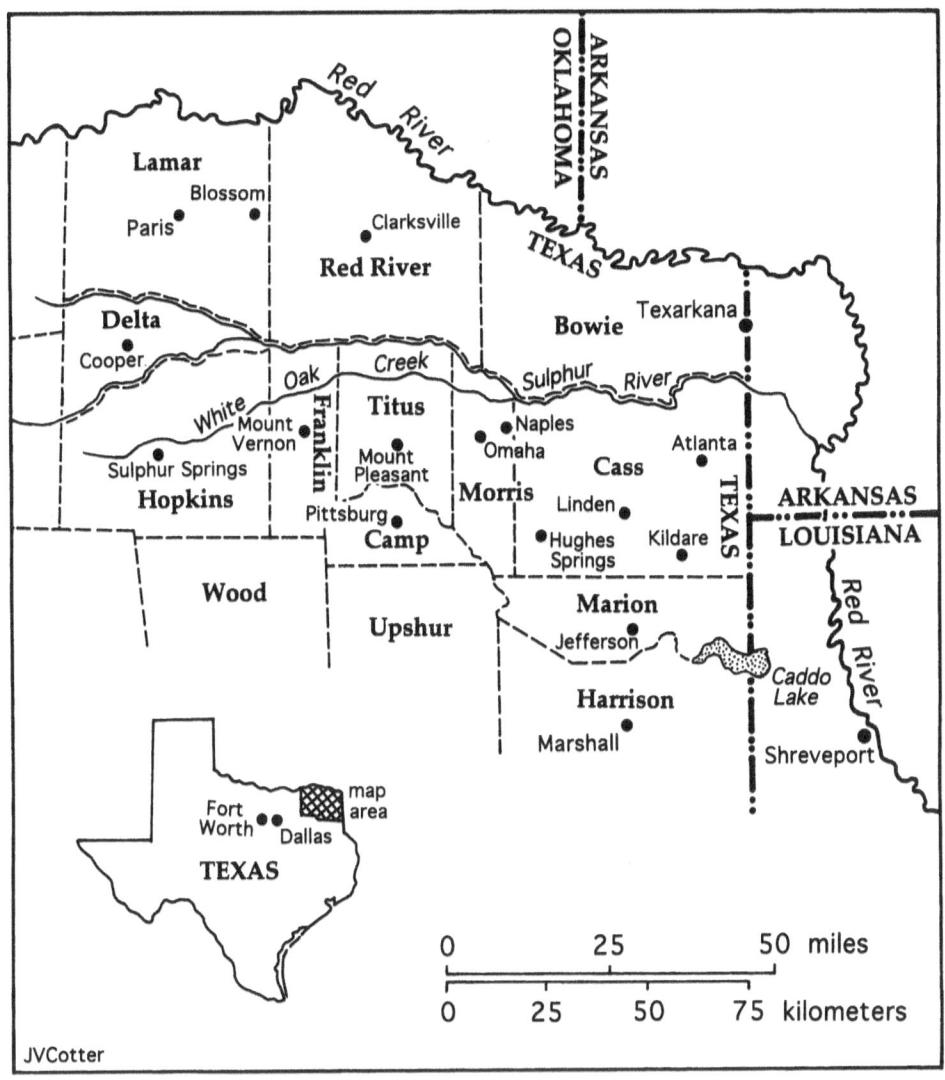

Northeast Texas. *Map by John V. Cotter.*

Clementine (Tiny) Hill, born in Alabama in 1856, were among the vast numbers of southerners who sought to rebuild their lives in Texas. Both came to Texas with their parents soon after the Civil War and settled near Kildare, southeast of Linden in Cass County. Like most Northeast Texans, their parents farmed. Tiny Hill married John Leonard in 1876. The young couple emulated their parents on a small neighboring farm. Their first child, Martha Ann, was born in 1878 and within ten years they had five children. Green Thomas was born in 1880 and Cora Suvelia August 9 in 1883. Laura Maranda joined the family in 1885 and Byrdie Clementine in 1888.[9]

Family portrait, 1901. From left: Cora, Obie, O. J. T., Enola, Tom, Marvin, Emma Clementine, Laura, and Byrd. Marvin's mother is holding a picture of her firstborn child, Martha Ann Harrison, who died July 25, 1900.

Despite raising a large family, John and Tiny avoided the trap that snared so many others. They carefully saved money and avoided debt so they could pursue their dream of owning a store. In the late 1880s they sold their farm, moved their family to Linden, and started a business, John Leonard, Dealer in General Merchandise. They probably moved when the Kildare and Linden Railroad, a narrow-gauge, short line that hauled lumber and offered limited common-carrier services, opened in 1889.[10]

Linden offered little competition and inexpensive entry into retailing. Unfortunately, John Leonard did not foresee the economic downturn that began even before the severe Depression of 1893. He also overestimated the impact the Kildare and Linden would have on the local economy. At best passengers and freight faced expensive and inconvenient changeovers and delays. At worst its narrow gauge and shaky finances meant it offered only irregular freight service. It soon folded, leaving Linden without rail connections to the outside world until 1911. That was why Linden had few merchants.[11]

Without a railroad, merchants paid more for incoming goods and had to offer lower than market prices for cotton because of the added cost of hauling freight to and from the terminus in wagons. More-affluent customers, who purchased staples and sold cotton on a larger scale, went a few extra miles to do business with the merchants of Hughes Springs, Daingerfield, Jefferson, or Atlanta, all towns on the Texas & Pacific or Missouri, Kansas & Texas railroads. That left John Leonard with more-marginal customers who lacked the means to go to nearby towns. When cotton prices turned down, they were unable or unwilling to pay their debts. By the start of the Depression of 1893, John Leonard had gone back to farming full time. He blamed his lack of success on those who failed to pay their debts, but his timing in entering business was poor and he underestimated the importance of the railroad. His son Marvin would have better timing in starting his business and a better understanding of railroads.[12]

During the years they ran a store in Linden, no children were born to the Leonards, but between 1892 and 1898 Tiny gave birth to five more children, a second family. Twins born on January 25, 1894, died at birth. The other three survived the dangers of a nineteenth-century childhood and later moved to Fort Worth. Emma Enola was born on April 28, 1892. Marvin came along in 1895. On September 4, 1898, Obie completed the family. All were reminded of the fragile nature of farm life, however, when the oldest sibling, Martha Ann, died at age twenty-one in the summer of 1900.[13]

Enola, Marvin, and Obie were born and spent their early years on a farm bordering the city limits of Linden. Their father purchased twenty-one acres after giving up the store, and he rented another twenty acres. In a 1983 interview, Enola remembered Marvin as "sick a great deal" when young. He twice contracted pneumonia and was a frail child. Obie, on the other hand, was exceptionally healthy. All three helped around the farm. Because they were close to town, the Leonards devoted much of their effort to truck crops, milk cows, and chickens. They sold fruit, vegetables, eggs, and milk in town or to the lumber camps near town. In the fall, cotton, sweet potatoes, and peanuts provided an infusion of cash that allowed the family to purchase shoes and clothing for the next year.[14]

Farming still depended heavily on hand labor. Mule-drawn machines aided in preparing and planting the fields, but unless the acreage was large and the farm prosperous, the machines were typically of the "walk behind" variety. Late in life Marvin still remembered the discomfort of roots and clods of dirt hitting his shins as he followed the plow. Harvesting and cultivating cotton, fruit, and most vegetables was done largely by hand. Feeding and tending chickens, cattle, and mules all required intensive labor. There were no air-conditioned cabs astride gigantic tractors or sophisticated feeding and milking machines. No wonder Obie picked up the habit of always thinking about a better machine, or that later, when he could afford it, Marvin hired labor rather than sweat himself.[15]

Social life in the Leonard family was typical of farm families of that time and place. The family went to church twice each Sunday and every Wednesday night.

They often alternated attending the Baptist and Methodist churches. Friends and neighbors gathered on the front porch of the Leonard home for singing in the summer. Guitars and mandolins played by older children provided accompaniment. The three youngest Leonards were very close companions. The two brothers slept in the same bed, and they joined their sister in games in the barn and in the fields. Enola and Obie played basketball and ran track in the public schools; Marvin hunted raccoons with his pet dog and fished. All three took pleasure in making extra money by doing odd jobs or selling the products of the farm for their parents.[16]

A few stories about the Leonards' childhood entrepreneurial ways illustrate their contribution to the family. The two boys planted potatoes two weeks earlier than their neighbors so that they could have the first crop in the spring. They sold them in nearby lumber camps to workers hungry for fresh vegetables and willing to pay a premium price. In the fall they gathered baskets of pine cones to sell to the lumber mills for fuel and cut extra firewood from the family woodlot for sale in town. All three children took eggs to a grocer in Linden, and all three heartily resented his broken promise to pay promptly once he sold the eggs. Hunting and fishing were more than sports; they put meat on the table. Enola joined the boys in the hunting and fishing expeditions. Until late in life she remained a crack shot and enthusiastic angler. The help of the children kept the larder full and the family out of debt.[17]

Staying out of debt was crucial to the family's increased prosperity. Conditions improved for some in Cass County after the late 1890s. Lumber companies built short-line railroads throughout the region and began harvesting the virgin timber, creating jobs and a market for those like the Leonards who sold supplies to the lumbermen. Cotton prices crept upward and stayed at a more consistent level. After 1900, population grew in the county and in the precinct that contained Linden. Yet every dip in cotton prices drove less efficient and indebted farmers into tenancy. Every rise in cotton prices pushed land prices further from the reach of young farmers. By 1910, tenants increased to about 45 percent of all Cass County farmers.[18]

Unlike the majority of small-scale farmers, John and Tiny Leonard bought land in these perilous but promising times. In about 1903, they purchased a hundred-acre farm a mile and a half from Linden. Witnessing the effect of indebtedness on other farmers reinforced John Leonard's reluctance to use credit. He paid cash for the farm. Given the depressed economy of the mid-1890s and the small size of their farm, that level of savings testified to the family's thrift and hard work. Making the purchase when they did demonstrated good business sense. Farmland doubled in value from 1900 to 1910.[19]

Ownership of a hundred acres also put Marvin's parents squarely in the middle class of rural Cass County. As more farmers became landless tenants, the Leonards acquired land. Their acres did not number in the thousands. No tenants and few hands worked for them. Yet at a time when, with the best mules and equipment, a family was hard pressed to raise more than forty acres of cotton a year, a hundred acres divided between cotton, other crops, a woodlot, and pasture was all a family could work without additional labor. John and Tiny Leonard owned land and valued their independence. Debt was their enemy not just because it hurt their pocketbook, but because creditors forced farmers to raise cotton, the most familiar cash crop. Debt forced farmers into dependency upon the whims of the cotton market instead of allowing them to raise their own food or experiment with potentially more profitable crops. In contrast, the Leonards practiced a mixed form of agriculture, supplemented by hunting and seasonal work off the farm. They retained a measure of control over their lives. Their ability to save and their experience as storekeepers further separated them from the majority of farmers in Cass County. Marvin and Obie Leonard's family was not poor, but it was frugal and lived within its means. Their parents passed on the values, outlook, lifestyle, and habits of an acquisitive, upwardly mobile middle class.[20]

Yet the Leonards' improved status came at a high cost. While Marvin Leonard loved his mother intensely and often spoke fondly of her, he seldom spoke of his father. On Sundays between the morning and evening church services the family sat in absolute silence as John read the Bible. The children's transgressions were severely punished, and as Enola remembered, "Papa was pretty hard." The same discipline, some would say the same obsession, extended to saving money. Marvin told only one story about his father. He lost a nickel between the floorboards of the porch. The nickel rolled after it hit the ground and wound up buried in the dust. John Leonard forced his son to spend the entire day looking for it. When Marvin found the coin his father had little to say except that he should never have lost it in the first place.[21]

Although she did it in a kinder way, Marvin's mother reinforced the lesson that nothing should be wasted. One night she served spinach that Marvin refused to eat. As he told his youngest daughter years later, she smiled sweetly and said, "All right, you can eat it for breakfast." Thinking she was joking, he went to bed without eating his spinach. All he got for breakfast was that same spinach, and his mother told him firmly he would get nothing more to eat until he finished it. Part of the incentive to succeed that John and Tiny Leonard gave their sons was the desire not to have to look for every nickel or to eat every bite of spinach.[22]

By 1900, leaving the life of a small-scale farmer behind required more than an elementary school education. When the younger Leonard children began their education, the Linden school had three rooms. That was a step up from nearby rural Lamar County, where the author William A. Owens went to school. There the schools had two rooms at best. Students were lumped together in crowded classes taught by overworked and inexperienced teachers. Indifferent students made a bad situation worse. Owens recalled, "I went to the little room, in something like the third grade. Miss Era, the teacher, was young and thin, and in her first year of teaching. She was having trouble with the big boys, and had little time for two more pupils. She had me share a desk with a boy sixteen years old and six feet tall. His name was Thummon and he could not read the third grade reader. Miss Era stood him in front of the room and kept him there while he spelled out each word and then said it."[23]

Most Cass County schools offered no advantage over the rural schools of Lamar County. In 1907 a local newspaper reported that the white children of the county attended school an average of only fifty-six days per year. The black children did slightly better, averaging sixty-three days per year. The editor asked, "What kind of progress can our children ever make with this amount of attendance?" He went on to comment that this meant schoolchildren attended only half the time. He called this "appalling" and pointed out, "We did last year just half as much good toward the education of our children as our school facilities made it our reasonable duty to do."[24]

At a time when most did not finish high school, Marvin got within a few months of finishing and Obie graduated from high school. Unlike tenant farmers and others lower down the social and economic ladder, the Leonard family stayed in one place, and their parents kept the boys in school. In the fall and spring they missed school to help with the harvesting and planting, but most of the time their mother and father sent them to school. According to Enola, their mother insisted that they complete their lessons each day before they began chores and play. Both mother and father could read, write, and keep books. Their children would do better. Fortunately for them, others in their community shared these values.[25]

Because it was the county seat, Linden had a small but aggressive professional class of lawyers, doctors, merchants, newspapermen, and progressive farmers determined to spend more money on education. Calls for better-trained teachers and improved facilities filled local newspapers. Early in 1908, local leaders formed the Linden Independent School District. Particularly important to the Leonard boys was the creation of a consolidated high school that drew from the surrounding countryside. Marvin and Obie did not have the best educational opportunities, but they were better than they would have been a few years earlier, and much better than if they had lived farther from the county seat.[26]

Marvin talked little of his school days. When pressed, he mentioned that arithmetic was his best subject and credited the Linden schools with giving him the analytical abilities to understand a balance sheet. Adding numbers rapidly in his head, he compared current and past performance figures. Numbers from several years back quickly came to mind, and if profit, expenses, and turnover were headed the wrong way he knew it instantly. He also picked up the habit of reading the newspaper from front to back every day. By soaking up information like a sponge, he always knew how the local economy was doing, where the best investment opportunities were, and what his competitors were doing. Conversations with bankers, lawyers, and community leaders were sprinkled with ideas and information picked up by constant reading of the newspaper. Yet throughout his life, he was reluctant to speak in public. Perhaps this was because he felt self-conscious before a generally better educated crowd, but he was also shy and disliked the limelight. Obie, three years younger than Marvin, had the advantage of receiving most of his schooling after Linden's educational reform movement began. Unlike his brother, he graduated from high school and attended a few months of college. Although not as avid a reader as Marvin, Obie enjoyed and usually did the public speaking for the brothers.[27]

Marvin and Obie Leonard did not grow up in the most progressive and prosperous community in Northeast Texas. Nearby Jefferson, Texarkana, Pittsburg, and Daingerfield all had healthier economies and better school systems. When Marvin entered the first grade, his school was much like that described by Owens. Yet as the creation of a consolidated high school indicated, Linden changed rapidly during the decade before Marvin left home in 1914. Its citizens embraced reform. Joining education on the list of reform movements were attempts at greater racial harmony, a new status for women, prohibition, a restructuring of the political system, and attempts to improve transportation. Not even a catastrophic cyclone and flood in May, 1908, slowed efforts to improve the town. Although Marvin and Enola were left with a lifelong fear of strong winds and high water, the town bounced back from the destruction of about one-third of its buildings and the loss of several lives.[28]

The decade before World War I was an age of optimistic town building. As the editor of the local newspaper stated less than a year after the cyclone, "We hear a rumbling somewhere and we hope it will develop into a mogul engine." The editor and other leading citizens were "rustling to upbuild the town of Linden and the surrounding territory."[29]

Yet the past never quite left Linden. Progress remained more a hope than a certainty. After the 1908 storm, citizens quickly began to rebuild, but city leaders left the repairing of the Confederate Monument on the town square until last. This enraged some area residents who, eyes fixed firmly on the past, demanded the immediate restoration of the town's symbol of commitment to the South's honor and heritage.[30]

Still, in some respects, the town's citizens moved beyond a southern heritage.

Chief among these efforts were attempts to improve relations between whites and blacks. Lynchings and other forms of racial violence were common in the Leonards' childhood. In nearby Jefferson whites murdered two blacks in 1897 because they refused to leave politics to white folk. In 1908 a white mob lynched six blacks in Hemphill, a few counties to the south. That same year, vigilantes took a black man from the custody of the district attorney and lynched him in Naples in adjacent Morris County. In 1909 a mob in Marshall attacked two blacks indicted for the murder of a deputy sheriff. The mob broke the blacks out of jail and lynched them. This brutal act enraged the editor of the Linden newspaper. He declared, "There may be circumstances when such conduct is justifiable, but those negroes were under indictment by a special jury, with a special court ready to try them, with no chance of escape if they are guilty of being connected with the crime. Yes it shows a spirit of savagery, and not of justice."[31]

Despite calls for reform, in 1915, at about the time Marvin Leonard left for Dallas, a mob killed two blacks in nearby Sulphur Springs following another brush with a local sheriff. After burning the body of one black victim already dead from gunshot wounds, the mob bound the other and set him afire while he was still alive. Marvin and Obie grew to manhood at a time of extreme racial violence, but it was also a time when calls for reform were common. Such calls did little good, but they surely helped make the boys aware of the ambiguous place of blacks in the South. They were necessary for a healthy economy, yet often faced intense prejudice.[32]

Women's roles were also a subject of popular debate. Echoing the words of many other progressive reformers in 1909, John Banger of the *Cass County Sun* praised women as "the redeeming glory of humanity, the sanctuary of all the virtues, the pledge of all perfect qualities of heart and head."[33] Women were seen as different from men not only in the obvious physical ways but in their basic goodness and morality. This gave them a particular role in society—the educators of the next generation in matters of the "heart and head." While believing men and women had gender-specific roles, reformers in the Cass County area still called for equality of opportunity for women. Neither physical nor moral differences should force women into a narrow range of activities. Instead Banger insisted "it is not apparent why they should not engage in masculine occupations as freely as they like." Even a decade before women could vote in Texas, some supported women candidates for the office of county clerk.[34]

Broader roles for women coincided with efforts to rebuild and reform society. Much of this effort eventually centered on the prohibition campaign. In 1911 Texans voted on statewide prohibition of the consumption and production of alcohol. By a narrow margin the prohibitionists lost. In Cass County, however, prohibitionists won 55 percent of the vote. Reform, defined by the standards of the day, was making headway in Cass County and with the Leonard family. Marvin, although fond of an occasional drink, remained an advocate of prohibition into the 1930s.[35]

Among other social reforms were efforts to improve the public appearance of Linden. Street paving, tree planting, and park construction all received attention around 1910. As with education improvements, these changes were part of a package to make Linden a more attractive place for new settlers. Civic boosters trumpeted the arrival of the Jefferson and Northwestern Railroad in 1911 as their crowning achievement. They predicted great things for Linden, and the town did begin to grow. Yet it was too late. The town moved too slowly into the railroad age and contained too many people who put Confederate monuments ahead of economic progress. Greater opportunities lay elsewhere for those willing to leave home.[36]

FROM LINDEN TO FORT WORTH

While Linden meandered into the twentieth century, Dallas and Fort Worth roared forward. In 1900 Dallas had a population of almost 43,000. Ten years later, it had more than doubled, to 92,000. Fort Worth experienced an even greater rate of growth. In the same period, its population climbed from 27,000 to more than 73,000. The early stirring of the oil industry, the arrival of new industries such as meat packing, and the westward expansion of cotton production all aided the growth of the two cities. Construction of new lines and the consolidation of older systems made the two cities railroad centers, giving their merchants access to vast trade areas and the opportunity to buy the cheapest possible goods. By 1910 Dallas and Fort Worth attracted a steady stream of rural Texans.[37]

As the pull of Dallas and Fort Worth increased, Marvin came within a few months of finishing high school. About 1912 he announced that he was quitting school. He refused to complete the requirements for graduation because, as Obie recalled, he did not want to burden the family with the expense of buying him a graduation suit. Remembering his ill health as a young child, his mother hoped that he would become a Methodist minister. Marvin did not listen, closing off opportunities in the professions that demanded formal education.[38]

Instead of graduating, Marvin hired on for fifty cents a day to drive jobbers and drummers in a horse-drawn buggy from one country store to another in Cass, Morris, and Marion Counties. Acting as wholesalers and distributors, Marvin's employers promoted a varied line of merchandise and helped merchants with displays and promotions. On the drive from retailer to retailer, these salesmen kept up a running commentary on the quality of the storekeepers. This gave Marvin an opportunity to observe and learn exactly how country stores operated. He soon understood what sold and why. He saw how merchants purchased their

Marvin with his high school class. Marvin's shoes needed shining, which may be why he put his hat over one of them, but his clothes had no patches.

goods and learned the importance of displaying merchandise in ways that appealed to the typical country customer. He observed shopping atmospheres that attracted customers and those that did not. Thus, he furthered his informal education in storekeeping begun by stories of his father's general store.[39]

Marvin's trips through rural Northeast Texas coincided with a new trend in retailing. Merchants who competed primarily on their ability to furnish credit and supplies and market cotton began to fade away even in rural areas. Increasingly, stores advertised that they did business on a cash-only basis and competed on price instead of the availability of credit. R. N. Traylor, a mercantile firm in Daingerfield with a six-county business advertised, "The advantages of this store are many. All the advantages we enjoy are yours also. Oftentimes a manufacturer gives us a special price concession to win our trade. We share this with you to gain or retain your patronage and good will. Very frequently we have the pick of style and exclusive control of patterns. This again rebounds to your advantage. How much return we can give you for your money and how much satisfaction in service, is our first thought as daily we control the methods and policies of this store." Once the automobile and improved roads made transportation easier, this type of store drove traditional merchants out of business across Northeast Texas.

Stores like J. J. Segal's in Jefferson, "the bargain center of Northeast Texas," became the model for success. By 1912 Segal's was the biggest competitor of the Linden merchants.[40]

Marvin Leonard observed the shift of rural and small-town trade away from local furnishing merchants toward higher-volume, lower-priced retail stores in larger towns. Accompanied by the trained eyes of traveling salesmen, he toured the major retail establishments of his area. He observed that merchants no longer compensated for the failure of some customers to pay their bills by high markups and steep interest rates on credit. Instead they increased their trade by cutting prices. They reduced risk by eliminating credit. Many abandoned the cotton business, leaving it to larger firms directly linked to domestic and foreign mills. Just as his father observed the birth of the small-town southern furnishing merchant, Marvin observed that system's replacement with more modern retailing methods. His Fort Worth store became the epitome of this new cash-only, price-sensitive, high-volume retailing system. In the mid-1930s, Marvin and Obie Leonard's store appeared to the writers of the Works Project Administration to be an "old-fashioned general merchandise store." In other words, Marvin modeled the look and feel of his store after the innovative stores he observed on the eve of World War I.[41]

Marvin's part-time work for traveling salesmen did not excuse him from farm chores. In the early spring he turned the soil with a mule-drawn plow to prepare for planting. When the soil warmed a bit, he planted potatoes. Later he planted corn, sweet potatoes, and then cotton. He fed and cared for the livestock—the mules so essential to agriculture and the cows and hogs that supplied meat, milk, and a little extra income. He cut, baled, and hauled hay. Once a heavy bale fell on his feet, leaving him with flat, aching feet for the rest of his life. In the June heat he hoed cotton. In the even higher temperatures of late August and September, he picked cotton. Dragging a long heavy cotton sack through the fields never evoked nostalgic memories for Marvin. Indeed, in later years he often commented that he had no desire to invest in any agricultural pursuits. Obie also recalled farmwork as difficult and frustrating. He was especially vehement about his difficulties with mules, something that helps explain why he loved automobiles and tractors. Yet Obie retained a fondness for the land. He liked the challenge of making pecan orchards and ranches turn a profit. Marvin had his fill of farming as a teenager. He was tired of "being tied down by a rake and a plow and a grubbing hoe."[42]

Marvin had reason to leave the farm but lacked an opening. The start of World War I in Europe disrupted his routine and pushed him from the farm. When war broke out in August, 1914, cotton prices fell rapidly. U.S. cotton exchanges closed for most of August and September to stop the slide in prices. By October, a panicked market offered prices almost 50 percent lower than they had been in October, 1913. Prosperous times suddenly turned for the worse. While the exact date that Marvin left remains unclear, he probably helped with the fall harvest and then departed for Dallas in November or December, 1914. The family needed his labor during harvest, but did not need another mouth to feed over the winter. While prospects on the farm looked grim, wartime demand for petroleum and manufactured goods had already quickened the pace of economic growth in Dallas. The Christmas season sparked hiring in retailing. Marvin had reason to leave and a place to go. His brother G. T. "Tom" Leonard already lived in Dallas, and it is likely that Marvin lived with him for a while. He joined the thousands of black and white Texas youths who left the farm for the city during the 1910s. Unlike his parents, opportunity for his generation lay in the city.[43]

Once in Dallas, Marvin worked as a stock boy and a clerk in a grocery store. From early until late, he swept the floors, stocked the shelves, and rang up sales. While Obie finished high school and remained on the farm, Marvin learned to weigh merchandise on a scale and how to talk to customers. He acquired, as Obie put it, "a line of chatter." He also added to the small savings he had built up by driving traveling salesmen. He may have resented looking for the nickel, but he retained the frugal habits of his youth. When he wore holes in his shoes, he cut out two pieces of cardboard and placed them in the bottom of his shoes. The calluses from those ill-fitting shoes left another painful, lasting example of frugality carried too far.[44]

Marvin learned many of the practices responsible for Leonards' early success from his Dallas employer, Mr. Gardiner. While earning $27.50 a week, Marvin absorbed the valuable lesson of how to make money in the salvage and grocery store business. Gardiner specialized in unclaimed and damaged railroad freight purchased at as low a price as possible. He turned his inventory quickly to accelerate cash flow and free storage space for more purchases. He also featured bargain items even if they fell outside his main product lines. It was from Gardiner that Marvin learned to evaluate diverse merchandise. He estimated what to pay for railroad salvage by judging what customers would pay. Gardiner also demonstrated the efficacy of displaying merchandise in bulk and attracting customers through advertising.[45]

Every morning at four o'clock Marvin met Gardiner at the rail yards to buy unclaimed freight. They began the day with a bracing shot of whiskey. Moving from the disciplined world of his childhood to the more free-wheeling world of urban retailing must have been as exhilarating as that shot of whiskey for young Marvin.[46]

Equally exhilarating was the breakneck pace of economic expansion after the American entry into World War I in 1917. By 1920 Dallas's population stood at

158,976, making it the second largest city in Texas, trailing San Antonio by only a few thousand. Fort Worth's population was 106,482. Both cities were regional hubs for the wheat, cotton, railroad, and petroleum industries. Both were also wholesale and trading centers. Dallas controlled much of the trade of East Texas and southern Oklahoma. Fort Worth wholesalers focused on West Texas and eastern New Mexico. Selection of Dallas in the 1910s as the site of the regional Federal Reserve Bank solidified its position as the leading banking and insurance center in the Southwest. Fort Worth benefited from the expansion of meat packing during the war and from the location of a General Motors plant on its eastern border. By the end of the war, thanks to the discovery of the Ranger Field in 1917 and increased demand for oil, it had more refineries and pipelines than any other Texas city.[47]

Moved by calls for citizens to do their duty, Marvin volunteered for the army. Denied service because of poor vision and bad feet, he continued working in Dallas until the fall of 1918. Then he quit his job and volunteered for Red Cross work. The war ended before he received his assignment, leaving him without a job.[48]

In the meantime, his brother Obie graduated from Linden High School and went to Texas A&M College to train for military service. War's end, November 11, 1918, found him still struggling with entrance exams at A&M. He worked for a time as a carpenter and took a course in auto mechanics. Enola worked in Dallas but returned to the farm in Linden when Tiny Leonard died on December 26, 1917. A few weeks before, when the horses pulling her wagon bolted, their mother fell and broke her hip. While bedridden she contracted pneumonia. Tiny Leonard died the day after Christmas at age sixty-one. As long as they lived, Marvin, Obie, and Enola remembered their "wonderful mother."[49]

Tiny Leonard died just before Marvin's twenty-fourth birthday. She had worked hard and enjoyed modest economic success. Her family occupied much of her time, but they never had the chance to ease her later years. Enola carried on in her mother's image—devotedly maternal, but also independent, self-assured, and competent in business. She called Marvin "Son" until he died. She had her own life, but she always looked after her brother. In future years, Marvin provided every material comfort, every possible ounce of economic security for his wife and daughters. Perhaps this was a reaction to his mother's untimely death.[50]

In his attitude toward women, as in much else, Marvin took much from Linden. In good southern fashion, Marvin Leonard's past was never past. His friend Walter Humphrey commented when Marvin died that he "didn't put on the show of a great man." His most distinctive quality was "modesty." What made him special was that people wanted to work hard for him. They did so in part because he treated them as if they all grew up together in Linden.[51]

More than country manners explains Marvin Leonard's success. In Linden and in Dallas he learned to trust his judgment. Since most people who worked for him, especially in the early decades, came from a similar background, he trusted them. Those who worked for him understood and appreciated this level of trust. Until the late 1940s, Leonards did not need elaborate bureaucratic systems to ensure employee productivity and honesty. Operating on a smaller scale allowed high levels of personal loyalty and provided all the control the store needed. Managers and clerks alike wanted to make money for him and the store.

When he opened his store in downtown Fort Worth in 1918, Marvin could take the pulse of his customers and his suppliers. He was a great observer and a quick learner. He discerned the basics of retailing before he left Linden. He learned more in Dallas. He understood what to pay for goods and how to price them to achieve rapid turnover. Like Segal's and Gardiner, he avoided credit and emphasized price, not high fashion. Salvage and special purchases offered a chance for eye-catching promotions. Shopping should be fun, because at its best that was how it was in Linden—a Saturday in town away from the toil of farm life.

Marvin Leonard seldom originated new techniques. He did not invent the practice of selling salvage or cash-only stores. He copied what worked and made it better. He adapted to changing conditions by being experimental and pragmatic. These skills also derived in part from his early experiences. He grew up in a time of rapid social and economic change, where people experimented with prohibition, fought a war in Europe, and moved from the country to the city. Trying new ideas and new techniques as long as they made sense was normal. As a boy, he sold potatoes and pine cones. As an adult, he sold dented canned goods and refrigerators. As his customers, suppliers, and competitors changed, he tried anything that offered profit. Rather than originality, Marvin's great strengths were evaluating opportunities and knowing what best fit the time and the market.[52]

Profit was the key. He intensely wanted to succeed in business. Much of this incentive came from his sense of being deprived. Leonard never experienced the true poverty and hurdles to success so obvious to William A. Owens and William Humphrey. Marvin, however, recounted only four stories from his childhood: hunting for a nickel, eating spinich, wearing patches, and not graduating from high school because he did not want his family to buy a new suit. It was not that his family could not or even would not buy him a suit. He did not want to ask them to spend the money. Instead, he pursued success, status, and financial security with a focused intensity developed in Linden.[53]

By carefully nurturing the legend of Marvin and Obie, never overplayed, never gaudy, the Leonard brothers used the "poor boys make good" overtones of their story to inspire those who worked for and shopped with them. Workers and shoppers were proud of the brothers and proud to aid their success. The story helped

Marvin forge intense personal bonds with people from a similar background. He was the head of a family, not some cold and distant boss. He was a "normal guy," not a merchant prince.[54]

Yet this use of history, of myth, obscures a more complicated and more interesting story. Marvin Leonard succeeded not despite his past, but because of his past. In keeping with his changing and rapidly evolving early years, he always adapted to his time. In the 1950s, he even moved beyond his Northeast Texas roots to make his the first fully desegregated department store in Fort Worth. In reality, the patches on his clothes were marks of a disciplined, pragmatic, goal-driven family, not dire poverty. They were an incentive to rise in the world. Combined with his "capacity for quick and wise decisions," that drive and those qualities provided wealth and status impossible to achieve on a hundred-acre farm near Linden.[55]

"Razors and Cheese," 1918–27

His plan to serve in the Red Cross scuttled by the end of fighting in Europe, Marvin Leonard looked for work. When he could find nothing that approached the $27.50 a week Gardiner paid, Marvin gathered his savings, determined to open his own store. Rather than compete with his old boss in Dallas, in November, 1918, he moved west to Fort Worth. There he found a grocer wanting to leave business and willing to sell his stock. Peddling those goods at discount prices, Marvin parlayed his small investment into a larger stake. That money together with funds from his father, brother Tom, and sister Enola was enough to rent his own retail space and stock the shelves.[1]

The new store opened for business Saturday, December 14, 1918, in the one hundred block of N. Houston Street in the morning shadow of the Tarrant County courthouse. It offered an odd assortment of bargain goods that lured customers downtown to buy "razors and cheese" or "cabbage and peas" and probably looked like an abbreviated version of Gardiner's salvage store in Dallas. Its first day's sales totaled $195.26 on $600 worth of inventory. In 1927, store sales topped $1 million.[2]

Such success required adapting to new market realities. Between 1918 and 1927, Fort Worth experienced dynamic growth interspersed with sharp, brief recessions. In good times or bad, Fort Worth's population and the population of its large trade area in West Texas spiraled up. Economic and demographic change led to equally dramatic changes in retailing. Marvin began business at a break point in the history of Fort Worth retailing. In 1918 most stores were locally owned and stressed full service and credit. During the next few years, national grocery and general retailing chains, attracted by Fort Worth's growth, entered the market, introducing self-service and lower prices to the city. In reaction, local merchants copied some of the new trends and countered others by going upscale and stressing service and credit even more. Those that did neither or could not survive the swift reversals of the local economy went out of business.

Unlike scores of other small retailers, Marvin read the market changes taking place and positioned his store for success. When others went out of business, he bought their stock and sold it at bargain prices. Instead of going upscale, he beat the national chains at the low-price game. He built his trade by appealing to blacks, workers, and farmers. Stacking merchandise high and crowding unexpected items onto cluttered counters added excitement and an element of the hunt to their shopping experience. By selling both necessities and semiluxuries at bargain prices, Marvin allowed the less affluent to share the 1920s consumer culture.[3]

Leonards began selling mostly groceries and salvage items. Before long, Marvin crowded other kinds of merchandise into his store until it defied simple classification. By 1927 its appearance and atmosphere resembled an old-fashioned general store, but behind the scenes Marvin built a more contemporary organization. By the late 1920s, Leonards operated like a modern department store, albeit one that catered to a less affluent customer than the Fort Worth emporiums established in the 1880s and 1890s.[4]

Just as Leonards moved from selling a motley and random assortment of goods to becoming a department store, Marvin moved from above the store into a highrise apartment. Family influence remained strong at Leonards, but by 1927 it was less pervasive and less constant. Success brought the opportunity for Marvin and his brother Obie to do other things. This success might not have been possible without the time to learn and the opportunity to acquire capital provided by the spectacular growth in the Fort Worth economy immediately after World War I.[5]

Fort Worth's Boom and the Birth of Leonards

Well-timed and generous rains ensured good crops for West Texas farmers in the fall of 1918, but did not interfere with oil production launched the previous year around Ranger. Fort Worth benefited from higher yields in the wheat and cotton fields and in the oil patch. Burrus, Bewley, and the city's other mills transformed the region's wheat into thousands of barrels of flour and ground sorghum and other grains into fodder. Numerous elevators stored the shipments of unmilled grain that Fort Worth track and transit dealers drew from Texas, Oklahoma, Kansas, Nebraska, Colorado, and New Mexico. Four large oil mills processed seeds from the region's ginned cotton, while the city's cotton exchange served as the largest inland cotton concentration point in the state. Good rail connections allowed Fort Worth to take full advantage of cotton's expansion westward during the war and the increasingly intensive cultivation of the nearby Blackland Prairie region.[6]

Cotton and grain dealing complemented the city's livestock market and packing houses. Close proximity to cattle producers, ample supplies of fresh water, and good rail connections attracted Armour, Swift, Fort Worth Packing, and Texas Dressed Beef to Fort Worth. These advantages and the ability of Swift and Armour to pour capital into new plants made meat packing Fort Worth's largest industry by World War I.[7] After the first packing houses opened in 1902, practically all West Texas cattle came through Fort Worth. Cattle receipts at the stockyards grew from $132,174 in 1902 to $1,384,594 in 1918. Sales of calves, hogs, sheep, horses, and mules also increased tenfold.[8]

Dealing in agricultural commodities solidified what good rail connections began: Fort Worth's strong commercial ties to a flourishing region. Fort Worth wholesalers did business as far away as Arizona and dominated the trade in much of West Texas, eastern New Mexico, and southwestern Oklahoma. By the mid-1920s, this area was one of the most dynamic rural regions in the country. Rates of population growth and land values passed those of rural counties in the eastern part of Texas as both oil and agriculture fueled growth. The city's regional prominence grew steadily so that by 1927 local wholesalers did more than $200 million in business.[9]

Oil field equipment added to the goods distributed through Fort Worth as it became the refining, distribution, and financial center for the oil industry in the western part of the state. Refining capacity jumped in large increments—first in 1912 when Gulf Oil and Pierce Oil opened units and again in 1915 when the Magnolia Petroleum refinery came on line. By 1918, all three drew from Ranger's Brewer pool, which produced $2 million worth of oil that year. Further strikes in Desdemona and Burkburnett in the fall of 1918 signaled the magnitude and richness of the region's oil deposits. Fort Worth sizzled with excitement.[10]

Each new discovery stimulated more exploration so that almost overnight Fort Worth teemed with new citizens bent on getting rich in oil or ancillary businesses. All the hotels and office buildings in town overflowed. The city's population increased by 45 percent from 1910 to 1920, and at decade's end more than thirty thousand new citizens claimed Fort Worth as their home. By the time Germany and the Allies signed an armistice on November 11, 1918, ebullient shopkeepers, merchants, oilmen, workers, and manufacturers in Fort Worth had much to celebrate.[11]

Entrepreneurs and industrialists initiated more than $1 million of construction in the first month after the end of the war. All the industries central to Fort Worth's economy—livestock and meat packing, refining, oil and gas transmission, oil field supply and brokering, cotton dealing, grain milling, agricultural storage and distribution, and the wholesale houses and railroads—geared up for growth. Swift and Armour led the way with major capital expansion plans, budgeted at $800,000 and $500,000, respectively. More than 60 percent of the oil trunk pipeline mileage in the state radiated out of Fort Worth, and weekly newspaper reports declared that construction on new refineries with their own pipeline networks would begin as materials became available. Even residential construction accelerated after the U.S. government released lumber for building purposes. Only Fort Worth's military installations (Hicks, Everman, and Benbrook Air Fields and Camp Bowie) faced an uncertain future.[12]

Fort Worth retailers shared the boom. L. G. Gilbert's ads reminded customers that it was "Fort Worth's Fastest Growing Department Store," but many others could have made similar claims. Most of the major retailers added on in the final months of 1918 or slated expansions for the following year. To make shopping more convenient, grocery stores opened branches throughout the city rather than enlarging their existing stores. New stores sprouted between, beneath, and above the major renovations and expansions. Meat markets, groceries, millinery shops, salvage stores, and unclaimed railroad freight dealers squeezed into small storefronts. Among the new signs in downtown Fort Worth was one hung in December, 1918, by two brothers drawn to the bustle of Fort Worth, Marvin and Tom Leonard. Christmas shoppers making last-minute purchases might not even have noticed their 25-by-60-foot store.

In later years, Leonards could honestly claim to sell almost everything imaginable, but at first it was more accurate to say it would sell anything vaguely related to groceries. The store's first-day inventory consisted of unclaimed freight, mostly canned goods, bought at a railroad auction. Marvin spent much of that morning pretending to sweep the sidewalk in front of the store and arranging and rearranging the tubs of merchandise bargains he had placed there. No store prospered without customers, so putting aside his natural shyness, Marvin struck up conversations with passing pedestrians. His optimism shone through as he convinced them to step inside and buy.[13]

A can of condensed milk, possibly dented, brought the first nickel into the store. The sale typified Leonards' merchandise that day and hardly portended future sales of hay harvesters, the finest silks, or 175 varieties of cheese. Distressed goods—grocery salvage, fire sale and bankrupt stock, and jobber specials—comprised the store's merchandise for the first two years. While special purchases remained important for decades, Leonards eventually became what Neil M. Clark described in the *Saturday Evening Post* as a business that dealt "in standard goods, at all price ranges, much of it nationally advertised, bought through regular channels at prices no lower than any other merchant similarly situated pay."[14]

Marvin built on the store's meager beginnings by keeping a close eye on cash flow and relying on his family. He lived in an apartment on the second floor above the store to reduce expenses. At first, his older brother, Tom, worked at the store on weekends, but three weeks after the grand opening, he quit his job with the Dallas Coffin and Casket Company to join Marvin full time. Tellingly, he kept his place in Dallas and rode the Interurban back and forth everyday for several months until he was certain the venture would last. Finally, in the spring of 1919,

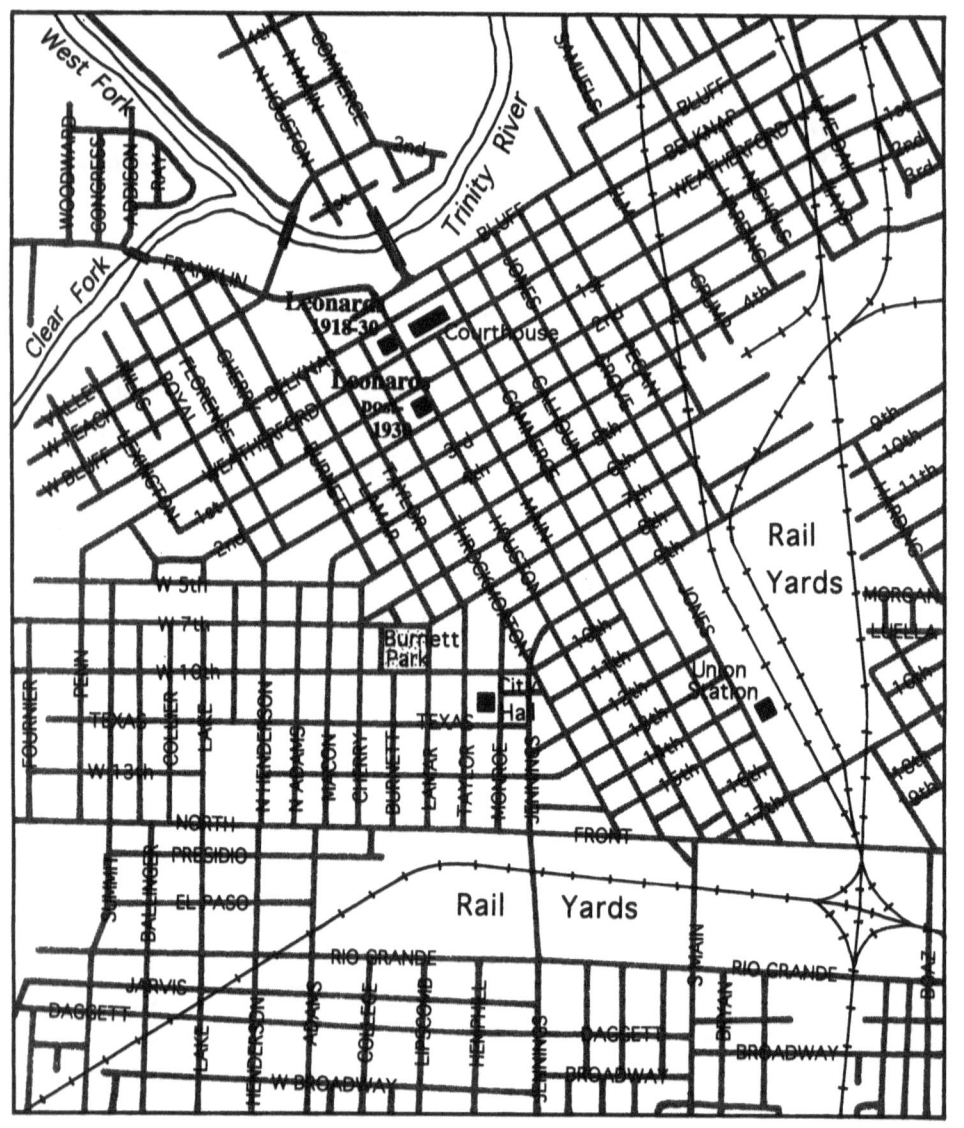

Downtown Fort Worth, 1918–30. *Map by John V. Cotter.*

Tom had enough confidence in the store's future to move his wife, Mabel, and their three children to Fort Worth. The following November, younger brother Obie moved in with Marvin above the store and joined the Leonards operation. Enola Leonard kept house for her single brothers and worked part time in the store. Mabel Leonard also pitched in at the store on high-traffic days and at inventory time. John Leonard soon made it a houseful when he came to live with his sons and daughter above the store.[15]

Leonards remained very much a family business through 1922. Father, daughter, and the two unmarried sons continued to live on the premises. The siblings purchased the merchandise, swept the store, greeted the customers, and rang up sales. They hired extra help only on Saturdays and during really busy times. In 1922, after the brothers expanded the store, the family moved to a nicer apartment on Camp Bowie Boulevard. Enola seldom worked at the store after that because her father required more care and because Leonards employed more clerks.[16]

Tom Leonard's trepidation about moving to Fort Worth and the family's frugal living arrangements and hiring practices were understandable. The oil boom had attracted crowds of merchants eager to display their goods, and many had more experience and a stronger financial footing than Marvin and Tom. Grocers representing every conceivable competitive angle served Fort Worth, and Leonards was one of many salvage stores specializing in groceries.

In 1919, more than fifty local groceries ran ads in the *Fort Worth Star-Telegram*, and fifteen companies similar to Leonards advertised discount prices on single or limited lines of merchandise, most of it war surplus. The number of war surplus purveyors dwindled after 1919, but Fort Worth's position as a railroad terminus ensured a constant flow of bargains on unclaimed and slightly damaged freight. In an attempt to combat rising inflation, even the Housewives' League of the Chamber of Commerce advertised it would sell a carload of "canned sweet corn from the doors of the freight car standing at the corner of Commerce and Seventh Street at cost price without profit." Leonards, Four States Salvage, and Dobson and Co. parlayed humble beginnings in salvage into major retailing operations. Most of the others faded away.[17]

Despite posting respectable first year's sales receipts of $76,000, thin margins kept Leonards' profit low. Business was attractive enough to lure Obie away from his mechanics job in Dallas and to provide a living for the family, but there was no extra cash for newspaper advertising. The young merchants waited almost two years, until September 19, 1920, before splurging on a newspaper ad.[18]

It was about that time and perhaps for the purpose of paying for his first ad that Marvin took the initial step in building a lasting relationship with Fort Worth National Bank. Thirty years later, Robert Ellison Harding reminisced about his first encounter with Marvin Leonard. As he remembered, Marvin walked into the bank around 1920 and came over to Harding's desk in the lobby. Harding, who was then a vice president, looked up and saw a young but confident merchant with figures in hand. Marvin energetically explained he needed a line of credit because he could not enlarge fast enough from store profits. Harding gave him what he wanted because "I knew he was a winner." Marvin would need all the resources Fort Worth National would make available because by that time, Fort Worth's grocery industry was on the verge of a revolution.[19]

THE GROCERY WARS

As Marvin recognized, founding a grocery store in Fort Worth in 1918 required few specialized assets, only a modest capital investment, and little technical know-how. Most grocers did business as they had for years. National powerhouse A&P still had a few outlets in Fort Worth in 1918 but within three years withdrew from Texas to concentrate its resources in other regions. Piggly Wiggly, the Memphis-based chain, tiptoed into the city in the summer of 1918, but had not yet blanketed Fort Worth with self-service stores and price-oriented advertising. Small, independent grocers operating in a traditional manner far outnumbered larger, more modern rivals.

Before World War I, rivalry usually played out along three dimensions in the grocery business: service, availability of credit, and location. Grocers typically emphasized full-service shopping, where customers placed orders, either in person or by phone, and relied on the grocer to select and assemble the order. Many grocers offered credit accounts to simplify phone and delivery orders. Credit was particularly important for grocers with large numbers of rural customers who had money when the crop came in, but depended on credit the rest of the year. Location counted in the strategic mix because shoppers replenished stocks frequently, and thus tended to patronize convenient locations. Credit accounts also tied shoppers to one or a few grocers, and full service created a trust relationship between the grocer and the shopper. These conditions led most people to rely primarily on their neighborhood grocer.[20]

As Marvin had observed in Northeast Texas, cash-only stores emerged as popular alternatives to credit operations between the Panic of 1907 and the end of World War I. Selling for cash simplified bookkeeping, eliminated delinquent customers, and allowed merchants to maintain or lower prices in inflationary times. Offering credit, on the other hand, forced higher overhead and linked prices to the cost of money. Frustrated customers became acutely aware of the impact of inflation and high interest rates. For a time, customers remained tied to credit merchants by habit and debt. Yet, even in rural areas, increased prosperity in the 1910s allowed customers to switch from credit to cash. As a result, customers had fewer ties to their grocer and could choose their store based on price.[21]

In Fort Worth, wartime inflation accelerated the move to cash-only stores, and wartime prosperity encouraged expansion. Turner and Dingee, Fort Worth's oldest grocery store (established in 1878) switched to a cash-based business in 1917, promising the "Best for Less for Cash." Its main rival, Sandegard's, soon adopted the practice in all but its main store. Grocers with available cash flow or access to capital also recognized the potential in expanding to several locations. At the close of the war, Turner and Dingee's sign hung on ten stores throughout the city, while Sandegard's boasted "Fifteen Economy Cash Stores." These local chains dominated Fort Worth's grocery business, but with continued prosperity and population growth came new competitors—at first a flood of small entrepreneurs and later national chains such as Piggly Wiggly, Clarence Saunders, A&P, and Helpy Selfy.[22]

At this juncture between the dominance of local chains and the arrival of national chains, Marvin Leonard began business. When Marvin rented his first selling space, four stores similar to his already operated on the same block. New grocers, mostly independents like Leonards, opened for business every week, each one trying to appeal to customers in a unique way. Unlike most of these, Leonards survived and thrived.

After 1920 Marvin adapted his store to the emerging realities of the grocery business in Fort Worth. More than anything else this meant adjusting to wild price swings and rapid changes in grocery sales volume and merchandising techniques. During the 1920s, all sectors of retailing experienced rapid growth and change mixed with sharp reversals in sales volume, but inflation and deflation hit groceries first. To complicate the roller-coaster ride further, local grocers, even more than department stores, faced intense competition from national chain stores. To adjust to these new conditions Leonards transformed itself from a tiny salvage operation into a grocery giant. Ironically, its success also led it away from groceries toward general retailing.[23]

Marvin's original retailing strategy—buying unclaimed freight and salvage stock, keeping margins slim, turning inventory quickly, featuring bargain items even if they fell outside the store's main product lines, and guaranteeing all merchandise—produced an early version of a general deep-discount store. His shrewd ability to assess and price inventory made this approach work. Marvin's intuition and practical knowledge of his customers allowed quick and accurate bidding on a diverse range of items. He instructed Obie to do the same, telling him "when you go to buy unclaimed freight, make a quick decision. If they have two cases of one item you want and a hundred cases of another, give them their price on the two cases and talk them down on the hundred."[24]

Careful buying undergirded Leonards' pricing policy. Low prices attracted customers, while a money-back guarantee lowered their risk. This combination ideally suited postwar Fort Worth. As prices across the city crept up in the summer of 1919, boosted by inflation and profiteering, Leonards and others able to secure low-cost stocks and willing to earn smaller margins attracted bargain-hunting customers and kept them when the economy turned down the following year.[25]

Marvin also recognized the importance of cultivating special ties to the railroad companies. Annual contracts with railroad companies allowed Marvin to secure a steady stream of low-priced goods, but the same contracts meant that Leonards' selection depended upon what the railroads had to offer. Marvin's first ad on September 19, 1920, highlighted the volume and price savings but also the randomness of a stocking strategy that depended on available unclaimed freight.[26]

Unclaimed Freight Sale

Beginning at 8 o'clock Tuesday morning, Sept. 21 at 111 N. Houston St. West of the Court House:

4,800 cans of No. 2 California Sun Sweet Prunes, 15 cents per can, Ready to serve seven portions.

17,200 cans of 1 lb. net Libby's Best Red Salmon, 50 cents kind, 25 cents a can.

24,000 cans of No. 3 Yellow Yams, 15 cents a can.

3,340 cans of No. 2 Tomatoes; red, ripe, hand packed, 11 cents per can.

3,120 cans of No. 2 Stringless Beans, 12½ cents per can.

1,800 gallons of Syrup, $1.00 per gallon.;

160 rolls of extra heavy Roofing, regular $5.00 selling for $3.60.

Many other things too numerous to mention. Everything sold under an absolute guarantee.

Leonard Bros. Selling Agents for Unclaimed Freight.

Marvin supplemented railroad goods with fire stocks, damaged merchandise, and later, inventory from bankrupt stores. Obie joined Marvin in searching for volume bargains offered by manufacturers on closeouts and discontinued stock. For many years, Leonards' advertising copy followed the pattern set by its first ad. Small but bold print drew readers' attention to special items, available at extremely low prices until the stock was depleted. At various times the store featured: thirty-five thousand pounds of prunes; fifty thousand pounds of chicken feed at 2.5 cents per pound; 1,740 men's collars; "spuds"; several carloads of pure sugar cane and ribbon cane syrup; pure hog lard; 7,200 packages of Jiffy-Jell; several tons of cabbage; hundreds and hundreds of pairs of women's shoes for $1.85; a carload of bananas; two carloads of oak lumber; and a special offer for razors and cheese. These items generated cash that the brothers plowed back into more inventory.

By 1921, Leonards had added enough merchandise bought through regular channels to drop the moniker Selling Agents for Unclaimed Freight and call itself a Grocery. Despite the new name, its merchandise remained a hodgepodge of branded items, railroad leftovers, and surplus. Tom, tired of trafficking in unpredictable and irregular inventories, parted with Marvin on amiable terms. He started a more traditional grocery called G.T. Leonard Grocery on the other end of Houston Street. His first ad ran May 12, 1921, and by October he was generating enough business to become a full-service, complete-line grocer. When Tom left, Obie still worked for Marvin for wages, but Marvin soon gave his younger brother a working partnership in the store. Enola also owned a small percentage of the store through the 1920s. Employees and customers alike looked forward to Enola's frequent visits to the store. Stopping to chat, perhaps to buy something, she added a note of gracious southern country hospitality to the bustle of the store.[27]

As Tom left and Obie took over as the other half of Leonard Brothers, tumultuous change rumbled through the retail grocery market in Fort Worth. By late summer, 1921, Turner and Dingee had expanded its holdings to twenty-one branches, many equipped with meat markets, and Sandegard's operated eighteen units. Their market coverage and purchasing economies afforded by expansion did not keep the national chains from marching into Fort Worth.

Piggly Wiggly, with one store when Leonards opened, had four stores in place and the promise of many more by August, 1921. Despite the recent emphasis on lower prices, Fort Worth grocers (including Marvin and Obie Leonard) still pulled groceries from their shelves and filled the market basket for their customers. Larger grocers took phone orders and delivered. In contrast, Piggly Wiggly, a cash-only, self-service store, offered nationally advertised, name-brand merchandise. The store layout also contrasted with traditional groceries, with one continuous aisle that wound through the store, ending near the front door and checkout stand. Its simple but bold advertising emphasized price, convenience, and value.[28]

Piggly Wiggly's arrival ended the dominance of traditional grocers and brought new retailing methods to Fort Worth. Sandegard's quickly abandoned credit and full-service in favor of self-service. At the same time it re-emphasized the traditional value of customer-grocer relationships. Neither Sandegard's nor Turner and Dingee lowered prices to match Piggly Wiggly. Instead, they peppered their ads with claims of "honest and true value" and "wonderful values." Both Sandegard's and Turner and Dingee reminded shoppers of their many years of successful merchandising in Fort Worth. They were "A Home Institution."[29]

About twenty-five independent grocery operators formed the Neighborhood Grocers Association to cooperate on purchasing and advertising and to present a unified position against Piggly Wiggly and other encroachers. Their ads emphasized "better prices, better merchandise, and better service."[30]

Piggly Wiggly countered in late 1921 that "the old-style grocery store cannot compete with Piggly Wiggly because they have too much overhead, and they haven't sufficient purchasing power to own merchandise at the right price which forces them to ask higher prices or go out of business." The number of grocers advertising in the *Star-Telegram* jumped as merchants tried to solidify gains made during the early oil boom and protect themselves from Piggly Wiggly's advance.[31]

Piggly Wiggly hammered away, opening nine new stores in 1922. Two local bakeries attempted to exclude the chain from their delivery routes because it consistently cut the price of bread below the bakers' recommended level. Piggly Wiggly responded by baking its own bread products, thus driving community prices down.[32]

The Neighborhood Grocers Association attracted more members in late 1922 and launched a new ad campaign in early 1923. For weeks Piggly Wiggly and the Association tossed salvos back and forth—the independents directing shoppers' attention away from "Foreign Competitors" back to hometown merchants, and Piggly Wiggly responding that such propaganda emanated from "weak sister competition" and that "nobody cries like a crybaby." The vituperation subsided after that exchange, but the ad campaigns continued well into the summer. Piggly Wiggly dedicated weekly ad space to inform shoppers of the advantages of patronizing its stores, while the Neighborhood Grocers Association did the same for its members.[33]

Despite cooperative efforts like the Neighborhood Grocers Association, most grocers could not compete with a rival that turned its inventory an average of twenty-five times each year, operated with lower than half the expenses of local establishments, and generated two to five times more volume in the same floor space. The robust economy allowed less efficient grocers time to adjust and find their competitive focus, but the basis of competition had changed permanently. In July, 1923, Sandegard's sold its entire operation to Harry J. Adams, who closed a third of its locations and modernized its procedures and policies. Early the following year, Turner and Dingee consolidated with H. H. Pittman, the second oldest grocery business in Fort Worth. Still operating under the name Turner and Dingee, the newly incorporated concern sold all but its downtown store to M-System, a local company that operated and contracted for grocers in Texas, Oklahoma, New Mexico, Kansas, North and South Carolina, Alabama, Georgia, and Florida.[34]

Marvin and Obie's first response to the grocery wars was to expand their food

Leonards was famous for selling large quantities of bananas and other produce. In the original store, Marvin stacked the produce high and let displays spill out the door and onto the sidewalk.

offerings to increase selection and volume. In the earliest days, Leonards depended on grocery customers attracted by low prices. At the end of 1921, as the grocery wars heated up, Marvin realized that sticking with unclaimed grocery freight limited the store's potential profits. He told Obie they could continue as they had and earn a satisfactory living or risk building the store into a much larger organization. With Marvin's encouragement, Obie agreed they should expand. They began by adding a meat market. Early in 1922, Marvin convinced brother Tom Leonard that if they both sold meat, they could buy jointly and gain price breaks from their suppliers.[35]

The store added produce to the mix later that year when an enterprising man suggested that he go to various vendors and buy overripe bananas and sell them in front of the store. He promised Marvin and Obie half of the profits. According to Obie, "This man would go down and buy bananas when he could find them. . . . He would stand on the front [sidewalk] and sell these and put the money in his pocket, and every night we would have a settlement for that day's business.

This worked out very successfully and for many, many years most of the overripe bananas of Fort Worth were sold at Leonards."[36] From this beginning, Marvin and Obie added other fruit and vegetable items, until they operated one of the largest produce stands in Fort Worth.

Leonards also took advantage of Piggly Wiggly's disruption of the local market that year. When Texas Co-operative Supply Co., Fort Worth's largest co-op grocery, succumbed to competitive pressure, it liquidated its entire stock at wholesale prices and offered its fixtures to the highest bidder. Marvin and Obie grabbed the inventory for cents on the dollar and sold it for a small markup. This purchase substantially expanded Leonards' standard grocery inventory, but still allowed lower prices than Piggly Wiggly. Purchases of bankrupt stock soon became a standard source of supply.[37]

It was in instances like the purchase of the entire inventory of Texas Co-operative that access to credit proved crucial. Marvin knew how to sell and he knew how to buy. Fort Worth National supplied the third key ingredient: the money to buy at the lowest price. Because of the line of credit Marvin had established at Fort Worth National and his good relationship with R. E. Harding, he had access to the capital to buy in bulk. He never forgot the bank's contribution to his success and remained its loyal supporter for decades.[38]

Marvin and Obie did not confine their special purchases to groceries. After 1922 they acquired merchandise traditionally labeled hard lines—nonfood and nontextile items—if there was profit in it. They also sought out sources of supply that allowed them to pass along low prices to their customers. This meant, as Table 1 demonstrates, that the store's identity changed continuously as the brothers found new product lines to stock and new merchandising approaches.

The move into nonfood items began gradually as buying opportunities presented themselves. During the winter of 1922–23, Marvin and Obie accumulated a small stock of used furniture and some light hardware. They rented a little more space next door, segregated the hard goods from the grocery inventory, and started merchandising those items. One clever pitch called attention to their collection of "Dressers, Beds, Springs, Mattresses, Sewing Machines, Stoves, and Refrigerators: Everything in Furniture AND Everything for the Camp at Lake Worth."[39] Shoppers unwilling to purchase used furniture for their homes might buy campware. With the onset of summer, Leonards also touted a complete line of garden tools and lawn mowers.

In the fall of 1924, Marvin extended his supply network to include manufacturers' closeouts when he bought three popular lines of merchandise at bargain prices: Bluebird Electric clothes washers, Davis rotary sewing machines, and Davis bicycles. With no room for such bulky stock in the Houston Street locale, Marvin rented a storefront next door to Sanger Brothers for the sale.

TABLE 1. THE MANY FACES OF LEONARDS IN THE 1920S

Date	Advertised Store Name
Sept. 19, 1920	Leonard Bros. Selling Agents for Unclaimed Freight
Mar. 13, 1921	Leonard Bros. Groceries
Feb. 10, 1922	Leonard Bros. Grocery and Market (added a meat market)
Oct. 22, 1922	Leonard Bros. Grocers and Traders (bought the stock of Texas Co-operative Supply Co.)
May 11, 1923	Leonard Bros. Groceries, Meats, Furniture, and Tools
Dec. 12, 1924	Leonard Bros. Groceries, Meats, Hardware, and Auto Accessories
June 22, 1925	Leonard Bros. Groceries, Meats, Vegetables, Hardware, and Auto Accessories
Oct. 26, 1925	Leonard Bros. Groceries, Meats & Vegetables, Field & Garden Seed, Hardware & Notions, Auto Accessories
Apr. 19, 1926	Leonard Bros. Wholesale and Retail

SOURCE: *Fort Worth Star-Telegram*, 1920–26

Obie's interest in auto mechanics prompted Leonards' next expansion just a few months later. Through a broker, he obtained 1,500 seat covers and around twenty barrels of wrenches, spark plugs, and automobile accessories that jobbers had discarded. Leonards Bros. Groceries, Meats, Furniture, and Tools became Leonard Bros. Groceries, Meats, Hardware, and Auto Accessories.[40]

At about the time Leonards added auto accessories and Turner and Dingee consolidated with H. H. Pittman, competitive conditions in the Fort Worth grocery business settled into a quasi equilibrium. The healthiest independent grocers and butchers (Harry J. Adams, Packing House Market, Model Grocer, 1st Street Grocery) advertised weekly or biweekly. Leonards advertised sporadically, usually when it needed to push a large volume of deeply discounted items. Piggly Wiggly dominated the market with sixteen stores but appeared content to share customers rather than drive competitors from business.[41]

Fort Worth's expanding economy and growing population tempered competition and gave merchants room to maneuver. In January, 1925, the *Star-Telegram* inaugurated a photo series chronicling major construction projects in the city. At year's end, investment in new construction outstripped the previous year by over

$2 million. In June, citizens excitedly predicted the addition of two thousand more jobs to the community's industrial payrolls within the next year, including a 22,000-spindle cotton mill planned for construction. West Texas farmers enjoyed the best wheat crop in five years, which promised that wholesaling, shipping, and milling would remain strong.[42]

Before independent grocers settled comfortably into following Piggly Wiggly's lead, more national competitors arrived forcing new readjustments in the grocery industry. Charles Saunders, founder and ousted chairman of Piggly Wiggly, announced the opening of his first Fort Worth "Charles Saunders, Sole Owner of My Name" Grocery Department Store with a full-page ad on July 17, 1925. Saunders competed with his former company by offering improvements such as a broken rather than continuous aisle and no turnstile to regulate customer movement. Also in contrast to Piggly Wiggly, Saunders's stores accepted personal checks and carried a more complete inventory of meats, produce, and groceries.[43]

Just six months after Saunders arrived, the Great Atlantic and Pacific Tea Company (A&P) further disrupted the Fort Worth market when it announced plans to open an unprecedented seventy-five new stores in Fort Worth. According to J. H. Genung, the Sales Director of the chain's Southern Division, A&P would open five new stores by February 1, 1926, and after that would open five stores every thirty days until it had all seventy-five in operation.[44]

A&P's strategy centered on service and value as well as price. Its policies called for systemwide pricing in its fourteen thousand stores. As Genung explained, "Our entry in Texas means that our stores will have stable prices at all times. Our prices are the same everywhere. As an illustration of what conditions exist now, you can buy sugar in Dallas 2 cents a pound cheaper than you can in Fort Worth. Butter is cheaper in Dallas than Fort Worth. When we open our stores we will give Fort Worth the best prices that exist." The chain's $325 million in sales for 1925 also gave it considerable buying clout with manufacturers. The chains were winning the grocery wars.[45]

Marvin recognized the implications of the grocery wars for his business. Price competition made customers more aware and appreciative of the bargains he offered. Because his buying skills and contacts depended on the secondary market rather than traditional distribution channels, he could take advantage of the fallout from chain competition. He also benefited from a growing reputation as a fair dealer and a local citizen. This meant customers could blame greedy chains for driving their favorite grocer out of business, then switch to Leonards and enjoy low prices in goods bought from the failed ventures. Marvin also realized that although low grocery prices drew customers into his store, competition kept margins very low. The best way to profit from this situation was to continue seeking higher volume and to supplement his stock with plenty of nonfood items.

This practice, already begun by 1925, separated Leonards from other grocers and produced a more robust bottom line.

FROM GROCERIES TOWARD GENERAL RETAILING

Each new line changed Leonards' merchandise mix, insulating it a little more from the chain grocers while reinforcing the store's appeal to its target customers—working and middle-class Fort Worthians, recent arrivals from the Texas countryside, blacks, and Saturday shoppers from farm counties. Between 1919 and 1925, the number of hourly wage earners in Fort Worth industries increased by 50 percent, with many of these new workers coming from nearby rural areas. Among these workers was a growing number of blacks, whose population increased by 40 percent in Fort Worth in the 1920s. Shoppers from as far west as Lubbock and Amarillo rode the trains into the city. These folks were accustomed to stores where general merchandise abutted groceries. Leonards' homely look—no artfully styled display windows, no walnut cases featuring handbags from Paris—made shopping a comfortable and familiar experience. In addition, by buying bankrupt stocks and closeouts, Marvin and Obie could set prices far below the standard retail price, in a range that even families with the most pinched budget could afford. Demographic change favored Leonards.[46]

During 1926 price wars and advertising battles brought new excitement and challenges to the Fort Worth grocery industry and underscored the need for Leonards to shield itself from direct competition. A&P and Saunders upped the stakes by advertising twice each week (usually Mondays and Fridays) and buying full pages of space. Piggly Wiggly did not stand idle. It, too, poured money into its advertising budget, allocating funds to semiweekly (Tuesday or Wednesday and Friday) full-page ads. On three occasions that year, its ad manager reached into reserves to fund double-page ads. The three chains also raced each other for prime store sites. By year's end, Piggly Wiggly operated at twenty-three locations, fourteen containing meat markets. A&P did not quite keep pace with its promise of five stores a month every month, but its twenty-five new stores exceeded Piggly Wiggly's total. Saunders could not match the other two in volume (it opened only eight new stores in 1926), but did compete aggressively on price and value. Expansion slowed in the first part of 1927 as the grocery chains paused to observe developments in the local and national economy and to consolidate their gains. In January, pundits predicted a lull in local oil production, cotton prices displayed some weakness, and wheat prices broke sharply when investors holding long positions suddenly liquidated. The consolidation of Fort Worth National Bank with Farmers and Mechanics National Bank at the first of the year also signaled some underlying weaknesses in the local economy. Nationally, a less optimistic business outlook unsettled the stock market briefly.[47]

By the mid-1920s Obie and Marvin no longer wore aprons and worked behind the sales counter. Here, Obie (front and middle) smiled while visiting with customers.

Fort Worth's economic engine, however, soon resumed its robust pace. Local baker Mrs. Baird's took out a full-page ad announcing that "in April 1927 there were 305,491 loaves more of [its] bread eaten than in April 1926."[48] The Fort Worth Grain and Cotton Exchange inspected more carloads of grain that April than in any previous April on record. They paid out $3 million for 2,204 cars. The record-breaking trend continued in the summer, when the Exchange smashed previous July business, handling 6,456 cars of grain.[49]

Even a downturn in cotton production did not slow the local economy in 1927. Boll weevil damage and irregular rains cut the West Texas cotton crop to its lowest level since 1922. Yet robust corn, grain sorghum, and hay crops and a higher market price for cotton dampened the effect of a reduced cotton crop.[50] The Fort Worth economy barely stumbled. Construction continued on a record-setting pace. The city issued close to $4 million in building permits in December, which pushed total construction to $17,111,430, passing its 1926 record of $17,022,467.[51]

Jack Long, a Fort Worth native, took the opportunity afforded by the upbeat business climate in the summer of 1927 to launch an assault on the grocery chain giants. In July, the locally owned and operated Helpy-Selfy Grocery chain held its grand opening. By year's end, thirteen stores operated under the Helpy-Selfy banner. The national chains responded to Long's challenge by opening more new stores, remodeling their older locations, and adding meat markets and delicatessens to existing operations. Piggly Wiggly launched an ad campaign to reinforce its image with shoppers: "All Over the World—First in Quality, First in Price, and First in Cleanliness." Saunders Sole Owner touted its annual local sales of $1 million and built its image around price, courteous service, clean shelves, and easily accessible merchandise. A&P continued to emphasize service and convenient locations.[52]

Small, single-location grocers suffered the most as the larger competitors duked it out. Unable to match the chains' advertising prowess, most independent grocers stopped running newspaper ads in 1926 and depended on customer loyalty and word of mouth to sell groceries. Many quietly closed their doors. Marvin and Obie, however, continued insulating their store from the craziness of the local grocery store wars by using nontraditional sourcing, diversifying the store's product mix beyond groceries, and stressing bargains that even the national chains could not match. These tactics drew on the brothers' unique skills and experiences and allowed Leonards to avoid head-to-head competition with much stronger rivals. Chain stores drove many traditional grocers out of business, but as Marvin recognized early on, that disruption brought opportunity to Leonards.

Despite forays into hard lines, before 1927 Leonards remained vulnerable to grocery competition because the bulk of its cash flow and profits came from food. Indeed, Marvin's insistence on pursuing all avenues to profit made it more like a traditional full-line grocery store even as it diversified into other merchandise. Early in 1926, the local "Self-Serving" grocery chain went out of business, and the brothers grabbed its varied inventory at deep discount prices. Leonards, however, did not adopt the self-serving format for another decade. Instead, like a traditional, full-service store, its clerks sold the bargain merchandise from behind a counter. Around the same time, the Southern Wholesale Grocery Company failed, making its large inventory available at far below wholesale prices. Marvin and Obie added the wholesale operation to their expanding enterprise and changed its name to Fort Worth Wholesale Grocery and Produce Co.[53]

MANAGEMENT AND FAMILY

Until 1923, Marvin and Obie, with occasional assistance from Enola and the help of a few clerks, waited on customers, weighed orders, wrapped packages, kept the books, and designed and placed the ads. As the scope of operations expanded and the tasks of securing credit, locating bargains, and negotiating for new inventory became more crucial, the brothers handed responsibility for managing the emerging departments over to capable employees. Marvin expected his growing staff to keep in direct touch with supply sources, ferret out the lowest prices on their lines of merchandise, keep overhead to a minimum, and respond quickly to customers. Marvin also delegated more responsibility to his brother.[54]

The two brothers who guided Leonards through these formative years were, as one observer put it, "as unlike as spinach and peas." Their skills and personalities complemented each other instead of overlapping. Marvin planned the strategy for the store and made all the major decisions. Obie learned to buy and sell and to shop for bargains. He increasingly took charge of the store's growing physical plant and helped move merchandise from storage into the hands of customers. Such a division of labor made for a harmonious working relationship. Harmony also came from the tacit agreement that, ultimately, Marvin was always in charge.[55]

Hiring new managers, defining their responsibilities, and decentralizing the daily operations of the departments freed the brothers' time to travel all over Texas to fire sales and auctions and personally inspect inventories hawked by agents and brokers. When a line of merchandise promised a reasonable profit, one of the brothers would travel to the site and make a bid. If transporting the goods added too much to the cost, they would put on a sale on the spot. Otherwise, they carted it back to Fort Worth. This type of sourcing required good contacts, ready cash, a knack for merchandising, and an ability to switch gears quickly. For instance, in 1925 Marvin and Obie became experts on tobacco and fancy dry goods when they took over the damaged stock of Lederman's Cigar Store and the Empress Fashion Shop after their buildings burned down. Soon after, a neighboring seed store filed for bankruptcy, and the partners added field and garden seeds to the store's growing list of departments.[56]

The brothers also had the time and capital to nurture a lifelong interest in real estate. Marvin and Obie developed subdivisions southeast of downtown near Glenwood and Sycamore parks and in North Fort Worth during the mid-1920s. Indeed, in August, 1927, the net worth of their real estate slightly exceeded the net worth of their store. For those with a cash-producing business like Leonards and a good line of credit, real estate in Fort Worth in the 1920s offered a quick and profitable return on investments. Reflecting their different interests, after 1927 their real estate investments increasingly diverged, with Obie focusing on farms and ranches and Marvin concentrating on urban tracts.[57]

Differences between the brothers extended to their personal lives. After moving from above the store in 1922, Marvin continued living with Obie, Enola, and their father. That same year Obie met Margery Fay Woolridge, the daughter of a Church of Christ minister. Margery and her family lived in Dallas, but relatives in Fort Worth introduced the couple. They dated for four years, and many times Marvin went along on their dates. The trio frequented the Golden Pheasant in downtown Dallas for dinner or picnicked in the park on Sunday afternoons. In May, 1925, Margery and Obie married. Their first child, Obie Paul, was born a year later on May 16, 1926.[58]

Marriage did not end the friendship between Margery and Marvin. Seventy years later she still remembered leaving Obie at the store while she went with her brother-in-law to watch the Fort Worth "Cats" play baseball. Obie liked to work and never enjoyed attending sporting events, but Margery and Marvin liked baseball. No one—not even the man left behind at the store—complained.[59]

Marvin's social life extended beyond baseball and keeping his brother and new sister-in-law company. He enjoyed taking dates to the night clubs that flourished despite prohibition. Bridge parties offered another diversion and a way to meet attractive and available women. Marvin also joined a large number of fraternal organizations, including the Masons and the Lions Club. Yet he still worked very long hours and may have joined some fraternal organizations simply for business reasons.[60]

Business demanded constant attention and a willingness to experiment. Not all of Marvin and Obie's forays into unusual stocks proved successful. Early attempts to buy dry goods presented the brothers with merchandising challenges because they did not know the hazards of buying odd sizes, bad colors, and out-of-fashion styles. But, as their competitors realized by the late 1920s, the Leonards learned fast.

JOINING FORT WORTH'S DEPARTMENT STORES

The general merchandise stores that contended with Leonards' phenomenal growth, customer loyalty, and aggressive marketing at the end of the decade probably did not notice its ascent. After all, Leonards began in a cubbyhole with hand-lettered signs promoting canned goods specials and an unpredictable assortment of grocery staples. In the heady days after the war, Fort Worth's general and specialty retailers focused on attracting customers and increasing consumption. Artful displays and fancy fixtures called attention to increasingly upscale merchandise. Shoppers crowded into Monnig's, Stripling's, and Meacham's department stores as they had for decades and overflowed into Sanger Brothers and L. G. Gilbert. These department stores began, like those established elsewhere in the last decades of the nineteenth century, as large dry goods stores with conservative, highly centralized management. As elsewhere, economic prosperity, skillful merchandising, and the increased urbanization of the previous twenty years transformed these department stores into some of Fort Worth's leading locally owned businesses by 1918.[61]

Despite the size of department stores, specialty stores still did a booming business. Women ran up their credit accounts at The Fair, Jackson's, Colton's Ladies Toggery, and The Style Shop and paid out cash for their purchases at Gan's, The Vogue, and Breacher's. Many male shoppers patronized shops catering exclusively to men, such as Washer Brothers and A. and L. August, rather than department stores. Besides these main stores, many other boutiques served Fort Worth's women and men.[62]

As the 1920s unfolded, Fort Worth attracted national general retailers much as it had grocery giants like Piggly Wiggly and A&P. Once Penney's, Montgomery Wards, and others entered Fort Worth, independents responded to the lower-cost, lower-priced competition by moving further upscale. They built fancier facilities, added more services, and upgraded product lines. After a shakeout that closed many smaller shops, Marvin positioned Leonards as both less expensive than most department stores and specialty shops and more in touch with local customers than the chain stores. Leonards' success, then, came not despite the increased competition and emphasis on fashion, but in part because of it.

One contemporary observer of the growth binge among department stores in the 1920s argued that most stores attracted customers with greater service and fancier facilities. New plants, fixtures, and merchandising policies inevitably added to operating costs and often forced merchants to raise prices.[63]

Fort Worth merchants followed this national trend by remodeling and expanding their operations with vigor and by upgrading their merchandise when possible. Virtually all of the major downtown merchants added to and spruced up their stores right after the war. Throughout the 1920s, ads in the local papers trumpeted grand reopenings, special renovations, and new enlarged stores. No merchant wanted to fall behind the others when it came to facilities, fixtures, or services, lest they lose the ability to lure the fashion-conscious.[64]

Just as in groceries, these national trends ushered in dramatic postwar changes in the well-defined dimensions of general retailing competition and offered Marvin new opportunities for profit. In 1918 Fort Worth merchants believed a downtown location was essential. For department stores, conventional wisdom demanded entrances on either Houston Street or Main Street. After that, store managers tinkered with various combinations of price, style, delivery conditions, credit terms, and services. Monnig's, Stripling's, and the other department stores often featured price in their newspaper ads, which allowed them to compare themselves favorably with the more exclusive specialty shops. Yet, while store ads screamed with promises of low prices, all of the department stores emphasized a more complete shopping experience, based on supplying a wide assortment of quality goods, reasonably priced and properly serviced. All the major competitors bore the costs of daily advertising in the *Star-Telegram*, *Press*, and *Record*, where merchants reached not only Fort Worth citizens, but North and West Texas households. The *Star-Telegram* was particularly effective in reaching rural households because during the 1920s it had the largest circulation of any newspaper in Texas and was delivered in most of West and North Texas.[65]

Advertising departments filled their ads with elaborate copy to announce sales events, special promotions, and new styles, lest customers be alienated by stale ads, dull merchandise, and humdrum events. All the major stores used timed advertising that coordinated the arrival of new merchandise with community events, holidays, or recurring sales. The annual Southwest Exposition and Fat Stock Show, the arrival of the West Texas Shriners, or any other local happening served as an excuse for every major store in town to plaster the newspaper and their store fronts with salutations and invitations to make special purchases. Community pride and good public relations made for successful retailing.[66]

Despite the similarities among the competitors, managers worked to build unique images for their stores. Washer Brothers ran more manufacturers' brands ads than its competitors, taking advantage of the name recognition of its suppliers. Gan's included an elevator in its remodeling plans to create a more upscale image and to signal its progressive management. Monnig's reinforced customer loyalty through membership in the S&H Green Stamp program. Advertising slogans, window displays, and special promotions reinforced distinctiveness that perhaps existed only in the imaginations of the merchandise managers and copy writers.[67]

Of the major Fort Worth retailers, Monnig's and Stripling's acted more like big-city department stores. Both maintained extensive wholesaling operations and a network of buyers and agents in manufacturing centers.[68] Stripling's usually led Fort Worth merchants in adopting practices introduced in New York, Atlanta, Chicago, or Philadelphia. It was first to operate a barber shop and beauty salon on its premises, and by 1924 its luncheon room served one thousand meals a day. Stripling's also pioneered behind-the-scenes operations, generating its own electricity, manufacturing its own electric lights, and maintaining a 2,400-head automatic sprinkler system to protect the store and its merchandise from fire. When the dog days of summer arrived, only the obstinate store manager or one hamstrung by corporate policy refused to follow Stripling's lead and close early on Saturdays.[69]

Despite efforts to mimic big-city retailing operations, Stripling's often reverted to habits learned as a small-town dry goods company. Management unabashedly and proudly advertised "an extraordinary sale" of navy surplus refrigerators and other salvage offerings just like Leonards, the shoestring-budgeted, cash-only store down the street.[70]

Monnig's acted with more caution than Stripling's. It ran less extravagant ads, delayed expanding its facilities until mid-decade, and refused to give up the moniker "Monnig's Dry Goods Company" in favor of the more modern "Department Store" until the 1940s. Instead, it used its bannerhead to call attention to its longstanding presence in Fort Worth, proclaiming itself "The Department Store With 29 Years Reputation."[71]

A follower in retailing, Monnig's dominated the local wholesaling market, and throughout the 1920s its wholesale operation represented a larger part of its business than the retail end. It serviced thousands of accounts with merchants in all parts of Texas, Oklahoma, New Mexico, and Arkansas. Monnig's wholesale volume expanded with the postwar economy until it reached several million dollars in 1923, a whopping 33 percent increase over the previous year. Each year the Monnig brothers chartered the largest boat on Lake Worth for a style show during the annual wholesalers convention and offered to pay the round-trip railway fare for visiting merchants who placed at least $750 in orders. Monnig's also vertically integrated by manufacturing overalls, work pants, and work shirts.[72]

Other stores worked equally hard to develop and maintain a unique image. Gilbert's and Sanger Brothers, relative newcomers to Fort Worth department store retailing, created a stylish and progressive image with shoppers. Meacham's, as a mid-decade ad admitted, was not the largest, the lowest priced, or the oldest department store in Fort Worth, but it did sell "Good Goods, at Low Prices, Intelligently Serviced [and these things] Always Will Be Appreciated." Despite adopting a conservative and unoriginal merchandising strategy, Meacham's expanded its customer base throughout the 1920s by carefully monitoring retailing trends and local conditions.[73]

In the early 1920s, the entrance of several chain stores into the Fort Worth market altered nongrocery retailing just as the entrance of Piggly Wiggly and A&P changed grocery retailing. Before the war, the community's stable economy had drawn only a few chains, most notably W. T. Farley, a national clothing store established in the 1890s, and S. H. Kress's and F. W. Woolworth & Co., the leading five-and-dime variety stores. The first wave of chain store expansion largely bypassed Fort Worth because its size fell between the big cities targeted by companies such as S. S. Kresge and smaller towns preferred by chains such as J. C. Penney. A combination of factors—excellent railroad connections and distribution facilities, steadily growing population, economic prosperity, and Chamber of Commerce boosterism—brought the area to the attention of expansion-minded retailers after the war.[74]

J. C. Penney, which had begun experimenting with locations in medium-sized cities, opened a new branch in downtown Fort Worth in 1920, as did the National Clothing Company. W. T. Grant Co., which combined features of a low-priced department store with those of an expanded-selection dime store, also targeted smaller industrial cities and chose Fort Worth in 1922. Two years later, mail-order giant Montgomery Wards carried its retail expansion plan into Fort Worth by taking over the defunct Chevrolet assembly plant on Seventh Avenue. The 236,000-square-foot building allowed Wards to expand its local mail order operation by 300 percent and open a 50,000-square-foot retail store on the premises. At announcement ceremonies, a company spokesman praised the vitality of the community, saying that "the expansion of the present plant is justified by business conditions in Fort Worth and in Fort Worth's trade territory. Fort Worth's position as a railroad center means quick delivery of mail orders and it was a factor affecting the decision to expand."[75]

After the addition in the mid-1920s of specialty merchandisers such as Kinney's Shoes, Western Auto, Frigidaire, and the Union Clothing Company, the retailing landscape in Fort Worth took on the form that would remain familiar to local shoppers for three decades. Like most chain stores, these firms charged into town eager to drive down prices and grab customers from local retailers. Although Leonards was not yet the dominant player it would become, the mid-1920s were crucial for its growth and positioning in the retail industry. The entrance of national chains caused similar consequences to those Marvin had observed a few years earlier in groceries. He and his managers knew there were opportunities in chaos. When new, strong competitors drove small merchants out of business and made customers more price-conscious, Leonards snapped up inventories for quick resale and highlighted prices below those of the chains.[76]

The way rivalry in retailing played out in Fort Worth mirrored the rest of the nation. Independent retailers all over the country felt the sting of increased competition from more efficient national chains, and by 1930, 58 percent of department stores reported an operating loss. Price pressure was especially intense. In Fort Worth, W. T. Grant vowed to "Bring New Low Prices to Fort Worth," while Penney's promised "Standard Quality Merchandise for Less Money." National Clothing stated that its policies took into account "all the family, all conditions, including financial; all problems, including the high cost of living; all desires, including style, fit, quality, and service," in brief, "Good Clothes for Everybody." Western Auto kept it simple, advertising that it carried the "Largest Stocks at Lowest Prices—a Savings of 20–50% Everytime." In large measure, those claims were accurate. One management scholar wrote in 1930 that Penney's and other well-managed chains operated more efficiently "because of (1) cheaper rentals; (2) a policy of cash and carry; (3) elimination of service of the costly type which does little for the customer but gratify her vanity; (4) a firm policy with reference to returns and allowances; (5) mass buying; (6) a modification of the traditional buyer status which is hampering the effectiveness of department stores; and (7) a faster turnover of merchandise, which aside from reducing interest costs, has a definite tendency to mitigate the extent of mark-downs."[77]

In the immediate postwar years, a healthy economy and a growing population muffled the effect of national competitors in Fort Worth, but merchants with limited buying clout soon felt the increased competition. The following figure suggests that the arrival of chains soon coincided with increased going-out-of-business sales. While the high number of failures in 1921 was partially attributable to a brief but sharp nationwide economic downturn and dip in cotton prices, the local economy rebounded by mid-1922. After that, chains, not a weak economy, put sole proprietorships and small partnerships out of business. Department stores and successful specialty stores staved off their new competitors by enhancing their product lines, upgrading facilities, and emphasizing service. Yet those moves strapped stores with increasingly high costs, leaving room for cost conscious operators like Leonards to expand their customer base.[78]

Montgomery Wards' managers took advantage of the bind facing the modern department store. Wards' ads claimed it offered more bargains because it was "like the first department stores of America in the simplicity of its layout." Instead of expensive equipment and furnishings, Wards had "no mahogany, no plate glass, no elaborate showrooms. It has it all on one floor, and the appointments are neat but not expensive. This is a cash and carry store, except for those who desire to pay delivery charges." Lower-priced chain store operators did not always compete head-to-head with Fort Worth's entrenched department stores. Increasingly, however, they diverted customers shopping for staples and semistaples from department stores to their stores. By the late 1920s, Fort Worth's chain stores and independent specialty stores that imitated their strategy sold vast quantities of linens, wash goods, sheeting, blankets, and certain kinds of yard goods. While department stores were making "class," style, and fashion their objectives, they neglected staples.[79]

Rapidly changing rules of competition and economic prosperity defined Fort Worth retailing during the 1920s. Boom times brought hundreds of new merchants to the area. Most started small, but well-managed chain stores also found Fort Worth an attractive place to do business. The trend of competing on price rather than credit accelerated, though as long as the economy expanded even some inefficient retailers generated enough cash flow to secure seasonal lines of merchandise and remain in business. By mid-decade, the smallest establishments failed, too undercapitalized and too similar in their stock to survive heavier competition and swings in the economy. Other failures stemmed from either exceptionally poor management or catastrophic fire. But despite the gloomy words of some business analysts and the arrival of new competitors, Fort Worth's larger, better-capitalized, and better-managed department stores and specialty stores enjoyed tremendous prosperity in the 1920s.

Fort Worth's booming economy accounted for some of the increase in sales

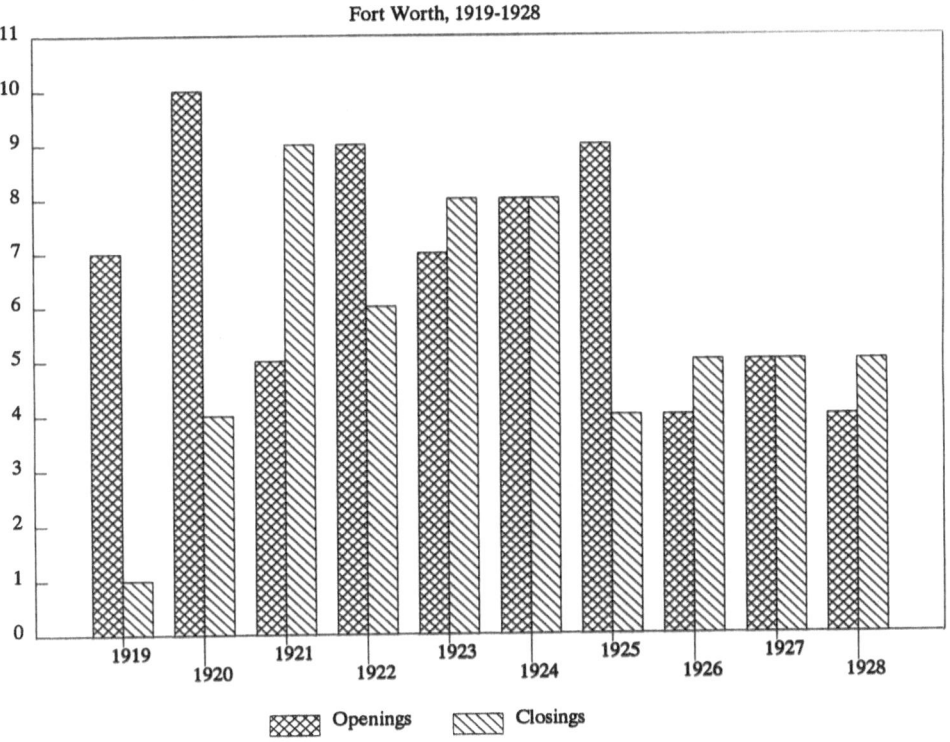

Nongrocery Openings and Closings
Fort Worth, 1919-1928

Note: Based on openings and closings advertised in the *Fort Worth Star-Telegram* from 1919 to 1928.

volume and profits, but the large department stores also changed with the times. To avoid competing primarily on price, larger retailers continued to follow the national trend of expanding product lines, upgrading facilities, and enhancing service offerings. They appealed to an increasingly affluent and increasingly fashion-conscious middle and upper-middle class by adding floral shops, drug departments, beauty salons, luncheon rooms, and by stocking live pets. Most found a way to provide shoppers with free parking. Stripling's even experimented with revolving credit when it introduced the Ten-Payment Charge Service, which spread payments for purchases of more than twenty-five dollars over ten weekly payments. Larger retailers also learned to promote their businesses and attract large crowds. More than twenty-five thousand people attended the Montgomery Wards Grand Opening in 1924. New buildings drew equally large crowds to well-established local firms. By the next year, Stripling's, Sanger's, and Fakes Furniture had moved into multistory buildings constructed specifically for them.

Despite its conservatism, even Monnig's responded to competitive pressures and opportunities. When the influx of independent and chain competitors threatened to undercut its position as the more moderately priced department store in town, Monnig's gradually upgraded its merchandise offerings and announced its plan to become "The Supply Base for the Better Dressers." It also began the policy of marking merchandise upon receipt to help track inventory and prevent older items from accumulating. In 1924 Monnig's expanded with gusto, tripling floor space and incorporating the latest fixtures and displays.[80]

Such substantial expansion left Chamber of Commerce boosters panting for superlatives. They boasted that in 1925 aggregate retail sales for Fort Worth would exceed $100 million and pointed out that Fort Worth was now a "Metropolitan City."[81]

Between 1924 and 1927, Marvin and Obie took advantage of the healthy Fort Worth economy and the lessons they learned from dealing with intensifying grocery competition. Local retailers had spent extravagantly to stay ahead of the chains and cash-only stores, creating opportunities for stores with leaner operations. At the same time, merchants attuned to the buying habits of locals could make more-responsive stocking and service decisions than chains hamstrung by national policies. Leonards did both, filling the niche below the other downtown department stores, while outselling the chain stores.

To reinforce efficiency, Marvin, Obie, and their managers continued to emphasize buying at the lowest possible price. The brothers had earned a solid reputation among their network of buyers and sellers in the regional secondary market and received regular calls from jobbers needing to unload stock or brokers with news of impending bankruptcies. As the number of bankruptcies among independent retailers increased with the intrusion of the chain retailers, Marvin and Obie's buying opportunities also rose. Buying bankrupt stocks allowed drugs, auto supplies, and various other departments to add additional items and carry more-complete lines of merchandise. Leonards never tried to upgrade in ready-to-wear in the 1920s. Instead it beat the chains on price. In fact, like the national chains, Leonards took customers from the established department stores.[82]

In 1927, after their first one-million-dollar sales year, Marvin and Obie consolidated the gains made by the store and strengthened the store's image. Piecemeal additions to its product line meant that the store already carried most items found in Monnig's, Stripling's, and the rest, but the brothers also wanted customers to recognize the store as more than a hodgepodge of leftover merchandise and storefronts with a common sidewalk.

To reinforce a unified image across the disparate departments that composed Leonards, the brothers added institutional advertising to the usual ad mix. One ad notified shoppers of the "reasons why you should shop at Leonard Brothers: many departments under one roof; dependable merchandise at bargain prices in every department; complete satisfaction or your money cheerfully refunded. Shop Belknap to Weatherford Streets on Houston Street—The Leonard Block." Other ads raised shoppers' awareness that Leonards offered value, service, and reasonable quality as well as bargains. One example introduced J. E. Bohrer, an agricultural expert, in charge of Leonards' seed department, stating that "he will gladly advise our customers regarding seed and planting problems, free of charge." Another promised customers that the store "is prepared to supply your needs with the right kind of merchandise." The brothers also encouraged the advertising department to make appropriate changes. The effect included spruced-up layouts, chattier copy and, for the first time, ads with drawings of sales merchandise. Leonards looked and acted more like a department store.[83]

Marvin and Obie made other managerial decisions in 1927 that moved the store further from its roots in salvage and groceries. During the spring the store added a fountain and sandwich counter so that shoppers could pause and refresh themselves while shopping rather than leave the premises. In June, Leonards became a regular, weekly advertiser in the *Star-Telegram*. Before then, the store had advertised irregularly (rarely more than once a month and often much less than that), usually when new inventory arrived or when stock was not moving. Leonards also began using advertising copy to shape buyers' habits. Ads in June offered special inducements to encourage weekday shopping in the form of super special sales on Mondays, Tuesdays, and Wednesdays. Marvin liked to see the store jammed on Saturdays, but realized that a full store during the week required advertising.[84]

As Christmas 1927 approached, the brothers took steps to ensure that holiday shoppers would not forget Leonards. For their customers' convenience, they relaxed the store's cash and carry policy to institute a layaway option called "the Reserve Plan," and every day an in-house factory produced enough fresh candy to satisfy any candy lover. Leonards also joined with other retailers to sponsor the city's annual "Santa's Pack" Contest. The biggest milestone that year, however, was the debut of Toyland, soon one of Leonards' most popular features.[85]

Like its competitors, Leonards had faced the overriding realities of the 1920s: a booming but erratic economy and the challenge of adapting to new retailing methods and chain store competition. First, the brothers had to find a way to set themselves apart in the proliferation of grocers and salvage agents drawn to Fort Worth's booming economy. Before the store could establish a solid footing, the economy briefly faltered, even while wholesale prices continued to climb. As Fort Worth roared back to life and prices stabilized, much stronger competitors targeted the city for expansion. In each instance, Marvin and Obie positioned the store to attract customers. They relied heavily on nontraditional sources for inventory and offered low prices on staple goods, backed by a strong money-back guarantee. They created an atmosphere where less affluent Fort Worthians and farm and ranch folk from surrounding counties would feel comfortable. The store's eclectic mix of products displayed in a jumble, its humble facility pieced together one lease at a time, and its knowledgeable and friendly employees combined to create an atmosphere that customers appreciated.

Marvin and Obie's determination to find and sell bargains led them to redefine the boundaries of the store. By continually expanding the store's product mix, they brought cash into the store and differentiated themselves from other grocers. They avoided direct competition with chain stores and other general merchandisers and took advantage of the crippling effect these larger competitors had on local merchants by buying their bankrupt stocks. As Leonards became a department store, its competitors did not consider it a rival—it neither looked nor acted like their own stores. Conventional department stores enhanced services, upgraded stocks, and occupied increasingly luxurious floor space. The Leonard brothers focused on keeping costs low. As these downtown giants soon discovered, Leonards was not too different or ragtag to attract large numbers of customers interested in its deep and wide stocks of bargain-priced merchandise. Furthermore, Marvin and Obie had proven adept at abandoning strategies that did not work. They would not stick to any strategy, even their reliance on nontraditional sourcing, if it alienated customers or lost money.

In the 1920s, Leonards took full advantage of the local prosperity, making and remaking itself as it grew. By 1927, it had established a reputation for selling bargain merchandise to the citizens of Fort Worth and the city's large trade area in North and West Texas. Competitors and bankers understood it could adjust to changing times and intensifying competitive pressures. This reputation and the ability to adapt to industry and economic changes—built upon, polished, and refined—propelled Leonards through subsequent decades.

"Not Content to Drift," 1920s–38

In December, 1932, a writer for the *Star-Telegram* remarked that after fourteen years of hard work, "the hours are still long for Marvin and Obie Leonard because they are not content to drift." That was an image the brothers always sought to project—planned, orchestrated, constant growth through hard work. In their use of the Leonards Creed and the phrase "here we grow again" they gave the store an aura of inevitable progress. In fact, between 1931 and 1936 Fort Worth's economy slumped and sales at Leonards stagnated.[1]

That same image of purposeful striding forward on a predetermined path also provided a convenient symbol of the brothers' life away from the store. It fit the portrait of poor farm boys made good that helped attract customers, even if it did not always fit their experiences. Marvin was only twenty-seven years old in 1922 when Leonards began growing rapidly. During the next decade and a half, he adjusted to life in a swiftly growing city and to his newly earned wealth and status. It was a period of significant and sometimes bumpy personal transition.

Still buried in this over-simplified image, there was a key insight: Marvin was "not content" to allow chance or changing economic circumstances to dictate his future. He pushed himself to the point of breaking his health to build a successful business and found ways to maintain profits even in the Great Depression. He also looked for happiness beyond the store. By 1938 the store could get along without his constant attention. In fact, the hard years of the Great Depression fixed in the public mind Leonards' image as the place to go and forced it to evolve into a store that offered everything. By 1938, Marvin also had married and begun a family. He had opened Colonial Country Club two years earlier and expanded his real-estate holdings. By then he had assumed the role of community patriarch that he would fill until his death. Marvin and his store had reached maturity. To insist that they inevitably assumed these roles in the 1920s diminishes the struggle and growth of man and store.

In Transition

By 1925, Marvin and his brother Obie increasingly followed different paths. That was the year Obie married and quickly settled into family life. After the birth of Paul in 1926, Margery and Obie had three more children: Robert Woolridge on April 15, 1928, Margery Ann on August 27, 1931, and Martha Jane on January 4, 1934. Obie reveled in being a father and husband. When bad dreams or illness woke the children, he tended them. He told Margery that it was only fair that he look after the children at night since she took care of them all day. Almost every Wednesday, the couple hired a sitter for the children, dined out at the Virginia Waffle Kitchen, and took in a movie. The rest of their social life was equally low-key and family oriented. The club scene and the country club life had little appeal. Margery was a dedicated member of the Church of Christ, but Obie, who did not join the church until late in life, preferred to spend Sundays fishing, hunting, or looking over his increasingly large land holdings. Even before his marriage, Obie had the idea of buying farmland and planting pecan orchards. He reasoned that with patience he could profit from the orchards. In 1933 he purchased his first four hundred acres. He built up his acreage gradually and eventually harvested 4.5 million pounds of pecans per year, making him the largest pecan grower in Texas.[2]

While his brother reconnected with the habits of Linden, Marvin embraced life in a booming city. Obie married early, preferred being with his family to being out on the town, and returned to agriculture. Marvin remained a bachelor much longer, enjoyed an active social life, and avoided anything resembling farm life. Obie was deeply rooted in his past. Marvin sought a new way.

Marvin and Obie's father, John Leonard, died in June, 1927, from heart disease, just after his seventy-fourth birthday. After their father's death, Marvin and Enola moved into the twelve-story Forest Park Apartments, then considered one of the finest buildings in town. Living in a high-rise was glamorous and far from the small-town world of Linden, but vestiges of Linden always remained. Both Marvin and Enola retained a healthy fear of high winds, a fear born in May, 1908, when a cyclone virtually destroyed their hometown. Whenever the wind picked up, they left their apartment and headed for the basement.[3]

When the wind diminished, Marvin and Enola enjoyed life in the Jazz Age. Both dated, went to sporting events and night clubs, and attended meetings of fraternal organizations and bridge clubs. Enola fished and hunted with Obie. She made frequent car trips back to Linden to visit her sisters, Byrd and Cora. Independent and self-confident, Enola gassed up her Hupmobile and made the long drive to Linden by herself. Her ability to shoot a rifle as straight as any man probably eased her mind when traveling lonely roads. Marvin dabbled with golf and played gin rummy. He also enjoyed having a drink with close friends like W. A. Moncrief. Prohibition failed to dry up their social life.[4]

Prohibition, however, was a cause that Marvin long supported, at least for other people. That support and other relics of life in Linden partially explain his membership in the Ku Klux Klan, which consistently advocated strict enforcement of prohibition laws. Like others in a prosperous but anxious white, urban middle class with a rural, Protestant past, he joined a seemingly righteous cause.[5]

Little about the Klan now seems righteous, but its historians warn against stereotyping "the Invisible Empire as an irrational movement that lay outside the major currents of American political and social life." The second version of the Klan, organized in Georgia in 1915, eventually included millions of average Americans from all parts of the country and from a broad range of social and economic classes. Like all its other incarnations, this Klan was racist, but racism was not the only reason people joined the Klan.[6]

At first, Fort Worth Klan Number 101 clearly was a mainstream movement. Founded in 1921 by Tarrant County Sheriff Sterling Clark and County Judge Hugh Small, Klan 101's most prominent member and effective leader was William A. "Bill" Hanger, a corporate attorney and former state senator. Mayor E. R. Cockrell and other city officials were also members.[7]

One indication of the complexity of the Klan was that William M. McDonald, Fort Worth's leading black businessman and politician, supported Cockrell despite the mayor's obvious ties to the hooded order. McDonald introduced Cockrell at a 1923 political rally at the St. James Baptist Church, one of the most prominent black churches in the city. The mayor distinguished between those who were good citizens and "negroes who are bootleggers and gamblers." He promised to use the Klan to end vice, but to protect "any unoffending negro."[8]

Cockrell's comments at the St. James Baptist Church clearly illustrated that the Klan grew out of a widespread sense that society was out of control. The Bolshevik Revolution and the Red Scare of 1919 left the impression that America could crumble at any moment. Growing organizations such as the National Association for the Advancement of Colored People and the American Federation of Labor seemed dangerously extreme to some Texans. Fear of radicalism increased in 1921 as Fort Worth endured one of its most bitter labor disputes, when the International Butcher Workers struck the local packing plants. Railway workers struck the next year. Divorce was up. Open violations of prohibition laws made a mockery of the legal system. Prostitution and vice flourished as the oil boom brought a surge in business at Hell's Half Acre, the notorious red light district near downtown. The Klan promised to regain control from these varied threats and restore order.[9]

For members of Klan 101, these goals required going beyond the law to save the law. Those believed guilty of immorality and vice, those who defied segregation, those who were non-Protestants, and those who flouted white middle-class values became Klan targets. A favorite Klan practice was to tar and feather alleged offenders, but other forms of intimidation were almost as common. The local Klan could take the law into its own hands because of its close ties to the sheriff's office and the police.[10]

To dramatize their moral crusade, Klan members, both men and women, held several large parades in downtown Fort Worth. In December, 1924, an "interminable line of white trudged slowly and in silence" behind a low-flying World War I biplane. Red electric lights beneath the bottom wing and tail section glowed in the shape of a cross. The marchers paused on Main Street and the "Klan Korus" sang "Onward Christian Soldiers."[11]

Klan influence extended beyond parades and vigilantism. The Fort Worth chapter played a pivotal role in politics and business. In 1922 a group of citizens who loudly criticized the Klan lost their attempt to control city government. Klansmen ran city government, including the police, until 1924.[12] That year Charles H. Hurdleston claimed that Bill Hanger and other local Klan leaders tried "to drive from business every person who was not 100 per cent American and who did not signify it by joining the Klan."[13]

The Klan seemed all-powerful and widely accepted. The Fort Worth Fat Stock Show even designated March 13, 1924, as Klan Day. Yet Klan influence soon waned. The *Fort Worth Press*, Judge Hal Lattimore, Sr., Henry Meacham, and other civic leaders joined the progressive wing of the Democratic party and the state's largest business interests in depicting the Klan's secrecy, brutality, willingness to exceed the law, and political manipulations as un-American and uncivilized. One indication of the slipping prestige of the Klan and the antipathy it had aroused was the bombing of the 4,000-seat Ku Klux Klan Hall. On November 6, 1924, two explosive devices went off and fire destroyed much of one of the largest meeting halls in the city.[14]

Opponents of the Klan also took a less violent tack. In the summer of 1925, the new city manager, O. E. Carr, fired all known Klansmen working for the city. Although Klansmen burned crosses throughout the city, Carr refused to back down, and the Klan abandoned its effort to run city government.[15]

Internal squabbles and disagreements with the national organization further disrupted the Klan. Many resented Hanger's dictatorial control. Others accused the local chapter of financial mismanagement. Klan 101 lingered on until 1928, but it rapidly lost members and influence after 1925.[16]

Given his occupation, background, and links to both the Masons and the Methodist church, two prime recruiting areas for the Klan, it was not surprising that Marvin was part of the Klan before 1925. He may have joined the Klan during its 1922 membership drive, but his first surviving membership card was dated June, 1924. In fact, Marvin briefly joined numerous organizations during the 1920s.

Although later calling them a waste of time, he belonged to the Masons, the Shriners, the Salesmanship Club, and the Lions Club.[17]

Despite obvious differences with other clubs, the Texas Klan's foremost historian insists that while it had many faces, the Klan "was first of all a fraternal order." It offered fellowship, business contacts, and a chance to improve the community. Klan 101 donated to the YMCA building fund and with the Lions Club ran the Ku Klux Klan Kiddies Camp for poor youth on Lake Worth. It aided the local Baptist and Methodist churches in promoting enforcement of prohibition laws. In a sense, the Klan encouraged members to serve the public good.[18]

After 1925, however, an anemic Klan offered few benefits. There is also evidence that Marvin was well aware of the Klan's violent character. Although he continued to pay his dues, he told his daughter Miranda that he was so sickened by the tarring and feathering of a Klan victim that he stopped actively participating in the organization. That he participated in the Klan at all puzzles many, for he never exhibited virulent racism and prejudice. Several of his early employees were black and he formed close bonds with some of them. James Morgan, for example, began working at the store in the early 1920s and for two decades held a variety of jobs. Marvin trusted and respected Morgan, even relying upon him as a witness in court. Nor was this a totally paternalistic relationship. Marvin called him Morgan, not James as was common among old-school southerners. Morgan was more than a boy.[19]

As Marvin's lack of virulent racism suggests, assigning causes for membership in the 1920s Klan remains complicated, especially since few records endure from the secretive organization. Insufficient evidence exists to say for sure why Marvin became a Klansman, but paying his dues as long as he did hints that he was more than a casual member influenced to join by a friend or drawn to the organization by its pageantry. Such members dropped out when the number in the local Klan shrank from several thousand in 1924 to a few dozen in 1927.[20]

The Klan must have offered Marvin something. He was too focused on building up his business to waste his time on anything that offered him nothing. Starting in Linden and continuing through the rest of his life, he viewed prohibition as a positive step and "vehemently opposed labor unions."[21] The Klan let him stand up for these principles. While Marvin's attraction to the Klan seems rooted in Linden, it grew in Fort Worth, where rapid economic and population growth made the appeals for order that undergirded these principles compelling. The Klan offered comparative newcomers, such as Marvin, a chance to exert control over a still-strange environment. Membership also conferred and confirmed status. Some members of the commercial and social elite condemned the Klan, but members of the political elite led the Klan. Marvin had obtained standing with his bankers, yet for a man who remembered the patches on his childhood clothing, further confirmation of his status mattered. Later, Marvin Leonard, community patriarch, would not need or want overt signs of his place in Fort Worth, but when he was still a striving young businessman, the Klan and all the other groups to which he belonged gave voice to his principles, anxieties, and fears.[22]

While his membership was understandable, in joining the Ku Klux Klan and maintaining his membership until 1928, Marvin associated with the most zealous defenders of a social order whose touchstones were xenophobic Protestantism and white supremacy. In testimony to his capacity for growth and his complexity, thirty years later Marvin led the way in ensuring equal treatment for blacks in Fort Worth. And in 1936, he ensured that Jews could be members of Colonial Country Club.[23]

After the Klan collapsed, Leonards purchased the old Klan Hall from the few remaining shareholders of the defunct organization and used it as a warehouse. The sloping floors of the auditorium make such use difficult, but Obie decided it would make an ideal pecan shelling facility. The brothers sold the building to Ellis Pecan Company and turned a profit.[24]

An incident concerning the city's attempt to condemn a lot Marvin owned north of the courthouse further demonstrated his drive to make a profit and his still-evolving place in the community. In April, 1928, the Fort Worth City Council initiated discussion with Leonard on acquiring a parking lot he owned adjacent to what was then called Bluff Park. The city hoped to purchase all the land in the rectangle formed by Bluff, Houston, Belknap, and Commerce Streets and enlarge the park. In June, 1928, the council voted to condemn Marvin's land between Belknap and Bluff Streets "if the owners will not agree to a satisfactory sale price to the city."[25] For a year Marvin dickered with the city over the value of the land. He originally asked $98,000 for the 9,000-square-foot parcel, but lowered his price to $88,000. At one point the city offered him $54,000 but withdrew the offer when an appraisal board set the price at $31,500. In June, 1929, the case went to the county court.[26]

Jenkins Garrett got his first legal experience in the case. The son of an attorney who gave up a lucrative practice to become a Baptist minister on the north side of Fort Worth, Garrett began working for Leonards in the summer of 1927 at age thirteen as an office boy and courier. He was paid five dollars per week and got to keep the old Columbia bicycle he used to deliver messages around town. One of his first tasks in the summer of 1929 was to collect evidence for the case. Carl Bruner, Leonards' office manager, stationed him at the corner of Commerce and Belknap Streets with instructions to make one mark for each car that passed by going north or south. James Morgan left his work at the meat market to man the corner of Houston and Belknap. Since Commerce and Houston both curved around the courthouse and carried heavy traffic to North Main, there were plenty of cars to count. Bruner and Marvin's attorney, S. F. Houtchens, intended to argue that all those cars could stop at any business built on Marvin's Bluff Park lot.[27]

Houtchens was a large man, with the voice and demeanor of a "small town Methodist minister." When Garrett testified in the county court case, City Attorney R. E. Rouer insinuated that Garrett so admired Marvin Leonard that he had made additional marks on his tally sheet. Houtchens approached the witness box. After fixing the jury with a ministerial gaze he leaned over toward the witness box and said, "Master Garrett, you just put one mark for each car, didn't you?" Garrett responded, "Yes, sir." Houtchens continued, "You would not do anything other than what you are asked to do?" "Yes, sir." "You would not lie, would you?" "No, sir."[28]

Morgan followed Garrett to the stand and faced the same line of questioning from the city attorney. Rouer closed Morgan's cross examination by asking, "You would do anything you could to help Mr. Leonard, wouldn't you?" Morgan looked down from the box and with simple dignity responded, "I would do everything but lie." The day was won. The six-person jury awarded Leonard $81,000 for the lot.[29]

Rather than pay this sum, the city moved to dismiss the case and abandon the condemnation process. The presiding judge, P. J. Small of County Court at Law Number 2, agreed. Marvin did not let the matter drop. He had Houtchens appeal the dismissal and in a precedent-setting case that Garrett would later study in law school, first the Court of Civil Appeals and then the State Supreme Court sustained Small's ruling. The courts found that "when property is condemned for public use the proceedings may be abandoned even after a judgment is rendered." The city could not be forced to buy the lot.[30]

This case was a benchmark in the move of Marvin Leonard from rough-and-tumble, struggling entrepreneur to established community leader and dedicated family man. A few years later, Marvin sold the Bluff Park lot to the city at its price, but he would not accept less than what he considered a fair price in 1929. This was especially true if the city, particularly city attorney Rouer, would not give him the respect he believed he deserved. Throughout his lengthy legal battle against the city he insisted he was not "uncivic." Pointing out that his income rose and fell with the city's economy, Marvin insisted that no one was "more ambitious for the city of Fort Worth than I am." It was a matter of equity, honor, and status within the community.[31]

A Growing Store and New Managers

After 1929 few needed to be reminded of Marvin's or Leonards' place in the local community. Sales at Leonards went from $1 million in 1927 to $2.5 million in 1929, one of the sharpest percentage increases in the entire history of the store. Not surprisingly, this three-year period was one of pronounced prosperity in Fort

Worth. Despite intensifying competition, rapid economic growth buoyed sales at all the better-managed stores. Yet not every store made a profit, and some grew too large for their traditional style of management. Taking advantage of prosperity required an increasingly sophisticated managerial structure and the recruitment of talented managers.[32]

Things did not begin well in 1927. On January 10, a fire broke out in the second-floor storage area of the Leonards building and did about $10,000 worth of damage. Water flooded part of the grocery store on the first floor, but the mess was cleaned up and quickly repaired. Acting with characteristic alacrity, Marvin opened his store for business the next day.[33]

Getting the grocery store back in top shape was critical because it remained the largest volume department. As would be true for decades, low prices in the grocery department, the bakery, the meat market, and the produce department drew customers to the store. Fierce competition with chain stores and Marvin's insistence on selling bread and other easily identified items at the lowest price in town, however, kept margins in groceries very thin. Slightly higher markups in meat and produce helped keep overall food sales profitable.[34]

Leonards continued to rely on shrewd buying to increase profit margins. Marvin, Obie, and department heads scoured the region searching for bargains on distressed merchandise. Between 1927 and 1929, the brothers also expanded Fort Worth Wholesale Grocery and established Fort Worth Wholesale Produce. These wholesale operations secured lower prices for goods purchased through regular channels. Both sold primarily to the stores owned by the Leonard family. On a cash and carry basis, however, they sold to other independent grocers. As a Leonards publication stated, the store's close affiliation with wholesaling operations meant "the Chain Stores have never been able to stop or hamper progress."[35]

Leonards also supported its high-volume, low-margin strategy with an efficient, friendly, and service-oriented work force. More than 60 percent of Leonards' employees worked in foods, and Marvin and Obie did not hesitate to hire more people as the store grew. From September, 1928, to November, 1929, the number of employees in the four food departments increased from 51 to 124. By the close of 1929, the food departments did more business than any Fort Worth competitor, and Leonards was the largest single-site purveyor of meat, groceries, baked goods, and produce in Texas.[36]

Higher profit margins in nonfood departments also allowed Leonards to undercut prices offered by its grocery competitors. Groceries brought the customers in, but from its founding in late 1926 until the early 1930s, the drug department typically enjoyed both the highest profit margins and the highest annual increase in sales. Drugs never had the same cutthroat competition as groceries, yet that department faced competition from at least three major chain stores and from drug departments in other large department stores. In fact, Leonards followed Monnig's into the drug business. In 1925 Monnig's built a new building and added a drug department; Leonards did not add drugs until the following year.[37]

Leonards started its drug business and managed it much as it did other departments. When chain stores and department stores drove traditional drug stores out of business, Leonards often purchased their bankrupt stock. The store passed the savings on to its customers and supplemented low initial costs with volume buying and selling. These moves undercut the price of most local competitors and still ensured impressive profits. Drugs epitomized Leonards' strategy in the late 1920s. Enter each new line of sales as cheaply as possible. Build up a base of loyal customers by keeping prices low and selection broad. Rely on the large volume of customers generated by the food departments to attract additional sales.[38]

Marvin and Obie's success in selling drugs also demonstrated their skills at selecting managers. The original drug manager was F. T. Massingham, a registered pharmacist. In late 1928, the brothers made Morris E. Erwin manager and Massingham the assistant manager. Erwin, who was born in Linden, was twenty-nine years old when he came to Leonards. Since Obie and Erwin were nearly the same age, they may have been friends in Linden. Certainly the Leonards knew Erwin and trusted him. Erwin also had many years of experience in the wholesale drug business. As the time Marvin spent traveling with salesmen around East Texas taught him, wholesalers really knew the ins and outs of buying.[39]

Since he came from the same place, Erwin also shared Marvin and Obie's perspective on their customers, many of whom had moved to the city from places like Linden, or who came into town on Saturdays from the small towns and rural areas surrounding Fort Worth. Understanding these customers helped Erwin know what to buy.

Enough other managers and employees fit the general profile of Morris Erwin to say that three principles guided hiring at Leonards in the 1920s and 1930s. First, hire someone with whom you already had or could form a close personal relationship, a relationship that allowed the employee instinctively to understand and act upon Marvin's low-margin, rapid-turnover merchandising concept. Second, hire managers who knew their merchandise and how to buy it as cheaply as possible. Third, hire employees who possessed the background and imagination to sell that merchandise to the store's customers. Hobson Mack and his brother Robert Mack, for example, managed the wholesale grocery business. They were born in Sulphur Springs, another Northeast Texas small town. They had experience working wholesale in the larger town of Paris, Texas, and in Fort Worth. They shared a common background with Obie and Marvin and quickly formed a close relationship. They understood grocery wholesaling, Leonards' customers, and Marvin's basic merchandising concept. Even entry-level employees often fit this pattern.

Lloyd Shockley and his brother Lee Roy, who both began work at Leonards in the 1920s in the grocery department, had grown up in southeast Morris County, just across the county line from Linden. Sometimes Marvin used Rice-Stix and other wholesalers to suggest potential employees, but even then, new hires fit the well-established mold.[40]

In some ways even Carl Bruner, Marvin and Obie's most important early-day manager, fit the pattern. Bruner started work with the store as office manager and head of accounting in 1927. In 1929 he either purchased or was given as a bonus a percentage of the store, the only nonfamily member ever to own a part of the store until it was sold to Tandy in the late 1960s. Clearly Marvin considered him partially responsible for the phenomenal growth of Leonards in the late 1920s. In 1930 Bruner became secretary-treasurer of the organization, and combined those duties with those of a general manager and personnel director.[41]

Bruner was born near the village of Kerens, in Navarro County, Texas, in 1900. His family was part of the distinctive Texas German community found in the central counties of the state. He grew up in Frost to the west of Kerens but still in Navarro County. The county lay in the rich Blackland Prairie region south of Dallas and was the first center of oil production in Texas. Reflecting the county's and his family's prosperity, Bruner graduated from Frost High School and attended Baylor University. He moved to Fort Worth in 1919, the year Obie joined Marvin, and worked in the wholesale grocery industry. By 1927, he was the general credit manager of the James McCord Company, a local wholesaler. Thus Bruner shared the rural, small-town background and the experience in wholesaling common to most Leonards managers in the 1920s and 1930s.[42]

Unlike most managers, however, Bruner had some college education. Bruner was a studious man, a self-taught expert in business and tax law. He also understood the grocery trade on a national level and carefully analyzed sales trends, advising Obie and Marvin about future prospects for the economy and about potential new lines of business. He was a planner and a thinker. A good understanding of his contribution comes from a letter Marvin sent Bruner from his honeymoon trip in March, 1931: "In going over the papers, wouldn't it be a good idea to have Quit-Claim deeds instead of Warranty on all the transfers—also for the Corporation to assume all liabilities. You know what I mean. Would also like to have you transfer back the $24,000 worth of stock to Miss Enola's account which you transferred to me (I said $24,000—I don't remember the exact amount but of course you do.)" Marvin sketched out the big picture. Bruner filled in the numbers and the details.[43]

Bruner was one of the main reasons that Leonards successfully expanded into wholesale groceries and competed head to head with the largest grocery store chains in the country. He was an independent, self-confident man who bluntly offered a different perspective from Marvin's. Unlike other managers, however, coworkers had a difficult time forming close, personal bonds with Bruner. He was perceived as being arrogant and aloof, some said a stereotypical Texas German. Perhaps he was only studious and shy. At any rate, he was very direct in dealing with Marvin and Obie and with employees. He did not mince words or waste time. He cared about maximizing profits and efficiency, not southern hospitality. That cultural difference added to the stress of running a large operation like Leonards and may be why he left day-to-day management of the store in 1938.[44]

Next to Bruner, the most important manager to join the company in the late 1920s was R. D. T. "Doc" St. Clair. His career offers an instructive contrast to Bruner's. Like Bruner, St. Clair came from a different background than Marvin and Obie's: he grew up in Fort Worth. St. Clair and Bruner were also born the same year, 1900. After attending the public schools in Fort Worth, St. Clair worked with the Nash Hardware Company and the Trav Daniels Sporting Goods Company acquiring good experience in buying and selling hard lines. Unlike Bruner, he was a charming and personable man. Throughout his long tenure at Leonards, he formed close personal bonds with all his coworkers.[45]

One of the most frequently told stories about Leonards concerned how St. Clair went to work for Marvin Leonard. In late 1927 Marvin Leonard walked into Trav Daniel's store and asked St. Clair to fix him up with everything needed to play golf. St. Clair sold him the best set of matched clubs in the store and a good many other items as well, all the time convinced that "I've got myself a pigeon." Marvin, however, was sizing him up as a manager. Early in 1928 he offered St. Clair a job running the hard line departments at Leonards. At first, St. Clair refused. He did not want to deal in distressed merchandise targeted to bargain-hunting customers. He practically ran Trav Daniels and believed he would have to work so hard at Leonards that it would cut into his fishing time. Marvin told him not to rush his decision and to investigate the offer. St. Clair made $150 a month at Trav Daniels, and Marvin offered $200 a month and a percentage of the profits. Both Daniels and his banker urged him to take the offer, pointing out that Leonards was the fastest-growing retailer in town. With reluctance St. Clair accepted, thinking there was no harm in trying it for a year or two. He worked at Leonards for forty-four years and by 1936, hard lines was the most profitable section of the store.[46]

Hiring the right department managers and forming a personal relationship with them was critical to the success of the store. Department managers, also called buyers, decided what to stock and determined pricing strategies. They designed the layout of merchandise and played a major role in promotions. Marvin, Obie, and Bruner still kept a close eye on managers, who had less autonomy than they would be given in the late 1930s. The trio made major purchases and dealt daily with suppliers in all fields. They watched cash flow, inventory, and turnover. They ensured that there was money available for any purchase because they wanted buyers to cut costs by purchasing in bulk. Managers were not independent operators, but part of a large, centrally managed concern that could compete with any national chain on any product line. In terms of ordinary buying and pricing, however, managers were remarkably independent, going months without direct supervision by Marvin. Yet because they admired and respected him, they worked hard to earn a profit and stay within his merchandising concepts. In return, Marvin demonstrated his faith in them by giving them freedom. A few months after he began work at the store, St. Clair asked Marvin how he was doing. Did he need to do things differently? Marvin responded that he would suggest a change if conditions warranted, but that until then St. Clair should do what he thought best.[47]

By the late 1920s, not only had Leonards added numerous departments to its core food business, it described itself as a department store. It advertised a full range of products at everyday prices, not just special promotions. Selling thousands of cabbages at absurdly low prices still made it famous, but selling a normal line of products at competitive prices on an everyday basis made it profitable. Its managerial structure increasingly resembled a typical department store of its day, not a general store.[48]

Yet with its old building and jumbled wares, Leonards looked like a general store—a very large and very crowded general store. Adding new departments, new managers, more clerks, and more merchandise in existing departments made quarters tight in the one hundred block of North Houston. The store had taken over all the available space on the block by 1929 and it was still crowded. Moreover, the buildings were old, run down, and inconveniently laid out. Each time Marvin and Obie expanded the store, they knocked out a passageway to the new section, but load-bearing walls separated sections of the store and broke the natural flow of customer traffic. This architectural impediment divided the store's floor space into a series of long, narrow shopping areas connected by a hall at the front of the store running parallel to Houston Street from Belknap to Weatherford. Shopping was difficult, and the store did not have the look or feel of a modern department store. Leonards called itself a department store, but to be one required a new building.[49]

A New Store and the Arrival of the Great Depression

In later years, company legend pointed to the decision to build a new store as one taken in the face of an approaching depression. Building in 1929 demonstrated Marvin and Obie's vision, courage, and wisdom. As one chronicler of the Leonards' story put it, "With pessimism cloaking the city and the country, Marvin and Obie started talking of growth."⁵⁰ Actually it was not the bold decision in the teeth of the Depression later described. Nor did the brothers act in isolation. Leonards needed more space, but their competitors also forced the store to act because most of them moved into new buildings between 1925 and 1929. In addition, the local economy would not feel the full impact of the Depression until 1931. Even then, as the Chamber of Commerce pointed out in early 1933, progress in the city continued.⁵¹

Popular conceptions of the Great Depression usually peg its starting point as October 24, 1929, the day of the big crash in the stock market. In Fort Worth, however, conditions that fall seemed more promising than in the recession of 1920–21, and optimism, backed by the reality of good sales figures at local retailers, remained high through the next year.⁵²

First among the many related reasons for the city's prolonged economic health was Fort Worth's significant advantage over its neighbors in handling agricultural commodities. From 1928 to 1931 the cotton, wheat, and railroad industries enlarged and modernized their yards, mills, and handling capacity in Fort Worth. When the Texas & Pacific Railroad completed new shops and yards in 1928, it transferred workers and tasks to Fort Worth until more than two thousand shop employees and trainmen did the work formerly done in scattered locations. Encouraged by the expanding presence of the railroad companies, Universal Mills built two mills with a combined capacity of three thousand barrels of flour per day in 1930–31. These improved facilities meant that while commodity prices slipped after 1929, the volume of grain and cotton moving through Fort Worth increased until 1933. Fort Worth made its money on the volume of the trade and on the spread between what local dealers paid and what they sold commodities for.⁵³

The relatively good health of the West Texas economy also augmented the flow of trade from Fort Worth and the flow of customers to Leonards. Large new oil fields opened in several West Texas counties, helping Texas oil production double from 1925 to 1929. Much of the production was developed by Fort Worth companies, and Fort Worth remained the refining center for the region. At the same time, the development of irrigated agriculture around Lubbock meant that Fort Worth wholesalers had a giant new market. Mules, other livestock, and a wide variety of tractors and farm implements moved from Fort Worth to the South Plains. Fort Worth's major trade area remained insulated from depression until 1931.⁵⁴

Increased economic activity in West Texas and at the mills and rail yards spurred construction in Fort Worth. By 1929, residential construction, including that done by Marvin and Obie, was slowing down. Commercial construction, on the other hand, gathered steam. Texas & Pacific opened the Union Depot for passenger service in 1931 at a cost of $1.5 million. Responding to the discovery of the huge Yates Field in Pecos County and other new fields, the refineries expanded capacity and modernized their plants in 1930–32, spending more than $3.5 million. Office and retail space also increased dramatically in the late 1920s and early 1930s. Montgomery Wards opened a $2 million building to handle its regional mail order business and house its local retail store. The Fair moved into a new store in 1929 and the Sinclair Building was completed at about the same time. W. T. Grant and S. H. Kress built new stores in the early 1930s. In part, construction continued because large commercial structures took longer to plan and build than residential construction. Plans made in 1929 often took two years to become reality. Yet it was also true that for a time the construction boom in primary industries like refining and transportation kept the economy strong enough to justify new stores for Leonards and its competitors.[55]

One final factor accounts for the delayed onslaught of the Depression and Marvin and Obie's decision to build a new store. Banks continued to lend money for interim financing of large real-estate projects. As in other Texas cities, the fast pace of economic growth during World War I caused a rapid expansion of the number of banks in Fort Worth. The brief economic downturn in 1921–22, however, triggered a round of bank consolidations. Four relatively large banks emerged: Fort Worth National, First National, Continental National, and Farmers and Mechanics National. In 1927 Fort Worth National, Marvin's bank, absorbed Farmers and Mechanics. As a result, by 1929 banking in Fort Worth was far more concentrated than in any other Texas city. Indeed, three of the sixteen largest Texas banks were located in the state's fourth-largest city. Consolidation reduced the number of incompetent managers and lessened competition between banks. Less competition encouraged Fort Worth banks to avoid risk in the boom times of 1927 to 1929.[56]

In early 1930, just as work began on Leonards' new building, a run on First National Bank briefly disrupted the local economy, but the scare soon passed. If anything, the February, 1930, run put to rest fears of weakness in the local banking system. Spared the collapse of the real-estate market that plagued banks in other cities and having demonstrated the strength to survive a panic, there was little reason for banks to shut off credit to a thriving business like Leonards.[57]

Because the Fort Worth banking system and economy remained strong into 1931, tales of the Leonards' brave move into a new building in the face of the Great Depression were a bit like tales of catching the biggest fish. The deed grew more daring as time passed. That is not to say that investing $519,000 for the land and $450,000 for the new building and fixtures was without risk. The old location had been very good to Marvin and Obie. With about $800 in start-up capital, they had built a business that generated $2.5 million in sales and allowed the brothers to diversify into real estate and other businesses. They realized, however, that quarters were tight and that their space was not as usable or as modern in appearance as their competitors' stores. They had no choice but to move if they planned on future growth.[58]

In November, 1929, Obie and Marvin announced the purchase of all but the northwest corner of a block bordered by Houston, Throckmorton, First, and Second Streets. This lot was two blocks south of their original store. In January, 1930, site preparation began. The old buildings were torn down and a basement dug by the end of May. Construction of the store began in June, and by the first week of October, the new store was ready. It was a two- story building with a full basement and twice as much floor space as the old store.[59]

Obie oversaw every detail of construction and did his best to ensure that the store could be run efficiently and economically. Generators in the subbasement burned cardboard and other packaging to produce electricity, and the store had its own water well. The first floor was designed so that customers could move through the entire area without obstruction. No longer would load-bearing walls divide the store into odd-sized pieces. Two large, centrally located stairways allowed easy movement down to the basement and up to the mezzanine. The basement housed a well-equipped creamery designed by Obie. The store purchased raw milk and cream from area farmers and converted it into butter, buttermilk, pasteurized milk, cream, and ice cream. On the top floor was a bakery that produced more than seven thousand loaves of bread per day. In fact, portions of the new store resembled a factory more than a department store. Besides the bakery and creamery, Leonards manufactured candy and pasta, roasted and ground coffee, and operated a laundry. No wonder Obie insisted on his own source of water and electricity.[60]

Saturday, October 4, 1930, was the last day of business in the old location at 100 N. Houston Street. For the previous week, the Chamber of Commerce had used the new store for a home show. That done, it was time to move. The doors closed at 10:00 P.M., but anxious employees began moving from the old to the new store an hour earlier. Wives and husbands of employees came downtown to help. Young part-time workers helped out, too. Using trucks, pushcarts, and wheelbarrows, several hundred workers moved all the merchandise south to the new store. They worked all night, all day Sunday, and well into Monday morning. It was like a large party. Helpers passed out sandwiches, coffee, cakes, and pies. Workers sang as they hauled boxes and barrels of merchandise to the new store. Anxious family members who came to check on their loved ones stayed to help out. By early Monday morning, the task was completed; the new store opened at 7:00 A.M. on Monday, October 6, 1930.[61]

A few hours earlier, Doc St. Clair saw Marvin Leonard standing alone at the back of the old store with tears in his eyes. He asked, "What is the matter Mr. Marvin?" Shaking his head, Leonard replied, "I just don't know, I just don't know. This old store has been pretty good to us. I just don't know." Few ever saw such emotion or doubt in Marvin Leonard. It was testimony to the difficulty of leav-

The week before the new store opened for business on Monday, October 6, 1930, customers lined up at the old store to take advantage of bargains.

ing a proven business location and making a large investment in a new store. The old store was comfortable and familiar. Sentiment tied him to the place where he had started business.[62]

Marvin did what he could to ease his customers into the new surroundings. One oft-told story, which may not be entirely true, still indicates Marvin's insistence that the new store fit his old customers. The story has him telling his employees, "If you see someone who seems to be looking for a place to spit, just walk in front of them and spit on the floor so they'll know it's all right. Make them feel at home. If a mother wants to nurse her baby, get her a chair. Or let her sit on the piece goods counter."[63] Few spat on the floor of the new store, but telling the story over and over made an important point. Black and white customers felt at home because employees retained "a relaxed country atmosphere."[64]

In 1996 Catherine Symington still remembered what it was like for her and other blacks shopping at Leonards in the 1920s and 1930s. Her mother gave her brother and her three dollars for groceries and two dimes to ride the street car back. They walked to Leonards, made their purchases, saw their friends, and rode back with their heavy sacks of food. She remembered tubs of merchandise out on the sidewalk in front of the old store and "blind people with their cups out" wandering through the crowd on the street. While Marvin probably believed that blacks had a place and should stay in it, blacks shopped at Leonards from the beginning because the prices were good and they felt welcome. Leonards, like most stores in the South with black customers, had segregated rest rooms, drinking fountains, and eating facilities. Many department stores in Fort Worth, however, did not bother with providing segregated facilities; they simply excluded blacks. Within the limits of segregation, Leonards made blacks feel at home. As Symington said, "that was the place for us."[65]

Leonards was also the place for country folk of both races. Elba Crumby's family was typical of this type. She was born in Winnsboro in Northeast Texas in 1922. Her family, like thousands of other white farm folk, later moved to West Texas, settling sixty miles west of Lubbock near the New Mexico boundary. In the mid-1930s, her father lost all his teeth and was reluctant to spend the money to have a custom set of dentures made. A cousin told him to go to Fort Worth and buy a set of teeth from Leonards. Crumby's father traveled 350 miles to Fort Worth where in a corner at Leonards he found a tub of teeth. He looked through the teeth, trying on one set after another until he found a pair that fit. He proudly wore them for many years. The incident reveals not only that Leonards' reputation for good merchandise at a fair price reached a long way, but that Texans knew if you could buy teeth, you could probably buy anything else you wanted at Leonards.[66]

While Leonards kept much of the feel of a town square on a Saturday, it added a vital ingredient to the mix. Marvin and Obie fostered an exciting, circus-like atmosphere that made shopping fun. The same gift for attention-grabbing promotions, the same willingness to try anything once continued in the new store. A few months before the opening of the new store, the brothers purchased six boxcars of preserved figs from the Imperial Sugar Company for the bargain-basement price of $.25 per gallon. After debating whether to sell them for $.49 or $.59 a gallon, Marvin suggested they sell them for $.39 a gallon as part of their grand opening sale. Extensive advertising and the excitement of the Grand Opening brought long lines of customers to the special counter where the figs were sold. According to company legend, one man got in line without knowing what the line was for. He waited patiently until he reached the head of the line. Taking his wrapped package he asked the clerk, "What is this?" The bemused clerk asked why he stood in line to purchase an unknown product. He replied, "If this many people want it, it must be a real buy."[67]

Thanks to this flair for promotions and the continued health of the Fort Worth economy, business increased after the move. In fact, sales were so good in 1931 that brokers began writing Marvin to see if he was interested in selling the store. He responded that he would sell, but for a high price "since our business is one of the few that has increased in both profit and volume continually for a number of years." He could not again say that sales and volume increased over the previous year until 1935. The Depression arrived in Fort Worth by late 1931, and not even Obie and Marvin could make sales go up in the hard times that followed. Oil prices, the shipping of agricultural commodities, meat packing, and all types of manufacturing declined.[68]

One memorable sign of that national calamity was the Bank Holiday of 1933. For the good of the community and the stability of their own investments, civic leaders were expected to prevent bank failures, maintain the flow of currency in the local community, and restore public confidence during times of panic. Marvin and Obie learned the lesson well. In March, 1933, faced with the complete collapse of the American banking system, newly inaugurated President Franklin D. Roosevelt closed all the banks in the country. This stopped the massive withdrawals that threatened even healthy banks, but it also meant that those living from paycheck to paycheck lacked the means of converting those checks into currency.[69]

Out of this adversity grew an image of Leonards that persisted in the public mind for decades. In the absence of banks, Leonards offered to redeem all payroll checks if the customers would accept part cash and part scrip. Marvin had a local printer make up paper scrip in various denominations with the Leonard name on it. Leonards accepted the scrip for any purchase, and other local merchants soon followed. In part because of Leonards, there was no currency shortage in Fort Worth, and business went on as usual during that tumultuous month of March, 1933. That scrip endeared Leonards to a generation of customers who remembered that when they could not cash a check anywhere else, Leonards gave them the chance to buy what they needed. So many people kept a bit of the scrip as a memento of the Bank Holiday that Leonards paid for the cost of printing and made a small profit besides. As often happened, doing good for the community created loyal customers and increased profit.[70]

Issuing scrip during the Bank Holiday signaled that Marvin and Obie Leonard had a new place in the community. They joined Amon Carter, W. T. Waggoner, William Monnig, and a few others in an elite group that the community turned to in difficult times. When a state- and county-financed program to feed hungry school children ran out of funds in 1933, Marvin contributed $35,000 to feed the children. With the help of the Community Chest, he made sure that the school meals program continued until the government was better able to handle the problem. Through the store, both brothers supported the Lena Pope Home for orphans, which was founded in 1930 and depended upon the generosity of local citizens to survive the Depression. Marvin admired Lena Pope, who, despite being married to a wealthy local businessman, devoted much of her life to the care of neglected and homeless children. He regularly contributed food, clothing, building supplies, and money, philanthropy that the Leonard family still practices.[71]

BUILDING COLONIAL AND A NEW FAMILY

Building Colonial Country Club furthered the transition of Marvin Leonard from boom-time businessman to influential community leader. The country club life, however, was only half the story, for at about the same time he became a committed family man.

As he recounted the story in later years, Marvin first tried golf in 1922 when he joined the Glen Garden Country Club on the southeast side of downtown Fort Worth. The game was too slow and time too short, so he put away his clubs. As he recalled in 1960, "I found out it took about four hours to get around the course. I thought that was silly. How could anyone stay away from work that long?" A few years later, the long hours at his desk caught up with him, bringing chronic fatigue and stomach trouble: "I woke up one morning in 1927 feeling so low that I went to my family doctor, and he said to start playing golf or start preparing for a crack up." Leonard paid up his back dues at Glen Garden and began playing nine holes in the morning before breakfast. He lived nearby and after playing half a round he returned home, where Enola fixed his breakfast. As he said, "It wasn't long until I was eating a good breakfast—oatmeal, eggs, bacon—really eating a good breakfast and enjoying it." For many years, he made it a point of playing at a minimum every Sunday, Tuesday, and Thursday at either Glen Garden or River Crest Country Club. Golf, with a wager thrown in to heighten his interest, took his mind off business and gave him a little exercise and fresh air. He remained healthy into the 1950s.[72]

By the early 1930s, Leonard was a director of the Glen Garden Club and actively involved in an experiment with bent grass greens. Hole number 18 was planted with bent grass and with plenty of water it thrived, yielding one of the smoothest, most consistent greens in the state. Better courses in the North and West all had bent grass greens, and Marvin saw no reason for Forth Worth's golfers to settle for less than the best. Most of Glen Gardens' directors still considered bent grass too delicate for the extreme heat, cold, and wind found in North Texas and resisted expanding its use. The experiment, however, convinced Marvin of two things. He liked thinking about how to build a better golf course, and bent grass could flourish in Fort Worth.[73]

Determined to build a true "championship course," Marvin set to work in 1935, constructing his course on 140 acres along the Trinity River. Colonial Country Club opened on January 29, 1936. Perry Maxwell and John Bredemus designed and built the course, preparing as many as ten plans for each hole. Marvin walked

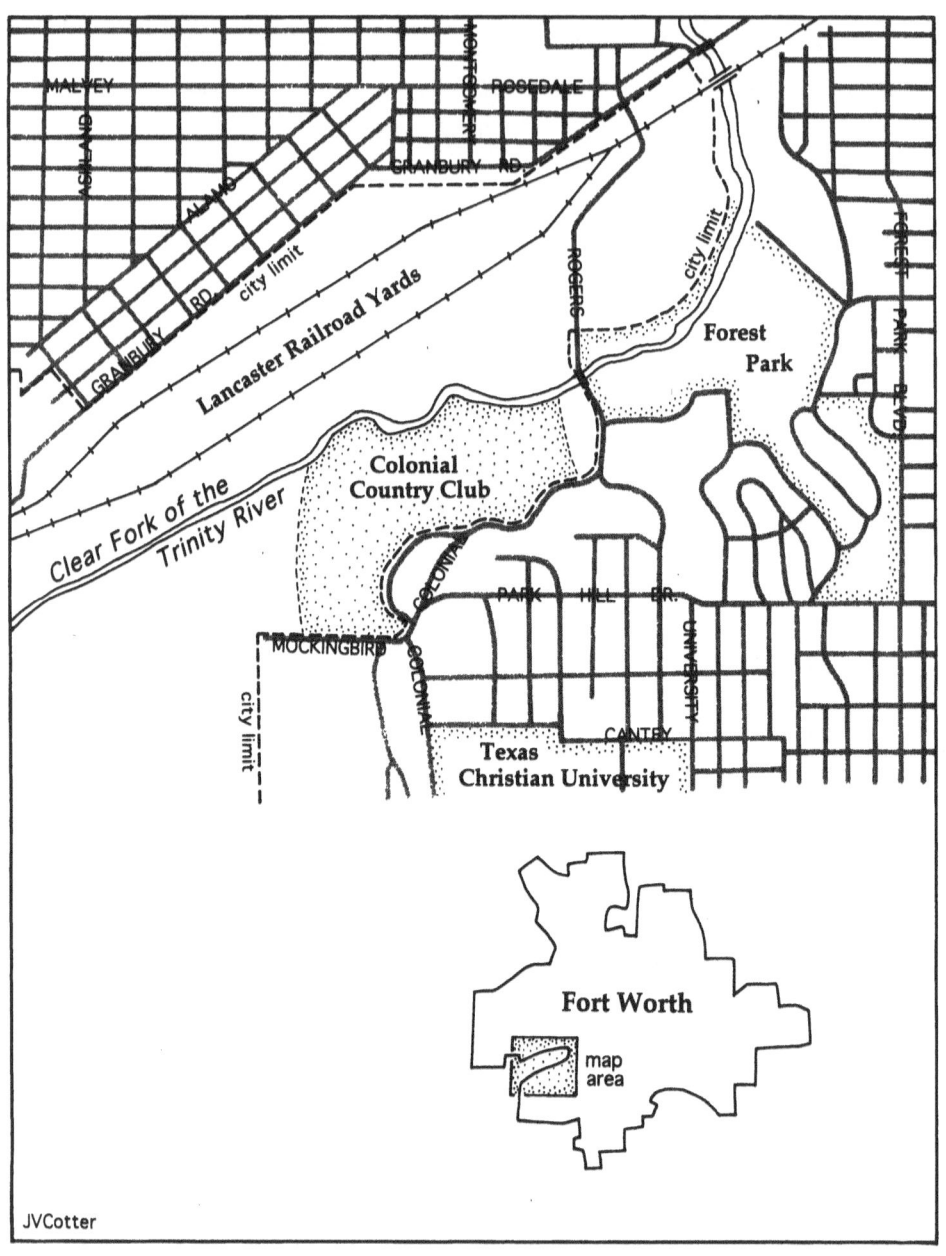

Colonial, 1936. *Map by John V. Cotter.*

the ground on which the course was to be built with them, and he made the ultimate decision on each hole. Colonial boasted Bermuda grass fairways and healthy bent grass greens. An irrigation system pumped water out of the Clear Fork of the Trinity to keep what was initially a 6,800-yard course in top shape. There were also tennis courts, a swimming pool, and a club house fronted by four white columns in keeping with the name Colonial. Total cost was about $250,000.[74]

During its first two years the club lost money, but in 1938 it began to show a small profit. Profits increased over the next few years as membership increased from about 100 in 1936 to 450 in 1941. Slot machines were an interesting contributor to profit. Marvin kept 80 percent of the take, and the owner of the machines kept 20 percent. The owner kept the local police from disturbing the nice arrangement. Marvin's continual improvements were another reason membership and profits increased. Gradually he transformed Colonial from primarily a men's golf club to a family club. Construction of a new ballroom in 1941 marked the end of this transformation. Men could play golf and talk business over a drink and cards. Women and children joined the men on the course. Couples danced in the ballroom, and the whole family took advantage of the club's other amenities. Among those who joined were several prominent Jewish families. Unlike clubs in many other parts of the country and some of the more exclusive clubs in Houston and Dallas, Colonial always had Jewish members. Perhaps this reflected the relatively small number of Jews in Fort Worth, but it also reflected Marvin's lack of religious or ethnic prejudice. Like other clubs, Colonial excluded blacks, but otherwise, if you could pay your bills and had good references, you could join Colonial. As oil and defense spending buoyed the local economy and increased the city's

Marvin's characteristic swing did not always send the ball a great distance but it usually sent it straight.

population, Colonial became the fashionable club for the up-and-coming.⁷⁵

Many of this rising class settled in the residential neighborhood that Marvin developed around the club. He recalled that the residential development was an afterthought: "Houses have followed the golf course, not the golf course following the houses." Colonial Hills was a hugely successful development, one that made Leonard a good deal of money and added a host of potential new members for the club. Golf, however, was always more than a matter of money for Marvin, and by the late 1930s golf, work, and family filled most days.⁷⁶

At the start of the 1930s, Marvin's family life still centered on Enola and Obie. He enjoyed visiting Margery and Obie's rapidly expanding household. He still lived with Enola, but both soon started their own families. Enola married J. C. Moulton on December 26, 1931. The couple had one daughter, Laura Mae, born February 12, 1934.⁷⁷

Marvin married earlier the same year. He met Mary Elinor Vaughan in early 1930 at a bridge party, and they began dating regularly. Mary, the fifth of six children, was born in Oklahoma on January 12, 1907. Her father, Frank O. Vaughan, worked for the railroad and the family moved often. They lived in Big Spring, Texas, and New Orleans before coming to Fort Worth in the 1920s. Mary's mother, Annie May, was in ill health by the time Marvin met her daughter, and she died in 1934. Mary came from an artistic family filled with musicians, and one of their favorite activities was listening to opera on the radio. She was also a dedicated member of the Episcopal Church.⁷⁸

Marvin courted Mary at her family's home in the Mistletoe Heights subdivision near Forest Park. He also sent Jenkins Garrett, again a courier at the store, on his bicycle to deliver boxes of candy to her. Doubtless the candy helped, but the two seemed attracted to each other from the first time they met. In the midst of planning and completing a new store, Marvin and Mary planned a wedding. When they married, on March 8, 1931, he was thirty-six and she twenty-four. It was a small ceremony limited to family. With tongue in cheek Marvin notified friends and employees, "Personally, I don't particularly enjoy being showered with rice and old shoes, but the wife would enjoy it immensely." A crowd gathered at the Texas & Pacific depot to see the newlyweds off on their honeymoon.⁷⁹

On January 12, 1932, their first child, Mary Elinor, was born. She shared a birthday with her twenty-five-year-old mother. Marvin hired a nurse for the baby without asking Mary and told her never to do anything he could hire someone to do for her. His wife was not to know the hard physical labor of his mother and his sister Enola.⁸⁰

Mary would also influence Marvin. In 1932, she encouraged him to take over the leadership of the Little Theater, a community playhouse. She also helped convince him to take on a larger role at the Lena Pope Home. As Lena Pope recalled later, she visited Marvin in about 1933 and told him "the Lord has led us to you." She wanted him to join William Monnig and Charles Lupton on her Advisory Board. After giving her a characteristic wry smile, Marvin responded, "The Lord will agree that I have enough problems on my hands without taking over some of His." But he went on, "In a hassle with you, Charley Lupton, and my wife, I would get approximately nowhere, so write me in."[81]

When Marvin and Mary first married, they lived in the Forest Park Apartments, but they soon moved into a house on Monticello Drive. Located between downtown and the River Crest Country Club, the house provided convenient access to the store and the golf course. One friend remembered the house as "a plain two story house," with three bedrooms. Another daughter soon came to live at the house on Monticello. Miranda was born on March 26, 1934. Space was getting tight, and the Leonards began construction on a house adjacent to River Crest Country Club soon after Miranda's birth. In 1936 they moved into a large home at 600 Alta Drive just in time for the birth of a third daughter. Martha Vaughan was born on November 3, 1936. Her parents called her Martha, but to her sisters and friends she was Marty. On June 20, 1944, a fourth daughter, Madelon, completed the family.[82]

Like his brother Obie, Marvin took parenthood seriously. He made it a point to be home for the evening meal with his family and helped discipline and train the children. He taught his children by example, but also intervened directly in their lives. As a teenager, Marty's temper sometimes flared on the golf course. Once, while vacationing in California, she threw down a club in anger and disgust. Her father said, "All right, that is enough." He put the clubs away for two weeks, leaving Marty without the thing she enjoyed most about vacations.[83]

Marvin encouraged his daughters to participate in sports and school activities and tried to ensure that they had a normal childhood. He took them to the doctor and the dentist, and he attended their school functions. The girls and their friends trailed along behind him to the store. One friend remembers going to the bakery with Marty for a fresh loaf of bread and then to the grocery cooler for a stick of butter. With bread and butter in hand, the two headed for Marvin's office to eat their snack.[84]

While Marvin played an active part in his daughters' lives, he was in many ways a traditional father. Mary and Marvin had clearly separate functions as parents. Mary took charge of religion and education. She tended to school activities and took the children to school every day. She selected their clothing, taking care that it not stand out from their classmates at the public schools. Marvin was in charge of fun: deciding when and where they would go on vacations; leading the family pony around the yard, girls astride; or later watching cowboy shows with Madelon.[85]

In 1934 Marvin and Mary were very much in love and proud of their first house at 3912 Monticello Drive.

Marvin and Mary had fixed ideas on the proper roles of men and women. While Marvin's mother and sister Enola had worked hard and were competent in business matters, apparently he never considered that any of his daughters would take part in the management of Leonards. Mary, Miranda, Marty, and Madelon all worked briefly at the store, usually during the Christmas rush, but Marvin made little effort to train them to take over the store or to prepare them for the business world. In elementary school, Marty played quarterback on a football team with the neighborhood boys and was the only girl on the team. They challenged other neighborhood boys and played them on the River Crest golf course, winning about as many games as they lost. When Marty was eleven or twelve, Mary and Marvin made her give up football because it was not ladylike. A limited definition of being a lady would eventually cause problems between husband and wife. Still, in the 1930s and 1940s, Marvin Leonard and his family were happy.[86]

Even after he married, Marvin worked long hours. James Blair, who started work for Leonards in the early spring of 1931, remembered that Marvin came to work shortly after eight o'clock. He arrived after the department managers and after his brother Obie, but he still put in a long day at the store. He kept close tabs on what went on, close enough to know when a supplier shorted them a few pounds of cheese.[87]

Marvin even carried this attention to detail and close association with the store with him on his honeymoon. After a rousing send-off, complete with the usual gags and marginally humorous notes about the difficulties Mary could expect with an old bachelor, the couple traveled toward New York. Along the way Marvin wrote back to the store with tips on buying new merchandise and how to improve the layout of particular items. He remained very focused on the store.[88]

Hard Times and Retailing

Marvin's attention to detail was crucial in the grim early 1930s. Changes in the gross annual sales at Leonards were one indication of the depth of the Depression in Fort Worth. After reaching $3.5 million in 1931, sales dropped more than $200,000 in 1932 and remained at about the same level through 1936. Not until 1937 would sales surpass the 1931 level. For five years Leonards experienced slow growth or an outright decline in sales.[89]

To some degree, a decline in the cost of merchandise offset the decline in sales. From 1917 to 1927, the cost of goods to merchants and to consumers went up dramatically. Indeed, one of the reasons that Leonards initially grew was that it offered consumers a way to beat inflation. From the late 1920s to 1940, however, the consumer price index generally went down. The cost of buying goods went down for all merchants, and Leonards' well-developed buying ability allowed the store to reduce its expenses even further. In some cases, particularly when faced with competition, the store also reduced its markup on merchandise. Usually, however, it kept the margins near the pre-1931 level. Thus, annual sales went down far more than profits. Even in the worst days of the Depression in 1932–34, Leonards still made an annual net profit of more than $200,000.[90]

Marvin and Obie also met the challenge of marketing in the Great Depression by opening another store. During the 1920s, the brothers occasionally used the name Everybody's for salvage stores they operated in various spots in the downtown area. If they acquired a large stock of lower-quality merchandise, irregulars, and seconds, they simply found the cheapest retail space available and advertised in the local newspapers. By 1929 they operated a grocery and meat market on Weatherford Street called Everybody's. In 1931 they took the half-block fronting on N. Houston Street that once housed part of Leonards and opened up a new Everybody's. This 19,000-square-foot store featured lower-quality and lower-priced inventory than Leonards and catered to those more interested in bargains than a nicer shopping atmosphere. Its original stock was made up largely of seconds, irregulars, and other merchandise Marvin did not want transferred to his new store. Like Leonards, Everybody's sold groceries, meat, produce, drugs, hardware, dry goods, seeds, and shoes, but did not carry as wide a selection as the main store. This was especially true of clothing and other dry goods, where Everybody's concentrated on work clothes and other low-priced products. Like the main store, Everybody's was supplied by Obie and Marvin's wholesale companies.[91]

Ted Leveridge, who began working under Carl Bruner in the accounting department in 1928, managed Everybody's and had the idea of opening up an alternative to Leonards. His original idea was to keep Marvin's low-price, rapid-turnover concepts, but to feature slightly lower-quality merchandise. Being smaller let Everybody's operate much like Leonards in the early 1920s. No collection of merchandise was too small or too bizarre if the price was right. The store fit the times. Although it operated until the early 1960s, some of its most successful days were during the Depression. In 1931 Everybody's total sales were $525,000. By 1935 total sales exceeded $700,000. Expanding sales at Everybody's offset declining sales at the main store.[92]

Lower production, distribution, and sales costs also helped Leonards maintain a steady profit level in the 1930s. One of the most famous examples was bread. The bakery used the most efficient ovens available. Once baked, a conveyor belt with slots for each individual loaf delivered the bread down to the grocery store. The smell of hot bread permeated the store, and employees pulled the loaves off the conveyor and put them in sacks for eager customers. Customers were eager because not only was the bread delicious, the price was right. In 1932 the normal price was five cents, but Leonards often ran specials featuring bread at two loaves for a nickel. Because Leonards did not have to store the bread and did not pay to distribute it to numerous sites, its expenses were low. That advantage, along with the large volume of bread sold, allowed Leonards to maintain the lowest bread prices in town. Low-cost, high-quality bread marketed by the common sense approach of letting customers see it and smell it repeatedly drew customers into the store.[93]

Meat was another example of how Leonards profited despite the drop in total sales. High volume at Leonards combined with what was sold at Everybody's and G. T. Leonard meant they could buy in bulk. Since they paid up front, hard-pressed meat packers gave the company a price break that was passed on to its customers. As with bread, selling at only three sites in downtown Fort Worth reduced distribution costs. The customers came to them.[94]

In one final way, Marvin and Obie adjusted to the Great Depression. They put increased emphasis on nonfood sales. When they moved into the new store in 1930, groceries, produce, meat, and delicatessen sales made up about 70 percent of total sales. Taking advantage of the increased space in the new store, the brothers expanded the amount of merchandise in the nonfood departments. In 1931 food made up only about 55 percent of total sales, and by 1937 it made up only about 40 percent of total sales. Groceries would remain an important part of Leonards for decades, bringing in new customers and keeping old customers coming back. By 1937, however, hard lines and other nonfood departments were the heart of the business. Food had always been very competitive and during the Depression already slim profit margins got slimmer. Drugs and hardware had higher markups than bread and meat.[95]

Increased sales of nonfood items required more space. In 1937, Marvin and Obie purchased the northwest corner of the block where their new store stood. They knocked out the walls between the former Rosenthal's Furniture and Leonards and expanded to cover the entire block bordered by Houston, Throckmorton, First, and Second Streets. The new space housed enlarged departments for men's clothing, furniture, and shoes. While Leonards still had the feel of a country square on a Saturday night, its product lines increasingly mimicked major department stores across the country.[96]

The image and product mix of Leonards were well established by January, 1938. So were the image and interests of Marvin Leonard. He had a happy family and a fine new home. The citizens of Fort Worth admired him for helping them cope with the Depression and for building Colonial Country Club. Golfers watched with interest his efforts to build and maintain a championship course. Bankers and corporate executives knew of his success in retailing and real estate. They stood ready to ask him to join their boards of directors. Marvin and his store now filled the roles in the city for which they were best remembered: a respected family man; a voice of reason, compassion, and optimism among city leaders; a promoter and benefactor of golf; a businessman of mature judgment and remarkable vision; and a store that dominated Fort Worth retailing by contributing to the community while offering everything to anybody at the lowest possible price.[97]

MY PRICE OR NO PRICE, 1938-48

By 1938 Marvin Leonard rarely bade departing employees goodbye at the door. The growing store had too many doors, and too many other things occupied his time. Besides, a more mature store with a well-defined image, clear merchandising philosophy, and hierarchical management structure no longer required constant oversight. A new era, for Marvin and for Leonards, had begun.[1]

Marvin increasingly used the store as the headquarters and bank for his rapidly expanding investments in oil, real estate, and regional corporations. Community service and philanthropy filled a larger part of each day. His passion for golf and the appeal of time spent with close friends and family also pulled Marvin away from his former routine. Marvin and Obie even considered selling the store—for the right price.[2]

Marvin's willingness to sell and willingness to turn managerial responsibility over to others arose from a pragmatic search for security. Leonards yielded an income that pushed Marvin into the highest tax bracket. His reputation for integrity, ingenuity, and deal making flowed from the store. Community leaders and business associates knew they could find him at 200 Houston Street, and investment proposals from aspiring entrepreneurs collected on his desk. Leonards' growth and success created an ever-widening network of contacts for Marvin, and resulting appointments to charitable and corporate boards established his place among Fort Worth's elite. Yet while Marvin was proud of the store and liked to recall its earliest days, he viewed the store with a detached eye for the bottom line.[3]

Marvin anchored Leonards. He worked at his second-floor desk every day—taking and making calls, sifting through correspondence and operating figures, and following up on projects—but no longer roused himself at three o'clock in the morning to search for bargains on Produce Row or to make an auction sale on time. Instead, he slipped up the back stairway just before ten o'clock and stayed until mid-afternoon. Marvin joined Obie in the cafeteria often enough for Alma

Bennett Robertson, who worked there, to remember saving a dish of carrot salad for him whenever she made it. Just as often, though, he ate at his desk, quickly finishing a sandwich and banana from home or a lunch sent in from a cafe down the street. This let him work efficiently then leave for Colonial Country Club or another golf course. He enjoyed this flexible schedule, but he knew the store needed his strategic planning, marketing ability, and clear focus on low prices.[4]

THE STORE IN 1938

Marvin could leave the store early because it had grown up. Customers saw the obvious evidence. Professionally lettered signs announcing sales and directing customers around the store replaced crude, hand-painted ones. Newspaper ads grew more detailed and featured the store's depth and breadth of stock along with popular prices for all merchandise. An advertising staff and a display department planned and carried out increasingly sophisticated marketing and promotional efforts. The building (three floors and a basement) straddled a full city block, and every day six hundred employees punched in to ensure that retailing, wholesaling, and behind-the-scenes operations ran smoothly.[5]

The basics remained: the twenty-year-old business still carried a motley collection of merchandise, still featured bargains over fashion, and still appealed to Fort Worth's working families with country roots. What customers could not easily see was the increasingly sophisticated strategy and organizational structure that supported the larger, modernized retail operation. During the 1930s, Leonards had added and expanded departments and services, experimented with new merchandising and promotional techniques, cultivated more-varied suppliers, and built a managerial hierarchy to coordinate and control the extensive operations. These moves solidified the strategy it would follow for its second twenty years—giving customers as many reasons as possible for visiting the store and every opportunity to buy something once they were there.

The grocery, meat, and produce departments and the delicatessen operated next to each other on the first floor, each with its own management and staff. The variety of products and services offered would have startled out-of-town visitors who wandered, unsuspecting, into Leonards. The grocery department took up much of the ground floor—partly because it stocked five thousand different items and partly because it had recently rearranged its operation to offer both full- and self-service to customers. A 108-foot display case featured the store's meats, cheeses, fresh fish, poultry, and deli offerings—from pigs' feet to strip sirloin. The twenty-two butchers and butcher's assistants trimmed, packaged, and sold thousands of pounds of bacon, steak, and roast every day. Depending upon the season, shoppers would find up to one hundred different fresh produce items. C. R. Ferguson, fruit and vegetable manager, trucked in goods from local sources and bought from area farmers if possible. He also used regional and national vendors to supply Fort Worth produce-lovers with strawberries from Arkansas, green beans and other field crops from Colorado, apples from Washington, and potatoes from Idaho.[6]

Across from groceries—taking up the western portion of the first floor—Armour Hann operated his drug department. The huge number of prescriptions filled by the department's three registered pharmacists pleased area doctors because, according to Hann, "physicians know that our volume insures fresh drugs at all times." The department also stocked a broader range of merchandise than a typical independent pharmacy. While they waited, customers could shop for knickknacks in the gift section, replenish the kids' school supplies, or try on jewelry. Women could wander over to the adjacent cosmetic department to browse the latest colors and styles or sip a soda at the fountain.[7]

J. B. Moates, recent high school graduate and soda jerk extraordinaire, launched his Leonards career from behind that fountain counter. Having taken a job scooping ice cream and mopping up after messy customers for thirteen dollars a week in 1935, Moates soon viewed store operations with an eye to his own advancement. He listened to the vendors and jobbers gabbing when they stopped in for a doughnut or quick sandwich and overheard their exchanges with department buyers as they haggled over the right price for a big sale. From his vantage point behind the counter, young Moates watched the traffic flowing in and out of the men and boys department across the way. Perhaps he also heard that Al Smith's department added substantially to the store's total profit each year. He pestered Smith for a job so persistently that he eventually earned a transfer. The department's place on the convenient northeast corner of the first floor guaranteed heavy traffic, and its selection of stock with a heavy emphasis on work clothes—durable and priced to move—ensured ample sales. Moates, hired as an extra for the Christmas selling season, parlayed his opportunity into a full-time job. He led his new department in sales his first year and every year after until he was promoted into management in 1940.[8]

Claude Hamrick's shoe department occupied space adjacent to men and boys in the center of the east side of the building. Clerks kept countertop displays filled with shoes for the family so that passing shoppers might inspect them for style and sturdiness. Fifty leather-upholstered chairs also enticed customers to stop and shop. Leonards' plan for selling shoes—stocking a full range of sizes (from infants' sizes to men's size fifteen) and styles (for dress, work, and casual wear), keeping prices affordable, and giving customers reasons to shop and to buy—succeeded splendidly. The department sold around 125,000 pairs of shoes each year.[9]

Groceries continued to dominate the store into the late 1930s, both visually and in terms of gross sales. The food departments generated the most sales and required half of the store's inventory investment, but increasingly, departments in other parts of the building drove profits.[10] By the mid-1930s, hard goods, housed on the south side of the basement, contributed the most to store profit, in actual dollars and as a percent of sales.[11]

Hard goods included an almost unmanageable range of merchandise: hardware, housewares, sporting goods, plumbing, lighting, paints, wallpapers, and a variety of items falling under the rubric of five-and-dime goods. That varied inventory reflected Leonards' commitment to stocking complete lines of merchandise, not just items in the bottom price bracket. Locals shopped for the bargains; contractors stopped in for builder's quality hardware supplies and construction material; others came from several counties away because they knew that Leonards "could supply them what they wanted from [its] large stock at a price they wanted to pay." As with foods earlier, growth in hard goods rendered management and control increasingly difficult. In 1938 Marvin broke hard lines into three smaller departments—hardware, sporting goods, and housewares—each with its own manager.[12]

Another high-margin department, Cliff Bigby's seed and pet department, shared basement space with hard lines. The very nature of this department's inventory meant that shoppers viewed a different stock of merchandise almost every time they visited. As seasonal demand swung from seeds to insecticides to fertilizers, Bigby and his seven full-time clerks arranged and rearranged the shelves, tables, and counters. Some days, clay pots took up all the space beneath the display tables. At other times, bags of fertilizers and pet food congested the aisles. During the Easter season, potted lilies overflowed from every nook in the department, creating the illusion of entering a sanctuary.[13]

Good smells from the cafeteria, also located in the basement, mingled with and masked some of the earthier garden-center odors. The eatery may not have added much to Leonards' bottom line (less than one thousand dollars and only a 2.5 percent return on sales in 1936), but it did entice people to the basement, generating traffic to high-margin departments. Lois "Steve" Drennan, one of Leonards' three female department managers, and her fifteen-person staff served an average of one thousand meals in their corner of the basement every day.[14]

Wedged in the southwest corner of the basement, between the seeds and sporting goods, sat the automobile supply department. Leonards carried such a complete stock of automotive parts, accessories, and supplies that manager Ed Dyer claimed owners of the three most popular automobiles in the low-price range could, figuratively speaking, "jack up their old frame and body, and let the automobile supply department at Leonards build a new car from scratch underneath." The remainder of the basement space housed the store's creamery operation and, tucked in a niche along the east wall, the newly established shoe repair business.[15]

The mezzanine held a less diverse set of departments. Roy Bledsoe's furniture department had moved upstairs when it began encroaching on other departments' floor space downstairs. As the largest single-floor furniture showroom in Fort Worth, it occupied a section one block long and a half-block wide. Customers could choose from the fifty-five different bedroom suites on display or furnish any other room of their home. There was also an extensive selection of floor coverings, decorating accessories, and several long rows of large appliances.[16]

Ready-to-wear and fabrics shared space with furniture. As in Cliff Bigby's seed department, the inventory and displays in these two departments reflected the changing seasons. Each spring, piece goods manager W. A. Banks highlighted cotton, silk, and linen lace. As the weather warmed, featured shelf space yielded to hopsack and rayon linen. Fortsman wool and various wales of corduroy found their way to the countertops as winter approached. Featured items made good advertising copy but price and variety in staples—basic fabrics, buttons, zippers, and other notions—drew customers back again and again. In similar fashion, the ready-to-wear department carried a full line of clothing all year and filled in the line with new items as the seasons changed.[17]

Customers found "more merchandise for less money" at Leonards, but they also found more services. While a customer shopped, he or she could buy automobile license plates or pay the local poll tax. Sportsmen could secure their hunting licenses in the store and after a successful outing bring their buck back for Leonards' butchers to skin and quarter it at no charge. The well-manned package check stand meant shoppers could store their purchases for curbside pickup rather than lug them around while they shopped.[18]

The unique check-cashing operation continued to provide an easy way for folks to convert checks into cash. Locating the check-cashing cage at the back of the basement meant that patrons passed by a lot of merchandise before and after cashing their checks. Many spent part of the more than $500,000 per week in cashed checks before leaving the store. This operation was so large that Leonards cashed more checks than any downtown bank. The operation was a perfect example of Marvin's merchandising skill. Instead of worrying if prices were too low, he worried if they were too high. Instead of being concerned about bad checks, he was concerned when the number of bad checks declined. Fewer bad checks meant a decline in the number of people using the check cashing stand. He also knew that by placing the cage at the back of the basement, customers spent enough on their way out of the store to more than pay for the service and the loss on bad checks.[19]

Marvin and Obie would give almost anything a try that brought more people into the store or made buying simpler, easier, or more convenient. One story has Marvin witnessing a mother spanking a crying child. Reasoning that the problem stemmed from a tired child and an equally tired mother, he set out to devise a baby shopper, a buggy with storage space for packages. Thereafter, parents wheeled their weary tots around the store in free, conveniently placed strollers.[20]

In most cases, the extra services served the same function that the store's promotional efforts did: they drew customers to the store. Sometimes Leonards' managers exhibited such creativity that customers could not tell the difference between a standard service and an event designed to generate customer traffic and goodwill. For instance, in 1929 Leonards began sponsoring an annual party for the children of Fort Worth. By 1937 this event had grown into a spectacle involving a fleet of chartered buses that hauled twenty-seven thousand local children to Lake Worth for the day. The children enjoyed hot dogs, cold drinks, and watermelon and had plenty of games and activities to keep them busy. The goodwill from the event and the registration procedure, which required a trip downtown to Leonards, generated a substantial bulge in the store's late-summer school supply sales. Later, Leonards replaced the day trip to Lake Worth with tickets to Leonards' Night at the circus and complimentary ice cream and popcorn, but the effect remained the same. Parents brought their children to Leonards to pick up the free tickets; once there, they bought school supplies.[21]

In an industry where the ease of imitation—in product lines, services offered, hiring practices, and compensation schemes—dominates competitive dynamics, promotions are a key tool for building store image and customer awareness. Department stores such as Leonards had a wide array of tools to draw from to whip up customer excitement. Industry observers suggested that "by plugging one promotion after another, a store builds and maintains an atmosphere of aliveness, alertness, and movement." Leonards certainly found that true. It supplemented its heavy newspaper advertising with sales events, promotional stunts, and any scheme that would build customer excitement.[22]

These promotional efforts supported Marvin's fundamental selling philosophy: "The quickest way to sell a piece of merchandise is to put it out where a prospective buyer can see and feel it." Given the importance of customer traffic for the success of this approach, it is hard to imagine that Leonards overlooked any promotional opportunity. The biggest ones provide former employees and customers with some of their most vivid memories.[23]

The biggest selling season and the opportunity for the most-impressive promotions came in the weeks before Christmas. Many Fort Worth natives grew up believing that the real Santa Claus stayed at Leonards when he came to Fort Worth because the store's Toyland was so much larger and more spectacular than any other toy department in town. Every afternoon at 4:00 from Thanksgiving through Christmas, children tuned to radio station KGKO to hear Santa's broadcast from Toyland. Lucky tots talked their parents into a trip downtown to help Santa air his program. Doc St. Clair guaranteed Toyland's prominence in 1937 by launching the Christmas selling season with a huge promotional event. He hired a local fireworks manufacturer to put on a one-thousand-dollar show at Meacham Field to herald the arrival of Santa. More than twenty thousand people attended. For many years, fireworks were a regular part of Santa's arrival at Leonards' Toyland, and each year the display and the crowds grew larger. The last show cost Leonards five thousand dollars—money well spent on customer relations.[24]

Many of Leonards' most memorable promotions were built around onetime, rock-bottom bargain, huge-volume items. Much as Sam Walton envisioned every Wal-Mart store having a power alley where managers could feature manufacturers' deals and special buys, Leonards promoted special-purchase merchandise at vastly reduced prices. The humble fig featured prominently in several promotions, including when the new store opened in 1930. In the spring of 1938, the opportunity arose again. A Gulf Coast canner miscalculated and found itself stuck with eight train carloads of fresh figs put up in one-gallon cans. Leonards bought the entire stock so cheaply it again could sell cans, ordinarily priced at $1.50, for thirty-nine cents. The mountain-sized stacks of canned figs attracted attention, and the price lured enough customers to wipe out the entire stock in three months. For this kind of promotion, the nature of the featured product mattered little. Having a huge stock at a ridiculously low price mattered more. At various times, Leonards negotiated similar bargain purchases on bananas, sugar, syrup, coffins, white enameled iron bars, tin cans, and steel-shaft golf clubs. In turn, the manager/buyers turned the deals into publicity opportunities.[25]

The best bargains did not always end up on Leonards' shelves. Expanding on its Depression-era contacts, buyers at Everybody's often located eye-catching bargains. They continued to offer lower-quality goods at even lower prices than Leonards. In late spring, 1938, Everybody's featured a branded sneaker for ninety-eight cents. Montgomery Wards did not want to lose sales to Everybody's, so it cut its price on the same sneaker to eighty-nine cents. The price seesawed back and forth, neither store wanting to be undercut, until sneakers were flying out the door at twenty-nine cents a pair. Over a six-week period, the manager and his sales clerk, Wilbur Newsome, sold between seven and eight thousand pairs of sneakers. Because of the deal Everybody's had secured with the manufacturer, it made money on each pair until the price dropped below forty-four cents. Soon after that, the price war bottomed out.[26]

Leonards and Everybody's were not the only stores in Fort Worth trumpeting their products and image through promotions. Every merchant in town celebrated sales spectaculars, coordinated seasonal inventory pushes with contests and demonstrations, and sponsored special events to attract crowds. Mimicry ran rampant. Stores copied good promotional ideas from each other, tailoring them to fit the style and image that their customers expected. Leonards borrowed and was borrowed from. For instance, in the 1920s some of Leonards competitors pioneered the practice of giving away theater tickets. By the late 1930s, Leonards had upped the ante, sponsoring free motion pictures in Fort Worth's parks from May through October. Leonards' size made the economics of those types of promotion feasible and, to a certain degree, inimitable. It could take a promotion tried elsewhere, tinker with it, expand it, and make it uniquely Leonards. For example, other firms could put their names on school book covers and other trinkets, but who else in town could supply 250,000 book covers to Tarrant County's schoolchildren every year or distribute its own brand of milk in cone-shaped containers that could double as megaphones for high school pep squads?[27]

The look and feel of the store—its layout and product lines, the wide variety of departments, the energy ignited by its continuous promotions—reflected deliberate choices made by Marvin, Obie, and their managers. Unlike many entrepreneurs, Marvin and Obie had no difficulty moving beyond successful but increasingly less useful strategies. The evolving range and types of Leonards' merchandise exemplified their thinking. Leonards had gradually expanded its supplier pool, parlaying the relationships formed with railroad companies and agents in the early years into a larger, more-varied network of contacts. Many traditional suppliers—manufacturing wholesalers and jobbers—preferred doing business with Leonards because it paid its bills on time, took advantage of cash discounts, and handled adjustments on returned merchandise.

Rather than severing ties with the old contacts, Everybody's continued the job of handling most odd lots and job lots, closeout items, and salvage and fire sale inventories. Having Everybody's down the street eased the move away from that successful formula at Leonards. While Leonards expanded and upgraded, Everybody's continued to serve the shirtsleeves trade with a general-store concept that included a variety of bargains derived from nontraditional sources of supply mixed with traditional department store merchandise.[28]

Leonards also took advantage of a loophole in the law that allowed a store to own and operate a wholesale business with its own retail operation as a captive customer. Through its various wholesaling arms—Fort Worth Wholesale Grocery, Fort Worth Wholesale Produce, and Fort Worth Wholesale Merchandise Co.—Leonards and Everybody's bought from manufacturers in larger volume and at wholesale prices without having to maintain a sales force or the other trappings of transacting business in the market. Tom Leonard also continued to buy for his store through these wholesale operations. Everybody's, Leonards, and G. T. Leonard's paid cost plus 3 percent. The wholesale businesses did sell to other retailers, but only on a cash-and-carry basis and at regular wholesale prices. This policy allowed the wholesale operation to spread its volume a little further without additional investment. It also allowed them to avoid prosecution

During the 1930s and 1940s Everybody's expanded to fill the entire block where Marvin first began business. This picture taken from the Tarrant County Courthouse in the 1940s shows the Houston Street entrance.

under the Robinson-Patman Act that forbade stores setting up wholesale units for their exclusive use.[29]

Leonards experimented with other forms of vertical integration and quasi integration as well. This was especially true in food lines. As part of its full-line, popular-price strategy in groceries, Leonards had added several production operations when it moved to the new building in 1930. These facilities—the bakery and pastry plant, the fresh candy manufactory, and the coffee roasting and grinding operation—continued to contribute to profits and Leonards' image. The basement egg-candling operation ensured that Leonards' customers bought the freshest eggs available from local farmers, and the creamery still provided a major outlet for area dairy farmers. To supplement its third-floor workroom operations, Leonards contracted with canneries and manufacturers to produce private-label products as diverse as canned vegetables, salad dressing, motor oil, and refrigerators, which it sold under the Leonards brand name. These products, often priced lower than more-familiar brands, underscored the store's commitment to reasonable quality, maximum variety, and enticing bargains.[30]

Although a few salesmen with well-established connections or extraordinarily large lots still called on Marvin or Obie, department manager/buyers made most of the stocking decisions. One story credits Obie with buying the eight train carloads of canned figs in 1938. Another time he bought so much sugar that it required one solid train of freight cars, plus four extra cars to haul the sugar to Fort Worth. Before long, however, key managers had stories of their own to tell about buying huge inventories of bright red pants, pale yellow pants, and odd-sized chambray shirts.[31]

Decentralized buying created both flexible response to demand and some discontinuity across departments. By 1938 national brand names figured more prominently in storewide advertising and displays, but a quick look at the ads in Leonards' twenty-two-page special birthday section in the *Star-Telegram* illustrated how the adoption of name brands varied from department to department. The grocery section carried nonbranded staples such as bulk rice and dried beans alongside local (Light Crust Flour milled at Fort Worth's Burrus Mills), regional (Texsun grapefruit juice from Weslaco), and national (Heinz and Pillsbury) brands. For certain items, especially coffee, candy, and dairy products, Leonards offered a privately labeled house brand. Hard goods departments also carried heavy stocks of nationally promoted items: Speed Queen washers; General Electric ranges, vacuums, and lightbulbs; Newton's "Ghost" fishing line; and Eastman Brownie cameras. Yet hard goods also stocked many private labels. In comparison, clothing and soft goods departments struggled to find name-brand suppliers willing to distribute through Leonards, but by 1938 the men's department had begun to carry Hyde Park suits, Hawk and Lion uniforms, Red Cap work shirts, and Beaver Shirt Co. polo shirts. Buyers for women's clothing often had to settle for local labels made in the fashion of better-known brands. Occasionally, manufacturers would send closeouts and overstocks to Leonards, as happened when Marshall Field made three hundred dotted Swiss frocks available for the store's 1938 birthday sale.[32]

Despite the efforts to stock better-known brands, Leonards continued to have problems with some prominent manufacturers because of its well-deserved reputation for refusing to maintain manufacturers' suggested retail prices. Texas had never enacted enabling legislation to put federal resale price maintenance laws into effect. Since these so-called Fair Trade Laws were not in effect, Fort Worth's largest retailer was under no legal obligation to avoid deep discounting. Yet well-known national firms like Sunbeam, Prestone, Arrow, and Simmons would not accept Leonards' orders because to do so would put their regular customers, who held the line on price, at a competitive disadvantage.[33]

Leonards' manager/buyers went to great lengths to outfox recalcitrant manufacturers and secure seemingly unavailable products. They cultivated relationships with small dealers in the towns around Fort Worth who would overbuy merchandise through regular distribution channels or through legitimate retailers and then resell it to Leonards. In turn, when Leonards' managers bought a large lot of some desirable merchandise at a low price, they sold that merchandise at cost to the compliant dealers.[34]

Doc St. Clair once got caught in one of these buying schemes. A local merchant who carried Sunbeam products bought a Sunbeam mixer over the counter at Leonards after the manufacturer's sales representative had assured him an exclusive run in Fort Worth. A check of the mixer's serial number revealed that it had originally come from the merchant's own store. Apparently, a dealer from Mineral Wells had bought it there and resold it to Leonards. Sunbeam sent a representative to visit St. Clair, with instructions to buy all the Sunbeam mixers and razors Leonards had so that the regular merchant could maintain price for the Christmas rush. St. Clair sold him all fifty-seven mixers and twenty-seven razors he had, but soon after the first of the year, he started stocking Sunbeam products again. Eventually, the Sunbeam salesman agreed not to hassle St. Clair about his bootleg merchandise if he would not advertise the deeply discounted prices in the Fort Worth papers.[35]

Sunbeam may have supplied Leonards unwillingly, but many manufacturers viewed the store as a desirable outlet for their goods. Benny Rubin, who with his wife owned and operated a Fort Worth dressmaking plant, typified the strength of the bond Leonards formed with its suppliers. In the earliest years of their relationship, a Leonards manager would approve Rubin's line of dresses or blouses at his factory and okay delivery to the store's receiving room. As the amount of business generated by Rubin's lines increased, managers no longer approved the line. Instead, Rubin brought his newest offerings to the store and merchandised them himself. If they sold, Leonards paid his invoice, usually twelve to fifteen dollars a dozen. If not, Rubin would take the dresses out and try something else. By the time Leonards moved into the new store in 1930, the business generated by Rubin's lines had grown so dramatically that it earned him a prominent display spot—directly in front of the stairs on the mezzanine. By the mid-1930s, Rubin visited his racks at Leonards every morning at eight o'clock to check what sizes and colors had sold the previous day so that his seamstresses could fill in the line. No matter how many dresses he sold, Marvin joked with Rubin that it was not enough.[36]

Manager/buyer autonomy at Leonards sometimes caused Rubin problems. At least once, he pulled his entire stock out of Leonards when a new buyer wanted to reassert control over what was placed in the store. Marvin had not heard about the incident, so when he bumped into Rubin a couple of weeks later, he asked how the dressmaker liked his new buyer. Rubin replied that he did not know much about him since he no longer did business with Leonards. After hearing the explanation of the falling out, Marvin told Rubin that when he hired a man to do a job he expected him to do it. Rubin assumed that both the conversation and the business relationship ended at that moment. Before Rubin got back to his office and behind his desk, the buyer appeared and told him that Marvin had informed him that anyone who could not get along with Benny Rubin could not work for him. The buyer invited Rubin back under the old terms. He accepted and stocked his ready-to-wear lines at Leonards until he closed his shop and retired.[37]

Adjusting to Growth: Decentralizing, Restructuring, and Remodeling

Despite Marvin's interference on Rubin's behalf, Leonards' managers typically ran their own show. Yet as the incident with Rubin illustrated, that did not mean they were free to act totally on their own. Marvin set policy and enforced that policy. Eugene Whitmore observed in his 1949 article that Leonards' managers have "high-level management skill, with authority to act. The Leonard men are not the type of merchants who must perform every operation themselves. They delegate authority and responsibility perhaps more than others. They refuse to get bogged down in the detail, yet maintain close supervision of operations."[38]

Department managers not only had buying autonomy, but Marvin's decentralized management style created another competitive edge. Each department could meet local competition head on. Housewares, originally a subdepartment of hard goods, provides a good example. Sales growth for housewares accelerated at a phenomenal rate in the mid-1930s because other stores could not offer comparable bargains. According to housewares clerk Janie Witcher, not even Stripling's, Leonards' closest direct competitor for household goods, matched its prices or selection, and in many instances, Stripling's could not beat Leonards' quality. Within a couple of years the stock and sales of most housewares lines had doubled or tripled. The store's structure and management philosophy easily accommodated housewares' emerging dominance in the local market.[39]

In 1938 Marvin and Obie rewarded C. L. Stocks for his sales efforts by promoting him to manager of housewares and allocating to him two-thirds of the basement floor space to house his newly established department. Like other department managers, Stocks had complete profit responsibility that included all backroom activities. This meant that he ran his own warehouse operation and was charged a certain percent of sales for the space. He also bought all of the department's merchandise. If he thought popular-priced cosmetics, drugs, infants' wear, or gift bric-a-brac would sell, Leonards allowed him to carry such stock, even if it duplicated lines carried in other departments. As department manager, Stocks oversaw the display of merchandise, set prices, trained and supervised employees, and planned his department's promotional activities.[40]

The breakup of hard lines into departments and Stock's promotion to department manager typified Marvin and Obie's store: it grew like topsy. Departments added assistant managers for particular lines of merchandise as growth in the line merited it. If sales continued to rise, management elevated the subsection to a department. This created both a very responsive retail organization and opportunities for ambitious employees, a lesson not lost on J. B. Moates. About three years after finagling a job in the men and boys department, one of Leonards' suppliers, National Shirt Shops, offered him a job. When Marvin heard Moates had tendered his resignation, he called the young man (not yet twenty) into his second-floor office and asked him why he wanted to leave. The always frank Moates explained that he could earn more money and move up faster at National. Marvin refused to counter the offer. Instead, he asked whether Moates had a particular department he would like to run, to which Moates replied that any of them would be fine. As he closed the interview, Marvin promised Moates neither a raise nor a promotion. Rather, he encouraged the young sales clerk, telling him that one day he might run his own department. Having witnessed other young, hustling employees take charge of new departments, Moates chose to stay, thoroughly convinced that in the long run he would prosper with Leonards. Several weeks later Moates received a raise, not as an enticement to stay, but as a reward for his work. Even better, within a couple of years he began climbing the managerial ladder and sharing the prosperity of the company.[41]

Marvin and Obie had long recognized a department store rule of thumb: "As stores expand the number of departments and the variety of items carried, it becomes impossible for one or two individuals to personally supervise the store's entire merchandising activities." While Leonard's managers probably had slightly more autonomy than many, nurturing independent managers followed a trend set by the best-run department stores. The department manager structure worked fine until stores approached annual sales of $5 million. Then the industry practice was to split the store into divisions and add divisional merchandise managers to keep track of initial markups, markdowns, turnover, inventory, expenses, and net profits across related departments. This intermediate managerial position, inserted in the hierarchy between the store manager and the department managers, improved stock planning and control, curbed the tendency of buyers to operate their departments as small fiefdoms, aided interdepartment promotions, and created a better-coordinated flow of goods through the store.[42]

Leonards reached that critical size and created three merchandise manager positions in 1938. Doc St. Clair took charge of the hard goods division housed in the basement, and Jack Hester became merchandise manager for food and other ground-floor departments. Marvin and Obie reached up to Grand Rapids, Michigan, to staff the third slot—upstairs merchandise manager. They hired J. S. (Jim) Leach, a silk buyer whose name they may have gotten from their New York source for soft goods, Felix Lillianthal. It took three trips to Michigan before Marvin finally convinced Leach that he was the man to exert control over Leonards' dry goods, appliance, furniture, and accessories buyers. Marvin and Obie added three more desks to the mezzanine balcony to accommodate their new merchandise managers, who began asserting more control over Leonards' stocking, selling, and promotional decisions. They also organized more buying trips to New York and Chicago.[43]

The addition of merchandise manager positions to the hierarchy complemented other features of the increasingly complex organizational structure at Leonards. Carl Bruner had served as the store's general manager (GM) for more than a decade, but his roles as legal advisor, tax expert, and controller and his partial ownership status made him a far more pivotal figure than a traditional GM. Although he continued to act as a consultant to Marvin for another decade, the independent-minded Bruner left day-to-day management to pursue his own business interests at about the time the merchandise managers were added to the hierarchy. When Elam Henderson took over the GM slot in August, 1939, the position reverted to its traditional role of handling personnel, service, and maintenance duties for the store. B. V. "Bill" Haberer, a Notre Dame–trained lawyer who came to Leonards from Sanger's, served as office manager, but his real duties encompassed those usually assigned to the controller: accounting, expense control, and general merchandise control. Dealing with Leach, Hester, and St. Clair instead of a stable full of department heads made Haberer's job much easier. It also moved Marvin one rung further from department managers.[44]

Leonards supported its executives with a well-developed back-office operation and numerous staff departments. The store handled its own advertising, displays, public relations, and hiring. The comparative-shopping department housed a staff of mostly women who shopped at competitors' stores and recorded their price lines, sales, and markdowns in an effort to make sure no one in Fort Worth priced lower than Leonards. Under Obie's watchful eye, chief engineer M. B. Barksdale supervised the four-unit power plant in Leonards' subbasement that provided power for a one-hundred-ton refrigeration unit, produced five tons of ice each day, drove pumps for the store's artesian wells, powered the store's manufacturing facilities, and, after 1939, fueled its air-conditioning system. All of these nonselling operations, especially the air-conditioning in a Texas summer, gave customers another reason to visit Leonards. One look at such diverse procedures demonstrates why Leonards increasingly decentralized management and control.[45]

Another crucial addition to the executive suite was a new personal secretary

Elam Henderson, Obie, J. Frank Norris, the best-known Baptist minister in Texas, and Marvin, circa 1948.

for Marvin and Obie, Juanita Branham. Branham already had a job in Dallas when she presented herself for an interview on the mezzanine at Leonards, but she wanted to avoid the daily commute and work closer to home. Marvin gave her a two-week trial. Rather than quit her job before she had secured a new one, Branham arranged to take her vacation days during that fortnight. She impressed the brothers and accepted the permanent job when they offered it. During her first year, Branham brought order to the jumble she found in the store office and its files. For the next twenty-nine years she kept that order, acting as secretary to both men, handling both store business and their personal affairs.[46]

A revamping of the bonus incentive system accompanied the 1938 reorganization and eased the transition to the new structure. Before the change, all employees received the equivalent of two weeks pay each Christmas. Marvin, Obie, and Carl Bruner also supplemented their own salaries at year's end, divvying up some of the profits and leaving the rest in retained earnings. With Bruner's role reduced, Marvin replaced this system with a discretionary end-of-the-year bonus based on departmental or divisional performance. Managers quickly realized that record sales brought record bonuses and willingly traded some autonomy for higher earnings.[47]

Partially tying compensation to store results not only mitigated any possible negative effects of usurping some of the department managers' powers, it reinforced the importance of sales growth. Leonards consistently paid higher bonuses than the industry average—usually between 1 and 2 percent of total store sales. The generosity and sagacity of this bonus system becomes apparent when comparing Leonards to other department stores. In the mid-1930s, the 303 department stores that, like Leonards, had annual sales of more than $3 million earned just 0.8 percent on sales—one-tenth of Leonards' net profit before taxes in 1938 and less than it paid in bonuses.[48]

Such profit figures also demonstrated that the problems plaguing department stores around the country had not yet visited Leonards. In the mid-1930s the average expense ratio hovered above one-third of department stores' total sales. This put pressure on stores to inflate gross margins with high markups on merchandise. E. B. Weiss attributed the high expenses in America's department stores to a variety of factors. Customers returned merchandise more often—"in some departments, one of every four purchases are returned." In larger stores, behind-the-scene nonselling-personnel expenses accounted for up to 60 percent of payroll. In addition, most stores had lost track of inventory control. In essence, "buyers had created unbalanced inventories, promoting no- or low-profit items, creating slow turnover, encouraging heavy markdowns, and leaving departments short of wanted items and long on slow-moving items." Department stores across the nation had also begun experimenting with various forms of consumer credit, including installment selling, letters of credit, preapproved credit limits, seasonal credit, and layaways. Expenses associated with approving, administering, and collecting from customers added to the increasingly bloated expense ledgers. In contrast, expenses rarely rose above 23 percent at Leonards, and until the 1950s, they usually were under 20 percent of sales.[49]

Low expense ratios derived from policies Marvin put in place. Of primary importance was his close attention to turnover. Quick sales reduced the cost of storing and handling merchandise and eliminated the need to mark down prices. Marvin was also reluctant to abandon the old cash-only policy he grew up with, and this meant that Leonards did not bear the cost of an elaborate credit system. As late as 1943, 87 percent of sales were for cash. Of the remaining 13 percent, almost three-quarters were layaway sales. Open-account sales made up the remainder of the credit purchases (around 4 percent of total sales), and much of this was credit sales to employees or to commercial accounts.[50]

Insulated, at least temporarily, from climbing expenses due to credit operations, Leonards might have succumbed to other expense woes without a careful eye on expenditures. For instance, it accepted returns unconditionally, but as a rule, managers attempted to satisfy the customer with an exchange on the floor first, offering a refund only after investigating other avenues. This policy created goodwill and did not excessively inflate Leonards' return expense. Leonards also staffed a relatively large number of nonselling positions. Many of those extra employees, however, worked in manufacturing operations, contributing both to the bottom line and to cost savings. The number of strictly administrative positions remained low into the late 1950s.[51]

Despite efforts to control expenses, unsystematic buying persisted even after the creation of merchandise managers, and that created the potential for a bloated, slow-moving inventory. A revitalizing Fort Worth economy in the late 1930s, however, once again mitigated most inventory problems. In a rebounding economy even the wrong merchandise sold if priced right. The Frontier Centennial celebration in 1936 and three successive years of Billy Rose and John Murray Anderson's glittering musical show, Casa Mañana, signaled that Fort Worth was ready to leave the Depression behind. Thanks to federal- and local-government spending (about $15 million and $5 million, respectively), Fort Worth added a variety of improvements during the mid-1930s: a new city hall, the Will Rogers Memorial Auditorium and Coliseum, and a public library. These expenditures stimulated the economy enough that by late 1937, the city council restored municipal salaries that had been reduced in 1931. President Roosevelt's visits in 1936, 1937, and 1938 as well as Texas Christian University's gridiron exploits gave local citizens even more reasons for optimism. Petroleum's return to health and cotton and grain markets' improved stability provided a strong base for that optimism.[52]

Leonards responded to improved conditions by undertaking its first major remodeling effort since moving into the new building. Growing sales in a number of departments put a premium on selling space. Jim Leach brought this up one Saturday evening in 1939 as Marvin and Obie passed by his desk on the way downstairs to the cafeteria, saying how awful it was that the store was losing money. This comment caught both men's attention. When questioned, Leach stated that rather than admire the view from the mezzanine down over the first-floor selling space and out onto Throckmorton Street, Marvin and Obie should use the huge white columns rising from the selling floor to the roof as supports for a full second floor. They agreed. Obie tackled the construction project, and by Wednesday, he had devised a plan. The following Saturday, after the store closed for the day, carpenters, welders, and laborers started work. By Monday morning, Leonards had a full second floor over the entire city block. This gave several departments, including draperies and carpets, room to expand.[53]

Not to be outdone by Leach, Doc St. Clair envisioned expanding sales in his division by adding a farm store that would handle large field equipment. In the summer of 1940, local businessman John A. Kee fell ill and decided to retire from business. St. Clair purchased his entire stock of International Harvester implements, McCormick-Deering dairy and farm equipment, and Farmall tractors and moved them to the corner of First and Taylor Streets across from Leonards. The buyout was a little more daring than many of St. Clair's ventures because he had to convince both International Harvester and Marvin of the practicality of Leonards entering the implement business.[54]

Traditionally, equipment manufacturers franchised authorized dealers to sell their goods because of the need to stock replacement parts, provide on-site service, and offer substantial amounts of credit to finance the purchases. St. Clair convinced both Harvester and Marvin that Leonards could finance the purchases, stock the replacement parts, and would hire contract mechanics to do the repairs. The appeal of the deal was Leonards' rock-solid reputation with area farmers. The store's wide selection of durable tools, seasonal seed stock, and low-price groceries had attracted farm families from surrounding counties to Leonards since it opened in 1918. By adding heavy equipment, fencing and roofing material, and other farming and ranching supplies, Leonards could further serve and satisfy these customers. The operation broke even in its first, partial year and added close to $27,000 to profits in 1941.[55]

Expanded selling space in the mezzanine and at the farm store stimulated increased customer traffic. Some of Leonards' customers caught the bus downtown, but an increasing number motored into the central business district from Fort Worth's expanding residential areas, putting pressure on downtown parking. The parking problem would never disappear for Leonards or for downtown merchants across the country. Marvin and Obie understood the importance of downtown access and worked continually so that scarce parking would not keep customers away. In 1940 they bought three-fourths of a two-block tract bounded by Throckmorton, First, Lamar, and Weatherford Streets and demolished the existing structures to make space for more free parking. The tract tripled Leonards' parking facilities.[56]

Parking was just one more adjustment to a growing business and a changing Fort Worth. There would soon be others. Before the full effects of all these adjustments were felt, however, a new challenge and a new opportunity presented themselves. The challenge was a wartime boom. The opportunity was to sell the store.

LOOKING BEYOND THE STORE AND FACING WORLD WAR II

With business in Fort Worth and at Leonards on the upswing in the late 1930s, Marvin and Obie again considered selling the store. Selling would free the brothers from the daily grind of retail and provide substantial financial security. Brokers like C. L. (Collie) Ettelson envisioned huge commissions if they could secure a cash buyer for the store and successfully negotiate its sale. Except for needing to oversee the preparation of a fairly detailed financial portrait of Leonards for potential buyers, the cost to the brothers for this independent prospecting activity was negligible. Ettelson presented Lehman Brothers with sales information on Leonards in early September of 1937. Negotiations never proceeded far, and by late October the possibility of serious negotiating evaporated.[57]

In 1938, a local agent, Durwood McDonald, began operating on Leonards' behalf in search of potential buyers. Armed with operating statements for 1934, 1935, and 1937, and detailed departmental financial reports for 1936, McDonald headed for New York. He made numerous unsuccessful calls but did reestablish contact with E. H. Scull, a New York–based department store consultant who had peddled Leonards around the industry several years before. Scull made his own attempts to locate a buyer the following year. He wrote Marvin that he had found an individual "thoroughly competent to operate your store successfully. He is young enough to have plenty of years of aggressive work ahead of him. He has had the entire responsibility of the management of a much larger concern than yours handling the same type of merchandise."[58]

Marvin rejected the notion of an individual buyer, writing back, "I don't want to have to depend upon any particular individual for a successful operation. . . . I would not want to have to be in a position to keep up with the operation in any way at all. . . . About the only way I think I would be interested in a deal of this kind would be to have some large company behind the deal—one that I would be taking no chance whatsoever of having it thrown back into my hands at some later date."[59]

Scull replied with some exasperation, "It seems to me that your store is of such a unique type and in many ways so different in its operation from other stores that I cannot at this moment think of any chain that is in existence at this time which would be interested in purchasing it now or in the future." It is unclear whether Scull was referring to Leonards' merchandise mix, its combination of grocery and department store operations, its size, or its tendency to stock merchandise from both traditional and irregular suppliers. The dearth of buyers no doubt also arose from Marvin's high asking price. Upon reconsidering, Scull suggested that the Kobacker Stores, based in Toledo, Ohio, might have a remote interest in Leonards. Nothing developed from that suggestion, and the beginning of the war put a damper on sales efforts until early in 1944. In the meantime, wartime prosperity brought other avenues to security.[60]

The outbreak of World War II infused Fort Worth and Leonards with money and energy. The city remained the largest livestock market and packing center, the largest terminal grain market, and the largest food distribution center in the South. All facets of the petroleum industry continued adding jobs and consumer spending to the local economy. The convenience of Fort Worth's many trunklines, highways, and airstrips and its historic role as a military outpost attracted an influx of defense dollars. On September 24, 1941, the city council bought 526 acres west of town near Lake Worth and turned the land over to the U.S. Army for a bomber plant site. Consolidated-Vultee (Convair) opened the facility the following April, and B-24 bombers began rolling off the assembly line. One example of the impact of the plant on retailing involves an agreement between dressmaker Benny Rubin, Leonards, and Convair's parent company, General Dynamics. Rubin contracted to manufacture the work uniforms for the Convair employees, and Leonards agreed to stock and sell them.[61]

Adjacent to Convair, the army built an airfield to train B-24 crews. In two-and-a-half years, the plant produced more than three thousand bomber and transport planes and four thousand bomber pilots received training. The war had a precipitous effect on other manufacturing concerns in Fort Worth. Between 1939 and 1947, the number of manufacturers increased from 284 to 382, the number of production workers increased by 257 percent, and payrolls jumped 708 percent.[62]

As a result of the jump in manufacturing jobs and the demand for men in the armed forces, labor still plentiful in 1938 became scarce by 1941. Young men with an eye to the future, like J. B. Moates, willingly accepted positions as clerks in the mid-1930s because it paid as well as most jobs and offered the chance for advancement. By 1941 manufacturing jobs did not always offer the same advancement opportunities, but they paid higher starting salaries. Increasingly, men took these jobs rather than working as clerks. Leonards not only had a difficult time hiring male clerks, it also lost some employees like Connie Powell and Jim Winters to the defense plants. At the same time, many established managers joined the armed services. Male employees exempt from service moved up the managerial ranks to take their place. Women increasingly filled the open entry-level jobs as clerks and began working their way up the ranks. Helen Love, for example, began working part-time during the war and at its conclusion began her managerial training under J. B. Moates. Limited employment records make any statement on hiring patterns tentative. Yet existing records suggest that during World War II, for the first time in its history, Leonards hired as many women as men. The store also began promoting them to a wider range of managerial positions.[63]

Hiring patterns were not the only new reality introduced by the war. After 1941, supply replaced demand as the biggest problem facing retailers. Products as diverse as bacon and shoes were scarce and sometimes unavailable. Often it took great creativity to secure hard-to-find items. At one point, Decker Meat Co. offered meat market manager James Blair the chance to bid on ten thousand pounds of bacon, with the hitch that he also had to buy five thousand pounds of spleens to make the deal. Blair badly wanted the bacon, but knew that much spleen would never move, even at Leonards. He arranged to sell the spleens to the Fort Worth Zoo as feed and took delivery on the bacon. Decker was glad to unload the spleen, and the zoo appreciated the price break Blair offered. Leonards also did well, clearing a substantial profit on the bacon and breaking even on the spleens. This careful cultivation of supplier relationships and its ability to dispose of very large inventories made Leonards an ideal customer for wartime vendors. The store's sales growth reflected this role. After several years of flat or declining sales, growth in sales passed 9 percent in 1938. During the next four years, Leonards posted double-digit increases in total sales. In 1941 sales increased almost 30 percent and remained above 25 percent for the next two years. Only in 1944 did the increase in sales dip back down to 9 percent. (See figure in chapter 6.)[64]

Total store sales after 1941 would have been still higher except for lagging food sales. In April, 1941, as the U.S. economy heated up and the country seemed on the brink of entering the war, President Franklin D. Roosevelt created the Office of Price Administration (OPA) whose charge was to prevent the high rate of inflation that characterized the World War I years. In January, 1942, Congress gave the OPA the authority to set price ceilings, and in April, prices were frozen at the March, 1942, level. This price freeze forced rationing. Price ceilings, rationing, and the expenses associated with demonstrating compliance all hit hardest on Leonards' food store, where nothing escaped regulation. From 1941 to 1944, sales from food increased 8.7 percent, but net profits declined by 21 percent. In comparison, nonfood sales increased 94 percent and net profits increased 73 percent. Since food made up only about one-fifth of sales by 1944, Leonards had an impressive balance sheet, and Marvin and Obie enjoyed significant wartime increases in their net worth.[65]

During these boom years, Marvin funneled an increasing portion of his earnings from the store into other ventures, particularly oil and natural gas leases. In the late 1930s, Mack Zachery, who worked for Neville G. Penrose, Inc., held promising leases in Andrews County, Texas, but had no money to drill them. He dropped by the store to discuss the situation with Marvin and found him looking for investments that offset a rapidly growing tax liability. Surging profits had pushed Marvin into the highest tax bracket because his income from the store was ordinary income instead of a capital gain.[66] Zachery sold a half interest to him and proceeded to drill several wells. By 1943 these investments had yielded assets in the form of producing leases, nonproducing leases, and royalty properties of $527,820.57, a total close to half as much as the book value of his partnership interest in Leonards. Income from oil was also taxed at a far lower rate than income from the store.[67]

The partnership with Penrose remained profitable throughout the war. On one occasion the company could not afford to drill on a lease, so Marvin paid to drill it. According to Zachery, "He got one of the best wells in the field." Since West Texas oil leases were going for around five dollars per acre with mineral rights for ten to twenty dollars per acre, Zachery encouraged Marvin to begin accumulating both leases and mineral rights. Marvin provided most of the financing—a blank commitment for $250,000—while Penrose spent $86,000. Within two years almost every bit of the investment produced. Marvin continued investing in leases and production contracts, and by 1945 they literally spilled out from the drawers of his desk.[68]

In addition to oil, Marvin invested in real estate and a variety of other ventures unrelated to retailing. He continued to hold property in the Colonial Hills subdivision and bought 136 acres and several lots in Bellaire Estates in a bankruptcy offering. Marvin also owned shares of the Tarrant Realty Company and the Seventh Street Realty Company. In buying real estate and in making other investments, he still relied heavily on Carl Bruner's leg work and advice, despite Bruner's departure from Leonards. In 1940 Bruner wrote a lengthy opinion concerning an opportunity to invest in a start-up business. Bruner's advice, as always, attended to every detail that Marvin raised and focused on the best way to structure the investment for tax purposes.[69]

Marvin's profits from the store also went toward buying Fort Worth National Bank stock. This was one of the ten largest banks in Texas and his store had long been one of the bank's most important customers. Historically, this stock had been closely held by the directors, but in 1940 scattered blocks became available. Marvin's interest in Fort Worth National may have centered on the need to safeguard his source of personal and business credit, or he may have seen the opportunity to gain a small measure of control over the bank. Marvin also felt a great deal of loyalty to the bank because of its role in financing the expansion of the store in the 1920s. Emotion, however, never overrode good business. Given his tax bracket, the stock was an attractive investment.

Early in 1941, Bruner responded to Marvin's request for information about the stock's prospects. In his usual deliberate style, Bruner gave a thorough accounting of the bank's situation—its capitalization, current book value, dividend history, earnings record, and investment prospects. He concluded his report with personal remarks about the value of the bank and his opinion of the tax ramifications of stock purchase. Whether on his own initiative or at Marvin's request, Bruner added the following handwritten comment under the bank's list of officers and directors: "Those checked are well up in years. It is doubtful if any of the others could carry the top load as well." Half of the top twelve officers and all but three of the directors had check marks by their names.[70]

Marvin weighed Bruner's conservative assessment of the appeal of the stock with his own reasons for wanting to buy, then during the next several years proceeded to acquire substantial blocks of the stock. The bank's president, R. E. Harding, whose ties to Marvin dated back to his earliest days in Fort Worth, encouraged his acquisition of stock. With Harding's blessing, Marvin became a director of the bank in 1944 and by 1957 owned about 13,500 shares, or 2 percent of the bank's stock.[71]

Marvin's expanding investments outside the store dovetailed with his swelling passion for golf, a passion fed by owning his own country club. After opening Colonial in 1936, he continued to play three times a week in foursomes drawn from a group of about twenty close friends. Club life attracted a group of men loosely connected by their club membership and overlapping business dealings who played golf and cards together regularly. Marvin met his buddies at the club, played a round or two of golf, then retired to the nineteenth hole for some hands of gin rummy. They traded gossip about promising oil leases and budding real-estate deals. Sidebets and drinking added to the fun. This routine left Marvin time to monitor the store, and it brought access to a network of businessmen connected with the pulse of the Forth Worth economy. Mainly, it allowed him to play golf regularly and enjoy the company of his friends.[72]

One close friendship that grew from golf was with Ben Hogan, a legendary figure among professional golfers. In Hogan's early days on the tour, Marvin sent him money to keep him going. In particular Hogan remembered Marvin's help in 1931 when he first tried the pro tour at age 19. By Christmas he was out of cash and stuck on the West Coast. Marvin wired him money, and there was enough for him to buy his bride-to-be a Christmas present. Hogan was always quick to point out that more than financial support made him an admirer of Marvin Leonard. He insisted that Marvin was one of the few men in Fort Worth who did not claim that he caddied for him. As Hogan wryly put it, "If I caddied for everybody who claims I did, I'd still be carrying a bag." Marvin always enjoyed watching Hogan play and was proud to count him as a friend. When Hogan won the Colonial tournament, as he did five times, it always held special meaning for Marvin.[73]

While Marvin never approached the skill of Hogan, he often shot in the seventies and maintained a low handicap for most of the years he played. He played quickly but deliberately—not for the exercise, but for the skill it required, the beauty of the sport, the release it gave him from his demanding lifestyle. He relished shooting around the diabolical hazards like Big Annie, the huge pecan tree on Colonial's 17th fairway, and navigating the most challenging holes. In short, everything about golf attracted him: following professional golf, playing, planning and building courses, and even visiting golf courses on vacation.[74]

The Colonial's course, rather than the surrounding real-estate development, remained Marvin's center of attention. In 1941 he told reporters, "I've got $250,000 in this club, and my only thought when I came out and bought what was then unbroken land along the Trinity river valley, was to build a first-class course that our town needed."[75]

As had been true of building the course, Marvin had distinct ideas about run-

Ben Hogan accepts the Leonard trophy from his friend Marvin after winning the Colonial National Invitational Tournament for the last time in 1959.

ning the club. Dissatisfied with the original manager, he sought someone he could train to do it his way, "a young man with a little, but not too much club experience." He found Vergal Bourland working as the maître d' at the Dallas Athletic Club and hired him. Bourland fit the profile of many of the managers Marvin had hired at Leonards—he had a small-town background, limited formal education, a lot of ambition, and a demonstrated civic-mindedness. Marvin gave him a great deal of latitude in the daily operations but guided him on big decisions. For instance, Bourland wanted to put craps tables in the club's basement during golf tournaments. Although Marvin willingly bet on cards and golf and had thirteen slot machines on the premises, he let Bourland know that he did not want craps games or other forms of open gambling in the club. According to Bourland, Marvin's philosophy of club management matched his philosophy at Leonards. He wanted it to remain open longer hours and to have an expanded range of club activities—book reviews, parties for couples, and events for women and children. Given that members paid a minimal fifty-dollar deposit and no initiation fee, he demanded more activities for less money.[76]

When Marvin built the Colonial course he insisted that its style and design place it high among the nation's premier courses. Once it was built, he focused on maintaining and improving the course. With help from greenskeeper Joe Cano, Marvin fought off drought and diseases such as Pythium and brown patch to keep bent grass on all the greens. As he walked the course, he thought of ways to improve and promote it. A chance to do both came with the announcement on May 25, 1940, that the Colonial Country Club would host the 1941 National Open golf tournament.[77]

Marvin and local golf enthusiast Dr. Alden Coffey had lobbied, cajoled, and coaxed the U.S. Golf Association (USGA) to bring the U.S. Open to Fort Worth. On one occasion, Marvin spent fifteen or twenty minutes on the phone to Boston with Harold Pierce, president of the USGA, reiterating the merits of Colonial. The call finally convinced Pierce: Any man who would spend $17.40 on a long-distance call was obviously committed to his mission, and if the same man would also guarantee to the association $15,000 for bringing the Open to the boonies, even better. For the occasion, Marvin bought a little extra land and revamped several holes, creating the Horrible Horseshoe, composed of holes number 3, 4, and 5. Golf aficionados considered the redesigned fifth, christened Death Valley, one of the toughest tee shots anywhere.[78]

Despite some rain, the 45th U.S. Open attracted big crowds, and Craig Wood finished ahead of the field by three strokes. The usually publicity-shy Marvin basked in the moment as he placed the victory jacket on Woods. The success of the Open stirred Marvin's desire for a big-time annual tournament in Fort Worth. The idea had to wait for the war to pass, but in May, 1946, the Colonial National Invitational held its first annual tournament. The first year, twenty-nine players competed for a $15,000 purse.[79]

A number of significant milestones marked the intervening years between the Open and the first Invitational. The excitement generated by the tournament finally prompted a reluctant Amon Carter, famed editor of the *Star-Telegram* and promoter of Fort Worth, to join the club in 1942. For him and others, the tournament confirmed the value of membership. Total membership of all types reached about seven hundred in 1946.[80]

In an even more auspicious move, in December, 1942, Marvin sold the club to its members for $290,000. Conscious of his mortality, Marvin acted to ensure the long-term stability of the club and to preserve the course. He joked that if he died, Obie, the executor of his estate, would plow up the course and sell it for home lots. As the joke indicated, the price was below market value. Yet he later commented that taking into account his cost and depreciation, on his 1942 taxes the transaction gave him "a net capital gain of $133,080.68." Considering the value of a 1942 dollar, that gain, plus the profit of previous years, explains why Marvin considered Colonial "a very excellent investment." The club also added substantial value to the residential lots he owned in the adjacent neighborhood. Clearly, there was nothing in the financial history of Colonial to discourage building another golf course.[81]

Marvin continued to operate Colonial as a private venture until January 1, 1943, when he passed ownership to the club's stockholding members. He retained managerial control over the club until he received the balance of the payment. Thanks to the relatively low sales price and the legacy of the slot machines, which he left in the club, the payoff came in four years. The lag in turning over control to the members meant that Marvin was still in charge when fire struck and virtually consumed the clubhouse on August 6, 1943. Jim Leach reported that Marvin met the disaster without despair, telling bystanders, "We probably won't start to rebuild until in the morning."[82]

While Marvin built and rebuilt Colonial and looked after his investments, he also became more active in local politics and philanthropy. In 1939, for the first time, his involvement in nonbusiness activities reached outside of Fort Worth. In recognition of his work in helping needy children, Governor W. Lee "Pappy" O'Daniel appointed Marvin Leonard to the newly created State Welfare Board that year. The governor, a former Fort Worth businessman, had presided over the Chamber of Commerce during the time that Leonard had served as a director. O'Daniel also knew of Leonard's tenure on the city's Civil Service Board, his contributions to the Lena Pope Home, and his involvement with the Fort Worth Little Theater during the 1930s. Marvin took these responsibilities seriously, and his increasing independence from the store and help from Carl Bruner in Austin gave him the time to serve without having to cut back on his weekly golf games.[83]

Leonards' success and maturity did not take Obie quite as far from the store. Obie still motored around the state scouting for big bargains and continued to tinker with ideas for improving store operations. Yet he too plowed profit from the store into other ventures, and the bargains he sought on his long car trips were just as likely to be farms, ranches, or orchards as salvage merchandise or fire stocks. At times, the brothers participated in the same oil deals, but increasingly their interests diverged. Obie did not drink and avoided club life. Paul Leonard reported that his father once carried a drink around at a party to make his guests more comfortable but put it down because it made him feel ridiculous. Instead of golf and urban real estate, his passions and his investments were tied to the countryside. He hunted and fished avidly and raised Herefords, pecans, sheep, grapes, and broad-breasted turkeys across the Southwest.[84]

Like his brother, by the mid-1940s Obie had more than enough to provide financial security and keep him busy outside the store. It was time to seriously consider selling the store. During the war, the Excess Profits Tax took a large bite out of their income from the store, while other investments offered a greater opportunity to lower their taxes. In addition, as Carl Bruner explained to R. E. Harding, Marvin had no sons and Obie's sons, Paul and Bob, then showed little interest in taking over. Because of high taxes, uncertainty about management succession, and the desire to pursue other interests, both brothers were ready to sell for the right price.[85]

A Serious Search for a Buyer

Early in 1944, Marvin and Obie formalized arrangements with the selling agents, Durwood McDonald and E. H. Scull, and their prospecting efforts became much more serious. Both men oiled the skids at Macy's hoping to generate interest. H. L. Churchill, Director of Research at Macy's, kept them on the line, raising their hopes without ever committing to anything but the need for more information. Scull also approached a vice president of the Allied Stores Corporation with information about Leonards. The executive appeared "enthusiastic" to make a deal until Scull mentioned the asking price of $7,613,000 and the assets involved. The Allied man responded "I may be crazy but not that crazy." Although Scull continued to court both Macy's and Allied, the first half of the year passed with little progress.[86]

In late June, a well-placed and glowing article about Marvin and Obie and the store appeared in the national weekly *The Saturday Evening Post*. Unfortunately, rather than giving the agents more ammunition when they called on prospective buyers, it had a dampening effect on the sales efforts. The journalist, Neil M. Clark, had been more fascinated with the stories about Leonards' daring purchases—a fire stock of steel-shafted golf clubs, discontinued WPA canned meats, and the white enamel iron bars that Leonards had turned into towel racks—than about its more prevalent standard product lines. Earl B. Puckett, president of Allied, read the story and decided that Leonards was "not of the class they wanted"; rather, "it belonged in the Hearn or Goldblatt class." Scull had to work hard to convince him otherwise.[87]

Despite the lack of success, Marvin, who took the lead in handling the potential sale, remained optimistic, saying he had expected that reaction. With confidence, he pointed to his store's "very low expense account" and insisted that with the war nearing an end and the tax situation soon to change the opportunity for profit was high. He also okayed Scull's request to expand the search for potential buyers to include City Stores and National Department Stores.[88]

Negotiations continued through the fall. Although Leonards attracted interest from expansion-minded New York department store chains interested in penetrating the South, most saw major stumbling blocks to a possible deal. In some cases, Leonards' customer base, appearance, and product mix, especially the grocery business, was a poor fit. For instance, Harold B. Wess and Mr. Chinlin, members of Macy's acquisitions committee, "felt the store was too cheap in character of merchandise it handled and that the building itself was very cheaply constructed and did not present at all a nice appearance." Chinlin commented further that "he thought it would endanger his own job if he were so foolish as to put up to the Board of Directors of Macy's the name of a store for acquisition that did over 25 per cent of its business in food stuffs." Other buyers questioned the way the deal would be structured. Neither Puckett at Allied or Saul Cohn at City Stores wanted to buy the property housing Leonards. Scull explained to Marvin that "chains have been so badly stuck with real estate in the past they will not consider any deal in which it is involved. Gimbel's charged off a real-estate loss of $6,000,000 last year. Allied charged off more than a million each of the past two years and are not through yet."[89]

The main impediment to serious negotiations, however, was price. Scull spent much of the fall trying to convince Marvin that his asking price soured any possible deal. On August twenty-first he wrote:

> I want to point out to you the fact that on December 31st the stocks as listed below were selling at the times earnings before taxes indicated on the New York Stock Exchange.
>
> | | |
> |---|---|
> | National Department Stores | 1.6 times |
> | Gimbel Brothers | 1.9 times |
> | Allied Stores | 2.6 times |
> | May | 2.9 times |
>
> The price you have asked me to get for your store is approximately five times your earnings before taxes. . . . If you would drop your price to what would be equivalent to three times your last year's earnings, it would amount to $4,232,637 and this price, you can well understand, based upon the above information, will be way out of line. I do not know whether you are willing to come down to a basis of two and a half times earnings which would be $3,700,000, but I do believe this would be the maximum amount it would be possible to obtain.[90]

Although frustrated with Marvin's intransigence over price, Scull continued to work toward the sale. In September he contacted Edgar Schnadig, head of the Chicago Mail Order Co. Schnadig had launched an active acquisition program and was also potentially interested in the General Motors building that Leonards had purchased as a long-term investment and a possible site for its expanding branch warehouse network. Scull again warned Marvin that his extremely high price and insistence on a real-estate sale would kill the deal. He suggested instead that Marvin accept cash for the net assets exclusive of real estate and a long-term lease for facilities. He closed his latest report, admonishing Marvin, "I can sell your store at a reasonable price, I am confident, because I have aroused the interest of several of the contacts I have made but none of them would think of touching the situation at the price asked and I think I have demonstrated to you in several ways that your price is a very exorbitant one."[91]

Marvin expressed a willingness to knock $650,000 off his price, but told Scull "I have not been able to get any more out and leave it a profitable transaction to us from our way of seeing it. Maybe at some future time, investors will have a better tax situation and be willing to pay more than they now are. I am sorry indeed and had hoped that something might be worked out." Scull's efforts on Leonards' behalf flagged after that. In December, he wrote that a representative of Gamble-Skogmo had inquired about Leonards, but once again high price stymied further negotiation.[92]

Carl Bruner replaced Scull and McDonald as the primary searcher for a Leonards buyer in 1945. He reestablished contacts with Macy's and Allied, and by working with R. E. Harding, attempted to stir up interest in the store. Late in the year, a deal put together by Bruner and brokered through Martin Fruhman of the Associated Retail Millinery Co. looked promising. Allen & Company, a Manhattan-based partnership, and Dallas Rupe & Son of Texas drew up an option agreement for the purchase of the store, including land, buildings, fixtures, and merchandise for $6,557,928.45. They never exercised the option, although Fruhman and his associate, Raymond Rossoff, continued hustling Leonards in various circles through the summer of 1946.[93]

Marvin's adamance about the price he asked for the store reflected both his assessment of its worth and his business attitude. Selling the store would have eased his tax liability and freed his time and attention to pursue investments with more favorable tax treatments. It would have also resolved management-succession issues and allowed him more time to devote to golf and other pursuits. These considerations did not lower his asking price because, as usual, Marvin wanted to strike a favorable deal. He was not desperate to sell, and he knew Leonards' value. The store was posting record sales. It had an impeccable record of controlling expenses and dominated Fort Worth retailing. Despite criticism from Scull and others, Marvin believed in the price he asked. As he wrote Scull in late 1944, "With people not willing to pay as much bonus as I had in mind, I do not believe we can ever get our minds together." In essence, he insisted on his price or no price. Bruner reiterated Marvin's sentiment a year later in his letter to Harding concerning the valuing of good will in the sale. The amount of good will built into the sales price was "reasonable," and "there is no reason to sell the business without a fair amount being paid for Good Will."[94]

Although the possibility of selling the store to outsiders would arise again in the late 1940s and the mid-1950s, Marvin never again pursued the option as seriously as he did in 1944 and 1945. He was content instead to further distance himself from the store. While he still watched the daily figures of the store, real estate, oil, and other investments took his attention, and golf took more of his time. The store prospered in spite of his reduced commitment. Its management structure easily accommodated the separation of strategic and operating control, and Fort Worth's economy provided a favorable climate for retail business.[95]

After the war, Fort Worth's citizens passed a referendum authorizing a $20 million bond issue for public works to keep employment and population figures up and avoid a post-war slump. City leaders worried that (as happened after World War I) a post-war slump would hit the local economy hard. Instead, employment remained high and the population grew. While there were a few months of turbulence in 1946, cold war concerns about the menace of communism soon caused an increase in government spending. Several thousand workers remained at the Convair plant working on a secret project, which turned out to be the B-36 bomber. On February 28, 1948, Tarrant Field was renamed Carswell Air Force Base and became part of the newly conceived U.S. Air Force. The new air base housed the Eighth Air Force, the country's atomic bomber force. Oil, wheat, livestock, and residential construction also kept the economy perking. Returning servicemen and wartime workers whose spending had been restricted by rationing drove sales up at Leonards and all other retailers. With little need to fund public works to maintain low unemployment, Fort Worth's leaders used the bond funds instead to expand municipal services. They needed these new services because in 1946, the city annexed forty square miles, including Kellis Park and Ridglea. Significant suburban expansion was on the horizon as the city's total area approached one hundred square miles.[96]

In 1948, however, downtown remained the heart of Fort Worth's economy. The city still lacked shopping malls and distant suburbs, and citizens did business and shopped in the central business district where most enterprises were locally owned and operated. Leonards, Stripling's, Meacham's, Monnig's, Washer Brother's, R. E. Cox, The Fair, Luskey's, Fake's, or Ellison's offered whatever customers needed. Most people attended church downtown. Downtown office buildings provided the regional headquarters for national oil companies including Pure, Continental, and Sinclair. Independents, such as Penrose, Moncrief, Roeser-Pendleton, Marshall Young, Ed Landreth, and Sid Richardson officed there, too. Downtown institutions stood poised to grow with post-war prosperity.[97]

Leonards, too, embraced the future. Managers and employees who had done wartime service returned to their old jobs or new ones in the store. Marvin lured Jenkins Garrett back to handle the legal affairs of the store, this time as in-house counsel rather than on outside retainer. Garrett's return to Leonards was a mark of the growing complexity of the brothers' outside interests and the maturation of the store's management. Marvin and Obie's oil and real-estate interests needed the constant attention of an attorney. The brothers could not toss the oil leases in a drawer forever. As it grew larger, Leonards also increasingly required legal help. A decade earlier Carl Bruner supplied that help while serving as general manager; now a much larger store required a more specialized and larger managerial system.[98]

Other needed changes were equally obvious. For Marvin and Obie, post-war prosperity confirmed what the failed sale of the store first suggested. It was time to further modernize and move upscale in furnishings, merchandise, and marketing. Each time a potential bidder backed out, he cited the look of the store and the lack of emphasis on fashion. A store without merchandise displayed on mannequins simply did not fit the retailing trend. This time it was a trend that had to be followed. Consumers flush with cash demanded fashion as well as value.

One change was less obvious. During the war the number of blacks, particularly in neighborhoods near downtown, increased dramatically. Like working class whites they had money to spend after the war, but they also increasingly resented segregation. Blacks had always worked and shopped at Leonards. When the store began offering credit options, such as layaway, it did not exclude black customers from the service. Lillie Bell Carter remembered the fair treatment she received when Leonards approved her to buy a radio on credit right after the war. Leonards' progressive attitude ended, however, when unwanted problems arose. Shortly after the end of the war, a black customer was served before a white one at the sandwich stand. The white customer got very angry and complained to Leonards' management. In response, Marvin and Obie excluded blacks from that serving area. Eventually they established a segregated stand for "colored only." Several black employees quit work over the issue, but the store went on—business as usual.[99]

Immediately after the war Marvin and Obie just wanted to avoid controversy and focus on growth. That growth led to even greater changes in Leonards. Among them was taking down the signs for white and colored in the mid-1950s.

Greater Leonards and Greater Fort Worth, 1948–60

When former employees described how Leonards changed over time, they typically responded, "It just got bigger." The store matched a fast-growing city and a dynamic market. Like Fort Worth, Marvin Leonard's interest in golf, golf courses, and his other businesses grew larger. Simply observing that each grew bigger, however, obscures that a change in scale meant a change in kind.[1]

For city and store, greater size altered their basic nature. Fort Worth's growth attracted a new wave of competitors and created new neighborhoods. Blacks moved into the city's inner core. Whites headed to the suburbs. Leonards responded to new competition and demographic opportunities, growing larger and offering a wider variety of merchandise. It also desegregated to serve its black customers and added more upscale merchandise and store fixtures to please suburban shoppers. Increasingly, Marvin relied on chain store methods and new layers of management to ease the burden of controlling and coordinating a gigantic enterprise.

Bigger was not altogether better, but it was a natural result of Marvin's long-term goals and ingrained management style. He went with what worked as far as it would take him and then changed course. Yet the objective remained greater size. In 1928 he claimed the store was "constantly growing bigger and better." In 1948 he still firmly believed that "a store must always grow, or else it's going to shrink."[2] After 1948 the store increasingly emphasized selection and credit. "You Can Find It at Leonards" supplemented "More Merchandise for Less Money" as commonly used slogans. This additional tag line symbolized a significant change in the character and identity of the store. By the end of the 1950s, the store was more like its competitors. It had higher expenses, was less flexible in its response to new economic conditions, and had lost some of its marketing flair.[3]

Changes in the scale and nature of city and store also affected Marvin. Fort

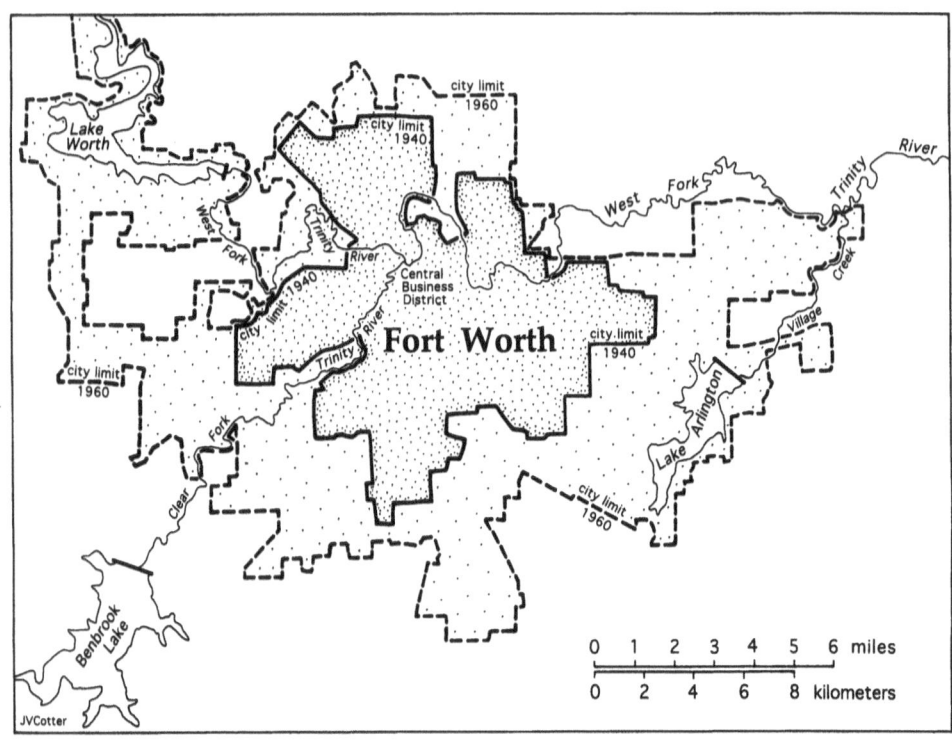

Greater Fort Worth, 1940 and 1960. *Map by John V. Cotter.*

Worth's growth brought new business opportunities and greater financial security. Adding new management and turning over the day-to-day business to his nephews freed his time to enjoy that security and pursue those opportunities. In particular, Marvin turned from the store to building and managing a new golf course and country club. Shady Oaks offered a creative preoccupation, a chance to add value to his nearby residential developments, and a focus for a restless mind.[4]

Greater Leonards and Chain Store Methods

In the summer of 1948, Leonards put the finishing touches on its largest expansion since 1930 and announced the opening of "Greater Leonards." Construction on the new building, occupying a half block facing Throckmorton and running from Weatherford to First Street, began in 1946. Upon completion, the varied food departments moved into new quarters, christened the Food Store. Other parts of Leonards were also renamed to reflect the larger, more image-conscious retail operations. The hard lines were consolidated into the Downstairs Store. Third floor clothing departments became the Fashion Floor, and the entire 1930 building was the Department Store.[5]

As was true of the 1930 building, corporate legend later stressed that construction began during a downturn in the economy. The brief lull in the Fort Worth economy in 1948 added credence to the legend. But in fact, World War II brought unprecedented growth to Leonards, and the company expanded as soon as the war ended and building materials and labor became available. Construction actually began at the peak of stunning increases in net profit and total sales.[6]

Fear of a recession similar to the one following World War I, however, encouraged the city to allow Marvin and Obie to connect their new building with the 1930 building over and under First Street. This use of public space by a private enterprise was new to Fort Worth, but at a time when city fathers backed a plan to sell bonds to finance public works designed to maintain high employment, a major construction project by a local business was more important than past precedent. Once again Carl Bruner handled the problem and articulated the argument in favor of private use of public property. Early in 1946, he worked out a contract with the city's attorneys allowing Leonards to rent city right-of-way above and below First Street. This was a far cry from the late 1920s when the city and Marvin clashed over the Bluff Park lot. The 1946 contract marked not just the

Children at Grand Opening. In the first week of September, 1948, Leonards opened its Food Store and gave away felt beanies emblazoned with the name Greater Leonards. Courtesy *Fort Worth Star-Telegram* Photograph Collection, Special Collections Division, The University of Texas at Arlington Libraries.

brothers' growing status but the increasingly close coalition between commercial interests and Fort Worth's government.[7]

Public and private cooperation allowed Leonards to build out instead of up. In Houston, Foley's, newly purchased by Federated Stores, built a six-story building on one city block at about the same time. In contrast, Leonards was able to limit the amount of time customers spent going up and down escalators and elevators by expanding horizontally. One obvious advantage was that shoppers could see, touch, and buy merchandise while moving horizontally. Thus, with the city's assistance, Leonards realized some of the advantages in design and layout of a modern shopping mall.[8]

Customers walked in air-conditioned comfort from the Department Store to the 22,000-square-foot Food Store located on the street level of the new building. With five floors plus a full basement, the new building also housed the creamery, bakery, and other food manufacturing and processing facilities.[9]

The Downstairs Store filled the 48,000-square-foot basement area of both buildings and carried expanded inventories of lines that had been Leonards' bread and butter for years—paint, wallpaper, hardware, sporting goods, housewares, automotive parts, lawn and garden supplies, plumbing supplies, and other hard lines. Tires of all types sold particularly well. The cafeteria, still located beside the hard lines, had expanded seating and now could serve 3,500 people on a busy Saturday.[10]

Hard lines also spilled out of the downstairs area and across the street to the Farm Store. Doc St. Clair's Farm Store had succeeded admirably and now sold tractors, combines, hay balers, dairy equipment, ranch supplies, lawn mowers, garden tillers, fence supplies, and numerous other gasoline- and electric-powered machines for home and farm. A large saddle shop was a special feature of the Farm Store, much to the delight of Marvin's daughters, who were avid horse lovers.[11]

With food departments moved to the new building, clothing and furniture departments had room to expand. On the first floor of the Department Store were the men's department, the new boys department, drugs, cosmetics, and an expanded men's shoe department. A new soda fountain with seating for seventy-two customers had a prominent spot just beside the Throckmorton Street entrance. Three women's departments—notions, accessories, and lingerie—moved to the first floor by the Houston and Second Street entrance. Reflecting an increased emphasis on higher-quality women's wear, these departments displayed the latest merchandise in new ash blond cases and shadow boxes.[12]

Furniture, appliances, and electronic equipment spread out, taking much of the space on the second floor of the Department Store. There was even enough space to devote an entire department to pianos. During the grand opening, Leonards brought in pianists to entertain shoppers, and a few years later a radio program featuring piano music was broadcast from the department. By then Leonards sold more pianos than any store in Fort Worth.[13]

Rugs, drapes, and other home furnishings filled another part of the second floor. The increased space allowed Leonards to display furniture and home decorations in completely furnished rooms like other large furniture or department stores. The days had passed when customers selected merchandise from crowded, jumbled stacks of basic furniture and home furnishings.[14]

Women's ready-to-wear took over the third floor when workroom operations moved to the new building. Obie, Marvin, and their managers wanted to give soft goods and hard lines a distinct personality separate from the rest of the store. In the case of women's wear, they also desperately needed to expand its appeal to a rapidly growing segment of the market. Since the 1920s, Leonards attracted women to the store with a large selection of attractively priced fabrics. In some years in the 1930s, they even sold fabric at a slight loss to maintain store traffic. By 1948, however, fewer women made their own clothes, opting instead to buy fashionable attire. Leonards' fabric selection remained large, but placing it near the women's clothing department encouraged customers to buy ready-to-wear.[15]

One device Leonards used to pull women from fabrics to ready-to-wear was attractively outfitted mannequins. Major department stores used mannequins as early as the 1890s, but until after World War II, they did not have a place at "Fort Worth's only complete one-stop economy shopping center." The appearance of mannequins more than anything else signaled Leonards' commitment to upgrading its clothing lines and revamping its image. An ad for the grand opening touted Greater Leonards as the place to "Aim High for Fashion—Low for Price." Marvin's long-held disdain for artistically displayed solitary items gave way to the reality of post-war buying habits. Leonards increasingly relied on artistic displays of the latest fashions along with price to sell clothing.[16]

Leonards' soft goods managers also accommodated women's more specialized fashion needs. After the war, both birthrates and the availability of merchandise for mothers and babies accelerated. The store's expanded space and decentralized managerial structure allowed buyers to continue the practice of creating new departments with fresh inventories. Not wanting to lag behind the times, Leonards opened a maternity shop and infant wear department on the third floor and in adjoining space established a children's furniture shop called the Stork's Nest.[17]

It was difficult to tell who came up with the ideas for the layout of the store, its new image, and expanded product lines. Clearly, Marvin had a hand in every major decision. Obie, however, controlled construction and the store's physical plant. He or a department manager would tell Marvin that the meat market needed a new freezer case but would seldom wait for his approval before acting. For larger, more expensive building projects, the brothers consulted extensively. Marvin usually handled financial matters and for the 1948 expansion set up a loan from a group of New York banks through Fort Worth National Bank. Naturally, he took a greater role planning such an important project. Still, Obie made most basic decisions about construction methods and the physical setup of the store.[18]

One example of Obie's contribution to the store was the construction and installation of escalators at the close of World War II. Before the war escalators were too expensive for even Fort Worth's most exclusive department stores. Yet escalators moved customers more quickly and easily from floor to floor than elevators, allowing multiple floors to seem like one floor. Shoppers who used escalators in other parts of the country reported back favorably, and most trade journals recommended them. Obie decided Leonards needed escalators to accommodate the store's growing crowds. Inquiries immediately after the war revealed that escalators remained expensive, and escalator companies had a large backlog of orders. Obie consulted with local engineer Robert F. Lockridge and decided to build rather than buy escalators. Working with local craftsmen, they successfully fabricated and installed the first escalator in Fort Worth. Obie spent so much time supervising the project that his wife, Margery, took their younger children down to the store to eat supper with him so they could see their father.[19]

Most customers were not used to riding an escalator, and it took a while to work the kinks out of Obie and Lockridge's design. To prevent accidents, Obie stationed employees at the top and bottom of the moving stairs to instruct riders to hold on, watch their toes, and step on and off at the correct time. After a few months, however, the escalators worked efficiently. The escalator monitors went back to their other duties, and Leonards began advertising that it had the only escalators in town.[20]

Vendors loved to demonstrate new merchandise near the escalators. The technology caused people to stop and stare, and traffic patterns led many people through the small space at an escalator's entrance and exit. One day, a factory representative might have a large display of new small appliances. The next, someone who could have passed for a barker at the county fair hawked special knives that cut tomatoes as smooth as silk or sold wooden monkeys on a stick. Contributions like Obie's escalators added to the sense of excitement that made Leonards a fun place to shop, while enhancing merchandise sales.[21]

As the escalators demonstrated, the layout of the store strongly influenced merchandising. Because of this, Marvin often joined his brother in creating the look and feel of the store. He wanted the goods out where customers could see them and feel them. He okayed the use of mannequins but still wanted full displays. White space between items on display characterized upscale stores, but for Marvin, too much white space remained a sin. He tried to modernize while preserving the old image of Leonards as a place where the merchandise spilled out of washtubs into the aisles.[22]

The first in Fort Worth, Leonards' escalators helped move crowds through the enlarged store. Through the 1950s even farmers still came downtown.

Once the new displays and the reorganization into more-distinct divisions was completed, Greater Leonards took on even more of the attributes of a modern shopping mall. Within a horizontal floor plan, customers passed from one distinct area to the next. Managers of each of these divisions, and to some extent department managers, even shared many characteristics of an independent operator. Just as proprietors paid rent to the mall owner, the central office deducted a fee for the amount of selling space and storage space they used from a manager's gross profits. Compensation was linked to sales and profits by the bonus system. Managers also enjoyed numerous opportunities for experimentation, innovation, and independent action. The key difference between Leonards and a shopping mall, however, was that the ultimate control and the ultimate risk for each department remained in Marvin and Obie's hands. They changed the system as the situation warranted, and they kept managers within the bounds of Leonards' basic merchandising philosophy.[23]

When Doc St. Clair went to work for the store in the late 1920s, Marvin told him to run hard lines like his own business. The merchandise manager position, created in the 1938 reorganization, removed some discretion from department managers. By 1948, however, the increased size and number of departments forced Marvin, Obie, and the merchandise managers to again increase the autonomy of department managers. St. Clair's various Downstairs Store managers bought their own merchandise, sometimes directly from manufacturers at markets in Dallas, New York, and Chicago. More often, at least until the mid-1950s, they bought from manufacturers' representatives who visited the store weekly. Department managers also purchased job lots or distressed merchandise as it came available. St. Clair still offered advice on major purchases and would travel with new managers until they learned the buying process. He also coordinated promotions across departments. For example, power tools and hardware might run complementary specials that appealed to the building trade or the home owner. Still, many basic merchandising decisions had reverted to the hands of department managers.[24]

Department managers' actions, however, were limited by the central office staff. Together with division heads, the central office allotted floor space and warehouse space to each department. Within that space, department managers could arrange displays, position cash registers, and decide other layout details. This arrangement allowed department mangers considerable input into the creation of Greater Leonards. Helen Love, the head of women's sportswear, for instance, helped design the Fashion Floor, and meat department manager James Blair added his input to grocery store design. Yet even in the case of store design, ultimate control was centralized.[25]

Fred J. Ross, a store designer since 1915, drew up much of the actual layout of the 1948 store. Ross had consulted for Leonards for many years, but worked almost exclusively for Marvin and Obie from 1946 until the opening in 1948. His goal was to achieve "step saving convenience" in the arrangement of merchandise. He also tried to sell more merchandise in less space. Ross claimed that the Food Store could do "several times the volume of business possible in huge food markets several times its size in other parts of the country."[26]

This emphasis on layout and its centralized control was not new. Obie always worked hard to increase sales per square foot, and this effort contributed to the store's success. Piggly Wiggly in the 1920s revolutionized the grocery industry by selling higher volume in less space. Greater Leonards took the process one step further. In the Food Store, wider aisles, larger shopping carts, a 200-foot refrigerated self-service meat counter, and a 150-foot pastry counter let customers buy more in less time. Across the entire store customers still bought more merchandise for less money, but they also purchased more types of merchandise in less time.[27]

Clearly, increased size and a new layout had advantages, but it also had risks.

Getting bigger meant that with available technology and Leonards' decentralized managerial practices, inventory and employees could not be controlled and managed with the store's traditional efficiency. Expenses eventually increased and floor space was not used to its ultimate capacity. Marvin responded to these problems by tightening, not loosening, centralized control. Greater Leonards did not evolve into a shopping mall. Instead, it increasingly acted more like Sears or Montgomery Wards.

In 1948, few probably realized the downside of greater size. Changes in the retail industry and new population patterns forced Leonards to adjust its image upward and grow larger. Hard line departments, like tools, sporting goods, or lawn and garden products, drew customers from what Mary Barton described as "all walks of life." Soft goods and food departments, however, depended more heavily upon farm folk and the working class. As late as 1956, when Doris Richeson began working for Leonards, she was struck by the large number of less affluent farmers and blue-collar workers shopping at Leonards. She observed them eating food in virtually all parts of the store as if they were on a town square. They felt right at home in a store that, unlike fancier department stores, still did not have standardized fixtures in all departments.[28]

Unfortunately for Leonards, the demographic tide was turning. Across Texas, farmers and ranchers moved to town. As rural towns grew into mid-sized cities, Penney's, Sears, Safeway, and eventually chains such as Wal-Mart recognized and responded to demographic trends. They entered places like Wichita Falls, Denton, Weatherford, Granbury, and Cleburne, forcing community merchants to expand and modify their offerings. West Texans and North Texans found more shopping opportunities at home, and trips into Fort Worth to visit Leonards became less frequent.[29]

Rural folk also moved to Fort Worth, providing a host of potential new customers, and Leonards made a special effort to attract their business. The city, however, grew so large that it became difficult for customers living on its fringes to reach downtown. Neighborhood grocery stores in particular were more convenient than Leonards. At the same time, the local meat-packing industry entered a period of decline, and growth in blue-collar jobs leveled off. Marvin and his managers had the task of expanding the appeal of Leonards among clerical and managerial workers while keeping customers streaming into the grocery store. The 1948 expansion made a solution possible: appeal to busy shoppers by improving the quality and variety of their merchandise. Leonards became a one-stop shopping center that offered selection and good prices. The store could not standardize all its fixtures and still keep prices low, but it could work to build a new image through better public relations.[30]

In 1947 the store hired Travis P. Young as its public relations director. Young was a past president of the local Junior Chamber of Commerce and had served as vice president of the Texas Junior Chamber of Commerce. He had worked as an executive vice president for Arlington Heights Ice Company and was extremely active in numerous church and civic organizations. His job was to reach out to a younger and rapidly growing Fort Worth population and to maintain the store's connections to the local business community.[31]

In early 1952, Charles Ringler replaced Young. Ringler also was active in the Junior Chamber of Commerce. He got to know Marvin when the two served on a committee to select the Jaycees' Outstanding Young Man. He also grew up across the street from Carl Bruner. When Obie's children visited the Bruner children, Ringler sometimes joined the party. In addition, his father, a leading Cadillac salesman, was well known and respected in the business community. Ringler was educated at Texas Christian University and worked at Ralston Purina and Magnolia Petroleum. In many ways, Ringler brought a perfect combination of skills and experiences to Leonards. He had some personal connections to the store and to Marvin, yet he had been trained outside the store and had established contacts that did not depend upon Leonards.[32]

Ringler was also a man of considerable initiative and determination. At the start of World War II, Ringler tried to get in the Army Air Corps. His entrance exam was misgraded and he wound up in the Coast Guard. When the error was discovered, he was told it was too late to switch out of the Coast Guard. He took the exam again, wrote to Washington to plead his case, and became a Marine pilot.[33]

After joining the store, Ringler introduced a series of innovations. He installed phones around the store, and customers could call the switchboard to help locate products. They could also suggest new products that the store should carry. New mothers and newcomers to Forth Worth received personal letters from Ringler inviting them to come to the store and redeem the gift certificates included with the letters. Ringler also continued and updated the tradition of special promotions and prizes. Leonards gave an automobile to the customer who guessed when a six-foot candle would burn out. Another prize went to the person who predicted when a ton of ice would melt. Leonards continued running free movies for children in the local parks during the summer. New promotions, however, highlighted the store's increased attention to fashion and electronics equipment. It sponsored a Miss Texas style show and outfitted the pageant's winner. When the race to build atomic weapons drove up the price of uranium in the mid-1950s, Leonards held a drawing for Geiger counters and displayed uranium ore. All of this was part of Marvin's charge to Ringler to "build an image."[34]

With the right image, greater size offered Leonards new potential. Thousands of customers recognized and trusted Leonards and enjoyed the flamboyant promotions and eye-catching bargains. It remained a familiar and reassuring place where people could meet their friends. Established contacts with manufacturers and distributors, coupled with increased buying volume, delivered low prices to customers. Strong cash flow ensured that department managers could buy what and when they wanted. Promotions and special attention to new customers kept crowds coming through the doors. Total sales and net profits surged after 1948.[35]

Yet greater size put pressure on Leonards' simple management structure and systems. One reflection of this was that in 1956 Ringler was put under Harry Rooke, the head of a newly created division called Sales Promotion. Rooke was in charge of all department publicity, major sales events, advertising, exterior and interior store displays, and had general oversight of public relations. A larger store demanded greater coordination.[36]

Adding more mid-level managers and central staff was a new departure. Marvin and Obie traditionally kept expenses low by keeping the store's bureaucracy small and inventory system simple. Mangers often did more than one task and the managerial levels were kept to a minimum. Unlike large department stores and chains, Leonards relied on a physical inventory rather than a paper trail to track merchandise. Except for large items sold on credit, the store kept no copies of sales slips. Unless hurried clerks paused to count what was on hand and compare it to what had been purchased, no one knew with certainty what remained unsold. Leonards office staff kept some records, but department and divisional managers attended to planning, cost control, and inventory management with little centralized oversight.[37]

Growth in sales, the number of employees, and the variety of merchandise made keeping an eye on turnover and coordinating the activities of varied departments increasingly difficult. Marvin's fast nickel turned into a slow nickel because no one knew that a particular type or brand of hammer went unsold for weeks. Perhaps a buyer working from inaccurate inventory estimates even purchased more of that same hammer. Besides adding new managerial positions, Marvin turned to chain store men to bring order to buying and selling systems and reduce the cost of carrying inventory.[38]

C. F. Kelley was one of the first chain store men hired after the 1948 expansion. Like Charles Ringler, he had one foot in the old world of Leonards and the other in the new world of modern corporate management. He was born and grew up in Wise County to the northwest of Fort Worth, and as a child he often accompanied his family on shopping trips to Leonards. After graduating from North Texas State University in 1940, he went to work for S. H. Kress & Co. He served as a B-52 pilot during the war and then returned to Kress. During the next four years, he worked in Kress stores in San Antonio, rural Oklahoma, and Idaho Falls, Idaho. In 1950, Elam J. Henderson, Leonards' general manager, recruited Kelley to take over several hard line departments. As Henderson well understood, the large number of stores and the geographic extent of chains required rigid bureaucratic control of inventory. Henderson told Kelley to use his chain store experience to revive the sagging fortunes of his hard line departments. While enjoying the greater freedom of action as a Leonards manager, Kelley also saw the necessity of bringing the systematic and disciplined habits of a chain store organization to his departments. He kept inventories down and made sure his buyers purchased merchandise that would sell quickly even without sensational promotions.[39]

Ray Shea came to Leonards the year after Kelley and solidified the chain store system in hard lines. Shea grew up on a farm in Fargo, North Dakota, and in 1931 began working for Montgomery Wards. He worked for Wards in North Dakota, Florida, Pennsylvania, and New York and also spent some time in the main office in Chicago. In 1946 Shea went to work at Joske's in San Antonio as the head of the hard line division. In the spring of 1951, Paul Leonard and Doc St. Clair went to San Antonio to meet with Shea. St. Clair was contemplating retirement, and Leonards would need a new hard lines manager if he left. The pair did not mention to Shea their interest in him, but a few days later Henderson called to ask Shea if he was interested in the job. Shea traveled to Fort Worth, toured the store, and wound up in Marvin's office. Marvin offered him the position of merchandise manager of hard lines and outlined his salary and bonus. Continuing the practice begun with St. Clair in the 1920s, he did not give him any specific instructions, except to say he "wanted him to take charge of the hard line divisions." Marvin clearly realized, however, that meant changing the managerial style and structure at Leonards.[40]

Almost immediately, Shea began installing the systems he learned at Montgomery Wards. Besides bureaucratic control of inventory, chains encouraged a rigid code of employee behavior. Managers were taught to be interchangeable parts that made the store's system work equally well in Chicago or Fort Worth. Indeed, as was true of both Kelley and Shea, chain store organizations moved men from store to store to break down their individuality and envelop them in the corporate culture. Shea reduced the independence of department managers and forced them to work within his general guidelines. He discouraged them from buying job lots and distressed merchandise. He wanted uniform quality merchandise, bought in bulk directly from the manufacturer. For example, he reduced the number of brands of clawhammers carried at Leonards and made sure they were better-quality products that would sell without price cuts and promotions.[41]

Chain store methods brought mixed results to Leonards. Under Shea, gross profits in hard lines went up and the company gained greater control of inventory. Net profits, however, did not go up as sharply as gross profits because expenses charged to the division by the central office rose after 1951. Increased local competition demanded more and varied advertising. The larger store and increased use of accounting controls meant adding more nonselling personnel to the payroll. Chain stores, however, also faced the problem of the cost of bureaucracy and solved it by improved turnover and the enthusiasm of their managers for the system. Shea, Kelley, and the other chain store men that followed them never completely grafted chain store methods onto the managerial culture of Leonards. Several of Shea's department managers bought what they wanted when they wanted it despite all that he said and did. Eventually they left, but not before they damaged Shea's efforts to control the expense of carrying inappropriate inventory.[42]

There was, however, a kernel of truth in criticism of chain store methods. It was difficult and costly to make the store something it had never been. The public never took to the name Greater Leonards. They still called it Leonard Brothers or Leonards. They liked the old ways and the old name. Those old ways, especially the job lots, indirectly added a great deal to net profit because they increased the turnover of many different products. The markup on job lots was seldom high, but if promoted and priced correctly they sold fast and therefore added little to expenses. They also brought in crowds who purchased other items. The crowds and splashy promotion of odd lots stimulated the creativity and salesmanship of all department managers, not just those directly involved in the promotion. Special promotions remained a fixture at Leonards and managers always enjoyed greater autonomy than at any chain. Yet reducing each manager's individuality and limiting the buying of distressed merchandise slowed the impressive growth in net profits so common to Leonards before the 1950s.[43]

Virginia Garrett, wife of Jenkins Garrett, remembered once buying two buckets with holes in them for a ridiculously low price. The buckets were clearly marked as seconds, indicating they had defects. What other store would think to market buckets with holes? The idea was amusing. The display encouraged creativity. Customers could repair the buckets or use them for flower pots. Under Ray Shea, holey buckets gradually disappeared from the store.[44]

Buckets with holes and the excitement that went with them disappeared because Leonards was too big and the market too different for the old ways to continue. A burgeoning inventory gave them little choice but to move toward chain store methods. New market conditions confirmed that choice. By the mid-1950s, there were fewer consumers with the time and talent to repair buckets and more competitors selling bargain merchandise. Leonards needed more and better-quality merchandise and tighter inventory controls.

Greater Fort Worth and Retailing

Understanding the new competitive dynamics requires revisiting the phenomenal post-1940 growth of Fort Worth. During World War II, defense spending at

General Dynamics and other Fort Worth–area plants and increased demand for petroleum pushed economic activity in the Fort Worth area to record levels. The city's population grew by more than 100,000 (about 60 percent) in the 1940s. While there were periodic slowdowns in the economy, prosperity and population growth continued into the 1950s. More people, more money to spend, and more jobs made the city a very attractive place for national retailers. Major chains either entered the Fort Worth market for the first time or placed increased emphasis on their Fort Worth stores.[45]

In 1949, for example, J. C. Penney moved F. W. Laughbaum, one of its most experienced and successful managers, to its downtown Fort Worth store. Laughbaum was charged with competing with Leonards and building up Penney's business. He started by stressing Penney's nationally advertised brands and uncluttered appearance in soft lines. Building on the chain's national experience, the local store displayed merchandise in the most attractive and modern way possible. This was particularly effective in women's fashions and in better-quality men's suits and shirts. Penney's promoted its own well-known "Town Craft" brand and other Penney's labels made by Hart, Schaffner, & Marx and other prominent manufacturers. Penney's filled the niche between Leonards and high-end stores such as Stripling's, Washer Brothers, and The Fair, blocking Leonards' expansion into better-quality women's and men's fashions. The problem was made all the more difficult by the continued presence of Monnig's in the middle and upper-middle segment of the clothing market. In addition, during the 1950s, television and radio advertising made nationwide retailers like Montgomery Wards, Sears, and Penney's—not to mention the expanded variety stores and the reinvigorated traditional department stores—more competitive.[46]

Leonards responded energetically by using its comparative shoppers to visit other stores and keep management apprised of competitors' sales and promotions. If possible, Leonards tried to find out about these sales in advance and run sales in similar merchandise. The company also continued advertising in the local newspapers virtually every day. Throughout the 1940s and 1950s, it was the largest single advertiser in the *Star-Telegram* and *The Shopper*. It also ran ads in the *Press* and the city's black newspapers: the *Call*, the *Mind*, and the *Como Monitor*. In 1957, for example, Leonards spent $1,091,671 on newspaper advertising, a $500,000 increase from the previous year. Although heavy advertising and special promotions reduced net profits, Leonards had to bear the cost to remain the dominant retailer in Fort Worth.[47]

In competing with department stores such as Monnig's and Stripling's, Leonards also faced the continuing problem of getting an adequate supply of nationally advertised brands. Many manufacturers still refused to do business with Leonards because it sold below the recommended price. Arrow, for example, sold shirts through several Fort Worth retailers. Leonards acquired a supply of Arrow shirts from department stores in rural areas of Texas and sold them below the company's suggested retail price. The shirtmaker responded by trying to block access to its product, but Leonards found new sources every time the company dried up an outlet. Eventually a truce was declared. Leonards could sell Arrow shirts at any price it wanted as long as it did not advertise that price. In return, the company ceased its effort to block the sale of Arrow shirts to Leonards.[48]

Botany 500 suits, Prestone antifreeze, and other popular national brands proved even more difficult to obtain than Arrow shirts. The 1950s was a time of heavy brand promotion by which manufacturers bypassed retailers and appealed directly to consumers. Both the rapidly expanding television industry and national magazines were filled with advertisements touting specific trade names and products. After a heavy barrage of advertisement, price and quality often mattered less to shoppers than the brand. Customers looked for branded merchandise in stores and would shop elsewhere rather than buy nonbranded items. Stores carrying heavily advertised products benefited because customers often bought other items once they found the item they were searching for. When Monnig's sold a Botany 500 suit, the shopper purchased a new shirt and tie to go with it.[49]

Groceries became even more competitive than soft goods. The extra space provided for the Food Store in 1948 allowed growth in food sales to keep pace with Fort Worth's surging population, but the rosy economy and the growing number of potential customers attracted a new wave of national chains to Fort Worth. Well-heeled competitors could afford to run a loss to establish their presence in the area. These efforts to dominate the Fort Worth grocery market cut deeply into Leonards' profit margins.

This surge in grocery store expansion in Fort Worth began in the early 1950s and was led by Safeway. After building several stores in the Dallas–Fort Worth area and establishing a distribution network, the company initiated a price war in Fort Worth. In 1955 Safeway promised to make all advertised prices on any grocery item in Fort Worth its everyday price. This included special promotional prices and loss leaders on coffee, sugar, and cigarettes. Safeway's willingness to operate at a loss in Fort Worth signaled its commitment to dominate that market. Marvin told Jack Hester, the head of the Food Store, to meet Safeway's prices and promised it would not affect year-end bonuses. True to his word, Marvin paid more than $60,000 in bonuses to Food Store managers in 1956 even though the Food Store suffered a net loss of about $55,000.[50]

Jenkins Garrett joined the officers of two other local grocery stores and brought Safeway's anticompetitive actions to the attention of the U.S. Department of Justice. Using the provisions of the Sherman Antitrust Act, the Justice Department filed a complaint against Safeway in United States District Court in late

1955. Safeway officials eventually signed a consent agreement effective January, 1957, promising to stop offering artificially low prices and subsidizing money-losing stores in Fort Worth with profits from its other stores.[51]

Despite the legal victory, Safeway's multiple locations away from downtown and its extensive advertising hurt Leonards. Net profit after bonuses in the food division in 1957 was only about $4,000 on $4.5 million in sales. In comparison, in 1944 the food division at Leonards made a net profit after bonuses of $180,000 on about $2.5 million in sales. Although legal action stopped the red ink, the Food Store never completely rebounded. In 1960 it made a net profit after bonuses of about $46,000 on more than $5 million in sales. While escalating food sales increased customer traffic throughout Leonards, bigger sales no longer translated into bigger profits in groceries.[52]

Price was not the only reason Safeway cut into profits in food. It also enjoyed greater ease of access for those who did not live near downtown. Marvin and Obie faced a difficult dilemma. A bigger Fort Worth promised increased customer traffic, but a bigger Fort Worth also made driving downtown and parking a nightmare. During the Christmas season of 1953, Leonards inaugurated a bus service from a large parking lot by the Henderson Street bridge over the Trinity. Shoppers parked on the edge of downtown and rode to Leonards for free. Because of heavy traffic, the bus was slow. The ride was cold in the winter and hot in the summer. Despite efforts to enhance customer comfort—paving the lot, heating and cooling the bus stop, and running the service continuously from 7:00 A.M. to 7:30 P.M.—the shuttle built frustration, not customer loyalty. Through the 1950s, improving parking and access to the store remained a largely unsolved problem.[53]

Expanding the use of credit was more successful in building store traffic, building customer loyalty, and meeting the needs of a changing population. Leonards offered credit as early as 1939, but until after World War II, all but the largest sales were still for cash. Credit was used extensively in the Farm Store and for furniture and appliances, but most other departments used layaway. The post-war economic boom increased the chance that consumers would pay off their credit, and credit became increasingly common in all parts of the country. It fit in well with the heavy brand advertising and promotion of consumption that characterized the 1950s. Marvin encouraged the use of credit as long as two criterion were met. He insisted that managers run at least a 4 percent loss on credit. Less than that indicated the managers' credit standards were too tight. He also mandated that credit be offered without regard to race. There was to be no discrimination in the credit department. Use of store credit expanded rapidly through the 1950s and early 1960s.[54]

Meanwhile, Everybody's also offered credit and grew larger. Everybody's did not spend money on nicer fixtures and did not build a new store. Instead, from the 1930s on, it steadily expanded in the block where Marvin first opened his store in 1918. In June, 1948, two months before the opening of the new Food Store, Everybody's finished its most substantial renovation project. A complete second floor was opened on a store that now took up the entire block bounded by Belknap, Houston, Weatherford, and Throckmorton. Most of the load-bearing walls on the first floor were replaced by columns concealed behind shelving. This gave both floors an open look reminiscent of modern discount centers. The store also had a partial basement and all three levels were connected by an elevator and three stairways.[55]

Like Leonards, Everybody's opened new departments and carried a full range of groceries, meat and dairy products, soft goods, and some hard lines. Its almost seventy thousand square feet of selling space bulged with merchandise aimed at making it "a complete one-stop shopping center."[56]

Even more than Leonards, Everybody's drew customers from the working class of all races and ethnic backgrounds. By the 1950s, more than half the customers at Everybody's were Mexican or black. Between the end of World War II and about 1958, low inflation, relatively strong unions, and good economic growth increased the purchasing power of the working class. As it did with other Americans, heavy advertising encouraged the working class and minorities to consume brand name items and better-quality clothing. Everybody's, still managed by Ted Leveridge, responded. In an effort to live up to its stated goal "to strive always to be known as the working man's friend," Everybody's continued buying closeouts, fire sale items, bankrupt stock, irregulars, and seconds. Because they still remained a relatively small operation, they responded very quickly to any unique opportunities to purchase low-cost merchandise. Yet in categories such as shoes, work clothes, and food, they pushed toward the middle of the market. Some items, such as evaporative air conditioners, became a specialty at Everybody's, and in hot, dry summers salespeople would stand all day writing tickets for these items.[57]

Increasingly, Everybody's department managers directly competed with Leonards and took pride in outdoing the larger store. When asked to name their number-one competitor, they typically responded—Leonards. Everybody's growth reflected the success of these efforts. From 1951 to 1955 total sales at Leonards increased about 1 percent. Meanwhile total sales at Everybody's increased 22 percent. Total sales at Leonards were still more than four times those at Everybody's, but in some departments the gap narrowed dramatically. In 1951, for example, drug sales were $476,000 at Leonards and $246,000 at Everybody's. By 1955 Leonards' drug sales had grown to $496,000 compared with $370,000 at Everybody's. Low prices and low overhead partially explain Everybody's growth. Leveridge also often used more striking promotions than those at Leonards. Once, Everybody's gave away a barrel of money to the customer who came closest to guessing the exact amount in the barrel. As Leonards moved upscale, Everybody's continued to build an image as a place for bargains and good fun. Low costs, aggressive advertising, and entertaining promotions helped Everybody's achieve twice the rate of growth of Leonards. By 1960, Everybody's took business from Leonards in the middle range of the market.[58]

Greater size and scope at Everybody's and Leonards made it more difficult for Marvin and Obie to manage their retailing empire. Increased age made them less willing and less able to devote long hours to the store. Besides, the opportunities presented by the rapidly expanding regional economy made their time better spent elsewhere. Neither brother ignored the store. Both knew it was the base of their financial success but were ready for others to take a larger role in the store.

NEW MANAGEMENT AND PROFITS

Marvin continued to provide direction for the store. During his daily visits, he made or approved strategic decisions, hired key managers, and helped train his nephews, Paul and Bob Leonard, to take over the business. Marvin kept in touch with the store through his top managers and set the tone by exchanging a friendly and open greeting with employees. On rare occasions, he visited departments to offer praise or recommendations. He remained the major connecting point between Leonards and the civic and financial institutions of the city. By the late 1950s, however, the story of the store was more often the story of new managers brought in to change things.[59]

Obie also became preoccupied with other business interests. After 1950, he continued to office in the store but spent much of his time taking care of his personal investments. Beginning in the 1930s, he had purchased farm and ranch land and planted pecan orchards. By the 1950s, he was the major producer of pecans in Texas. Shrewdly buying and selling rural property brought him as much pleasure as any other business activity, and he pursued it with great enthusiasm. Mentioning a piece of property often elicited detailed descriptions of its advantages and disadvantages. This one had good water, but rocky soil. Here was one that could be developed with the right care into a fine pecan orchard.[60]

One of Obie's more interesting ventures took advantage of his engineering talent. In the 1940s he formed a company that manufactured and installed automobile air conditioners. By 1950 the company supplied Ford, Chrysler, and General Motors. Obie was determined that Amon Carter, the city's most recognizable leader, should have one of his air conditioners. Carter refused. Obie borrowed his car anyway and installed an air conditioner for free. Carter liked the air conditioner, as did many others. In 1954 Obie sold the company for $815,463.81.

Obie loved making deals. Like two of his favorite pastimes, hunting and fishing, it was a sport. For Obie much more than Marvin, making money by taking a risk excited and energized him. Obie did not need golf; he made deals. He did not win every time—that probably would have been too predictable—but he loved to play. And as the case of the auto air-conditioning company demonstrated, instead of rounding off the sale price, he liked to get his eighty-one cents worth.[61]

During the 1950s, Obie also devoted more time to community service. He gave generously to the Boy Scouts, serving as president of the Longhorn Council and a member of the National Executive Committee. The O. P. Leonard family also donated 250 acres of land near Granbury for a Scout reservation. In 1955 Governor Allan Shivers appointed him as one of the original members of the Trinity River Authority, and he was reappointed for terms that stretched into the 1970s. He worked to build reservoirs, improve water quality, and allow barge traffic to use the Trinity.[62]

As Marvin and Obie turned from the store to other pursuits, Obie's sons, Paul and Bob Leonard, took over more of the managerial duties of running a large enterprise. While attending the Fort Worth public schools, the brothers spent much time in the store. They were paid a dollar per day in the 1930s for stocking shelves and sacking groceries. In the summer of 1938, they went into business for themselves, opening up a soft drink stand in the store. They paid Leonards half the profits as rent and still doubled their investment. During the school year, they maintained the soft drink machines in the store.[63]

After high school, Bob Leonard, who was two years younger than Paul, attended Texas A&M and Texas Christian University. He married Virginia McGinley and went to work full time in the store. He began in the appliance department but also worked in hardware and sporting goods. His main interest remained the hard lines division, and he was particularly fond of sporting goods.[64]

At age ten, Paul Leonard began going down to the store on a regular basis and was soon working Saturdays and summers. His father and uncle moved him from department to department so that he could get a good feel for the entire operation. He attended the public schools in Fort Worth and in 1942 entered Washington and Lee University. After a year there, he transferred to Texas Christian University, but the war interrupted his college plans. In 1944 Paul joined the navy and served as an electronics technician until July, 1946. After the war, he graduated from Southern Methodist University with a degree in business while working in the advertising department at Leonards. He married Nancy Alice Powell in May, 1948, and from that time Paul was actively involved in the daily management of Leonards.[65]

Paul moved rapidly up the ranks and soon worked closely with General Manager Elam Henderson. Henderson fit the traditional mold of managers at Leonards. He was born in Athens in East Texas and moved to Fort Worth in 1915. In the 1920s, his father worked in the grocery department at Leonards, and Henderson formed close personal ties with Marvin and Obie. After working for two decades with a wholesale grocery firm, in early 1939 Henderson took charge of Leonards' newly created credit department. Later that year he moved into the position of general manager, working directly under Marvin. His handling of all routine managerial chores, including most personnel decisions, freed Marvin and Obie to pursue their varied interests outside the store. Henderson was a calm man, friendly and seldom ruffled by even the most irate customer or employee. He did the small things that endeared him to employees. When they were sick, he helped them find a hospital room. When they lost a parent or spouse, he helped as best he could. He said little, observed much, and let his actions speak.[66]

Two other managers were on a roughly equal footing with Henderson. Bill Haberer, the head of the accounting and financial operations, joined Leonards around the time Henderson did. Unlike Henderson, Haberer was a university graduate and a lawyer. He supervised bookkeeping, billing, deliveries, and credit and specialized in financial planning and analysis. He also monitored Leonards' changing tax obligations and insurance needs. Having replaced Carl Bruner as the numbers man, he focused on the hard reality of cash flow and profit. When Marvin looked over the store's year-end figures, he did so in the company of only Haberer and Jenkins Garrett.[67]

Garrett, the third top-level manager, had long-standing ties to the store.[68] After working at Leonards on weekends and in the summers as a teen, he went off to the University of Texas in September, 1931. Marvin told him to call if he ever needed a loan. While Garrett never asked for that loan, he worked most summers and holidays for the store until he graduated with a law degree. After receiving a Masters in Law from Harvard University, he was associated with Walker, Smith, and Shannon, the Fort Worth firm that handled legal matters for Marvin, Obie, and the store. During World War II, Garrett served in the FBI and afterwards Marvin persuaded him to become the store's legal counselor. He dealt primarily with the Leonard brothers' outside interests, helping set up their insurance company in the mid-1950s, overseeing their oil and gas deals, and handling land transactions. Like Charles Ringler, he also represented the brothers on numerous civic boards. To the extent that Marvin was involved in local and state politics, it was usually through Garrett. He also handled all legal matters for the store and when needed helped Henderson with general management duties. Together Garrett and Haberer handled Marvin's most intractable problems.[69]

One such difficult problem involved Carl Culps, the head cashier, who had worked for Leonards since 1920. In about 1950, discrepancies began to show up between the sales totals and the cash totals at Everybody's. The problem soon appeared in the figures for Leonards. All signs pointed toward an employee taking funds from the vault. Drawing on his experience at the FBI, Garrett had the drawers removed from two filing cabinets in the vault. He got inside one and Haberer got in the other. When they saw Culps pocketing money, they pushed a button that rang a bell in Obie's office. They saw him pocket money a second time before Obie came down and asked Culps to come with him to his office. Culps admitted taking about $70,000. Marvin soon came down to the store and cried when he heard the news. Culps was the second employee Marvin had ever hired and had been with him as long as his brother had worked in the store. Marvin refused to prosecute. Instead, Culps turned over all his assets to Leonards, which amounted to about $55,000. Marvin sent him to California to start over with a car and $3,000.[70]

Leonards was an organization built on trust, economic incentives, and personal bonds. Even those like Ray Shea who came from the clinical, bureaucratic world of the chain store developed a profound personal loyalty to Marvin and Obie. They wanted to make money for the brothers.[71]

Something loosened the hold of loyalty and incentives on Culps. No matter what the reason for the crime, the incident illustrated another important change forced by increased size. In an increasingly large organization, trust, incentives, and an opportunity to profit did not by themselves guarantee honesty and hard work. Acculturating new employees in the corporate ethos of making money for the Leonard family became more difficult. If a longtime employee with a close personal relationship with the boss could take funds, what of the scores of recently hired people? Greater size demanded not only greater cost control, but more-formalized policies and more-careful bookkeeping practices to ensure employee compliance. Size demanded a bureaucracy and standardized procedures.[72]

Besides rules and accounting procedures Leonards also began publishing a company newsletter to help standardize employee expectations. In 1956, Edith Loughlin began issuing the *Lenco News*. Among its first articles was a piece encouraging acceptance of sales quotas and suggesting that employees keep track of their own sales and strive each month to improve. In 1958, a more elaborate publication called *Hi, Neighbor* replaced the *Lenco News*. It too touted quotas and sales competitions and helped build a corporate ethos. Friendship and loyalty to Marvin no longer sufficed in the larger, more bureaucratic Leonards of the late 1950s.[73]

Bureaucracy had its benefits, especially when tempered by Leonards' flair for promotions. After absorbing the cost of opening the new building in 1948, a more systematic approach helped net profits quickly bounce back to near the level of the World War II years. Meanwhile, old-timers like J. B. Moates taught Marvin's brand of merchandising to chain store men like Woody Graham, a long-time employee of Penney's who headed Leonards' boys department. In the mid-1950s, Moates purchased fifteen thousand pairs of red cotton pants at $8.00 per dozen.

On Marvin's advice, he sold them for $1.38 per pair or three for $4.00. Every employee in the men's and boys departments dressed in red pants, and the store ran full-page adds in color in the local newspapers. Between April and May they sold all but six pairs.[74]

New bureaucratic methods were also not automatically extended to all departments. Armour Hann, who headed the drug department and had worked at Leonards since 1932, refused to accept new bookkeeping and accounting methods. He stuck to his old ways and was left alone because he always made a profit. Hann was famous for squeezing every nickel and seeking every advantage for his department. When hiring was centralized he complained that the personnel office always sent him the worst prospects. Actually, he made so much noise that personnel always sent him the best prospects.[75]

After World War II, Hann objected strenuously to increases in the minimum wage. Marvin patiently explained that raising the minimum wage was good for Leonards. Because it was a national standard all employers paid the same wages; competitors had the same labor costs as Leonards. Yet because so many of their customers were from the working class, the group that most benefited from a higher minimum wage, every time the minimum wage went up, Leonards' profits increased faster than their competitors. As long as Marvin was around to see and explain the big picture, and as long as old-time managers like Armour Hann remained focused on profit, Leonards avoided jolting and abrupt changes.[76]

Leonards balanced the old and the new through much of the 1950s. Ray Shea put in chain store systems, but Doc St. Clair decided not to retire completely and remained to instill in new employees the creative, flexible, and entrepreneurial spirit of the 1920s and 1930s. Elam Henderson, more than any other manager, commanded enough respect to ease long-time employees into modern systems and to remind the chain store folks that Leonards had done very well before their arrival.[77]

Perhaps the transition from the old Leonards to the new Leonards would have proceeded smoothly into the 1960s without Henderson's untimely fatal heart attack on February 15, 1959. When Henderson died, Paul Leonard took over his duties. In July Paul hired hard-nosed and efficiency-minded Clifton Overcash as personnel director and, later, general manager. By 1960, Overcash, working with Paul, had ratcheted up the control systems and standardization of behavior at Leonards.[78]

Overcash was a native of High Point, North Carolina. His parents owned a string of food stores, and he grew up in the business. After attending several universities, he received a degree from the City College of New York. He also served nine years in the Air Force, retiring in 1949 with the rank of major. He then went to work for Gimbels Department Store and remained there until 1953. For the next six years, he worked first for Lit Brothers Department Store in Philadelphia and then for S. S. Kresge Company where he was general superintendent of its Newark, New Jersey, store. Overcash brought to Leonards a clear understanding of the latest retailing and management trends in the Northeast. He also added to the growing dominance of chain store men and the chain store mentality in the upper ranks of management. He spoke for them when he argued, "We should eliminate, combine, streamline and make uniform as many of our systems as possible."[79]

Weekly top-management meetings symbolized the growing chain store mentality. When Ray Shea came to Leonards, regular meetings would have impinged on managerial autonomy. Henderson inaugurated weekly meetings in the mid-1950s, and after he died, Paul and later Overcash continued them. Obie and Marvin almost never attended, but by 1960 the role of the meeting was entrenched and formalized with memorandum summing up the previous meeting. The process begun by Kelley, Shea, and other chain store men brought systematized and centralized buying, more inventory control, and new accounting procedures. To cut operating costs, top managers reduced the autonomy of department managers, and through meetings and increased training they encouraged more-uniform behavior.[80]

Chain store methods' downside, however, soon became apparent. Bringing order and systemization reduced Leonards' experimental, iconoclastic spirit. At decade's end, customers still flocked to Leonards for red pants and a wide variety of other goods, but big crowds were not enough to generate high profits. Escalating expenses associated with the move to chain store methods ate away at the bottom line while the more rigid code of managerial behavior limited creative responses to new competition and new conditions.

PREJUDICE AND PROFITS

Marvin remained outside the bounds of bureaucratic rigidity and standard procedures. In fact, in the mid-1950s he moved decisively against one of the most entrenched standard procedures of his time—segregation. Perhaps he was only responding to his shifting customer base, for increasingly blacks moved into Fort Worth's inner core and whites headed for the suburbs. Yet among all the downtown retailers he took the lead.[81]

During the 1940s, the black population of Fort Worth grew faster than the total population, and by 1950 blacks comprised 15 percent of the city's people. Annexation of primarily white outlying areas kept the city's racial balance at this level through the 1950s, but the black residential area in the core of the city expanded while whites moved farther from downtown.[82]

Before World War II, most blacks lived near the railroad tracks east of downtown and in the southeast quadrant of the city. More jobs and better-paying jobs during and just after the war increased black income and made home ownership possible. Blacks quickly filled in most of the formerly white areas in the southeast quadrant near downtown, and East Rosedale Street became the center of a thriving black business and residential area. By the early 1950s, however, few homes were available in either the traditional or newer black neighborhoods.[83]

North and east of a loop in the West Fork of the Trinity River lay a primarily white working class residential area referred to as Riverside. For decades, the river divided white from black, but in 1956 blacks began migrating into Riverside. White residents responded by hanging blacks in effigy and firing rifle shots. Police set up a twenty-four-hour guard at the home of one black family. Within a year or two, however, most whites moved out of Riverside, and blacks moved in. It was a scenario repeated in other areas near downtown.[84]

For Leonards this meant that increasingly the customers with the easiest access to the store were black. It also meant that the white working class, long the backbone of its customer base, lived farther from downtown. Safeway, Sears, Montgomery Wards, and a few of the early discount stores captured the business of some of these white, working class customers. As noted earlier, Leonards and Everybody's responded by broadening their product lines and trying to expand their appeal to the middle class. In an even more significant action, they totally desegregated their facilities.

Integration in Fort Worth remains a largely untold story. The testimony of white and black leaders and newspaper articles suggests, however, that desegregation started earlier and caused less strife than in most southern cities. In 1961, when a group of Freedom Riders stopped in the city on their way from Los Angeles to Jackson, Mississippi, they found the bus station and most downtown eating establishments already desegregated. Schools would take longer to integrate, but Jim Crow vanished from most aspects of everyday life before passage of the landmark civil rights laws of the mid-1960s. By June, 1963, all of Fort Worth's restaurants, hotels, department stores (including their lunch counters, rest rooms, and other facilities), theaters, athletic contests, and churches were "open to all persons without regard to race."[85]

Fort Worth did, however, experience some racial violence. In 1950, a black man who refused to get up from his seat on a city bus was stabbed by a white. Attempts to integrate schools provoked angry words. The hanging of blacks in effigy and the occasional rifle shots, as occurred in Riverside, occurred elsewhere as well. Yet compared to the 1920s in Fort Worth and to other southern cities in the 1950s and 1960s, violence was minimal.[86]

An obvious reason for the relatively easy end to formal segregation was that the Fort Worth business establishment worked to make a smooth transition. In

1956 and again in 1960, the city's mayor appointed biracial commissions. Seeking what they described as a "quiet, behind the scenes revolution," these two commissions talked to most of the major business owners in Fort Worth. The black leaders on these commissions pressed their community to remain calm. The city helped the effort by gradually appointing blacks to the park board and the library board. In the late 1950s and early 1960s, the city police department, the fire department, the county sheriff's office, and the district attorney's office all hired blacks, some in high-profile jobs. As Marion J. Brooks, a local physician and the first black to serve on the park board remembered, it was as if the business establishment decided to put profits ahead of prejudice.[87]

Fort Worth, like other Texas cities, had a group of businessmen who, as legend has it, controlled events for the good of Fort Worth and their own bottom line. In the 1940s and 1950s, this group, called by critics "the Seventh Street Gang," met at the Fort Worth Club at 306 West Seventh. The group's recognized leader was Amon Carter. In 1954, the year before Carter's death, the directors of the club included H. B. "Babe" Fuqua, chairman of the Board of Fort Worth National Bank; Sid Richardson, an independent oilman and the richest man in Fort Worth; W. K. Stripling, president of Stripling's; J. B. Thomas, president of Texas Electric Company; W. P. Bomar, president of Bewley Mills; and Marvin Leonard. Through the club and through a series of interlocking directorships at Fort Worth National Bank, First National Bank, and Texas Electric, these men came into constant contact.[88]

The Seventh Street Gang was not a formal organization with fixed membership and a fixed schedule of meetings. It was, however, a powerful group that informally discussed local events on a regular basis. In politics and philanthropy, members of the group called on each other for support and were seldom refused. Carter helped Leonard secure the first U.S. Open in 1941. A year earlier, Leonard helped Carter build a regional airport to aid an industry in which Carter was very interested. Carter, Leonard, and William Monnig served together on the advisory board of the Lena Pope Home.[89]

The group was not all-powerful and was seldom as cohesive as its critics charged. In 1954 Jim Wright challenged incumbent Congressman Lucas Wingate in a campaign that emphasized Wingate's incompetence and his subservience to Carter. Wright won with 60 percent of the vote, including some of the votes of the Fort Worth establishment. Yet on most issues, including desegregation of downtown businesses, the Seventh Streeters played a decisive role. There would have been no biracial commission and, since they owned the businesses, no quiet desegregation without their support.[90]

Among all the downtown businessmen, Marvin led the drive to put profits ahead of prejudice. As early as 1948, the walls of separateness started coming down at Leonards when white and black employees began eating in the same lunchroom near the cafeteria. They also used the same restrooms and water fountains. While most areas open to customers remained segregated, Toyland did not. At Christmastime black and white children stood in line together to tell Santa what they wanted. Although parents usually ensured that they did not sit side by side, black and white children rode in the same train car around the fantasyland of toys and magical decorations. This less rigid attitude helped make Leonards the favorite place for blacks to shop. It was more than a shopping place; it was, as Kerven Carter put it, "the hub for meeting and greeting people."[91]

Despite this easier attitude, in 1952, when Charlie Ringler went to work for Leonards, the signs for whites and blacks that applied to the general public were still up. They remained in 1953 when John Maddux started work at Everybody's. But a year later, when Bobby Webber went to work for Leonards, blatant reminders of Jim Crow were disappearing. Webber, later one of the first black members of the state legislature from Tarrant County, saw blacks eating in the same cafeteria dining room as whites. They usually did not sit at the same table or even adjacent tables, but they were in the same room and they moved through the cafeteria serving line together. Willard Barr, an advocate of desegregation and mayor of Fort Worth in the 1960s, claimed that Leonards was the first department store in Fort Worth to desegregate. It could not have done so without Marvin Leonard.[92]

Marvin grew up in rural Northeast Texas where black challenges to white supremacy evoked brutal retaliation. He reached maturity in Fort Worth in the 1920s during a time of heightened racial tension. Yet, in some ways, the decision to integrate the store was a natural outgrowth of Marvin's past. When asked to explain her father's success, Miranda Leonard used three words: experimental, flexible, and pragmatic.[93]

Some of the racial attitudes of Northeast Texas at the turn of the century and Fort Worth in the 1920s may have lingered on in Marvin's heart and mind. Yet he realized that his customer base and the times had changed. More blacks than ever shopped at his store. Their money was just as green as anybody else's. As blacks grew more sensitive to the stigma of segregation, it was bad business to offend good customers. Pragmatism demanded a change.[94]

Marvin had always been a trader, a deal maker willing to buy and sell as the opportunity presented itself. He was not wedded to one piece of property or one set of ideas. Old money and old ideas did not impress him, but new projects and new ideas did. Despite a lingering sense that blacks had a separate place in society, he likely identified with them as outsiders that deserved an opportunity to prosper. He was willing to be flexible.[95]

Since the 1920s, Marvin enthusiastically backed new ideas brought to him by trusted managers. Above all others, perhaps, he trusted Jenkins Garrett. The relationship began in the late 1920s with Garrett testifying on his behalf and delivering candy to his sweetheart. During the intervening years, Marvin helped Garrett succeed in law school, as an attorney, and in business. This was not charity work. Despite the close bond between them, it was not simply something done out of personal commitment. Marvin knew talent and he knew how to recruit and retain that talent. One anecdote illustrates the point. In the late 1950s, while Marvin was playing a round of golf, Garrett brought him some papers to sign. The men playing with Leonard made fun of Garrett, referring to him as a flunky, an errand boy. Leonard stopped the match and in the clearest language possible stopped the joke. As he pointed out, Garrett was one of the main reasons he had time to play golf whenever he wanted. His people made him a success, and he was determined to back them. He trusted that their experiments would succeed.[96]

By the mid-1950s, Garrett was Marvin's link to the younger men working on the biracial commission that sought gradual and peaceful change. He suggested that Leonard desegregate the store, pointing out that the Interstate Commerce Commission had already forced the integration of train stations and was discussing bus stations. Besides, the Supreme Court in the Texas case *Sweatt vs. Painter* (1950) and in the more famous *Brown vs. Board of Education of Topeka* (1954) had made it clear which way the country was headed. Separate facilities could never be equal, and unlike the immediate post-war years, it was increasingly clear they were on the way out. Given their many loyal black customers it was better to be a trendsetter than to resist desegregation. It was worth the risk of offending a few white customers, and in an atmosphere of racial harmony most white customers would still shop downtown.[97]

Leonards followed a very low-key approach to desegregation, so low-key that there are no records and no clear memories of exactly when the transformation took place. No announcements mandated a change in store policy. One day Steve Drennan, the cafeteria manager, received notice from the central office to serve anyone who wanted to eat. Managers watched during the noon rush, but only one person complained. At the same time, the signs at the rest rooms, fitting rooms, and drinking fountains came down at Everybody's and at Leonards. By 1956 or 1957 both stores were totally desegregated.[98]

During the next few years, there were a few racial incidents at the store. Because it was well known, civil rights demonstrators anxious to attract media attention picketed Leonards. Store executives furtively took Marion Brooks's picture as he led one protest movement. Once, blacks from outside the city alerted the newspapers that they planned to desegregate Leonards' lunch counter. No one paid any attention because the lunch counter had long since desegregated. Although of minor importance, these periodic attempts to rock the boat upset Obie. Charlie Ringler recalled that Obie angrily denounced black dissidents as ungrateful for all that the store had done for them. Marvin rubbed his lips, turned to his brother, and said, "Now Obie, settle down. Settle down. This did not happen over night. It is not going away over night. It is going to work itself out. Just don't get excited. Don't get excited."[99]

That exchange captured the essential difference between the two brothers. Obie was a wonderfully creative man when it came to machines and production systems. He was friendly and got along well with individual employees. He could not, however, react as flexibly as his brother to a changing society and to changing market conditions. His was a different sort of pragmatism, one of nuts and bolts, not human foibles. Ultimately, Obie could not sustain the same level of experimentation and the same level of trust in those proposing the experiment. Each brother was a balance wheel for the other; each brought special competencies.[100]

Ringler recalled another time when he passed Obie's office soon after Marvin died. Obie called him into his office and with tears in his eyes confessed, "I don't know how I am going to get over losing Marvin. He has been my right hand all my life."[101]

OUTSIDE THE STORE

In reality, Obie's right hand had removed himself from most daily activity in the store long before his death. By the late 1950s, Marvin Leonard spent more time on building a golf course and developing the surrounding real estate than he did on store business.

As early as 1954, Marvin considered building a new course in Fort Worth. The economy was booming and the three major clubs in town had few slots open for new members. He wanted a piece of land with interesting topography and tried to buy about two hundred acres along the Trinity River in the city's Rivercrest subdivision. At the time, no other land suited him, and he considered building in California.[102]

In the 1940s and 1950s, the Leonard family escaped the Texas heat and spent their summers in northern California, often staying near Pebble Beach. Marty Leonard competed in local golf tournaments, and the entire family enjoyed various vacation activities. The family's second daughter, Miranda, attended Mills College in Oakland in the 1950s, which added to the attraction of the region. Gradually the idea took hold that Marvin should build a new course north of San Francisco. One of his favorite courses was Silverado in the Napa Valley, which was more a golf club with a congenial and select group of members than a country club. Marvin envisioned building something along the lines of Silverado, a beautiful course with a rustic club house.[103]

In August, 1955, Leonard found the ideal site north of San Francisco and was on the verge of buying it. Garrett intervened with a call from Fort Worth. Ap-

Mary, Madelon, Mary, Marvin, Miranda, and Marty (left to right) walk down the golf course at Santa Barbara, California, in 1952.

proximately twelve hundred acres on the western edge of the city owned by the estate of the recently deceased Amon Carter had become available. Leonard knew the land well. The year before, Carter invited Leonard and Garrett to tour the property with him. As they looked around, Carter told them of his plan to develop a residential area and a golf course in the flood plain of King's Branch which ran into the West Fork of the Trinity River. After Carter asked him what he thought, Leonard told Carter that the idea was sound, but the golf course was in the wrong place. The hills and live oaks on the eastern edge of the property provided a much more suitable backdrop for a golf course than the flat treeless area near the creek. Carter was obviously disappointed and said little more. He did not forget the conversation, however, for when he realized he was dying he left a note in his office saying the land should first be offered to Marvin. On the basis of that note, realtor H. H. Morse called Garrett after Carter's death to see if Leonard wanted to buy the land for $1,500 an acre. Garrett immediately telephoned Marvin with the news. Without suggesting a counter offer, he told Garrett he would take it. He evidently had been thinking about the King's Branch tract since his conversation with Carter and decided he wanted it.[104]

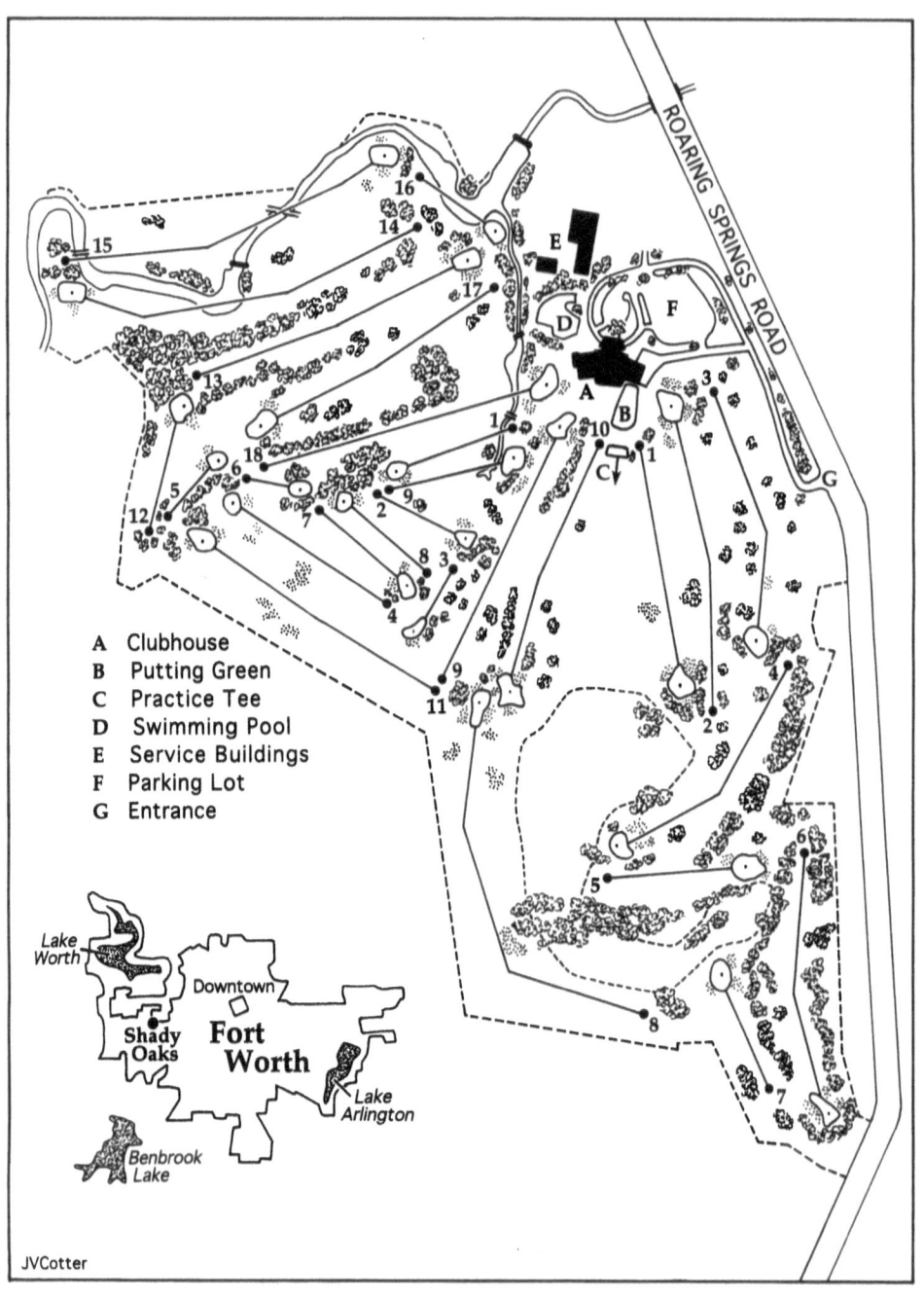

Shady Oaks, 1958. *Map by John V. Cotter.*

Marvin left on the night train from California. Even the prospects of acquiring a piece of land he had long admired could not cure him of his fear of flying. Within a few weeks of arriving back in Fort Worth, he finalized the purchase for $2.1 million. The *Star-Telegram* announced the sale on October 5, 1955.[105]

Carter had long planned to develop the area and had landscaped much of the eastern part. Those efforts along with the native live oaks made the rolling hills an ideal place for a high-quality country club and residential area. Leonard placed the golf course on about two hundred acres exactly where he told Carter it should be and called the country club Shady Oaks. He used one of the large oaks known as the "Hanging Tree" as its symbol.[106]

Robert Trent Jones, Ralph Plummer, and Lawrence Hughes designed and built Shady Oaks. Construction began in 1956 and, as he had with Colonial, Leonard took a personal interest in all aspects of the new club. He wanted the greens of the ninth and eighteenth holes to be visible from the Men's Grill. Every day he put a chair in the spot where the Grill's customers would sit. When workmen dug the Grill's foundation too deep, he had them fill it in. He was just as particular about each hole. Jones and Plummer wanted to avoid consecutive par-5s on the back nine, insisting that if fifteen was to be a par-5, fourteen must be a par-4.

Standing under the hanging tree in 1956, Marvin, Hunter Barrett, Jenkins Garrett, and Jimmy Alewine discuss the layout of the Shady Oaks golf course.

Without raising his voice Leonard settled the dispute. "It will be a par-5 and the green will be over there."[107]

Marvin intended Shady Oaks to resemble Silverado, but the project kept growing in scope. Because of its constant evolution into a full-scale country club and the extra care that Marvin lavished on the project, building the golf course, tennis courts, swimming pool, and clubhouse took almost three years and exceeded estimated costs. Leonard originally anticipated the total cost to be about $2 million. Actual costs ran about $3.5 million.[108]

The club building had a modern design with flat roofs and large windows overlooking the course. H. B. Friedman was the contractor for the project. Friedman and Marvin never had a contract; they simply trusted each other to do the right thing. Elam Henderson's wife, Jessie May, decorated the interior. As he did with store managers, Marvin gave her very few instructions. He simply told her to "make it look and feel like a beautiful home." She drew up and assembled a mosaic of semiprecious stones depicting a large live oak that filled an entire wall in the lobby and brought in local craftsmen to do the cabinets and paneling. Most of the furniture was custom-made in Fort Worth.[109]

Marvin and his wife, Mary, hosted the inaugural event at the club on June 7, 1958, with the wedding reception of their daughter Marty and her husband, John Griffith. The next month the club opened for its members. The initial membership fee was $6,500, the second most expensive in the state. Originally only about forty families joined. Marvin described Shady Oaks as "a second home" with "people of similar interests getting together in a social way."[110]

When construction began on Shady Oaks, the oil industry was flying high, but it slumped in the late 1950s. That slump partially explains the small number of members at Shady Oaks and why the club lost money during its first years. A slowdown in defense spending also hurt the local economy. Responding to poor revenue and a sluggish local economy in September, 1958, Marvin considered selling the club to its members, but no satisfactory arrangement could be worked out. In 1960, the club lost more than $150,000 and more serious efforts to sell began. During these early years, Marvin ran the club and, as with Colonial, made continual improvements. He intended Shady Oaks to be "unexcelled in the entire Southwest in the total magnificence of its facilities."[111]

Shady Oaks was a far different club than Colonial. Marvin wanted a member's course, not a championship course. It was meant to be fun and relaxing. One advantage of a relatively small membership was that no preset tee times were required. The club also had very few rules. Members were expected to use common sense and good manners. As would be expected of a club with a high initial fee, most members were businessmen. ("Men" is accurate. Like most clubs, at that time the membership resided in the hands of the male head of the household.)

The oil industry was well represented among the club's members, but many were merchants. One striking feature of the membership roster was the inclusion of several Jewish businessmen, the most famous of whom was Stanley Marcus of Dallas. Marvin relied on his friend Solomon Brachman to recommend Jewish members and by 1963 about 4 percent of the members were Jewish. Among them was Harry Friedman, the contractor for the clubhouse. Shady Oaks was one of the few exclusive clubs in Texas with Jewish and non-Jewish members.[112]

Whatever financial burdens the club brought were made up for many times over by profit from the development of the rest of the land purchased from the Carter estate. In late 1956, Marvin began developing a tract south of the club on the west side of Roaring Springs Road within the limits of the town of Westover Hills. Lots were large and deed restrictions required high-quality residential construction. In 1958, lot sales totaled more than $350,000. After that the slump in the oil industry slowed the pace of development, but by the end of 1960, lots in the first phase were sold and five more phases were ready for market. The area soon became the home of many of Fort Worth's wealthiest and most prominent citizens. Other substantial residential and commercial developments on the former Carter property would follow in the 1960s.[113]

Besides Shady Oaks and real estate, Marvin also became increasingly involved in the insurance industry. In 1955, together with Obie and Garrett, he set up the David Crockett Life Insurance Company. Actually, the insurance company was in some ways an extension of his interest in real estate. David Crockett Life bought the old General Motors building on West Seventh Street, the largest building in terms of floor space in Fort Worth, from Marvin. The next year the two brothers purchased controlling interest in State Reserve Life. That company was founded in 1924 and had more than $9 million in assets. State Reserve Life in turn purchased the Leonards Department Store buildings and leased them back to the brothers.[114]

Marvin's oil holdings also increased substantially after World War II. While Marvin originally invested in oil because of its tax advantages, by the close of the war it was rapidly becoming a cornerstone of his estate. Through the 1950s, he continued putting much of his income in oil-producing property. When Garrett went to work for Leonards in 1946, he took charge of the oil property. Eventually the task became too large. In the 1950s, Garrett hired Travis Cravens, an experienced land man, to help organize and supervise oil properties. He eventually also hired Bob Stahala, another attorney, to evaluate potential investments and keep track of oil properties in Alabama, Colorado, Florida, Louisiana, Mississippi, Montana, Nebraska, New Mexico, North Dakota, and Texas. As he had in the past, Marvin also depended upon his golfing friends for information on oil investments. He often participated in buying leases and drilling wells with Ben

Hogan, Gaylord Chizum, and other friends made on the golf course. He also relied upon trained geologists and geophysicists, having his property appraised by leading firms such as DeGolyer and MacNaughton.[115]

As his ownership share in Fort Worth National Bank increased, so did Marvin's role on the Board of Directors. For many years, he served on its Loan Committee, an important task in an era when Texas banks still depended upon their directors to evaluate the credit worthiness of major borrowers. Marvin was considered the mainstay of the Loan Committee and one of the most influential directors, especially after B. H. "Babe" Fuqua became chairman of the Board of Directors in the 1950s. Marvin served on the Executive Committee and usually supported Fuqua's initiatives. The two men were close friends, and board meetings were always brief and to the point because much of the business had already been decided in committee meetings. Marvin also owned stock in West Side Bank, Mutual Savings & Loan, and Fort Worth Savings & Loan, and he had a controlling interest in Bank of Commerce. This latter bank was originally a Morris Plan Bank. When it experienced financial difficulties, Marvin arranged its purchase and changed the name in order to better market its services. His son-in-law, John Griffith, served as president of the bank.[116]

Marvin also held stock in various regional corporations. He was the largest stockholder of Flour Mills of America, and Garrett became a director of that company on his behalf in 1953. Together with Garrett and Stayley McBrayer, he owned a chain of small neighborhood newspapers and a publishing company. Until it was sold to AMF in 1960 he owned 50 percent of the stock of the Ben Hogan Company, a manufacturer of golf equipment. Because Garrett, McBrayer, or Hogan handled the day-to-day details, managing these companies took little of Marvin's time. These diverse ventures did, however, prevent him from focusing as clearly as he once had on the store. Golf and his passionate effort to make Shady Oaks the best-possible country club took even more time and energy.[117]

Local charities and other attempts to improve Fort Worth also filled a larger part of his post-1948 years. Most, but not all, of Marvin's philanthropic efforts also built good will for the store. He continued to support the Lena Pope Home and feed hungry school children. After the war, he expanded the format of the City Junior Golf Tournament, which he originated in 1936, and tried to attract wider interest in golf. Even the free movies and parties for children in local parks sponsored by Leonards took on a larger scope. These were not new departures, simply expanded ones.[118]

Local churches, hospitals, and universities also benefitted from Marvin's philanthropy in a greater way. Much of his giving went to Methodist Hospital, All Saints Hospital, the Methodist church of which he was a member, and to Texas Wesleyan University in Fort Worth. His most famous ministerial solicitor, however, was J. Frank Norris, the controversial pastor of First Baptist Church in Fort Worth. When Norris had a crowd of visiting dignitaries to feed he routinely brought them from his nearby church to Leonards Cafeteria where Marvin let them eat for free. The next Sunday Norris would mention Leonards' generosity to the three or four thousand worshippers attending services. The same pattern was repeated in numerous black churches near downtown.[119]

In 1949, Leonards' mix of philanthropy and promotion reached perhaps its highest level. That March heavy rains caused widespread flooding. As the water rose, store personnel took every boat from sporting goods and used them to rescue people from the housing project to the west of Leonards. Later, Leonards repaired waterlogged stoves, refrigerators, washers, and even pianos for free and transported them to and from downtown. According to Jo Ann Vachule, "the offer was good whether or not the appliance had been bought at Leonards."[120]

By that time, Leonards and Everybody's sold a large amount of furniture and appliances on credit. If a customer's furniture was destroyed while he was still paying for it, the store extended new credit and eased the terms of the old credit. They also helped replace ruined carpet and other furnishings. Thousands of people trooped to Leonards to arrange for repairs, and while many needed store credit, the Red Cross and federal disaster relief funds gave others money to spend. Once in the store, they spent that money at Leonards or Everybody's. The 1949 flood and its aftermath again confirmed the public perception born in the Great Depression that while Leonards was a moneymaking enterprise, Marvin and Obie went out of their way to help people.[121]

In other cases, however, Marvin insisted on quiet giving. He gave money for an entire floor at Methodist Hospital, purchased needed equipment for All Saints Hospital, and donated to the United Fund without allowing his name to be used. He disliked ostentatious behavior unless it was meant to drum up business. Besides, as he once told Garrett, if he publicized every gift, long lines would form at his door.[122]

Marvin signed the checks, but he was not a meddling philanthropist. He relied on Garrett and Ringler to handle the practical details of community involvement and retained control of the big picture. This allowed him to give something back to Fort Worth and leave time for golf.[123]

More than age and a desire to play golf and build a golf course explains why Marvin turned over responsibilities to others. Doing something different, something new, especially if it related to golf, was fun. Others could handle the routine chores. After the long hours and hard work of the early years, doing something different may only have seemed his due, a reward for past effort. He also clearly focused on building up his estate. Through the 1950s, he increasingly transferred his assets to trusts created for his four daughters. Expanding his business interests beyond the store diversified what he intended to pass on to them. He wanted his children to be as safe and secure as he could possibly make them. Turning over more tasks to others was also a natural evolution of his long-standing managerial policies. He managed from a distance and could exist without immersion in the store.[124]

While he was generally happy in his later years, Marvin was not without problems. By 1960, he drank more heavily than before. What began during World War I with the practice of taking a shot of whiskey at the start of the workday continued through prohibition and World War II. Drinking and cigarette smoking were normal parts of Marvin's daily routine. These were habits common to many others; they were embedded in the cultures of the retail trade and the country club. There is little evidence that Leonard drank more than was normal for a businessman in that day and time or that drinking damaged his health before the late 1950s. Although some of the stomach trouble that prompted him to take up golf may have been caused by drinking, Margery Leonard remembered Marvin not drinking when they went out on the town with Obie in the 1920s. His children remember that he periodically gave up alcohol for months at a time to demonstrate that he controlled his habit instead of it controlling him.[125]

By 1960, Marvin knew his habits posed a risk to his health. For years he carried his cigarettes in his left jacket pocket to make them more difficult to retrieve with his right hand. In another bow to the possibility that cigarette smoke was harmful, he took up charcoal filters and became so convinced of their beneficial effects that he gave them to all his friends. He smoked with an eased conscience. As late as 1967, he still gave up drinking periodically. Yet none of these efforts lasted, and alcohol eventually damaged his stomach and liver. Perhaps Marvin's body chemistry changed and the need for alcohol increased with age. Certainly his tolerance for alcohol was high, and no one remembers him being drunk. Having several martinis while playing golf and more martinis while playing gin rummy left his card-playing skills intact, for he almost always won. He never had to be driven home from the club. He liked drinking and the camaraderie that went with it. He may also have drunk to ease his frustrations.[126]

Marvin's chief frustration was with his wife's illness. Mary Leonard was intelligent and artistic. She read continually and was skilled in all types of sewing and needlework. She created many fine needlepoint designs, including pieces for the chapel in the National Cathedral in Washington, D.C., All Saints Hospital, and St. Andrew's Episcopal Church. She played bridge and maintained a close relationship with a small group of friends. Marvin and Mary often attended parties and social functions. She was an accomplished ballroom dancer and according to her daughter Marty loved to dance more than anything. She also instilled in her daughters the love of good music.[127]

Mary Leonard supported philanthropic causes both alone and with Marvin. She first recognized the worth of the Lena Pope Home in the 1930s and interested Marvin in that charity. Mary was also a devout and faithful Episcopalian and donated numerous gifts to St. Andrew's Episcopal Church over her life, including beautiful handcrafted light fixtures and a carillon that she gave in memory of the Vaughan family. Her generosity was not limited to her own church. She and Marvin, along with Obie and Margery, gave bells to Arlington Heights Methodist Church in memory of Tom Leonard and his family. In the early 1950s, she convinced Marvin to buy several pieces of property in front of the First Methodist Church. The structures on the properties were run down, obstructed the view of the church, and detracted from its beauty. The sites were leveled and a new parking lot and landscaped entry area were constructed. True to Mary's artistic nature, the end result added to the beauty and appeal of the church.[128]

Mary enjoyed her home and took pride in dressing immaculately. At the very outset of their marriage, Marvin had told her that he did not want her to do anything around the house that she could hire others to do. Actually, Marvin lived the same way; he never shined his own shoes or pulled a weed out of the flower bed. Accordingly, as time passed, the Leonards employed a housekeeper, a cook, a laundress, a yardman, and any other help needed to keep the home and yard in mint condition. Several of her close friends, taking note of her lifestyle, called her "Queenie." In her later years Mary enjoyed and laughed about her nickname.[129]

Yet from the 1940s until her death Mary often felt melancholic and dejected. Despite her wealth, good friends, and ability to do good works, she believed herself constricted and confined by the role her husband asked her to play. Regrettably, from the mid-1950s, Mary was under the constant care of psychiatrists treating her for chronic debilitating depression.[130]

Eventually Mary realized that most of her problems were genetic because her mother had struggled with similar feelings of hopelessness and the reduction in vitality and vigor that went with them. At least that realization brought understanding and compassion for her mother, even while she struggled to make sense of her own feelings and relationships.[131]

Marvin loved his wife and grappled with her health problems—problems that remain ill-understood and often misdiagnosed. While he was a private person who seldom shared his thoughts with her, he tried his best to help her. He accompanied her to doctors around the country. The family ate breakfast together every morning, and Marvin waited until the girls left for school to leave for work. Despite his full schedule, he returned promptly each evening for dinner so that Mary would not be alone. He was a man used to solving problems. How many times must he have turned over in his mind possibilities to help her, and how many times had those solutions not panned out?[132]

Thus for Marvin Leonard and his store, the 1950s closed on an ironic note. Greater success and more security were not enough to bring him complete happiness. Becoming Greater Leonards brought problems in managing the store and eventually problems in maintaining the high levels of net profit so characteristic of previous decades. Yet Shady Oaks and the surrounding real estate offered a focus for Marvin's creative energy. The outside interests of Obie and Marvin thrived. Leonards continued to be a vibrant center of the Fort Worth retailing industry. The ability to find an answer to declining profits remained. As the next few years would demonstrate, the brothers retained the creativity and determination to respond to new market conditions in retailing.

Beyond all else Leonards retained intense customer loyalty—a loyalty that extended to the very young. One day in the late 1950s, Vera Pyle observed a mother and child out on the street headed toward Leonards. The little girl was crying and trying to pull away from her mother. The mother told her daughter, "Hush and I will take you to Leonards." The daughter stopped crying and started hopping along singing, "We're going to Leonards."[133]

6

SUBURBS, THE SUBWAY, AND SECURITY, 1960–69

Partings marked the 1960s. Marvin sold the store to his brother Obie in late 1964. Less than three years later, in October, 1967, the O. P. Leonard family sold the store to Tandy Corporation. While the increased age and diverse interests of the brothers influenced these sales, they also reflected the changing nature of downtown retailing.

Downtown had been the central business district, the heart of retailing in Fort Worth. Since 1918 Leonards grew as Fort Worth grew. By the 1960s, Fort Worth's and the store's growth brought more challenges than rewards. As suburbs and communities surrounding Fort Worth grew, discounters and chain stores in outlying shopping centers took away business and altered the shopping patterns of large numbers of Fort Worth citizens. Leonards responded by building a subway and a new Home Store. For a time these additions restored vigor to downtown and stimulated sales. But eventually, the needs of the city and the store parted.[1]

Marvin's withdrawal was completed during these years. Management modernized systems and controls to oversee the larger store and meet the competition. Early in the decade, Marvin still reserved the right to make the most important decisions. Despite diminished involvement, he remained the most visible symbol of the store. The business community held him, and by association the store, in high esteem, and customers felt his merchandising touch. Long after he turned management over to his nephews, he continued to insist that Leonards remain a fun place to shop—famous for low prices, wide variety, and extravagant promotions. The opening of the M & O Subway in 1963 crowned a long business career for Marvin and Obie. It combined splash with pragmatism—doing something no other department store had ever done and solving the parking problem that had confounded downtown merchants for years. As a local writer put it, the subway was "revolutionary, experimental and a step to the future."[2]

Honors and active pursuit of other business endeavors filled any spare time created from pulling back from the store. Developing real estate brought increased financial security, while Marvin's careful nurturing of Shady Oaks through the 1960s confirmed its reputation as one of the finest and most exclusive country clubs in the state. Through that decade, community groups repeatedly demonstrated their appreciation for what Marvin and Obie had contributed to their city.[3]

Public acclaim stretched beyond the Fort Worth city limits. Writers for the *New York Times* and *Time* drew special attention to the subway and the size of the store, emphasizing how it defied the odds and prolonged the vitality of downtown Fort Worth. The problems brought by Leonards' size and diverse merchandise were still hidden from public view.[4]

A Sprawling Enterprise in a Sprawling City

From its opening in 1918, nothing contributed more to the unique style and the remarkable profitability of Leonards than the managerial structure and ethos that Marvin created and nurtured. In the early years, ethos outweighed formal structure. Employees earned Marvin's trust through diligence and by modeling the boss's skills in buying and selling. In return, he rewarded them with autonomy. As the store grew, Marvin hired and promoted managers who understood and were motivated by his approach to retailing, and to a great extent he left them alone. This style also applied to his relationship with his two partners, Obie and Carl Bruner. Marvin allowed his brother maximum freedom over the things he knew best and delegated a remarkable number of operating decisions to Bruner. Gradually, the organizational glue provided by Marvin's personality and aspirations grew into formalized procedures and structures.[5]

During the 1930s, Obie and Marvin worked out a flexible and efficient division of power and responsibility between themselves and their managers. Everyone understood that ultimately, Marvin was the boss. He also played the role of "Mr. Outside," dealing with key manufacturers and suppliers, financial institutions, and the local government. Obie became "Mr. Inside," making sure the physical plant allowed maximum sales per square foot of selling space. Increasingly, Bruner orchestrated accounting, planning, advertising, legal services, and other aspects of day-to-day management.

When Bruner left full-time management in 1938, Leonards added merchandise managers to coordinate activities across its increasingly large and diverse departments and expanded the central office to include more specialized top managers. Marvin filled many of these slots by promoting men like Doc St. Clair and Jack Hester who knew and understood his way of doing business, and he forged personal relationships with managers who came to Leonards from elsewhere, such as Jim Leach. This new layer of management and the department managers beneath them retained much decision-making autonomy, but personal ties with the boss extended Marvin's reach down into the growing company.

Leonards kept this flexible and mostly decentralized system into the mid-1950s. Marvin did not double-check the work of his brother or managers. Instead he relied on numeric indicators of store and departmental performance. He checked sales, inventory turnover, and liquidity figures daily and tied key managers' bonuses to annual performance figures. Specialization of top management staff continued, but even Garrett, the store's lawyer, occasionally found himself pressed into selling ladders or pants when crowds grew too big. Department managers enjoyed remarkable independence, guided by the merchandise managers who helped maintain a consistent merchandising feel across the store. Throughout the store Marvin substituted loyalty, undergirded by an appealing bonus system, for centralized control. He gave out few instructions but made sure that managers profited as the store profited. He also provided intangibles. Marvin Leonard was a leader, a person to look up to, a reason to make a profit beyond simple self-interest. This system fit both Marvin's style and the managerial needs of the store.[6]

By the mid-1950s, the ever-expanding Leonards operation demanded more systematic management. Marvin's reach, even through his cadre of loyal and experienced managers, could not touch everyone. It became increasingly difficult to imbue every employee with the ideals that had brought Leonards success. As the distance between decision makers and frontline employees grew, management attempted to maintain close ties by using a monthly store newsletter and the Junior Executive Training Program. Yet bit by bit, employees felt the grip of tighter centralized control—introduced first on the divisional level with the arrival of people such as Ray Shea and eventually on the store level with the influence of Paul Leonard and Clifton Overcash.[7]

Inventory management came first in an attempt to control the expanding cost of carrying such a gigantic and varied inventory. Upper management also began collecting and analyzing other types of numerical data and following sales and expense trends more systematically. In 1959, Overcash called attention to problems that decentralized personnel practices engendered and suggested that Leonards needed to establish standards in all basic personnel functions such as "hiring, terminations, transfers, promotions, salary increases, counseling, and exit interviewing."[8]

The problems Overcash highlighted were natural outgrowths of decades of pushing decision making down to lower levels. Managers had developed different yardsticks concerning quality, salary, and work conditions. Criteria leading to promotion or dismissal varied across departments. Supervisors controlled salary and wage decisions, resulting in substantial inequities across comparable positions. Differences in personnel practices typically were handled through organizational norms and informal conversations among managers. This absence of companywide standards made sense when the store was smaller and information flowed more fluidly across departments and up and down the hierarchy. Larger organizations, observed Overcash, needed to establish personnel standards or risk wasting "money, manpower, time, sales" and damaging "public relations and employee morale."[9]

To Overcash's credit, he recognized that informal operating procedures strengthened the loyalty, dedication, and enthusiasm of Leonards' managers and employees and stressed that policy "must never harm or destroy [the feeling of individual responsibility and authority managers have for running their departments] in any manner." He suggested that all personnel actions come from the joint efforts of department managers and the personnel department. While this recommendation sounded reasonable, in practice it cut deeply into managerial autonomy. The creation of standards for hiring, terminations, transfers, promotions, and wages flowed from Overcash's office and ultimately usurped managers' control over many basic supervisory activities. It also marked the beginning of Overcash's ascendance and the acceleration of bureaucratization.[10]

To the executives running Leonards, the post-1948 increase in size and the growing formalization of management hardly seemed threatening or revolutionary. After all, flamboyant promotions and wide selection undergirded by low prices still drew large crowds to the store throughout the 1950s as they always had. Installing accounting and inventory procedures promised to curb some of the waste that seat-of-the-pants management engendered and add to the bottom line. The larger organization needed the discipline of policies that applied across departments to control costs and possible mismanagement. Leonards also needed to coordinate its merchandising efforts to deal with increasing competition, suburbanization, and the entry of more discounters into the Fort Worth market.

New demographic and competitive trends spread across the country in the 1950s, changing the landscape of general retailing. Increasing population and a healthy economy meant rising family income and more-even income distribution among all economic classes. In turn, these conditions escalated the demand for higher-quality goods. Madison Avenue hitched its wagon to this trend, and national manufacturers learned the power of pull marketing—building brand awareness by appealing directly to shoppers through advertising. As department stores and traditional retailers traded up for customers, discounters found more room to compete, much as the cash-only stores and dime stores had during the 1920s. Suburbanization accompanied rising income, prompting retailers across the country to accelerate branching efforts in suburban shopping centers. Downtown retailers suddenly faced a world full of new competitive pressures.[11]

Fort Worth's downtown merchants noticed the effects of these trends by the late 1950s. Many old downtown buildings were leveled, and few new buildings replaced them. Cox's and The Fair joined the flight to the suburbs, closing their downtown stores and moving to the Camp Bowie development. Those who remained supported the Downtown Fort Worth Association's efforts to pool resources and ideas to promote downtown shopping. Driven by Marvin's strong commitment to downtown and the knowledge that Leonards' downtown investment dwarfed all others, the store's managers looked diligently for solutions to the decay of the central business district. Drawing large crowds from a broad range of incomes, however, grew increasingly difficult.[12]

After 1960, downtown's share of the region's prosperity diminished further. With the effects of the mild late 1950s recession behind them, Fort Worth's citizens enjoyed a decade of rapid economic growth. Oil, agriculture, cattle, and defense provided the backbone of local productive power, but the city was also the South's top producer of candy, air-conditioning equipment, work garments, sports clothes, and uniforms. More Oldsmobiles, Buicks, and Pontiacs rolled off the nearby General Motors assembly line than were produced by all the rest of GM's American Olds-Buick-Pontiac plants combined. In addition to its thousand manufacturing plants, Fort Worth boasted more than thirty-five hundred retail stores and accounted for almost a quarter of all the retail sales in Texas. The opening of Six Flags Over Texas in August of 1961 between Dallas and Fort Worth brought visitors with open wallets from every state, and Carling Brewing Company's commitment to erect a $20 million plant south of town pushed Tarrant County into the ranks of the fastest-growing economies in the country.[13]

The healthy economy stimulated Fort Worth's population growth, and patterns of economic development influenced where people settled. During the 1960s, the city itself grew by 10 percent, while surrounding suburbs, where commercial activity was strongest, expanded by more than 90 percent. By 1970, Fort Worth proper had about 390,000 people. The suburbs had a population of about 280,000. Race differences increasingly divided city from suburb. About one out of every seven of the citizens of Fort Worth was black. In the suburbs whites outnumbered blacks fifty to one. Likewise, 85 percent of Tarrant County's growing Mexican population lived inside the city limits.[14]

Disparities in wealth also cleaved suburbia from the city—the poorest neighborhoods were within Fort Worth, the wealthiest ones ringed the edge of the city. Increasingly, residential areas closest to downtown housed poorer people of color. More-affluent citizens still came downtown to shop, but small shopping centers sprouted near their neighborhoods and provided shopping convenience close to home. Large shopping centers in Arlington and on Camp Bowie Avenue also attracted customers with new facilities, acres of parking, and a fresh collection of stores. These options made the drive downtown seem longer, more congested, and full of hassles.[15]

The challenge did not keep Leonards from making every effort to adapt to retailing and demographic trends. More and larger departments, upgraded merchandise, and greater selection all attracted customers to Leonards. More systematic, centralized management helped contain the costs of these efforts. These moves, logical within the context of the emerging competitive arena, sowed the seeds of Leonards' later struggles. Trading up ultimately made Leonards too much like its competitors and did not add enough to the bottom line. Centralization hampered its flexibility.

As the accompanying graph demonstrates, Leonards felt the effect on its bottom line. Net profit after bonuses fell off markedly after 1958. In the context of the economic dip and subsequent recovery after 1960, this decline in profit becomes all the more striking. Faltering sales due to recessionary times in 1959 explain only part of the steep downturn in profits. Even when sales rebounded, profits remained depressed. Rising expenses ate up profit faster than ever and accounted for the lagging net. Salary expense had increased during the 1950s, growing to six times larger than any other store expense. A recovering economy did not turn profit trends around. In 1962 sales rebounded, surpassing 1959 figures, but profit remained depressed, hitting its lowest mark for the post-1959 era. Expenses continued to climb, rising by more than $1 million from 1961 to 1962. All expense categories edged higher, but salaries and advertising increased the most. After the late 1950s, compensation expenses, which included salaries plus bonuses, no longer tracked sales. Instead they grew at a faster rate.[16]

Trends begun in the 1950s came home to roost in the early 1960s. Paul Leonard had pushed the store to position itself to respond to increasingly fierce competition. Expansion, upgrading, and control efforts prompted the installation of chain store methods which temporarily preserved steady increases in profitability. Modern management did not come cheaply, however, and eventually increased centralized control led to too much red tape. Department managers could not respond as creatively to competitors' moves as they once had. Promotions to guarantee store traffic demanded larger advertising budgets. An evolving customer base demanded the move into standard-quality hard lines and more-fashionable clothing, but expanded lines of merchandise necessitated stricter inventory control. It also cost more in salaries to have a larger store with enhanced centralized control. These managerial moves locked Leonards into a less appropriate, although perhaps inevitable, pattern. Leonards' dominance over Fort Worth retailing faltered. As one long-time employee observed, by 1960 Leonards was no longer "a first mover" in retailing.[17]

THE DRIVE TO MODERNIZE

Clif Overcash, Paul Leonard, and other key managers did not wait idly for Leonards to recover from its profit woes nor did they panic. Two main issues continued to

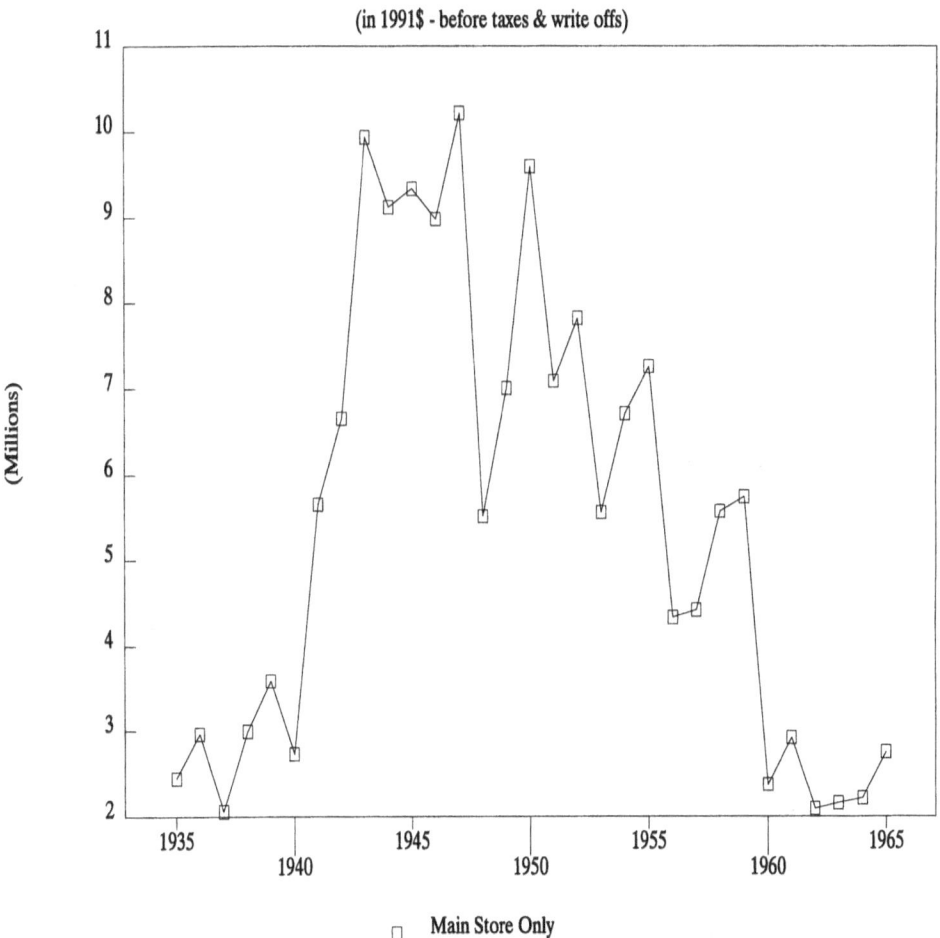

Net Profits After Bonuses, 1935-1965
(in 1991$ - before taxes & write offs)

☐ Main Store Only

Note: Based on net profits in "Sale of Store"; "1960 Expansion Files"; "Account Books, 1957–1965," LP. On conversion to constant dollars see John J. McClusker, *How Much is That in Real Money? A Historical Price Index for Use as a Deflator of Money Values in the Economy of the United States* (Worcester, Mass.: American Antiquarian Society, 1992), pp. 312–15, 330–32.

dominate top-management thinking as the decade began: reversing market share decline by making Leonards more competitive and controlling the sprawling organization. On Overcash's suggestion, Paul established the Executive Committee in 1960, composed of himself, his brother Bob, Armour Hann, Doc St. Clair, Bill Haberer, Jenkins Garrett, and Overcash and monitored by Marvin and Obie. This committee began a systematic appraisal of the store's competitive and organizational situation with an eye to reasserting Leonards' hold over Fort Worth retailing.[18]

Rising competition and the related issues of suburbanization and downtown deterioration dominated early discussions. Paul Leonard noted in a memo to his father, uncle, and brother that as the new decade dawned, Leonards would face tough competition from eight discount stores, plus a new Montgomery Wards and a new Sears. Moreover, different discounters presented different competitive challenges. Soft line discounters stocked very low-end, nonbranded merchandise and appealed to customers by store location, night and Sunday openings, and low price. Wards, Sears, and other national retailers offered sophisticated and often liberal credit programs with high customer appeal. In addition to the entry of strong discount competitors in Fort Worth, Leonards also had to contend with the rising popularity of suburban shopping, increased shoppers' awareness of trading stamps, and the expanding merchandising mix offered by many competitors. For instance, Kress added electrical appliances; Grants added power lawn mowers; and the Filling Station moved into boats and motors.[19]

Paul proposed a two-pronged strategy to counter the threats: incorporating many of the most current ideas in retailing and refurbishing practices that had contributed to Leonards' earlier success. His first concern was the specialty discounters, particularly soft goods sellers. For this class of competitors, Paul recommended meeting or beating price on branded items and emphasizing selection and price on nonbranded items. The creation of a soft line bargain basement operated on a self-service basis would also provide a less expensive but potent competitive tool. He also recommended the store consider more night openings for either Leonards or Everybody's or both.[20]

Sears and Wards provided an even greater challenge for Leonards, both because of their historic strength in hard lines and because of their marketing clout. In comparison to these retailing giants, Leonards looked decidedly outdated. The differences showed outwardly in store layout and furnishings, but also in contrasting store policies, most noticeably credit. Wards, Sears, and other national chains had built credit into a central strength in their organizations. In contrast, Paul viewed Leonards' "credit operation as creating more ill-will than anything else we do."[21]

Paul noted three areas that needed modernization. All departments, except those in the soft line bargain basement, needed to adopt first-quality merchandise and drop subquality items. Low-end basement merchandise would allow Leonards to meet soft line discounters' prices and encourage Leonards' customers to trade up to upstairs soft line departments. Home furnishings and soft line divisions needed more space to accommodate expanded lines and would require floor space, warehouse space, and refurbishing. Also, in rethinking design and layout issues across the store, Paul advised departments to enhance self-service opportunities as one way of curbing payroll.[22]

In addition to physical modernization, Paul recommended a complete overhaul of Leonards' credit program and urged Leonard family members to give serious consideration to suburban expansion, at least in a limited way. His idea was to introduce "twigs" of Leonards—suburban stores with only one or a few profitable departments represented. Twigging would allow Leonards to penetrate suburban markets without large increases in inventory investment, advertising expense, or administration expense.[23]

The Executive Committee, led by Paul and Overcash, took these ideas, studied, changed, and added to them, and eventually designed a series of major policy changes to respond to the internal and external challenges facing the store. Although Marvin neither initiated nor directed these strategy-making sessions, his final approval gave the plans legitimacy, and his stubborn loyalty to the downtown colored the committee's final recommendations. On January 22, 1962, Marvin announced Leonards' fourth major expansion and the construction of a subway to remote parking. Less newsworthy, but also part of the total plan was the merger of Everybody's with Leonards, consolidation of warehousing operations, an upgrade of Leonards' data processing capabilities, the creation of revolving credit, and the establishment of various internal programs for managing expenses and budgets. These initiatives—intimately tied to each other—held the committee's hope of revitalizing the store and bringing it up to the current standards of retailing.[24]

Leonards had added on before, but two aspects of this expansion stand out—its public appeal and the factors driving it. From the public's point-of-view, annexing another city block into Leonards' complex and modernizing existing facilities confirmed Leonards' commitment to and dominance over downtown. City officials celebrated private citizens funneling money into the central business district, and newspaper editorials lauded the plan. The proposed subway system, expected to connect Leonards with satellite parking along the Trinity River, garnered even greater praise. The sheer audacity of a business owning a private subway system took Forth Worth's citizens by surprise. That Marvin and Obie planned to operate it at no charge to riders stunned and thrilled them. A leading publisher hailed the announcement as imaginative and "too rare in this age of drift and resignation." Clearly, Marvin's stamp of approval on this latest expansion reconfirmed that neither man nor store would ever settle for the status quo.[25]

Although newspaper reports drew comparisons between this announcement and previous expansions, the underlying trigger and timing were tellingly different. Every other time Leonards had added on during the past forty-two years, swelling sales and increasing customer traffic had pushed even Leonards' most creative managers to plead for more space. In 1962, competitive pressures rather than clamoring customers stimulated the decision. Though it remained profitable, Leonards had struggled in the preceding years, and it expanded because of a declining market share and loss of distinctiveness.[26]

Leonards expanded as well because of its long-standing commitment to downtown. Downtown had always symbolized the "main tent" at the circus to Marvin, and during most of his years in business, it provided the heartbeat for Fort Worth commerce. The store benefited as much from the health of the Fort Worth economy and the vitality of downtown as it did from its own merchandising efforts. In 1962, Marvin's loyalty to the central business district remained strong, even though other downtown retailers doubted the area would ever recapture its vitality and centrality in the local economy.[27]

Marvin always knew that having strong competitors downtown made all the merchants better-off. In the past, one firm rarely invested in upgrades and expansions without the others following suit. This time skepticism and dwindling faith in downtown made a difference, for when Obie approached five other downtown department stores with the offer to share the building and operation of the subway, the plan fell flat. Stripling's chose to build a large parking garage east of its store to alleviate its parking problems, but the rest remained on the sidelines when Leonards made its announcement to expand. Other than supporting the rather weak promotional efforts of the Downtown Fort Worth Association, most had few ideas about refurbishing the neighborhood. Leonards stood virtually alone, ready to reassert itself and restore the downtown to its rightful position.[28]

TAKE A RIDE ON THE M & O

Marvin and Obie had continually simplified and expanded parking for their customers because handy parking was more than just a customer convenience. The store demanded a critical mass of patrons to ensure that its price-volume-turnover strategy worked. With that in mind, the brothers had bought and leased expensive downtown lots and provided free parking from the earliest days. They offered curbside package pickup for those who had to hike several blocks to retrieve their cars. After 1953, Leonards operated a shuttle bus service between the store and a remote lot that allowed shoppers to avoid the hassle of driving into downtown. Yet all these efforts paled in comparison with easy parking at suburban stores.[29]

Obie's idea to improve service and guarantee customer flow was to build a rail transit system a bit more than a mile in length between the store and its remote parking lot. About one quarter of the system would go under busy city streets, allowing subway cars to travel back and forth easily. This solution avoided rush-hour congestion and the store's reliance on meandering buses, while creating a major marketing tool for Leonards. The subway not only captured the imagination of Fort Worth folks, journalists and retail industry watchers from as far away as New York and London called attention to the feat.[30]

Obie took the lead in building the subway. The physical plant had always been his responsibility, and he had an affinity for things mechanical. Building underground transportation to remote parking appealed to his imagination, and he pushed the project doggedly until its completion. His leadership on the subway also foreshadowed his buyout of Marvin's share of the store in 1965. With Paul and Bob's expanded managerial roles and Obie's dedication to the subway project, Leonards increasingly became the O. P. Leonard family's store.

Despite Obie's identification with the project, it took the commitment and guidance of both brothers to tackle the most gigantic do-it-yourself project in store history. As usual, Marvin handled the financial side, arranging a loan from the Bank of New York with a participation by Fort Worth National. The project also required securing approval from several local government agencies. The Fort Worth Water Board granted permission to use the area by the river for parking, but retained the right to approve landscaping and construction so that the new system would not interfere with flood control. The Fort Worth Planning Department gave the store underground right-of-way. The City Council also approved the expansion, though legend still maintains that when excavation began a month later, Obie had not yet secured the building permits.[31]

From the start, Obie had his own ideas about the way things should proceed. He believed that open digging along the tunnel's projected path, except under the busiest cross streets, would raise fewer obstacles than burrowing underground. The Preston Geren architectural firm drew up the plans and appointed Woody Oliver, who had worked on the 1948 store addition, as its on-site representative. Leonards hired Haws and Garrett as the general contractor, and hundreds of workmen began excavating, bracing reinforcing steel into place, pushing dirt and rocks out of the way with giant bulldozers, and hauling in loads of fill sand.[32]

Construction on the tunnel began May 27, 1962, near the intersection of Franklin and Taylor Streets. An open trench was painstakingly dug south along Taylor, but digging that close to the Trinity complicated the job. Weep holes and springs seeped into the tunnel, saturating the floor. Three pumps operated constantly, moving more than ten thousand gallons of water each day out of the work site. Nevertheless, the threat of the sides collapsing remained, inspiring workmen to quickly secure bracing in the open trench. Next, forms were installed and concrete poured on top of arched sheet metal. Thick concrete soon lined the tunnel, ending the threat of cave-ins.[33]

Under Belknap, the subway's projected deepest point at forty-two feet, construction workers encountered an unusually hard stratum of rock. Because of the heavy traffic on Belknap and a thirty-six-inch water main that crossed above the

Construction of the subway began on May 27, 1962. Instead of boring a tunnel, contractors used a cut and cover method that required blasting through thick rock.

tunnel, workers bored this stretch through the rock instead of using the cut and cover method. Owners of the surrounding buildings sweated over the news that only dynamite would cut through the stubborn rock. Engineers used the minimum charge necessary to cut through the rock, while a seismographer monitored and recorded the intensity of each explosion. Although tedious, the process allowed the crew to burrow beneath Belknap and resume using the cut and cover method as they headed toward the new Home Store.[34]

The hard rock continued giving engineers and workmen problems. Using a boring machine, they drilled holes in the rock and then set off dynamite in the holes. An opportunistic funeral-home operator near the site of the explosions claimed that the detonations had caused some cracks in his building. Before Leonards had a chance to settle, a renter in the building spoke out that the cracks had been there long before.[35]

City water mains also posed a hazard. As the crew made the big cut between Weatherford and First Street, officials worried that if the water main running along one wall of the cut ruptured, the whole area would flood. Engineers designed giant concrete hooks to secure the pipe before digging went forward.[36]

Nearby property owners were not the only ones inconvenienced by Obie's project. In October, 1962, at about the same time that workers burrowed under Belknap, construction began on the subway's terminal beside the newly completed Home Store. An engineer periodically climbed out of the subbasement to warn employees to brace themselves for another jarring blast. During the winter, construction became more than a minor nuisance for the store's basement employees. Only a tarp blocked the cold winter wind that swooshed up from where workmen dug to connect the subway tunnel to the basement. Despite the noise, the distraction, and the cold wind, employees were thrilled by the subway plans and its promise of a renaissance for the store. Imogene Montgomery remembered "we were really in heaven—*the first subway.*"[37]

Eventually, trucks removed forty thousand tons of dirt and rock to make way for the tunnel. The 1,400-foot concrete corridor that remained held side-by-side standard gauge railroad track—just wide enough to carry the old Washington, D.C., street cars that Obie had found and refurbished. To add to the appeal of the ride, Obie had the blue and silver cars modernized and customized with air-conditioning and heating, new seats, and stainless-steel trim. Direct-current electricity from Leonards' own generators powered each car on the three-minute ride between the parking lot and the store.[38]

The subway project brought out the similarities and differences between Marvin and Obie. When Obie instigated the idea of remote parking ten years earlier, Marvin did not think much of the idea but trusted his brother's instincts. Marvin expressed even more skepticism when Obie proposed building the subway; he thought it would cost too much and expose the store to too much risk. Once Obie convinced Marvin that he could build it safely and for a reasonable cost, Marvin agreed and no longer involved himself in the details. Obie was different. He visited the site every day, even if it meant caking his shoes with mud and sweating through his clothes. He gleaned all the particulars from the various experts: architects, structural engineers, tunnel contractors, and inspectors. Above all, he wanted honest updates about mistakes and estimated costs.[39]

In the end, both men's career-long dedication to minimizing expenses kept the cost of the subway within reason. True to form, they found a way to have part of the cost underwritten because the underground passageway could serve as a bomb shelter and civil defense area. The final $500,000 price tag accounted for only about a quarter of the total outlay for the store renovation and the building of the Home Store. According to *Time,* "the whole shebang—lot, tunnel, subway cars, the works—cost only about $200 per parking space."[40] In comparison, a multistory parking garage would have cost $1,000 per space plus operating costs.[41]

Obie drove a golden spike into a cross tie on Monday, February 11, 1963, to signal the completion of the subway and to launch a citywide, two-week celebration of its grand opening. The press had a peek at the facilities the next night, and the two Leonard families sponsored an open house for employees and their families on Wednesday. More than five thousand folks joined the party, catching their first rides on the subway and browsing through the remodeled and expanded store. On Thursday night, Marvin and Obie showed off the facilities to their fellow downtown businessmen; the group adjourned to Shady Oaks Country Club afterward for dinner.[42]

The official Grand Opening made its splash the next morning. The subway was crowned the M & O Railroad, in honor of the proudest men there, Marvin and Obie Leonard, whose imagination and determination had brought new fame to Fort Worth. Then, at 9:00 A.M., Friday, February 15, 1963, city and county dignitaries crowded aboard one of the blue and white subways cars and chugged straight through a simulated brick wall in the store's basement terminal, officially opening the subway. After the various dignitaries convened to Lenwood Hall, the store's auditorium, for festivities and entertainment, Fort Worth's citizens at last got their chance to ride the rails.[43]

The subway attracted all sorts of riders—after all, Leonards charged nothing to park or to ride. Shoppers found that its design worked well. Color-coded terminals helped them find where they left their cars, and at top speeds of thirty miles per hour, the trip back and forth went quickly. Downtown workers appreciated that cars began running at 7:30 A.M., even though the store did not open until 9:00. The real draw of the subway, however, was its novelty. Certainly some of Fort Worth's citizens had traveled widely enough that subway transportation was old hat. Many had not, and for these folks—the backbone of Leonards' customer base—Leonards was now both a familiar shopping stop and a marvel.[44]

Downtown visitors also marveled at the latest store expansion. The Old Crenshaw Building and the Odd Fellows Lodge made way for a three-and-a-half-story brick and glass structure that filled an entire city block. Construction began in January, 1962, and by October the building was near enough to completion to begin moving all the home furnishings departments to their new quarters. The additional 212,000 square feet of shopping space brought the total floorspace of the Leonards' complex to slightly over half a million. Home furnishings, begun so modestly in the mid-1920s with shoddy furniture, spread over the first floor and mezzanine of the new building. While Leonards continued to offer a selection of furniture and accessories that all could afford, the new building also housed moderate and more-expensive furniture lines, including modern and traditional groupings and a complete Early American shop. The extra space also made it possible for Bob Johnson, merchandise manager for furnishings, to stock a selection of home office furniture for the first time.[45]

Because Leonards now covered so many blocks of downtown Fort Worth, the expansion of underground connections was crucial. As in the case of the 1948 expansion, the willingness of the city to allow Leonards to expand under the street meant that customers could move horizontally, buying and browsing as they went from department to department. After renovations, the underground shopping area stretched under three blocks and provided an unobstructed view for almost four hundred feet. This expanded space housed seven large departments and the Home Improvement center. Unless a customer needed bricks or lumber, he could find any home improvement tool, fixture, or supply at Leonards.[46]

The fact that many customers would now begin their Leonards shopping experience in the basement was not lost on Leonards' managers. The aisle between the subway terminal and the main stairs, perfumed by the smell of freshly made doughnuts, became the hottest selling space in the store. It had its own manager who coordinated promotions, and department managers paid a fee to display special promotional items in bins down the center of the aisle. Managers competed with each other for the space and haggled with manufacturers and wholesalers to find special bargain items that would sell quickly. One deal, struck by Bill Belz, manager of the western wear department, placed seven thousand pairs of "mellow" yellow slacks on a clothesline above the subway aisle. Within a week employees all over the store sported jazzy, yellow pants and sang along with Donovan as the intercom played "They Call Me Mellow Yellow" throughout the store. Despite the nontraditional color, the pants flew out of the door. Belz even saw strikers at General Dynamics carrying picket signs and wearing his mellow yellow slacks.[47]

Extra space, both above and below ground, gave existing departments more room to operate and made way for the creation of several new departments. Following the pattern set decades before, Leonards launched new departments whenever the sales of a particular line or lines of merchandise warranted it. The 1962 expansion conferred full-fledged department status to western wear and accessories, stamps and coins, books, musical instruments, and ready-to-wear for preteen girls. Also, a new beauty salon and professional portrait studio added to the ratcheting up of Leonards image as a full-service shopping center rather than a discounter.[48]

Leonards' 1963 Grand Opening ads did not just boast about adding more space and new departments. Construction of the store addition also brought technological triumphs. Obie's own lightweight aluminum concrete forms sped construction, and a huge concrete girder, thirteen feet deep and seventy-five feet long, possibly set a local record for the largest single support girder ever used in a construction project. Using steel rather than concrete support columns added elegance and practicality to the new building. This innovation took less floor space and intruded less into displays and traffic patterns. They also supported twice the load of concrete columns.[49]

No one at Leonards wanted the public to draw unfavorable comparisons between the new, modern-looking Home Store with its cantilevered construction and its frumpy companion buildings left over from previous renovations. Accordingly, all the parts of the existing store received a substantial face-lift as well. Starting with the structure opened in 1930 at 200 Houston, each part of Leonards made room for new fixtures, new lighting, and new department configurations. Managers arranged their expanded merchandise selections in "modern, scientific displays." The entire physical structure metamorphosed into an updated, color-coordinated, and refurbished modern Leonards.[50]

Management also invested in behind-the-scenes improvements. A new in-store package conveyor system expanded the always-popular curbside grocery pickup service. Shoppers left their purchases at check stands strategically located around the store and continued shopping unencumbered. A complex network of conveyors whisked the bundles to a central, car-accessible area, where at their convenience, customers picked up their accumulation of packages. Conveyors also played a role in the new loading and receiving dock. The design allowed trucks to back into the dock directly off the street and featured an automatic belt system to unload trucks and channel deliveries to predesignated areas within the store.[51]

Most of the improvements created a more unified image for Leonards and allowed for greater coordination across a mammoth operation. Expanding the basement under the street meant that customers did not notice when they moved from one building of the Leonards complex to another. Color-coordination and matching fixtures added continuity that the older version of the store lacked. Even the package pickup system helped convince shoppers that the Leonards experience was more than just shopping in one or two of the store's 185 departments. It was one large store, not a collection of smaller stores as in a modern shopping mall.

To supplement the automatic conveyor system for coordinating operations across the larger enterprise, management updated the telephone system. Although five-position switchboards were common in the Northeast, Leonards became the first retailer in the Southwest to adopt such technology. This type of switchboard gave store personnel the unprecedented ability to communicate with each other by providing access to five hundred in-store lines and forty-two incoming trunklines. The new public address system complemented the phone system, piping recorded music, locator announcements, or taped messages over the entire six-block area now occupied by the store.[52]

Almost everyone in Fort Worth heard of the changes taking place at Leonards. The local papers had charted the progress during construction and the *Star-Telegram* ran a giant twenty-four-page spread of advertising and news stories celebrating the grand opening. Fewer people shared the news of organizational changes taking place at Leonards. First, Everybody's retail operation was closed, and its merchandise and employees combined with Leonards. The previous September, a Leonards representative had announced the closing, explaining that the move would improve customer service because sales staff, service personnel, and management could work together rather than compete for customers.[53]

This motive, a publicly palatable one, certainly fit the situation facing the sister stores. Department managers in both stores had always had the latitude to buy whatever merchandise they thought their customers would buy. Consequently, shoppers could find similar or identical items in different departments and in both Leonards and Everybody's. The opposite was also true. Quality could vary substantially. Both of these situations confused customers and made it difficult for Leonards to present a unified and consistent image to its customers.

The amount of overlap, and thus the potential for confusion, between the sister stores had grown worse through the 1950s. As Leonards had traded up to attract more middle-income customers, Everybody's had followed in its wake. Its managers honed their buying skills, taking regular advantage of failing stores and special deals offered by manufacturers and wholesalers. Everybody's still targeted a more budget-minded customer, but aggressive buying by many Everybody's buyers escalated duplication with Leonards' product lines and the rivalry between the two stores.[54]

Rivalry was only one of several issues the Executive Committee discussed before merging Everybody's operations with Leonards. Of particular concern was accounting practices. Leonards had undergone several waves of accounting and bookkeeping changes since Ray Shea arrived in 1951. These efforts tightened accounting procedures to track expenses more accurately and allocate overhead costs more equitably. Because of Everybody's historic role in the company, it paid lower overhead and rent than other parts of the organization. Leonards' increasingly sophisticated accounting system revealed these bookkeeping inequities. For profit purposes, it probably mattered little whether Everybody's or corporate Leonards generated or showed the profit. But for management, which had increasing interest in setting consistent standards across the organization, the unit's special status presented a problem that merging it with Leonards solved.[55]

As the Executive Committee grew more serious about closing Everybody's, it turned its attention to the practicalities of doing so. At this point, the discussion about Everybody's and the store expansion dovetailed. Besides the other strategic roles expansion would play, adding on to Leonards would make it much easier to transfer and accommodate Everybody's volume to Leonards. The lowest-end customers would find similar products in Leonards' expanded basement operations, and other shoppers would be attracted to Leonards' greater selection.

In addition, the building occupied by Everybody's was added to the list of available space and became part of a master plan to consolidate the warehouse space serving the various retailing operations. By the early 1960s, Leonards operated warehouse space in a large number of remote locations. Over the years, Marvin and Obie had bought numerous tracts of land around the city at bargain prices. Whenever the store needed more storage space, Obie would throw up a concrete warehouse by using movable forms to pour the walls and ceilings on one of these lots. With construction costs of $2.75 a foot and no additional cost for land, Leonards had never worried much about the economics of its inventory operation. Each department manager ran his own warehouse operation, storing goods bought in large quantities and moving them to the selling floor when needed. Even when the store grew very large, decentralized control of warehousing persisted.[56]

By the 1960s, however, the diseconomies and inequities of manager-controlled warehousing had become apparent. Overcash suggested that consolidating warehousing and closing outlying facilities would lower taxes, insurance, and utilities. It would also reduce manpower, vehicle usage, and the cost of supervising such an extended operation, making restocking cheaper and more convenient. Besides the obvious cost savings of closing remote facilities and moving more operations to a centralized location, reallocating the Everybody's space to another use would help prevent that end of Houston Street from deteriorating into a skid row. Ralph Cook, who had replaced Haberer as controller, took on the unenviable job of recentralizing the warehousing operation.[57]

Overcash also hoped that tighter warehousing policies and consolidation would help further curb escalating inventory. After combining the warehouse space, he began charging managers increased fees for their assigned space. This practice irritated many managers. Woody Graham, manager of the boys department, disliked the idea so much he moved all his inventory into the aisles of his department to avoid the storage charges. Eventually, he gave in, moved his inventory back into storage, and grudgingly paid the rent on the space.[58]

Controls instituted to manage inventory on the floor accompanied the more sophisticated backroom systems. Leonards had always used handwritten receipts to record sales. This practice continued in the 1960s, but new, specially printed tickets required clerks to note much more information for each customer transaction. To complete a sale, the clerk recorded his department number, the type of sale, various customer and merchandise information, and other details that aided bookkeeping and made tracking inventory more systematic. Different transactions—layaway, charges, returns—required different tickets. Reminders in *Hi, Neighbor* instructed employees on the proper procedures for filling out the complicated forms—"How to Handle a Cash Refund," "How to Handle a Charge Credit for an *Employee* Returning Merchandise," or "How to Handle a Gift Certificate." Each month, a new set of instructions appeared, gently prodding employees to learn the ins and outs of the new system.[59]

Updating the store's data-processing capabilities and credit operation would have to wait a couple of years, but the remainder of the Executive Committee's master plan was in place by the end of 1963. The subway provided the most visible measure of its success. The lot beneath the Trinity River bluff provided about a fifth of the total parking spaces available to downtown commuters. At least two thousand downtown workers, including 90 percent of Leonards' employees, parked there each day and caught the subway. Another eight to ten thousand used the system for shopping, and this figure doubled during the Christmas season. Subway transportation was so popular that both the Downtown Fort Worth Association and the Fort Worth National Bank expressed an interest in extending the system. Like the Gruen Plan proposed in the mid-1950s, which sought to save downtown by transforming it into a huge pedestrian shopping mall, the idea had merit, but the potential participants could never resolve the practicalities of sharing building, operating, and maintenance expenses.[60]

While the Executive Committee's actions attracted customers, they did not dramatically increase profits. As expected, the expansion and subway construction generated more sales, but after increasing by $3 million in 1962, they remained flat, at around $29 million, for several years. Considering the closing of Everybody's, which had generated annual sales of around $6 million, the much-expanded selling space in the new store, and the robust local economy, the meager jump in sales must have disappointed management. Clearly, the revamped Leonards did not attract the same number of customers as the old Leonards and Everybody's combined. In retrospect, closing the smaller store was a mistake. Its flexible buying practices and appeal to working-class customers were lost. At the same time, expenses associated with the addition and consolidation of the two stores took a big bite out of net profit, reducing earnings by more than half from 1961 to 1962, from $423,589 to $204,333, and dragging them down again in 1963, when profit

In this aerial view of Fort Worth, the parking lot and subway route to Leonards is outlined. By the mid-1960s Leonards was north of most of the major downtown office buildings.

reached only $170,495. By the end of 1964, profits had recovered to preexpansion levels, signaling that the time was right for Marvin to sell his share of Leonards to the O. P. Leonard family.[61]

MARVIN SELLS THE STORE

Soon after the store began digesting the changes initiated by his nephews and Overcash, Marvin started collecting information relevant to selling his share of Leonards, Everybody's, Fort Worth Wholesale Merchandise Company, and the State Reserve Life Insurance Company. This was no simple transaction between two brothers and partners. The sale had corporate and personal tax consequences. Marvin had always controlled the majority of stock ownership in the corporations. For many years, however, both he and Obie had transferred stock to their children directly and in trust. The result was that Marvin and his family controlled the ownership of the businesses, while Obie and his family furnished the management. Joint and separate investments in oil and real estate further complicated breaking up the partnership. Since they had distributed some of these assets to the children, some properties had as many as eight owners. The State Reserve Life Insurance Company also owned property, and Everybody's, although now closed, retained numerous assets. Eventually, the two families worked out a series of swaps to untangle the commingled ownership of property and other assets. The transfer of Leonards to the O. P. Leonard family was the centerpiece of the deal.[62]

The brothers finalized the sale of the store at the end of 1964. The transaction was handled privately between the two families with Jenkins Garrett working out most of the details. The public knew only that Marvin was stepping down from active involvement in the running of the store. Newspaper descriptions of the reorganization painted Marvin in familiar hues and tones: grace, dignity, and class. Having served as the president of the firm since 1918, Marvin was now ready to yield his place to younger men and take the role as honorary chairman of the board. The formal announcement of personnel changes merely confirmed Marvin's cession of control to his nephews.[63]

Just as building and nurturing the store had forwarded Marvin's desire for security by creating a steady and substantial flow of income, selling the store completed the quest. He and his family received about $7.3 million in cash, assets, and property for Leonards, Everybody's, and Fort Worth Wholesale. Their part of State Reserve Life Insurance came to another $3.7 million.[64] The sale added to the endowment for his family he had begun building decades before. It also gave him enough liquidity to invest more heavily in the various real-estate opportunities growing Fort Worth presented. More fundamentally, it erased all his debts, leaving an uncluttered estate for his heirs. The need to provide for Mary and leave a legacy for his daughters had grown urgent as he had begun experiencing more-serious health problems.[65]

Marvin's health worsened after 1960. In May, 1961, problems with internal bleeding prompted a trip to the Oschner Clinic in New Orleans for a four-day battery of tests. Only a short time later, his Fort Worth physician diagnosed a potentially deadly aneurysm. His third daughter, Marty, accompanied him to Houston to consult with Dr. Michael DeBakey about his condition. DeBakey was frank with Marvin—the aneurysm could blow at any moment. Only surgery could take away the threat of a massive hemorrhage. Marvin refused.[66]

The knowledge that he could die alarmed Marvin and, ironically, perhaps desensitized him to other potential health problems related to alcohol and smoking. Yet it also made him more determined than ever to provide for his family. His daughters were grown, but he still worried about them and wanted to provide for them. When they were young, the process was simpler. He could demonstrate his care by buying savings bonds and giving credit to the schools they attended or by responding to a request from Madelon's gym teacher to send a television to the school for the children to watch the World Series games. As they grew up, fatherhood carried a much larger burden. The health of his oldest daughter, Mary, worried him. His youngest, Madelon, after a trying time with college, had moved to Italy. Miranda followed her own interests outside of his orbit. Proceeds from selling the store would not take his place in guiding his daughters through life, but it would make their journey more comfortable.[67]

Parting with the store he built from scratch and ran for forty-six years did not rob Marvin of his identity or affect his self-esteem. He loved the store—not because it bore his name, not because it was the biggest in town, and not because Leonards was Fort Worth. He loved it because he built it and because its success had allowed him to do everything else that he accomplished. Passing the store on to his brother's family gave him the chance to continue doing other things he found important—building and supporting Fort Worth.

That Marvin had accomplished much since he arrived in Fort Worth in 1918 was evident to the scores of people who attended various functions honoring him over the course of the decade. That he was not through was equally apparent. His name appeared in the local papers regularly, tracking his involvement in various organizations, his expanded real-estate ventures, and other activities.

The decade had barely begun before admirers started honoring him with dinners and ceremonies. In June, 1960, members of the Fort Worth section of the Texas Professional Golf Association presented him with a testimonial dinner at Glen Garden Country Club. Each year, he, along with many high-profile Texans, bore the barbs at the annual Gridiron Club roast. The most fitting tribute, however, came from the Exchange Club of Fort Worth, which honored both Marvin and Obie with the Golden Deeds Award for 1961. This award recognized the outstanding citizen(s) of Fort Worth in gratitude for their service to the community. The six-hundred-person turnout, the largest in the thirty-three-year history of the club, stood as a testament to the brothers' contribution to Fort Worth. Friends, business associates, and community leaders paid tribute with speeches and old stories.[68]

This award, conferred in April, 1962, recognized what many had always known about Marvin. In building his store, he made "vital contributions to the growth and development of Fort Worth." He attended to his businesses—serving the shopping needs of Fort Worthians and shaping their neighborhoods—while providing "unmeasurable benefits, guidance and inspiration to everyone who makes his home in this city." He took time to serve on the boards of numerous civic, cultural, and welfare organizations. In sum, the Exchange Club chose Marvin and Obie for the "indelible imprint" they had left on the life of Fort Worth.[69]

The following year, on June 14, 1963, Carswell Air Force Base held an appreciation day honoring Marvin and Obie as "Friends of the Air Force." The recognition served to remind the community again of the ways that the brothers had contributed to the city and its citizens. It also called attention to the role Marvin had played raising money to build a nine-hole golf course on the base.[70]

School administrators in Fort Worth had not forgotten the many times that Leonards and its owners had helped the city and its schoolchildren, making needed donations or footing the bill for school lunches when government funding dried up. In 1966, the Fort Worth Independent School District moved forward with plans to build the Marvin & Obie Leonard Junior High School (now called Marvin and Obie Leonard Middle School) in commemoration of the brothers' contributions. The new school symbolized the same spirit as the M & O subway. It incorporated the most progressive school design features—carpeting, air-conditioning, and a revised cafeteria setup—and economized on building and maintenance costs. It opened during the 1968–69 school year and had its formal dedication ceremonies May 6, 1969.[71]

Early the next year, Texas Wesleyan University named Marvin and Obie Business Executives of the Year. They were the first to receive this award that is now sponsored by Texas Wesleyan, the Fort Worth Chamber of Commerce, and *Business Press*. The award symbolized both their business accomplishments and their overall contributions to the community.[72]

Despite health problems and severed connections with the store, Marvin was not content to reap the laurels of a vigorous and service-filled life. He continued his long-standing involvement with Fort Worth National Bank and the Lena Pope Home, served as a trustee for Harris Hospital, and supported the Arts Council of Greater Fort Worth and many other worthy causes. In 1963 he and Obie voluntarily paid to feed 485 head of starving cattle abandoned by a bankrupt cattle and land company. The next year Marvin worked with fellow church members to found the First Methodist Church of Fort Worth Foundation. In the midst of this whirlwind of activities, he directed the development of the vast expanse of land west of town once known as the Johnson Ranch.[73]

SHADY OAKS AND RIDGMAR

Marvin Leonard had vision, especially when it came to real estate. When he purchased twelve hundred acres from the Amon Carter estate in 1955, he knew Fort Worth was growing westward toward his newly acquired property. As the map of Northwest Fort Worth in 1970 shows, this property, often referred to as Ridgmar, was shaped somewhat like a pear. It came to a sharp point in the north at the intersection of Roaring Springs Road and Highway 183, but was wide at its southern boundary. Eventually part of this wide base fell on both sides of the first major freeway in Fort Worth. This advantageous location and the addition of streets and utilities greatly multiplied the value of land originally purchased for about $2 million. By the time he sold the store, Marvin's annual profit from Ridgmar was greater than his annual profit from Leonards.[74]

A few months after the start of construction at Shady Oaks, Marvin began developing the adjacent residential area. This virtually simultaneous beginning characterized Marvin's development strategy. The club added value to the surrounding residential area, but new residents were also potential members for the club. Residential development began within the boundaries of Westover Hills, where lots sold briskly from October, 1956, until the fourth quarter of 1959. Sales picked back up in the fourth quarter of 1960 as the economy rebounded. The Westover Hills section had lots of an acre or larger valued in 1962 from $10,000 to $30,000 ($45,000 to $135,000 in 1991 dollars). In 1962 thirty new lots came on the market in Westover Hills. By early the next year, buyers could choose from about fifty available lots. Through the rest of the decade, Marvin and his agents gradually opened new sections. The most active year was 1970 when lot sales in Westover Hills totaled $523,000. By the end of that year, custom-designed and built homes, usually among the largest and most expensive in Tarrant County, filled Westover Hills. The lots' appreciated value indicates the planning and care that went into this development. By 1991 the larger lots in Westover Hills, exclusive of homes, appraised at about $450,000, a growth in value of more than three times the rate of inflation. Marvin Leonard knew how to select and market a product, whether it was shirts or real estate.[75]

Marvin actually marketed residential areas targeted to three price ranges. Westover Hills targeted the highest price range, but Ridgmar East, just to the west within the city of Fort Worth, quickly became an upper–middle class neighborhood with lots priced at from $5,000 to $10,000 and homes in excess of $30,000 in 1962. At that time, there were about eighty homesites available in Ridgmar East. Lots adjacent to Shady Oaks commanded higher prices, and some of the homes came close to the high standards of Westover Hills. Farther to the west in Ridgmar proper, about three hundred new homes stood by the close of 1962. Lot prices there ranged from $3,000 to $6,000, and homes averaged between $20,000 and $25,000 in value. Runway noise at Carswell Air Force Base lowered home and lot values in that section of Ridgmar.[76]

After 1962, newly constructed streets, sewers, and utilities made further development of Ridgmar possible. In early 1964, the highway department completed an overpass and freeway access ramps at the intersection of Ridgmar Boulevard and the West Freeway. This made getting in and out of Ridgmar much safer and easier. Sales picked up markedly after that point, topping $300,000 in 1965 for the two areas of Ridgmar. The growing Fort Worth economy, which created a record number of new jobs for the middle and upper-middle class, also boosted sales.[77]

Marvin's foresight in realizing Fort Worth would grow to the west paid off

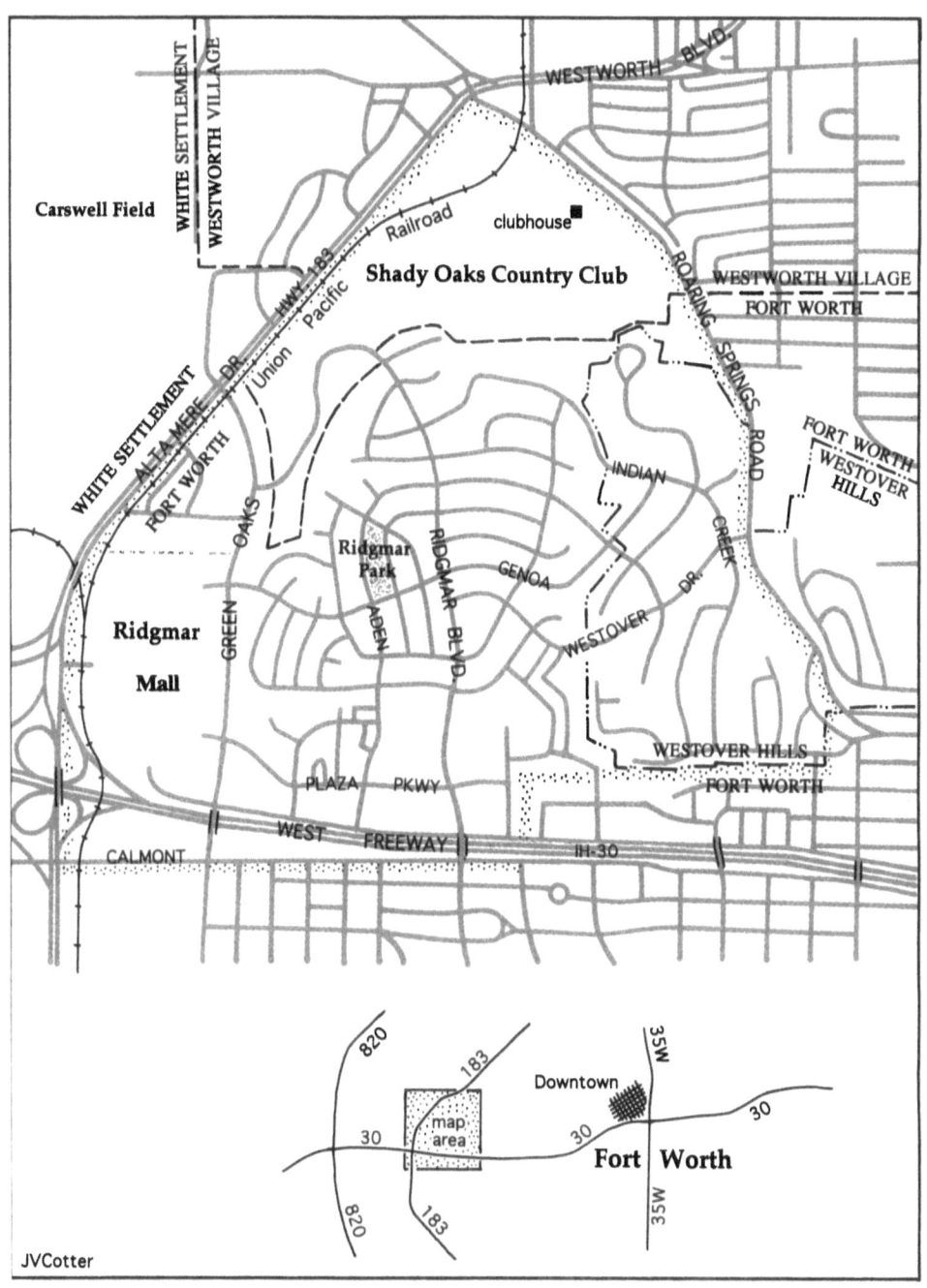

Northwest Fort Worth, 1970. *Map by John V. Cotter.*

handsomely once the economy picked up. Yet he did not rely upon simple intuition to develop his land. He employed land planners from Kansas City and used the local firm Carter & Burgess. Many of the concepts, including the name Ridgmar, came from preliminary plans for the California project that Marvin abandoned when he purchased the Carter property. Ridgmar meant "view of the sea" in Latin, but it worked well enough for the plains of Tarrant County. Streets names, such as Genoa, Dakar, and Juneau, evoked exotic vacation destinations. Most streets in the Westover Hills section ended in a cul-de-sac, which families preferred because fewer through streets meant less traffic in their neighborhoods. Within the boundaries of Fort Worth, streets curved instead of ending in cul-de-sacs because the city limited the length of dead-end streets. Using a curvilinear street design, however, served the same purpose of impeding traffic and avoided the square-block effect of so many post–World War II subdivisions. Even Ridgmar Boulevard wound about discouraging use by all except those going to and from their homes or businesses.[78]

Starting in January, 1961, John Maddux handled most of the details for the development of Ridgmar. In 1953, at age sixteen, Maddux went to work for Everybody's and continued working there until he graduated from Texas Wesleyan University in 1959. After graduation he went into real estate. The next year, he tried to sell Leonards a piece of property on Eagle Mountain Lake, arguing that the property would make a perfect employee retreat, a place for company picnics and meetings. Tom Whitley, who at the time handled real estate for the store and for the brothers, turned the idea down, but evidently Maddux impressed Whitley and Marvin with his enthusiastic sales pitch. A few months later Marvin hired him.[79]

When Maddux began working for Marvin, the first phase of Westover was already developed. Working with Bob Stahala, who handled most of the legal work, Maddux revised, finalized, surveyed, and platted lot layouts for five more development phases and oversaw the installation of streets, sewer systems, and utilities for each phase. He then marketed the lots and ensured that building restrictions remained updated and enforced. Maddux maintained standard quality within Westover Hills, Ridgmar East, and Ridgmar and helped convey each area's image to the public. As part of this goal he introduced the Life Parade of Homes in June, 1963. Maddux advertised the advantages of Ridgmar and invited prospective home buyers to view a dozen or so furnished and landscaped homes. Just as in the case of selling at Leonards, customers could see and touch the merchandise. Using this technique and others, Maddux developed twelve phases in Ridgmar and Ridgmar East during the 1960s.[80]

One quirky problem preoccupied Maddux. Four cities shared the legal jurisdiction of the property purchased from the Carter estate. The residential areas were in Fort Worth and Westover Hills, but the Shady Oaks clubhouse and part of the golf course lay within Westworth Village. The rest of the course was in Fort Worth and Westover Hills. And initially, the western edge of the Ridgmar addition along Highway 183 fell within the borders of White Settlement.[81]

Dealing with four different city halls created its share of obstacles. Fort Worth supplied the water and sewage treatment for Westover Hills, so Marvin built the lines in Westover Hills and then turned them over to the city of Fort Worth. In fact, to service the area immediately west of Westover Hills but in Fort Worth, the city had to build a line through Westover Hills. To some, these maneuvers gave the impression that Marvin was taking advantage of his political connections to enhance the value of his property. In 1959, a few members of the city council criticized the contract between Leonard and the city, but Jenkins Garrett argued before the city council that the Ridgmar development would add more than $30 million to the Fort Worth tax roles. Criticism died down.[82]

Developing the part of Ridgmar in White Settlement presented an even trickier problem because the runways at Carswell prevented that city from extending water and sewer lines to the new area. Garrett worked out a land swap between Fort Worth and White Settlement where both sides got easier-to-service territory. Now Marvin and his agents had to deal with only three city halls.[83]

In some ways, the state and federal governments played far more important roles in the development of Ridgmar than the local municipalities. After 1956, state and federal funding made possible the rapid construction of urban freeways that allowed cities to sprawl over an ever-increasing area. As much as anything else, the extension of the West Freeway (Interstate 30) made Ridgmar an attractive residential and commercial area. Marvin helped the process along by donating land for access roads on both sides of the freeway. By early 1965, the completed freeway, with access roads along each side and overpasses at Ridgmar Boulevard and Green Oaks Road, ran past the western edge of Ridgmar. A booming economy helped, but shorter and easier drive times to schools, shopping, and work contributed greatly to sales growth.[84]

Increasingly, these sales involved commercial as well as residential property. Traditionally, businesses concentrated in the downtown, adjacent to their clients and to the lawyers, insurance agents, and bankers they needed to see on a regular basis. The West Freeway, however, allowed corporations to move their headquarters away from the central business district without losing access to clients and professional services. In 1962, Ridgmar Plaza, north of the freeway on Ridgmar Boulevard, housed the Texas Crude Oil Co., while the Western Company and the Southern Baptist Convention announced plans to build major facilities nearby. By January, 1966, the area just north of the West Freeway at Ridgmar Boulevard emerged as a satellite business district with the construction of small strip centers on each side of the road.[85]

Several large apartment complexes arose adjacent to these commercial properties. The freeway eased the commute downtown, and those who worked at Ridgmar Plaza could walk to work. The Ridgmar Plaza Apartments opened in 1961 and in 1962 construction began on the nearby Imperial Terrace Apartments. There were thirty-two units in Imperial Terrace, each apartment exceeding fifteen hundred square feet and including many luxury features. The next year, A. B. Cass, Jr., of Dallas, who built Imperial Terrace, purchased forty-eight acres from Marvin on the northwest corner of the intersection of Ridgmar Boulevard and the West Freeway and announced plans for a huge apartment complex called Ridgmar Behind the Wall. As the name implied, a high fence shielded these exclusive apartments from the outside world. Construction began on the $25 million apartment project in early 1965. The apartments had an international flavor with the design of each cluster patterned after a different country, such as Spain or France. Cass also announced plans for an International Market Place filled with shops and restaurants and a high-rise apartment building.[86]

Under terms of his agreement with Marvin, Cass paid for the land as he began construction. Thus, in 1965, he paid more than $500,000 for about fourteen acres on which he built Ridgmar Behind the Wall. The next two years Marvin collected about $400,000 for additional acreage. In 1967, however, Cass began to have financial difficulties and never completed construction on the forty-eight acres. Yet his work meant that Fort Worth, like many other rapidly growing cities in the South and West, now had suburbs with much more than single-family housing.[87]

As long as the Fort Worth economy remained sound, apartment construction continued despite one builder's financial woes. In 1968, I. C. Deal purchased the land Cass had not used and some additional acreage between Aden Road and Green Oaks Road. The selling price exceeded $2 million. In 1969, Deal began construction on additional apartment complexes west of Ridgmar Boulevard.[88]

Extension of the freeway made Ridgmar a good location for hotels as well as apartments. In June, 1964, Marvin signed a fifty-year lease for $30,000 per year with Green Oaks Building Corporation on eleven acres in the southeast corner of Highway 183 and the West Freeway. In the area between the freeway and Calmont Street, the group constructed a 300-room luxury hotel designed to attract convention business. The West Freeway allowed easy travel downtown to the new convention center and Highway 183 offered quick access to attractions to the north and south. Within a year, Howard Johnson's announced plans to construct a motel adjacent to Green Oaks.[89]

While John Maddux handled the day-to-day details of developing Ridgmar, Marvin kept a close eye on all that happened. He met with Maddux daily through most of the 1960s, giving advice on designing new phases of Ridgmar's residential neighborhoods. He made the initial contact with large-scale purchasers such as H. S. Green and William T. Green of the Green Oaks Hotel. He also introduced Maddux to people potentially interested in buying lots in Westover Hills. When Maddux first went to work, Marvin drove him to Westover Hills to lay out a lot for a customer. He pulled right over the curb in his big Lincoln, crashed through the brush, and splashed through a creek. They got out and designed the lot to the customer's specifications. When it was time to close a deal, Marvin met with buyers, but he seldom haggled over the price. He simply said yes or no.[90]

Marvin's mastery of public relations and his contacts with various government officials contributed substantially to Ridgmar's successful development. His picture appeared whenever the local newspapers announced a sale, and his reputation for sound business practices gave Ridgmar a prestige and respectability lacking in some developments. As a member of the Good Government League and other civic organizations that had grown out of the Seventh Street Gang, he enjoyed easy access to city and state officials. Working through Garrett, he got things done, like the land swap between Fort Worth and White Settlement, that might have stymied others.[91]

As early as 1958 Marvin laid plans for the biggest commercial endeavor in Ridgmar, a giant regional shopping center. This development was first planned for the northwest corner of Ridgmar Boulevard and the Freeway. Construction of A. B. Cass's apartment complex pushed the proposed site westward, but Marvin remained optimistic about the soundness of the concept. Through the mid-1960s he pursued various leads, often working through Sid Uberman, who lived in Westover Hills. Finally in 1969 plans took shape for the purchase of 118.9 acres by J. C. Penney Company. The land, originally part of White Settlement, sat in the southwestern corner of Ridgmar, adjacent to the Freeway and Highway 183. The price of the land, $3,269,475, was so large that officials of Fort Worth National Bank came to John Maddux's office to oversee the wire transfer.[92]

In partnership with Kravco, a Pennsylvania company, Penney's developed Ridgmar Mall. Construction began in 1974 and the mall—"Fort Worth's first fully-enclosed, climate-controlled shopping center"—opened in 1976. Ridgmar Mall had five anchor stores: Penney's, Dillard's, Sears, Stripling's, and Neiman Marcus. It also had about 140 smaller specialty stores and restaurants on its two levels. Ironically, Marvin Leonard, who as much as any other made downtown Fort Worth the place to shop, helped replace downtown with suburban shopping malls.[93]

In 1968, during the initial stages of the land sale to J. C. Penney, Marvin sold Shady Oaks to its members for $2.7 million. In February, 1970, the club president estimated the replacement cost of the club at $7.7 million. The land alone was probably worth more than $2.7 million. Viewed in that light, the sale was an act of generosity done to preserve and promote Shady Oaks. Of course a stable, financially healthy Shady Oaks continued to add value to Marvin's unsold residential lots in Ridgmar and Westover Hills. As was often the case, good business and generosity intertwined. One might also view the sale of the club as another effort to provide financial security for his family. From 1958 forward, plan after plan to sell the club fell through. Through most of those years, Shady Oaks lost money. Selling the club recovered some of his assets, gave him a tax write-off, and stopped a small but steady drain on his income. For a man who realized his health was slipping, there was a final key point: selling Shady Oaks removed from his estate a difficult property to manage.[94]

Managing a country club required a special set of skills and competencies. A manager needed to know enough about growing grass to keep the greens and fairways in good shape, and Marvin rode the course with his greenskeepers on a regular basis. While he enjoyed working with grass, other aspects of the club caused more trouble. Selecting and retaining the right people to head up the clubhouse, food services, the golf shop, tennis and swimming, and other aspects of the country club required great care. Exclusive clubs need people that satisfy the members by offering good service, but they also must keep an eye on expenses because the cost of labor can easily escalate. This meant the general-manager position required a person of unusual skill in service delivery and cost control.[95]

Maintaining good customer relations presented a particularly difficult challenge, as an incident that occurred in October, 1964, illustrated. Because Shady Oaks consistently lost money, General Manager R. L. Crook made a special effort to attract private parties to the club. Parties added extra revenue, and the right kind of parties exposed potential new members to the charms of the club. Crook had high hopes when the Opera Association selected Shady Oaks as the site for their 1964 Opera Ball, but it brought as many problems as benefits. The ball began on Friday evening at eight o'clock and ran to two o'clock the next morning. At about three o'clock, as the catering manager was attempting to pay off the extra help and send them home, one of the organizers of the ball accosted him in his office. The angry man yelled and cursed at him for not providing enough help for a meeting of the Opera Association in the bar. The catering manager soothed the nerves of Opera Association members and explained that his staff had done its best to serve the unscheduled meeting. The next week Marvin stepped in and demanded an apology from the man who accosted his manager. He also tried to reassure the head of the Opera Association of his commitment to first-class service. The headache of dealing with ranting patrons and higher labor costs took the luster from what promised to be a way to advertise the club and make a profit.[96]

The incident at the Opera Ball highlighted the three major problems Marvin faced at Shady Oaks—expense control, service expectations, and low membership. Marvin set the service expectations quite high, which required heavy staffing. Yet if the club did not have enough members, the staff was underutilized. One waiter might easily serve four tables, but wound up serving only one. To serve the one the waiter had to remain. Thus, increasing membership became the focus of most attempts to ensure the financial health of the club.

Marvin noticed problems at Shady Oaks the first year it opened. In September, 1958, he agreed to incorporate the club as a nonprofit corporation with 650 shares of stock. After the sale of stock, this corporation would buy the club from Marvin for the $3.5 million Shady Oaks cost to build. A slow economy scuttled the plan, and in 1961 efforts began to merge Shady Oaks with the Fort Worth Club. When that too failed, Marvin returned to the idea of selling the club to its members.[97]

In October, 1962, Marvin helped organize Shady Oaks Country Club, Inc. Terms of the deal paid him $148,000 as a lump sum to compensate him for losses he incurred and provided a $7,000 per month fee for his continued involvement. The nonprofit corporation also set up a Board of Governors and elected a president to help manage the facility. Fred Hodge served as the first president of the corporation. This move and the hiring of Crook the next year alleviated, but did not end, the problems at Shady Oaks. In 1964 the club still lost more than $100,000.[98]

This second effort to organize Shady Oaks as a nonprofit corporation not only addressed problems of club management, it moved the members one step closer toward buying the club. According to the agreement worked out at that time, the purchase price was set at $3 million with much of that to come from the sale of new memberships. For six years, proceeds from the stock sales were placed in an escrow account. In the meantime, Marvin still ran the club with the help of the Board of Governors.[99]

Selling new memberships and convincing old members they should buy the club took time, but by 1968 Shady Oaks had enough members willing to buy shares of stock in Shady Oaks, Inc., for the deal to go through. By that point, Westover Hills was more completely developed, and new homeowners offered a good market for club memberships. Marvin also lowered the price to $2.7 million and included in the sale two pieces of property surrounded by the golf course.[100]

Between 1964 and 1968, losses at the club diminished, but still ran about $50,000 per year. This pattern continued for the first two years members owned the club. To help out, Marvin agreed to delay payment on the principle of the Club's purchase note. Eventually, Shady Oaks turned a small profit and the note was paid off after Marvin's death.[101]

Despite the fiscal problems of Shady Oaks, Marvin took great pride in the golf course and the club. He realized that the surrounding real estate earned several million dollars and that as the lots filled up the demand for club memberships would grow. He also knew that Shady Oaks made him money simply by adding to the value of those lots. He could afford to run Shady Oaks as he pleased. For him, the club and its golf course were as much a creative achievement as a moneymaking venture. The par-71 layout was 6,975 yards in length. Naturally, it had bent grass greens. Live oaks dotted the fairways planted in a type of Bermuda grass specially designed for Shady Oaks. In addition, he built a nine-hole course, probably patterned after the short course at Augusta and meant to serve as a practice facility. While having a small number of members contributed to the club's financial problems, it also made for a congenial atmosphere. Shady Oaks was Marvin's second home and the club members his second family. Selling the club for the price he received and in the manner it was accomplished took care of his first and his second families. It was in that sense characteristic of Marvin Leonard, who always sought security for those he loved.[102]

END OF AN ERA

Marvin's personal involvement in various business deals and community activities wound down with the decade. His age and his health slowed him, but his drive never failed. The people and things he loved drew his complete attention. He made the final investment in Leonards to assure its continued prosperity, moved the store and Shady Oaks into the capable hands of others, and built up his wealth with sagacious real-estate transactions. He even began work on a third golfing facility at his ranch near Tolar.

Yet as he withdrew from many activities, Fort Worth and the store missed his gentle touch. Marvin's faith in downtown rekindled interest in the central business district. Despite suburbanization, not all of Fort Worth's investment dollars flowed away from downtown in the 1960s. Willard Barr, F. W. Laughbaum, Jenkins Garrett, and others helped organize and focus the Town Hall movement in 1964. This group, supported by the Chamber of Commerce, the Downtown Association, and the mayor pushed hard for a variety of projects that would benefit greater Fort Worth. In 1965 it campaigned successfully for a local bond election to build a junior college and a downtown convention center in Fort Worth.[103]

Just as energetically, Paul and Bob Leonard and Clifton Overcash continued the modernization plan at Leonards and pursued efforts to bring customers downtown. In March, 1965, Paul Leonard proudly announced that the store had purchased its own computer, a Honeywell H-200, only the second installed in all of Fort Worth. The computer allowed Leonards to automate its billing system and credit accounts. The brothers also toyed with the idea of extending the subway system farther into the heart of downtown to the doors of the proposed convention center.[104]

The convention center was eventually built, but the wave of enthusiasm for extending the subway subsided. Because the Convention Center was at the south end of the downtown it did little to boost sales at Leonards, Stripling's, and other retailers on the opposite end of the central business district. Downtown merchants continued to lose sales to the suburbs. Meanwhile, external business opportunities grew for the O. P. Leonard family. They expanded their pecan and ranching businesses, and as the popularity of country retreats grew, developed lakeside residential areas and divided and sold some of their ranch land. They held valuable oil and gas property and owned a thriving insurance business and scattered properties throughout Fort Worth. Paul and the rest of his family recognized the need to reinvest heavily in the store to keep up with emerging retail trends but were unwilling to risk the family's entire capital base. It would mean shortchanging their growing investments in other areas. Rather than lock up their assets to make a go of suburban expansion, Paul hammered out a deal to sell the store to Charles Tandy for $8.5 million. On October 17, 1967, the local paper announced what many thought impossible: Leonards was now part of the Tandy Corporation.[105]

Paul, who continued as president of Leonards, explained the deal to employees. The O. P. Leonard family sold the Leonards name and all the stock and fixtures of the retail operation, including the subway. Paul expected "no changes in management, or in our lease agreement with those who are presently leasing department space in our store. No changes in policies or personnel are anticipated. Leonards will continue its merchandise policy of 'More Merchandise for Less Money' which has been in force since the firm was founded 49 years ago." Despite these assurances, many employees and even many customers would later reflect back on the store that they knew and remember the sale as the end of an era.[106]

Epilogue
"His Part in Our Times"

In the mid-1960s, Marvin Leonard purchased a ranch near Tolar, Texas. Having a clear plan in mind, he kept John Maddux, his real-estate advisor, from seeing the place until he had finalized the deal. He wanted no distracting voices. Although he did not play as often as he had a few years earlier, he intended to build one more golf course and to develop the adjacent land. By early 1970, his Starr Hollow Ranch featured a 2,900-yard, nine-hole course on the edge of a ninety-two-acre lake. It had its own clubhouse and a limited membership. Sketches were drawn up for the sale of lots for weekend homes.[1]

Despite worsening health, Marvin planned and worked until the end. During 1970, he was hospitalized several times and required frequent blood transfusions to combat a bleeding ulcer and cirrhosis of the liver. He died August 26, 1970, and was buried in the family mausoleum in Greenwood Cemetery in Fort Worth.[2]

Praise for Marvin Leonard and inventories of his accomplishments filled the local newspapers. The *Star-Telegram* numbered him among those few "who will take the broad and optimistic view, act upon it and make it reality." Writing in the *Press,* his friend Walter Humphrey, who had known him since 1926, pointed out, "When he died, all the many wonderful contributions he had made to the life of his community were spread out in the papers as a reminder to all of his part in our times. All the many personal things known differently to so many, could not have been. There would not have been space."[3]

Since his death, his friends and admirers have tried to sum up his contribution to retailing by insisting that Leonards pioneered many of the concepts now found in a Wal-Mart Supercenter. In the words of one, "Was not Leonards under JML's leadership an early Supercenter?" Both stores carried a wide range of merchandise, including groceries, stressed low prices, and benefited from low expenses. Sam Walton and Marvin Leonard both served as very personal symbols of their stores, men others trusted. Yet the men and their stores differed in many funda-

Marvin posed for this portrait at Colonial Country Club in May, 1970. He died in August.

mental ways. These differences offer a useful perspective on what Marvin Leonard meant to retailing and to Fort Worth.[4]

Insisting that Leonards was an early-day supercenter neglects the essential realities noted by Walter Humphrey—time and place. Marvin Leonard, whose training and background was in cash-only general stores and salvage, began business as downtown retailing entered one of its most dynamic eras, the 1920s. He left business in the 1960s as suburban shopping malls and strip centers replaced downtown stores as the hubs of trade. Through almost fifty years of doing business downtown, Marvin coped with continual changes in his competitor and customer base. From the 1920s on, national chains cut into the sales of groceries and soft goods at locally owned stores. In the 1950s, as Sears and Montgomery Wards expanded, hard lines became equally competitive. During its earliest days, rural Texans and local blue-collar families provided Leonards with the bulk of its customers. Over the years, Leonards expanded its appeal in the middle class and in some categories it sold to all classes. Yet the post–World War II decline in the rural population and the creation of rival places to shop in rural areas hurt business; so did the decline in the blue-collar work force that began in the mid-1950s. Leonards upgraded and refocused its business on the middle class. Unfortunately, the white middle class, in particular, moved farther and farther from downtown.

At about this juncture, Wal-Mart began. Sam Walton, a former chain store man, opened Walton's Five and Dime in Bentonville, Arkansas, in 1950. He took advantage of emerging demographic trends by locating stores in small towns in rural areas and eventually in suburbs. Wal-Mart helped dry up downtowns, not build them. In contrast, Marvin always insisted on remaining downtown. He also realized downtown was a total package. His business improved if other thriving merchants drew customers to the city's center. Conversely, his business declined when the other downtown merchants focused their attention on the suburbs. Instead of riding the wave of new demographic and retailing trends, as Wal-Mart did, Leonards fought them. In the 1990s few American department stores operate downtown. It is a different time. Even Marvin Leonard would have difficulty generating a profit downtown.[5]

As the post-1967 history of Leonards indicated, its strategies and business concepts did not transfer well from downtown to the suburbs. After Tandy purchased the store, it opened six remote locations, but most lost money. In January, 1974, Tandy sold Leonards to Dillard's for about $5 million. The Leonard name disappeared as all the stores became Dillard's. Eventually, the company closed the downtown branch.[6]

The downtown store had atmosphere and huge size—things that did not easily transfer to the suburbs. At its peak in the mid-1960s, Leonards operated in more than 550,000 square feet, and 350,000 of that was selling space. It employed twenty-five hundred people. For a brief time Wal-Mart experimented with Hypermarts, stores of about 225,000 square feet. It abandoned that concept because the stores were too large to manage efficiently. Supercenters require only about 125,000 to 150,000 square feet. Leonards was simply too big to copy except in another downtown. Indeed, the Hypermart experiment and Leonards' own troubles in the late 1950s and 1960s suggest that the store grew too large to manage efficiently even in downtown.[7]

This large size, however, allowed Leonards to maintain a unique atmosphere. It was a town square on a Saturday afternoon, a carnival with barkers pitching exotic merchandise, a place with red and yellow pants stacked to the ceiling. It was a place to meet and greet friends from all over town. Leonards got its personality from being one giant store owned by one family, a store whose merchandising characteristics came from one man—Marvin Leonard. Marvin realized to expand beyond one location would change forever the nature of Leonards. Even when it adopted chain store techniques in the 1950s, it was never as bureaucratic as a chain. It was experimental, flexible, decentralized, and impossible to duplicate.

When asked about what changed at Leonards when it was sold, employees had a standard response. As Elizabeth Dixon Nesbitt put it, "It was entirely different after it was sold to Tandy and then to Dillard's. The Leonards were always open to suggestions and if we needed something we were told to order it. It may not always have worked, but they let us try and always supported us."[8] Supercenters, like any chain, could never operate like Leonards because they are managed differently. Like other owners of well-managed downtown department stores, Marvin and his brother Obie "employed men and women with the qualities that saved them having to do the bossing."[9]

Then there are the questions of quality merchandise and customer service. Chains do not normally stock the wide range and high quality of hardware that Leonards always carried. Long after Model T's became scarce, Leonards still carried the spark plugs they required. In fact, as one former employee put it, "You could buy any item needed—all car parts." No supercenter and few chain hardware centers would do that. What supercenter has check cashing or package pickup to match Leonards? They may have a bank within the store but typically only cash the checks of established bank customers. In a recent survey of nineteen thousand readers of a consumer magazine, Wal-Mart Supercenters ranked twenty-nine out of thirty-five in customer satisfaction. To find out why, ask any customer standing in the long checkout lines—customer convenience does not come first at a supercenter. It always did at Leonards; Marvin demanded it.[10]

One other central difference separates Wal-Mart Supercenters or any other chain from Leonards. No chain, particularly one owned by a large number of stockholders, matches Marvin and Leonards' community contributions. Not even

Target, owned by Dayton Hudson, gives back to the many communities where it does business and adjusts to those communities in the ways that long-characterized Leonards.[11]

Marvin fit retailing to a changing customer base—adapting to Fort Worth rather than making Fort Worth adapt to a national marketing strategy. He led the way in selling to the working class and providing low prices for all during the Great Depression. Leonards "helped make life better for the poor by letting them pay on terms they could afford." As Fort Worth became a manufacturing center for the defense industry, Leonards adapted its trade to fill its customers' needs. As blacks became an increasing part of the urban landscape, Leonards led the way in erasing the stigma of segregated shopping and dining. Profit, not altruism, played the leading role in these changes, but the profit was there for all. Marvin Leonard acted while others stood on the sidelines.[12]

Marvin and the store's numerous and generous interventions aided a long list of charities. School lunch programs, the Lena Pope Home, local hospitals, educational institutions, and black and white churches all benefited from Leonards' success. Book covers, free entertainment in the park, and nights at the circus had a promotional flavor, but they also made the community a nicer place to live. Along with Toyland, these activities endeared Leonards to generations of families.

Ties between Marvin, his store, and his city were also strengthened by long involvement in real estate. Marvin constructed Colonial Country Club and Shady Oaks Country Club with profits from the store and by using the store as a source of short-term loans. When Fort Worth's population surged, the store's value secured financing for the construction and marketing of numerous subdivisions and commercial developments. The spatial arrangement of the city, the location of elite neighborhoods near golf courses and middle-class neighborhoods farther west, bear the indelible imprint of Marvin Leonard. As Ridgmar Mall and Ridgmar Square demonstrate, even suburban shopping felt his touch.

The popularity of golf and the importance of the professional tournament at Colonial also retain Marvin's imprint. He popularized golf as a spectator sport for the local community and reaffirmed it as a game to be enjoyed on a challenging course with the finest greens. His tournament continues to attract professional golfers of great stature and has proved to many that Fort Worth is not an isolated outpost devoid of sports except rodeo and football. Experts regard Colonial as the best course in Texas and one of the best in the Southwest. Every year the club awards the Leonard Trophy at the Mastercard Colonial.[13]

Leonards gave Fort Worth a special identity. Shopping at Leonards and attending fireworks displays in the park were part of the fabric of everyday life. Leonards instilled pride in Fort Worth's citizens and gave visitors something to remember.

Wal-Mart and Target cannot provide a city identity because they build the same store in every city. Without Leonards, Fort Worth's image and character changed dramatically. Margery Nordin echoed the thoughts of many when she wrote, "Downtown is really a drag since there is no Leonards."[14]

If Leonards gave something to downtown, the reverse also happened. Leonards was one of the last large, locally owned downtown department stores in the southwest—not a supercenter; not a suburban mall with multiple stores, multiple owners/managers, and multiple merchandising strategies; not just a department store. The interaction between Leonards and Fort Worth created a bigger, brassier store geared to the working and middle class. Like other such stores, however, much of its personality came from its location and its ownership.

In large measure, the impact of the store and the image it fostered was due to what Walter Humphrey called "the many personal things known differently to so many." Vera Pyle, who began work at Leonards in 1947, remembered, "My father had a severe stroke on a weekend. We called for a hospital bed on Sunday. Mr. Marvin had his furniture manager meet him at the store and arranged for the bed." Obie also contributed to the sense that caring and approachable people set the tone at Leonards. A friend told Elba Crumby "that her parents put their Christmas toys on layaway. Come Christmas Eve night and they had forgotten to get the layaway toys. By phone they got Mr. Obie, and he told them what time to come to the store on Christmas. Mr. Obie sat and talked with the people a good while." As Humphrey noted, a list of such small thoughtful gestures—each reflecting that Marvin and Obie took a personal interest in friends, employees, and customers—could go on for many pages.[15]

Part of the store's character also came from Marvin's ability to turn loose the reins of power. Had he focused totally on his store, as Sam Walton or F. W. Woolworth did, little time would have remained for small personal gestures, real-estate development, or almost anything else. Marvin was proud of the store and reveled in telling stories about its early days. Yet despite continuous emphasis on growth, Marvin had little interest in building Leonards as a permanent monument. He built it for his and for Obie's children, for their security. For the right price, he would have sold it in the 1930s or the 1940s. At some point within him the store was a vehicle, as one business associate put it in 1939, "to get your future assured."[16]

If there was a defining moment for Marvin Leonard, it may have been his father making him look for that nickel under the porch. Years of repeated insistence on saving for tomorrow left him with a lifetime drive to achieve security and a need to maintain order and control of all situations. His anxieties of the 1920s and his sale of Shady Oaks in the 1960s were part of this same package.

Of course, human beings cannot be explained quite that neatly. Marvin Leonard and his wife, Mary, had a great love for their family. As they stated in their will, "We love each of our children with all our being and desire that the benefits accruing to them from our estate shall be as equal as is possible and practical."[17] He also had unusual analytical abilities. He understood the store's performance from a few simple numbers. He could look at a piece of real estate and see what it could become.

Jim Leach often told a story that illustrated Marvin's vision. After Leach left Leonards, he served as a consultant or handled special tasks for Marvin just as Carl Bruner had. One day in 1966, Marvin asked Leach, who had recently sold a ranch in Parker County, to go out and look at a ranch near Tolar in Hood County. The request surprised Leach because Marvin usually spurned any real estate outside of the city. He responded, "Why not take Mr. Obie, he knows all about ranches?" Marvin insisted that he wanted Leach to accompany him and the two drove southwest fifty-five miles to the ranch.[18]

Marvin had learned about the property about a year before when he first began to think about buying a ranch. He knew the owner was financially troubled and figured that if he waited he could get the place for a good price. The ranch was run down, overgrazed, and fences and wells needed repairs. Still, the land was good. It had running water and a scenic location. As he drove Leach through the property, Marvin pointed to a cliff where according to legend the horse thief Belle Starr once camped. A stream flowed at the base of the cliff. He asked Leach how much it would cost to build a dam from the cliff to a point some distance away. Leach replied it would cost about $100,000, and wanted to know what he had in mind. Marvin replied that building a dam would create about a one-hundred-acre lake and provide water for a nice golf course. He outlined where he would put the lake and the course and where homes and a club house might go. An incredulous Leach asked why he wanted to build a course so far from town—no one would come that far from town to play. Marvin replied, "If you build a good course, they will come to play it." He thought big and thought long into the future, but as the success of his many projects demonstrated, he also thought carefully. The ranch was not an extravagance, but part of one more carefully laid plan. When he heard the news, an astonished Jenkins Garrett asked, "Are you going to become a rancher?" With a glint in his eye Marvin replied, "No, I've got some plans." He saw the potential of the valley as a weekend retreat for people like him.[19]

Marvin purchased the ranch and named it Starr Hollow after Belle Starr. About every third day for the four years before he died, Leach drove Marvin out to Starr Hollow. Leach supervised the mending of fences, the repair of water wells, and the stocking of the land with Black Angus. Marvin focused on the lake, golf course, and club house. He also built a house for his family that showed others the land's potential. He was near closing on several lot sales and had plans for more when death ended his last venture. He demonstrated once again that not only did he have vision, he had the capacity to follow through, to get things done.[20]

Starr Hollow remains in the Leonard family and is consistently ranked as one of the best nine-hole courses in Texas. Those who play on it are reminded of the care, energy, and creativity of its builder. In some ways, the link between Marvin Leonard and Fort Worth also continues. The physical makeup of the city—neighborhoods, golf courses, hotels, and shopping centers—bears his mark. Race relations in the city are not perfect, but they are better than they might have been without the peaceful and early integration of downtown stores and eating establishments. Those imprints, ironically, far outlived the store that made them possible.

While the store is gone and with it perhaps the possibility of its kind ever existing again, the managerial style of Marvin Leonard still offers lessons for our time. He took care to select the right person for a job, a man or woman who had initiative but would work within his general merchandising philosophy. Then he acted according to one of his favorite sayings: "You catch more flies with sugar than vinegar."[21] He treated those who worked with him with respect, got out of their way, and let them do their job.

Notes

Introduction

1. *Fort Worth Star-Telegram* (hereafter *Star-Telegram*), Aug. 31, 1948, p. 29. By 1940, Leonards was such a part of Fort Worth that it was commonly called "the store." See Marty Leonard interview by Victoria Buenger (VB) and Walter Buenger (WB), May 20, 1997; Larry R. Ford, *Cities and Buildings: Skyscrapers, Skid Rows, and Suburbs* (Baltimore: Johns Hopkins University Press, 1994), pp. 108–12.
2. *Star-Telegram*, Aug. 31, 1948, "Leonards Section."
3. Rosen Heights Baptist Seniors Group interview by VB and WB, Mar. 23, 1995; St. James Baptist Prayer Group interview by WB, May 29, 1996; Lillie Bell Carter interview by WB, Jan. 9, 1995. Also see Bob Ray Sanders, "Toyland Offered Children Warmth in a Cold Season," *Star-Telegram*, Dec. 25, 1994.
4. Joe Cano interview by WB, Feb. 8, 1994; Jenkins Garrett (JG) interview by WB, Feb. 8, 1994; JG interview by WB, Apr. 14, 1994; JG interview by VB and WB, Apr. 21, 1994; JG interview by WB, Feb. 15, 1996; Vergal Bourland interview by WB, Feb. 19, 1994; Willard Barr interview by WB, Apr. 14, 1994; Benny Rubin interview by VB and WB, Apr. 21, 1994; Tex Moncrief interview by WB, June 20, 1994.
5. Marty Leonard interview by VB and WB, July 14, 1994; Marty Leonard interview, May 20, 1997; Juanita Branham interview by VB, Feb. 19, 1994; Lloyd and Ruth Shockley interview by VB and Tom Born, June 1, 1994; Shockley interview by WB, June 28, 1995; Charles Ringler interview by WB, Apr. 14, 1994; Ringler interview by WB, Feb. 16, 1995.
6. On the most famous "Mr." see D. B. Hardemann and Donald C. Bacon, *Rayburn: A Biography* (Austin: Texas Monthly Press, 1987).
7. On the importance of department stores, see William Leach, *Land of Desire: Merchants, Power, and the Rise of a New American Culture*, pp. 134–38; Henry Givens Baker, *Rich's of Atlanta: The Story of a Store Since 1867;* Celestine Sibley, *Dear Store: An Affectionate Portrait of Rich's.*
8. For an introduction to retailing, see Peter Samson, "The Department Store, Its Past and Its Future: A Review Article," *Business History Review (BHR)* 55 (Spring, 1981): 26–34; Leach, *Land of Desire;* Susan Porter Benson, *Counter Cultures: Saleswomen, Managers, and Customers in American Department Stores, 1890–1940;* Susan Strasser, *Satisfaction Guaranteed: The Making of the American Mass Market;* Richard Tedlow, *New and Improved: The Story of Mass Marketing in America;* William Greer, *America the Bountiful: How the Supermarket Came to Main Street;* Stanley C. Hollander, "Retailing: Cause or Effect," in *Emerging Concepts in Marketing,* ed. William S. Decker; Stanley C. Hollander, *Restraints upon Retail Competition;* John Benson and Gareth Shaw, eds., *The Evolution of Retail Systems, 1800–1914.*

9. Leach, *Land of Desire*, pp. 15–152.
10. JG interview, Apr. 14, 1994; *Star-Telegram*, Aug. 31, 1948, "Leonards Section"; July 14, 1979.
11. *Star-Telegram*, Apr. 1, 1962. Also see Alan R. Raucher, "Dime Store Chains: The Making of Organization Men, 1880–1940," *BHR* 65 (Spring, 1991): 130–63; Godfrey Lebhar, *Chain Stores in America, 1859–1950;* James Brough, *The Woolworths*.
12. J. B. Moates interview by Robert A. Calvert and Larry D. Hill, Feb. 8, 1994; JG interview by VB and WB, Mar. 7, 1997. Also see Ralph Cook and J. B. Moates interview by VB and WB, Aug. 8, 1994; Connie Powell and Gayle Leonard interview by WB, Aug. 25, 1994.
13. Raucher, "Dime Store Chains," 130–63.
14. Ray Shea interview by VB and WB, June 11, 1994.
15. JG interview, Mar. 7, 1997.

Chapter 1

1. Miranda Leonard interview by VB and WB, Oct. 27–28, 1996; "33rd Annual Golden Deeds Banquet, Exchange Club of Fort Worth, 1962," Fort Worth Club, Apr. 27, 1962; *Fort Worth Press* (hereafter *Press*), Aug. 28, 1970, p. 8. Also see *Star-Telegram*, Aug. 27, 28, 1970, pp. 1, 18; *Press*, Aug. 27, 1970, pp. 1, 3. The celebration of the Leonard brothers' rags to riches lives was evident as early as 1932. See "Success of Store Due to 2 Farm Boys," *Star-Telegram*, Dec. 12, 1932.
2. Marvin Leonard left few letters behind. The major published sources on his life are Jim Trinkle, "Golf's Magnanimous Skinflint," *Golf Digest* 22 (May, 1970): 48–50, 70–71; Neil M. Clark, "Brother Act," *The Saturday Evening Post*, June 24, 1944, pp. 14–15, 59–63; Ruel McDaniel, "How Those Amazing Leonard Brothers Gross $8,000,000 a Year," *American Business* 8 (Oct., 1938): 22–24, 48–49; Eugene Whitmore, "The Miracle Merchants of Ft. Worth," *American Business* 19 (Apr., 1949): 8–9, 36–38; *Time*, Sept. 6, 1948, p. 84; Feb. 22, 1963, p. 44. Also see John Marvin Leonard, "Certificate of Death," Aug. 26, 1970, Fort Worth #2817.
3. William Humphrey, *Farther Off from Heaven*, p. 54.
4. Bureau of the Census, *Thirteenth Census of the United States: 1910, Population*, vol. 3 (Washington, D.C., 1913), p. 780; *Star-Telegram*, Dec. 4, 1932.
5. *Census: 1910, Population*, vol. 3, p. 810; U.S. Department of Agriculture, *Soil Survey of Cass County Texas*, 1937; *Texas Almanac and State Industrial Guide, 1904*, pp. 231–32.
6. *Texas Almanac and State Industrial Guide, 1904*, p. 92.
7. On the economic and demographic development of Texas in the late nineteenth century, see Harry Williams, Jr., "The Development of a Market Economy in Texas: The Establishment of the Railway Network, 1836–1890" (Ph.D. dissertation, University of Texas, Austin, 1957); John S. Spratt, *The Road to Spindletop: Economic Change in Texas, 1875–1901* (Dallas: Southern Methodist University Press, 1955); Samuel Lee Evans, "Texas Agriculture, 1880–1930" (Ph.D. dissertation, University of Texas, Austin, 1960).
8. Edward L. Ayers, *The Promise of the New South: Life After Reconstruction* (New York: Oxford University Press, 1992), pp. 55–80; Harold D. Woodman, *King Cotton and His Retainers: Financing and Marketing the Cotton Crop of the South, 1800–1925* (Lexington: University of Kentucky Press, 1968), pp. 243–359; L. Tuffly Ellis, "The

Revolutionizing of the Texas Cotton Trade, 1866–1885," *Southwestern Historical Quarterly (SHQ)* 73 (Apr., 1970): 478–508.

9. Emma Clementine Hill, "Certificate of Death," Dec. 26, 1917, Texas Department of Health #33984; O. J. T. Leonard, "Certificate of Death," June 28, 1927, Texas Department of Health #21520; John Leonard, Cass County Property Tax Receipt, Leonard Collection; Jo Ann Vachule, "Family Tree," in "The Brother Act," typescript, 1988, Leonard Collection. On the movement of southerners into Texas, see Terry G. Jordan, "A Century and a Half of Ethnic Change in Texas, 1836–1986," *SHQ* 89 (Apr., 1986): 385–90.

10. Vachule, "Brother Act," pp. 3–5; John and Clementine Leonard to Brothers and Sisters, June 12, 1890, Leonard Collection; Ron Tyler, Douglas E. Barnett, and Roy R. Barkley, eds., *The New Handbook of Texas* (hereafter *New HOT*), vol. 3 (Austin: The Texas State Historical Association, 1996), p. 1092; Charles P. Zlatkovich, *Texas Railroads: A Record of Construction and Abandonment* (Austin: Bureau of Business Research and the Texas State Historical Association, 1981), p. 76.

11. *Jefferson (Tex.) Jimplecute* (hereafter *Jimplecute*), May 5, 1911; John David Scott, "Obie," typescript, 1983, Leonard Collection, pp. 16–22.

12. *Texas Almanac and State Industrial Guide, 1904*, pp. 217–333.

13. Scott, "Obie," pp. 21–33; Vachule, "Brother Act," pp. 5–10.

14. Emma Enola Leonard Moulton interview by John David Scott, 1983, in Scott, "Obie," pp. 118–28. Quote on p. 119. Also see Hugh and Laura Mae Tyree interview by WB, July 1, 1994. (Laura Tyree is Enola's daughter.)

15. On Marvin's memories of farm life, see Miranda Leonard interview; JG interview, Apr. 14, 1994. Also see William A. Owens, *This Stubborn Soil*, pp. 5–269; Humphrey, *Farther Off from Heaven*, pp. 54–57, 76–80, 101–72; Jack Temple Kirby, *Rural Worlds Lost: The American South, 1920–1960* (Baton Rouge: Louisiana State University Press, 1987), pp. 25–50; Pete Daniel, *Breaking the Land: The Transformation of Cotton, Tobacco, and Rice Cultures Since 1880* (Urbana: University of Illinois Press, 1986), pp. 3–22.

16. Moulton interview, pp. 119–26; Miranda Leonard interview. Also see speech by O. P. Leonard to Leonard Brothers employees, circa 1938, in Marvin Leonard Papers (LP); Owens, *Stubborn Soil*, pp. 14–269.

17. Moulton interview, pp. 121–28; Tyree interview. Also see Scott, "Obie," pp. 23–26; speech by O. P. Leonard, 1938.

18. *Census: 1910, Population*, vol. 3, p. 780; *Census: 1910, Agriculture*, vol. 7, p. 660; Walter L. Buenger, "'This Wonder Age': The Economic Transformation of Northeast Texas, 1900–1930, *SHQ* 98 (Apr., 1995): 519–49.

19. Moulton interview, p. 126; *Census: 1910, Agriculture*, vol. 7, p. 660; Bureau of the Census, *Fourteenth Census: 1920. Agriculture*, vol. 6, part 2 (Washington, D.C., 1922), p. 667.

20. On the difficulty of acquiring land, see Shockley interview, June 28, 1995. Lloyd Shockley, who later worked for Leonards, was born in 1905 and grew up in neighboring Morris County. For a firsthand account of the class system among Northeast Texas whites in the early twentieth century, see Humphrey, *Further Off from Heaven*, pp. 101–228.

21. Miranda Leonard interview; "Success of Store Due to 2 Farm Boys," *Star-Telegram*, Dec. 4, 1932.

22. Madelon Leonard Bradshaw interview by VB, June 8, 1997.
23. Owens, *Stubborn Soil*, p. 110. Also see Vachule, "Brother Act," pp. 8–10.
24. *Atlanta (Tex.) Citizens Journal* (hereafter *Citizens Journal*), Nov. 21, 1907, p. 1.
25. One letter survives from John and Tiny to their siblings. While a few words are misspelled, it demonstrates both had at least some education. See John and Clemetine Leonard to Brothers and Sisters, June 12, 1890. Also see Moulton interview, pp. 118–28; Scott, "Obie," p. 24.
26. *Cass County Sun* (hereafter *Sun*), Feb. 25, Mar. 17, 1908, pp. 3–4; *Atlanta (Tex.) News*, June 25, 1908, p. 4.
27. Miranda Leonard interview; Ringler interviews, Apr. 14, 1994; Feb. 16, 1995; JG interview by VB and WB, May 12–13, 1997. Also see speech by O. P. Leonard, 1938.
28. Tyree interview; *Sun*, May 26, 1908, pp. 1–4; *Citizens Journal*, May 21, 1908, p. 1; *Atlanta News*, Apr. 9, May 14, 21, Aug. 27, 1908.
29. *Sun*, July 6, 1909, p. 4. Also see Buenger, "Wonder Age," pp. 521–33.
30. *Sun*, Sept. 8, 1908, p. 4. For a broader view of this phenomenon, see Dewey W. Grantham, *Southern Progressivism: The Reconciliation of Progress and Tradition* (Knoxville: University of Tennessee Press, 1983).
31. *Sun*, May 4, 1909, p. 4. Also see *Citizens Journal*, May 7, 1908; *Sun*, June 30, 1908; May 4, 1909; *Omaha (Tex.) Breeze* (hereafter *Breeze*), Aug. 24, 1910, p. 2; *Jimplecute*, Apr. 17, 1913, pp. 1–3; *Atlanta News*, Mar. 19, Oct. 1, 8, 1908.
32. *Jimplecute*, Sept. 2, 1915, pp. 1–3; *Pittsburg (Tex.) Gazette*, June 8, 1917, p. 2. On ritualized violence as a form of race control, see W. Fitzhugh Brundage, *Lynching in the New South: Georgia and Virginia, 1880–1930* (Urbana and Chicago: University of Illinois Press, 1993).
33. *Sun*, Jan. 5, 1909, p. 1.
34. *Sun*, June 29, 1909, p. 2. The editor of the nearby *Atlanta News* ran a long series of articles on the new status of women and on changing values. Many cited *The Ladies Home Journal*. See *Atlanta News*, Apr. 9, 1908, to July 2, 1908. Also see *Breeze*, Aug. 5, 1908, p. 2; Jan. 26, 1910; May 1, 1912, p. 1; *Pittsburg Gazette*, Jan. 18, 25, 1910, p. 2; May 10, 1912, p. 6; *Jimplecute*, Oct. 1, 1914, p. 1; *Sulphur Springs (Tex.) Gazette*, Aug. 7, 1914, p. 10.
35. Election Returns, 1887, 1911, Secretary of State Papers, Texas State Library. Also see Gould, *Progressives & Prohibitionists*, pp. 28–57; "PROHIBITION RALLY A BIG SUCCESS!" *Sulphur Springs Gazette*, July 23, 1911, p. 1; *Jimplecute*, Mar. 3, 10, 17, 1911, pp. 1–4; *Pittsburg Gazette*, Mar. 24, Aug. 4, 11, 1887, p. 2; Mar. 25, June 24, 1904; *Breeze*, June 28, 1911 p. 2; Marty Leonard interview, May 20, 1997.
36. *Breeze*, June 7, 1911, p. 2; *Texas Almanac and State Industrial Guide, 1914*, pp. 137–39.
37. *Census: 1910, Population*, vol. 3, pp. 795–96; Pate, *Livestock Legacy*, pp. 3–50; Michael Quinley Hooks, "The Struggle for Dominance: Urban Rivalry in North Texas, 1870–1910" (Ph.D. dissertation, Texas Tech University, 1979).
38. Scott, "Obie," pp. 27–28; Vachule, "Brother Act," pp. 9–10.
39. *Star-Telegram*, Dec. 29, 1929; "Success of Store Due to 2 Farm Boys," *Star-Telegram*, Dec. 4, 1932; Amos Melton, "Marvin Leonard," *Star-Telegram*, May 21, 1941.
40. *Sun*, Jan. 12, 1909, p. 1; *Jimplecute*, Jan. 20, 1911, p. 1. Also see *Jimplecute*, Sept. 19, Oct. 17, 1912, pp. 2–3.

41. Department Stores, "Works Progress Administration Guide to Forth Worth," unpublished manuscript compiled between 1938 and 1941 (Local History Division, Fort Worth Public Library), p. 16556.
42. Owens, *Stubborn Soil*, p. 232. Also see JG interview, Apr. 14, 1994; Marty Leonard interview, May 20, 1997.
43. *Texas Almanac and State Industrial Guide, 1929*, p. 106; Kirby, *Rural Worlds Lost*, pp. 275–333. According to Obie, Marvin worked in Dallas three or four years before opening the store in 1918. See speech by O. P. Leonard, 1938.
44. Speech by O. P. Leonard, 1938. Also see "Success of Store," *Star-Telegram*, Dec. 4, 1932; Vachule, "Brother Act," pp. 10–11.
45. Melton, "Marvin Leonard"; JG interview, Apr. 14, 1994; Vachule, "Brother Act," pp. 12–13.
46. Miranda Leonard interview.
47. Chamber of Commerce, "Petroleum," in *Fort Worth, 1924* (Fort Worth: Chamber of Commerce, 1924), pp. 5–8; *Star-Telegram*, Feb. 22, Dec. 15, 17, 1918; *The Story of Fort Worth from Outpost to Metropolis* (Fort Worth: Fort Worth National Bank, 1973).
48. Speech by O. P. Leonard, 1938; Vachule, "Brother Act," pp. 10–13.
49. Moulton interview, p. 123. Also see Vachule, "Brother Act," pp. 10–13.
50. Marty Leonard interview, July 14, 1994.
51. Walter R. Humphrey, "Quiet Measure of Greatness," *Press*, Sept. 13, 1970, 26A. Also see Shea interview; Stayley McBrayer interview by WB, June 20, 1994; Moncrief interview; M. J. Neely interview by WB, June 21, 1994.
52. This fits the pattern of what one student of retailing calls the great "merchant princes." See Hollander, "Retailing: Cause or Effect," pp. 228–29.
53. Owens, *Stubborn Soil*; Humphrey, *Farther Off from Heaven*.
54. Humphrey, "Quiet Measure of Greatness," 26A. Also see Moncrief interview.
55. *Press*, Sept. 13, 1970, p. 26A. Also see JG interview, Feb. 15, 1996; Bobby Webber interview by WB, Aug. 18, 1995.

CHAPTER 2

1. Vachule, "Brother Act," pp. 12–13.
2. *Star-Telegram*, Mar. 23, July 23, 1923. Also see Bradstreet Report, "Leonard Brothers," Aug. 20, 1927, LP; speech by O. P. Leonard, 1938.
3. On variety stores, see Simon S. Kuznets, *Cyclical Fluctuations: Retail and Wholesale Trade United States, 1919–1925*, pp. 20–33.
4. *Star-Telegram*, Sept. 30, 1928.
5. *The Whisper*, Nov. 13, 1929.
6. *Press*, Nov. 21, 1927; Oliver Knight, *Fort Worth: Outpost of the Trinity* (Fort Worth: Texas Christian University Press, 1990), pp. 155–205; L. M. Barton, *A Study of 81 Principal American Markets*; Karl Everett Ashburn, "Fort Worth's Relation to the Texas Cotton Industry" (M.A. thesis, Texas Christian University, 1928); Clarence Arnold Thompson, "Some Factors Contributing to the Growth of Fort Worth" (M.A. thesis, University of Texas, Austin, 1933).
7. Knight, *Fort Worth*, p. 165; Chamber of Commerce, *Fort Worth, 1924*.
8. In 1902, there were no calves, but there were 79,293 hogs, 9,767 sheep, and 4,872

horse and mules sold at Fort Worth's stockyards. This compares to 280,515 calves, 762,486 hogs, 334,596 sheep, and 78,881 horses and mules sold in 1918. See Chamber of Commerce, *Fort Worth, 1924*, p. 12.

9. *Census: 1920, Agriculture*, vol. 6, part 2, pp. 664–86; Bureau of the Census, *Census of Agriculture: 1925*, part 2 (Washington, D.C., 1927) pp. 1140–70; Bureau of the Census, *Fifteenth Census of the United States: 1930, Agriculture*, vol. 2, part 2 (Washington, D.C., 1932), pp. 1424–45; Gary L. Nall, "Panhandle Farming in the 'Golden Age' of American Agriculture," *Panhandle Plains Historical Review* 46 (1973): 94–112; Donald E. Green, *Land of the Underground Rain: Irrigation on the Texas High Plains, 1910–1970* (Austin: University of Texas Press, 1973), pp. 100–44; Walter L. Buenger, "World War I and Northeast Texas," *Locus* 8 (Spring, 1996): 114–16; "Monnig Dry Goods Co. Twenty-Third Anniversary Section," *Star-Telegram*, Apr. 7, 1912; *Star-Telegram*, Jan. 1, Nov. 25, 1928.

10. *Star-Telegram*, Dec. 19, 1915; Nov. 10, 1918; *Story of Fort Worth;* Roger M. Olien and Diana Davids Olien, *Wildcatters: Texas Independent Oilmen* (Austin: Texas Monthly Press, 1984), pp. 12–42; Richard R. Moore, *West Texas After the Discovery of Oil: A Modern Frontier* (Austin: Jenkins Publishing, 1971), pp. 1–87.

11. Fort Worth's population grew from 73,312 in 1910 to 106,482 in 1920. See Bureau of the Census, *Fourteenth Census of the United States: 1920, Population*, vol. 1 (Washington, D.C., 1921), p. 304. On the oil boom's impact, see *Star-Telegram*, Nov. 3, 10, 17, Dec. 1, 1918; Albert W. Atwood, "Rainbow's End," *The Saturday Evening Post*, Dec. 28, 1918, pp. 22, 32, 35. For the best scholarly treatment of the boom in Fort Worth, see Roger M. Olien and Diana Davids Olien, *Easy Money: Oil Promoters and Investors in the Jazz Age* (Chapel Hill: University of North Carolina Press, 1990), pp. 73–103.

12. *Star-Telegram*, Dec. 15, 1918; Knight, *Fort Worth*, p. 184.

13. Miranda Leonard interview; Vachule, "Brother Act," p. 18.

14. Clark, "Brother Act," p. 14. Also see *Star-Telegram*, Oct. 30, 1949.

15. On the store's opening and G. T. Leonard's role, see speech by O. P. Leonard, 1938; Vachule, "Brother Act," pp. 17–26; Scott, "Obie," pp. 35–36. Also see Margery Leonard interview by WB, Jan. 9, 1995; Tyree interview.

16. Margery Leonard interview; Tyree interview. Also see Scott, "Obie," pp. 65–67; Vachule, "Brother Act," pp. 19–21; *Star-Telegram*, Apr. 20, 1923, p. 4.

17. *Star-Telegram*, June 30, 1920, p. 6.

18. *Star-Telegram*, Sept. 19, 1920; speech by O. P. Leonard, 1938. Also see *Star-Telegram*, Jan. 1, 1919, to Dec. 31, 1919.

19. Interview with JG, Marty Leonard, and Madelon Leonard Bradshaw by WB, Sept. 17, 1997. Also see Reed Sass, "Since 1873: The Story of Forth Worth National Bank," typescript, 1952 (Local History Division, Fort Worth Public Library).

20. For an introduction to traditional southern storekeeping, see Ayers, *Promise of the New South*, pp. 81–103.

21. On Northeast Texas, see *Jimplecute*, Jan. 20, Feb. 10, 1911.

22. *Star-Telegram*, Dec. 20, 1918. Also see *Star-Telegram*, Jan. 5, Apr. 25, 1919; Feb. 27, Mar. 5, 12, 26, Nov. 5, 1920.

23. Kuznets, *Cyclical Fluctuations*, p. 7.

24. Quote from Vachule, "Brother Act," p. 20.

25. The rising cost of living was a frequent topic of news articles and advertising copy in Aug., 1919. See the *Star-Telegram*, Aug. 2, 6, 7, 1919.

26. *Star-Telegram*, Oct. 18, 1920, p. 3. For the first ad, see *Star-Telegram*, Sept. 19, 1920, p. 5.
27. *Star-Telegram*, May 12, Sept. 23, Oct. 21, 1921; Marty Leonard interview, May 20, 1997; "Agreement Between J. Marvin Leonard and Enola Leonard," Aug. 3, 1934, LP.
28. *Star-Telegram*, Oct. 25, 1918; Jan. 31, May 30, July 11, 1919; Jan. 11, Feb. 13, 27, Apr. 9, 18, July 30, 1920; Nov. 17, 1921.
29. *Star-Telegram*, Mar. 12, 1920, p. 13.
30. *Star-Telegram*, Feb. 4, 1921, p. 14.
31. *Star-Telegram*, Dec. 2, 1921 p. 6.
32. Piggly Wiggly bought newspaper space to describe alleged price fixing by two local bread companies who refused to deliver bread to its stores because it cut prices. See *Star-Telegram*, Aug. 30, 1922.
33. *Star-Telegram*, Feb. 9, 16, 1923. Also see *Star-Telegram*, Feb. 28, 1923.
34. *Star-Telegram*, July 3, 6, 9, 1923; Jan. 13, 18, 1924.
35. Speech by O. P. Leonard, 1938.
36. Ibid.
37. Ibid.
38. John Maddux interview by VB and WB, June 10, 1994.
39. *Star-Telegram*, May 11, 1923, p. 28.
40. Speech by O. P. Leonard, 1938.
41. *Star-Telegram*, May 30, June 1, 1924; Jan. 3, June 4, 5, 28, 1925; Jan. 1, 1926.
42. *Star-Telegram*, Jan. 3, June 4, 5, 28, 1925.
43. *Star-Telegram*, July 17, 1925.
44. *Star-Telegram*, Jan. 12, 1926, p. 1.
45. Ibid.
46. Bureau of the Census, *Fourteenth Census of the United States: Manufactures, 1919*, vol. 9 (Washington, D.C., 1923), p. 1456; Bureau of the Census, *Biennial Census of Manufactures: 1925* (Washington, D.C., 1928), p. 1467; *Star-Telegram*, Nov. 25, 1928; *Fourteenth Census of the United States: 1920, Population*, vol. 3, p. 1025; Bureau of the Census, *Fifteenth Census of the United States: 1930, Population*, vol. 1 (Washington, D.C., 1931), pp. 1063–86; *Fifteenth Census: 1930, Population*, vol. 3, part 2, p. 1082.
47. *Star-Telegram*, Jan. 23, 1927, sec. 3, p. 1; Jan. 27, 1927, p. 20.
48. *Star-Telegram*, May 11, 1927, p. 12.
49. *Star-Telegram*, May 3, 1927, p. 1; Aug. 3, 1927, p. 1.
50. *Star-Telegram*, Aug. 24, 30, Sept. 8, 23, 1927.
51. *Star-Telegram*, Jan. 1, 1928, p. 1.
52. *Star-Telegram*, July 1, 1927, p. 13. Also see *Star-Telegram*, May 13, July 8, 1927.
53. *Star-Telegram*, Jan. 11, 1926; *The Whisper*, Nov., 1929; James Blair, "Former Employee Questionnaire (FEQ), #412," July 5, 1995.
54. *The Whisper*, Nov., 1929, pp. 1–5.
55. Clark, "Brother Act," p. 14.
56. *Star-Telegram*, Aug. 5, 25, Oct. 26, 1925.
57. Bradstreet Report, "Leonard Brothers," Aug. 20, 1927, LP; *Star-Telegram*, Jan. 1, 1928.
58. Margery Leonard interview.
59. Ibid. The real name of Fort Worth's minor league baseball team was the Panthers, but they were commonly called the Cats. See JG interviews, Feb. 8, 1994; Apr. 14, 1994; Apr. 21, 1994.

60. Tyree interview; Moulton interview, pp. 118–28.
61. The best overview of the rise of department stores is Leach, *Land of Desire*, pp. 15–262.
62. Barton, *81 Principal American Markets*, pp. 109–10, lists sixty-seven men's clothing stores, forty-four women's clothing stores, and the same number of department stores doing business in Fort Worth in 1925. Also see *Star-Telegram*, Dec. 15, 1918.
63. Boris Emmet, *Department Stores: Recent Policies, Costs, and Profits*, p. viii.
64. *Star-Telegram*, Jan. 23, 24, Apr. 18, May 16, June 8, 18, July 13, Oct. 26, 1919; Jan. 4, Feb. 8, Apr. 8, 9, Aug. 15, 1920; Jan. 9, 16, Apr. 14, July 7, 8, Sept. 16, Nov. 3, 16, 1921; Feb. 15, May 10, 1922.
65. In June, 1920, the *Star-Telegram*'s circulation reached 75,000 daily and 90,000 on Sunday. The *Press*, a Scripps-Howard paper, began publication in 1921. The *Record* was sold to the *Star-Telegram* by William Randolph Hearst in 1924. See Jerry Flemmons, *Amon: The Life of Amon Carter, Sr. of Texas* (Austin: Jenkins Publishing, 1978), pp. 125–69.
66. Observations about newspaper advertising in this paragraph and those to come are drawn from ads carried in the *Star-Telegram*, 1918–28.
67. See ads in the *Star-Telegram*, 1918–28.
68. A 1924 Stripling's ad claimed that the store had added resident buyers in London, Paris, Berlin, Brussels, Milan, Barcelona, and Chemnitz to its list of domestic buying agents. See *Star-Telegram*, June 1, 1924. Monnig's bought most of its clothing and dry goods out of New York and its hard line goods in Chicago, St. Louis, Detroit, Philadelphia, and Boston. See Otto Monnig, General Manager of Monnig Dry Goods Company to Miss Betty Jane Jones, Jan. 11, 1934 in Box 3, #7 Business History, Miscellaneous Manuscripts, Local History Division, Forth Worth Public Library.
69. In 1920, the following stores announced that they would close at 1:00 P.M. through July and August: Stripling Company, Sanger Bros., Monnig Dry Goods Company, L. G. Gilbert, Jackson's, The Fair, Snaman & Co., O. H. Simpson, The Vogue, Norvell Corsett Shop, S. Breacher, Colton's, Gernsbacher Bros., Gans Company, The Fisher Company, The Empress, S. Bernhard, Cheney's, Miss Beulah Rucker, Seagal's, Field-Lippman Piano Co., Ladd Furniture Company, Pemberton Furniture Company, Loeb's, E. I. White & Company, C. C. Coleman, N. E. Rubin, J. N. Reagan, The Popular, Fakes & Company, Brooder's, L. A. Barnes & Company, E. R. Conner, and The Style Shop. See *Star-Telegram*, June 20, 1920 p. 6. J. C. Penney closed at 1:00 on Wednesdays and remained open regular hours on Saturdays. See *Star-Telegram*, July 9, 1920, p. 3. In the early 1920s, Stripling's added drugs, radios and gramophones, wall paper, draperies, rugs, floral, nursery, books, stationery, and a bargain basement. See *Star-Telegram*, July 13, 1919; June 1, 1924.
70. *Star-Telegram*, July 17, 1919.
71. *Star-Telegram*, Nov. 21, 1919, p. 2.
72. On the company's wholesale operation, see Monnig's ad in the *Star-Telegram*, Mar. 2, 1924, sec. 2, p. 6. For Monnig's offer to West Texas merchants, see *Star-Telegram*, Aug. 7, 1921; Otto Monnig to Jones, Jan. 11, 1934.
73. *Star-Telegram*, June 28, 1925, sec. 3, p. 22. Also see *Star-Telegram*, Nov. 23, 1919, p. 5; Jan. 11, 1920; July 6, 1921; Sept. 10, 1924.
74. More than half of J. C. Penney's stores were in towns of five thousand or fewer people in 1929. See Raucher, "Dime Store Chains," 130–63.

75. *Star-Telegram,* May 4, 1924, p. 1. Also see *Star-Telegram,* Apr. 23, 1920, p. 22; Sept. 10, 1920, p. 9; Oct. 1, 1922.
76. On Shaw's Jewelry, see *Star-Telegram,* Oct. 25, 1923, p. 6. On Kinney's, see *Star-Telegram,* Apr. 17, 1924, p. 9. On Kress's, see *Star-Telegram,* July 12, 1924, p. 7. On Western Auto, see *Star-Telegram,* Jan. 20, 1925, p. 11.
77. Emmet, *Department Stores,* p. 72. Emmet cites the 58 percent loss figure in the Harvard study on p. 10.
78. Emmet, *Department Stores,* pp. 9–83; Benson, *Counter Cultures,* pp. 31–74.
79. *Star-Telegram,* Aug. 7, 1924, p. 4. Also see *Star-Telegram,* Nov. 18, 1923, sec. 3, p. 7.
80. Otto Monnig to Jones, Jan. 11, 1934. Monnig's new three-story building (100,000 square feet) had 150 feet of frontage on Throckmorton, 125 feet on Houston, and 200 feet on Fifth Avenue. See *Star-Telegram,* Mar. 9, 1924, p. 1.
81. *Star-Telegram,* June 28, 1925, sec. 3, p. 29.
82. JG interview, May 12–13, 1997; Rubin interview.
83. *Star-Telegram,* Feb. 9, Mar. 9, Apr. 25, 1927.
84. *Star-Telegram,* June, 1927.
85. *Star-Telegram,* Nov. 20, 27, 1927.

CHAPTER 3

1. "Success of Store Due to 2 Farm Boys," *Star-Telegram,* Dec. 4, 1932.
2. Margery Leonard interview; Scott, "Obie," pp. 37–86.
3. O. J. T. Leonard, "Certificate of Death," June 28, 1927, Texas Department of Health, #21520; Margery Leonard interview; Tyree interview; *Sun,* May 26, 1908, p. 4.
4. Tyree interview; Moncrief interview; Moulton interview, pp. 118–28. Also see *Star-Telegram,* June 22, 1960; Vachule, "Brother Act," pp. 26–28.
5. In a billfold found in the Leonard Papers were five membership cards for Klan No. 101 with the signature J. M. Leonard dated June, 1924, to June, 1928. On Marvin's support for prohibition, see Marty Leonard interview, May 20, 1997.
6. Shawn Lay, "Conclusion: Toward a New Historical Appraisal of the Ku Klux Klan of the 1920s," in *The Invisible Empire in the West: Toward a New Historical Appraisal of the Ku Klux Klan of the 1920s,* ed. Shawn Lay (Urbana: University of Illinois Press, 1992), p. 222.
7. *Dallas Morning News* (hereafter *Morning News*), Nov. 17, 1921; *Press,* May 3, July 24, 1922; July 1, Sept. 8, 1924; July 23, 1926. Also see Charles C. Alexander, *Crusade for Conformity: The Ku Klux Klan in Texas, 1920–1930* (Houston: Texas Gulf Coast Historical Association, 1962), pp. 1–14; Charles C. Alexander, *The Ku Klux Klan in the Southwest* (Lexington: University of Kentucky Press, 1965), pp. 1–54.
8. *Press,* Mar. 29, 1923. Also see Tyler, Barnett, and Barkley, *New HOT,* vol. 2, p. 904; vol. 3, pp. 1165–66; vol. 4, p. 393; *Press,* Feb. 23, 1924.
9. Leonard J. Moore, "Historical Interpretations of the 1920s Klan: The Traditional View and Recent Revisions," in *The Invisible Empire in the West,* ed. Lay, pp. 17–38; Norman D. Brown, *Hood, Bonnet, and Little Brown Jug: Texas Politics, 1921–1928* (College Station: Texas A&M Press, 1984), pp. 50–252; Knight, *Fort Worth,* pp. 196–97; Steven A. Reich, "Soldiers of Democracy: Black Texans and the Fight for Citizenship, 1917–1921," *Journal of American History* 82 (Mar., 1996): 1503.
10. *Star-Telegram,* Aug. 7, 1921.

11. *Press*, Dec. 3, 1924. Also see *Press*, Feb. 17, 1922.
12. *Press*, July 24, Sept. 28, 1922; *Fort Worth American Citizen*, Apr. 13, 1923; Alexander, *Ku Klux Klan in the Southwest*, pp. 92–127.
13. *Press*, Sept. 22, 1924.
14. *Star-Telegram*, Nov. 7, 1924.
15. *Press*, Aug. 1, 5, 1925.
16. *Press*, Mar. 11, June 28, 30, July 1, 3, 4, Aug. 21, Sept. 3, 8, 1924; *Star-Telegram*, Mar. 14, 1924; Aug. 1, 4, 1925; Jan. 31, 1926; Alexander, *Crusade for Conformity*, pp. 69–84.
17. For membership cards to various organizations, see 1920s Billfold, LP. On Marvin's opinion that fraternal organizations were a waste of time, see JG interview by VB and WB, May 8–9, 1997; JG to WB, Apr. 24, 1997, authors' possession.
18. Alexander, *Crusade for Conformity*, pp. 33–34. Also see *Press*, Aug. 2, 1924; *Star-Telegram*, July 11, 1922.
19. Miranda Leonard interview; JG to WB, Mar. 11, 1997, authors' possession. Marvin Leonard was consistently praised as a man of integrity by members of the local black community. See Charles Hudson interview by WB, Feb. 16, 1995; Webber interview; St. James Baptist Church Prayer Group interview.
20. Hollace Weiner, "KKK Links Lurk in Tarrant Past," *Star-Telegram*, Feb. 25, 1990; *Star-Telegram*, July 9, 1927; Alexander, *Ku Klux Klan in the Southwest*, pp. v–viii. According to a recent study based on far more complete records than are available for Fort Worth, in Athens, Georgia, more than half the members of the Klan were small proprietors or white-collar workers. Most of them were born into farm families that owned a few acres and rented a few more. Klan members had climbed a rung up from their parents and feared slipping back. The Klan played on the anxieties and frustrations of some of the most driven of Americans—those determined not to fall back to the status of their parents. Although wealthier than an average Klansman, Marvin fit this profile. See Nancy MacLean, *Behind the Mask of Chivalry: The Making of the Second Ku Klux Klan* (New York: Oxford University Press, 1994), pp. 23–97.
21. JG interview, Feb. 15, 1996. Also see Marty Leonard interview, May 20, 1997.
22. Marvin was known and admired by local bankers, especially R. E. Harding of Fort Worth National Bank, but other businessmen, such as Doc St. Clair, knew nothing about him in 1927. See JG, Marty Leonard, and Bradshaw interview; Vachule, "Brother Act," pp. 26–28; Brown, *Hood, Bonnet, and Little Brown Jug*, pp. 251–52; Alexander, *Ku Klux Klan in the Southwest*, pp. 223–26.
23. JG interview, Apr. 14, 1994; *Star-Telegram*, July 9, 1927; "Klan Constitution," LP; Membership Roster, Colonial Country Club, LP; Fay Brachman to WB, Sept. 4, 1997, authors' possession.
24. In the 1920s billfold with Marvin's KKK membership cards were nineteen signed votes in favor of selling the Klan Hall to Leonard. Also see JG interview, Feb. 15, 1996; memorandum from JG to VB and WB, January 16, 1998, authors' possession.
25. *Press*, June 26, 1928.
26. *Press*, Apr. 10, 1928; June 26, 1928; June 7, 15, 1929; *Star-Telegram*, June 28, 30, 1928; July 3, 4, 1928; June 16, 1929.
27. JG interview, Feb. 15, 1996; *Hi, Neighbor*, July, 1958, p. 3; JG to WB, Mar. 11, 1997.
28. JG interview, Feb. 15, 1996.
29. Ibid. Also see *Star-Telegram*, June 11, 12, 16, 1929; *Press*, June 7, 15, 1929.

30. *Star-Telegram*, Oct. 17, 1930. Also see *Leonard v. Small, County Judge, et al.*, No. 12277, *South Western Reporter*, second series, pp. 826–30; JG interview, Feb. 15, 1996; *Star-Telegram*, June 25, 26, 29, 30; July 11, 17, 20, 1929; Apr. 5, 1930.
31. *Star-Telegram*, June 16, 1929. Also see JG interview, Feb. 15, 1996; Fort Worth Chamber of Commerce, "Annual Banquet and Election of Directors," Jan. 27, 1931.
32. Bradstreet Reports, "Leonard Brothers," Aug. 20, 1927, LP; *Star-Telegram*, Jan. 1, Oct. 3, 1928; Dec. 29, 1929.
33. *Press*, Jan. 11, 1927.
34. *Star-Telegram*, Dec. 29, 1929; "Financial Records, 1920s–1930s," LP.
35. *The Whisper*, Nov., 1929, pp. 10–11.
36. *The Whisper*, Nov., 1929, pp. 8–9; *Star-Telegram*, Sept. 30, 1928; JG interview, May 12–13, 1997.
37. *Star-Telegram*, May 31, Oct. 11, 1925; May 12, 1938; *The Whisper*, Nov., 1929, p. 8.
38. *Star-Telegram*, July 13, 1919; Apr. 20, 1922; Aug. 19, 1923; May 31, Oct. 11, 1925; Aug. 7, 1927.
39. *The Whisper*, Nov., 1929, p. 8; *Hi, Neighbor*, Sept., 1958, p. 3.
40. Thad Moser to J. M. Leonard (hereafter JML), Mar. 17, 1932, LP; Beno Weatherly to Thad Moser, Mar. 15, 1932, LP; *The Whisper*, Nov., 1929, pp. 8, 11; *Sulphur Springs Gazette*, Mar. 15, Nov. 29, 1912. Also see Shockley interviews, June 1, 1994; June 28, 1995.
41. *Star-Telegram*, Oct. 4, 1931; Dec. 4, 1932; May 12, 1938; JG interview, Feb. 15, 1996; *The Whisper*, Nov., 1929, pp. 1–2; Carl Bruner to Marvin and Obie Leonard, Dec. 12, 1938, LP; Carl Bruner to JML, June 3, 1944, LP; Memo to Marvin Leonard regarding work from Carl Bruner, Jan. 1, 1946, LP.
42. *Star-Telegram*, Oct. 4, 1931; Dec. 4, 1932; Tyler, Barnett, and Barkley, *New HOT*, vol. 3, pp. 17, 1075; *Texas Almanac and State Industrial Guide, 1925*, p. 326.
43. Marvin Leonard to Carl Bruner, Mar. 12, 1931, LP. Also see Carl Bruner to Robert Mack, May 21, 1931, LP.
44. Ringler interview, Feb. 16, 1995; James Blair interview by WB, July 6, 1995; JG interview, Feb. 15, 1996. Also see JML to Carl Bruner, Mar. 12, 1931, LP; JML to Hobson Mack, Mar. 12, 1931, LP; Carl Bruner to Marvin and Obie Leonard, Dec. 12, 1938, LP.
45. *Star-Telegram*, Sept. 30, 1928; *The Whisper*, Nov., 1929, p. 4.
46. Vachule, "Brother Act," pp. 26–29.
47. Ibid., pp. 29–31; Jim Leach interview by WB, Feb. 8, 1994; Blair interview; Cook and Moates interview; JG interview, Apr. 21, 1994; Blair, "FEQ."
48. *Star-Telegram*, Feb. 5, 12, 19, 26, 29; Mar. 4, 11, 14, 25, Apr. 1, 8, 15, 23, 30, 1928.
49. *The Whisper*, Nov., 1929, pp. 1–2; *Star-Telegram*, Feb. 9, Mar. 9, Apr. 25, 1927, p. 5; Nov. 13, 14, 1929, p. 1; Woody Graham interview by WB, May 6, 1994.
50. Vachule, "Brother Act," p. 41. Also see JG interview, Feb. 15, 1996.
51. Fort Worth Chamber of Commerce, *Five Years of Progress: Fort Worth, 1928–1932* (Fort Worth: Stafford-Lowden, 1933), pp. 1–2; Bill Fairley, "Depression Hit Fort Worth Later," *Star-Telegram*, Jan. 8, 1997. Also see JG interview, Feb. 15, 1996; Blair interview.
52. Fort Worth Chamber of Commerce, *Five Years of Progress*, pp. 1–5.
53. Ibid., pp. 13–22.

54. Knight, *Fort Worth*, pp. 187–212; *Texas Almanac and State Industrial Guide, 1931*, p. 194; Green, *Land of the Underground Rain*, pp. 100–44; Olien and Olien, *Wildcatters*, pp. 13–42; Samuel D. Myres, *The Permian Basin, Petroleum Empire of the Southwest: Era of Discovery* (El Paso: Permian Press, 1973), pp. 95–349.
55. Fort Worth Chamber of Commerce, *Five Years of Progress*, pp. 3–5; *Press*, Apr. 10, June 27, 1929; WPA, "Guide to Fort Worth," pp. 29,391–94; Bradstreet Report, "Leonard Brothers," Aug. 20, 1927; *Star-Telegram*, Jan. 1, 1928.
56. WPA, "Guide to Fort Worth," pp. 18,790–96; *Star-Telegram*, Apr. 17, 1927; Jan. 1, 1927. On Texas banking, see Walter L. Buenger and Joseph A. Pratt, *But Also Good Business: Texas Commerce Banks and the Financing of Houston and Texas, 1886–1986* (College Station: Texas A&M University Press, 1986), pp. 64–108. For an overview of banks in the Great Depression, see Elmus Wicker, *The Banking Panics of the Great Depression* (New York: Cambridge University Press, 1996), pp. 1–23.
57. *Press*, Feb. 19, 1930; *Star-Telegram*, Feb. 19, 1930.
58. *Star-Telegram*, Nov. 13, 14, 1929; May 24, June 18, Oct. 6, 1930.
59. *Star-Telegram*, Nov. 13, 1929; Jan. 20, May 24, June 18, Oct. 6, 1930.
60. *Star-Telegram*, "Leonard Brothers Celebrates 20th Birthday," May 12, 1938; Vachule, "Brother Act," pp. 45–51; Bruner to Marvin and Obie Leonard, Dec. 12, 1938; Blair, "FEQ."
61. JG interviews, Apr. 14, 1994; Feb. 15, 1996; Shockley interviews, June 1, 1994; June 28, 1995. Also see Vachule, "Brother Act," pp. 47–48.
62. Doc St. Clair, interview by Jo Ann Vachule, quoted in Vachule, "Brother Act," p. 48.
63. Vachule, "Brother Act," p. 49.
64. Max Lale and Cissy Stewart Lale interview by WB, May 15, 1996. For other descriptions of Leonards in the 1920s and 1930s as a big country store or a town square, see Francis Bird interview by WB, Aug. 26, 1994; WPA, "Department Stores," in "Guide to Fort Worth," p. 16,556.
65. St. James Baptist Prayer Group interview. Also see JG interview, Feb. 15, 1996; Webber interview; Hudson interview; Carter interview.
66. Elba Crumby, "FEQ, #087," July 24, 1995; Tyler, Barnett, and Barkley, *New HOT*, vol. 4, p. 850.
67. Vachule, "Brother Act," pp. 50–51. Also see *Star-Telegram*, Dec. 4, 1932; JG interviews, Apr. 14, 1994; Feb. 15, 1996; Shockley interview, June 1, 1994.
68. JML to F. T. Lipton, Mar. 25, 1931, LP. Also see "Financial Records, 1920s–1930s."
69. Wicker, *The Banking Panics of the Great Depression*, pp. 108–50.
70. JG interview, Feb. 15, 1996; Neely interview; Shockley interviews, June 1, 1994; June 28, 1995. On how local elites were expected to behave, see Walter L. Buenger, "Between Community and Corporation: The Southern Roots of Jesse H. Jones and the Reconstruction Finance Corporation," *Journal of Southern History* 56 (Aug., 1990): 481–510.
71. Vachule, "Brother Act," pp. 55–56; Shockley interview, June 1, 1994; *Star-Telegram*, July 26, 1939; Sept. 18, 1962; WPA, "Social Welfare," in "Guide to Fort Worth," p. 18800; Tyler, Barnett, and Barkley, *New HOT*, vol. 5, p. 269; Lena Pope, *Hand on My Shoulder: The Story of Lena Pope and the Home that Evolved from Her Dreams*, pp. 105–24.
72. *Press*, June 22, 1960; *Oklahoma City Daily Oklahoman*, Apr. 6, 1941; *Star-Telegram*,

June 22, 1960. Also see Amos Melton, "Chips and Chatter," *Star-Telegram*, May 3, 1935; Amos Melton, "Surprise Party for S. W. Golf Benefactor," *Star-Telegram*, Mar. 9, 1938; *Fort Worth*, June, 1960, p. 6; Moncrief interview.
73. Trinkle, "Magnanimous Skinflint," 48–50, 70–72; *Star-Telegram*, May 3, 1935; Mar. 9, 1938; Cano interview.
74. *Press*, Jan. 24, 1936; *Star-Telegram*, May 3, 1935; Mar. 9, 1938; *New York Herald Tribune*, June 26, 1940; Colonial Country Club, *This Is Colonial* (Fort Worth: Colonial Country Club, 1965); Russ Pate, *Colonial Country Club, 1936–1986* (Fort Worth: Motheral Printing, 1986), pp. 12–17.
75. "Statement of J. M. Leonard, regarding Shady Oaks," 1965, LP; Pate, *Colonial Country Club*, pp. 14–33; Marty V. Leonard to WB, Aug. 27, 1997; Fay Brachman to WB, Sept. 4, 1997; John Steele Gordan, "The Country Clubs," *American Heritage* 41 (Sept./Oct., 1990): 75–84; Peter Levine, "The American Hebrew Looks at 'Our Crowd': the Jewish Country Club in the 1920s," *American Jewish History* 83 (Mar., 1995): 27–49; "What Has Changed since 1928? Nothing," *Forbes*, Oct. 27, 1986, pp. 74–76.
76. *Oklahoma City Daily Oklahoman*, Apr. 6, 1941. Also see Pate, *Colonial Country Club*, pp. 28–29.
77. Tyree interview; Moulton interview. Also see Marty Leonard to WB and VB, Oct. 24, 1997.
78. Cricket McClure interview by VB and WB, Oct. 16, 1994; Libbie Vaughan interview by WB, Jan. 10, 1995.
79. "Wedding Bells," Marriage Folder, LP.
80. Vachule, "Brother Act," pp. 44–45, 51–52; Marty Leonard interview, July 14, 1994; Marty Leonard interview by WB, Feb. 14, 1996; Vaughan interview; McClure interview.
81. Pope, *Hand on My Shoulder*, p. 118. Also see *Star-Telegram*, May 19, 1932; July, 17, 1933.
82. McClure interview. Also see Vachule, "Brother Act," pp. 51–52; Marty Leonard interview by WB, Aug. 18, 1997.
83. Marty Leonard interview, Feb. 14, 1996. Also see McClure interview; Vaughan interview; Bird interview.
84. McClure interview.
85. Madelon Leonard Bradshaw interview by WB and VB, Dec. 9, 1994; Marty Leonard interview, Feb. 14, 1996.
86. McClure interview; Marty Leonard to WB, Aug. 27, 1997, authors' possession.
87. Branham interview; Blair interview.
88. Marvin Leonard to Carl Bruner, Mar. 12, 1931, LP; Marvin Leonard to Hobson Mack, Mar. 12, 1931, LP; Branham interview; Bradshaw interview, Dec. 9, 1994.
89. "Financial Records, 1920s–1930s."
90. Arsen J. Darnay, ed., *Economic Indicators Handbook* (Detroit: Gale Research, 1992), pp. 226–27; speech by O. P. Leonard, 1938; "Financial Statements, 1930–1938," LP.
91. Blair interview; *Star-Telegram*, June 10, 11, 1948; "Sales By Commodities, 1931," LP.
92. *The Whisper*, Nov., 1929, p. 10; JG to WB, Apr. 24, 1997, authors' possession. Also see "Sales by Commodities, 1931," LP; *Hi, Neighbor*, May, 1959, p. 5; Maddux interview.

93. Speech by O. P. Leonard, 1938; JG interviews, Feb. 8, 1994; Apr. 14, 1994; Apr. 21, 1994; Feb. 15, 1996; Blair interview; Woody Graham interview.
94. Blair interview.
95. In 1937, net profit in nonfood was 8.15 percent of nonfood sales. The net profit in food was 3.28 percent of food sales. That was typical of the decade. See "Sales by Commodities, 1931," LP; Main Store Sales, 1932–38 in "Third Party Sale, 1930s," LP. Also see Cook and Moates interview.
96. Speech by O. P. Leonard, 1938.
97. "Financial Records, 1920s–1930s."

CHAPTER 4

1. Powell and Leonard interview.
2. *The Whisper*, Nov., 1929, p. 14. Also see McDaniel, "Amazing Leonard Brothers," 49; Mack Zachery interview by WB, May 6, 1994.
3. Zachery interview; *Star-Telegram*, May 19, July 17, 1932; July 22, 26, Aug. 1, 1939; Feb. 4, 1941.
4. See responses to questions 88–91 in: F. J. (Joe) Kunze, "FEQ, #192," May, 1995; Eleanor Beers, "FEQ, #019," Apr., 1995; Blair, "FEQ"; Tommie Wade Smith, "FEQ, #410," June, 1995. Also see McDaniel, "Amazing Leonard Brothers," 24; Branham interview; Darlene Owens interview by WB, Aug. 16, 1995.
5. See *Hi, Neighbor*, 50th Anniversary Edition (Fort Worth, Tandy Corporation, 1968) for early hand lettered signs ("Honey $1.00/Bucket" and "4 Bread 25 cents—Full Weight Loaves"); and McDaniel, "Amazing Leonard Brothers," 24. For a description of the store and its employees in 1938, see the *Star-Telegram*, May 12, 1938, "Leonards Section"; McDaniel, "Amazing Leonard Brothers," 22.
6. *Star-Telegram*, May 12, 1938, "Leonards Section," pp. 13–14, 19; Shockley interview, June 1, 1994; Vachule, "Brother Act," pp. 66–67.
7. *Star-Telegram*, May 12, 1938, "Leonards Section," p. 15.
8. "Opportunity at Leonard's Praised by Mr. Moates," *Hi, Neighbor*, Sept., 1958, p. 3; *Star-Telegram*, May 12, 1938, "Leonards Section," p. 3; Vachule, "Brother Act," pp. 61–63. Also see Moates interview; Cook and Moates interview.
9. *Star-Telegram*, May 22, 1938, p. 21; Wilbur Newsome interview by VB and Tom Born, June 1, 1994.
10. In 1936, cost of goods sold in the food departments totaled $1,173,739 or 47 percent of the store's total cost of goods sold. Sales from those four departments totaled $1,459,298 or 42 percent of the store's total sales of $3,516,147. See "Leonard Brothers Statement of Operations, 1936," LP.
11. The hard goods department contributed $57,663 to store profits in 1936 on sales of $448,374—a 12.86 percent return. See "Leonard Brothers Statement of Operations, 1936," LP.
12. *Star-Telegram*, May 12, 1938, "Leonards Section," p. 6.
13. Ibid., p. 3; Vachule, "Brother Act," p. 68.
14. *Star-Telegram*, May 12, 1938, "Leonards Section," p. 10; "Leonard Brothers Statement of Operations, 1936."
15. *Star-Telegram*, May 12, 1938, "Leonards Section," pp. 5, 11, 22.
16. Ibid., pp. 7–8.

17. Ibid., pp. 10, 16.
18. Whitmore, "Miracle Merchants," 8, 36; Vachule, "Brother Act," pp. 70–71; *Fort Worth Shopper* (hereafter *Shopper*), Nov. 13, 1938, p. 2. Also see JG interview, Apr. 14, 1994; Jack McMurray interview by VB and WB on June 11, 1994.
19. JG interview, May 12–13, 1997; Clark, "Brother Act," p. 59.
20. Whitmore, "Miracle Merchants," 36.
21. McDaniel, "Amazing Leonard Brothers," 49; *Shopper*, Aug. 21, 1938, p. 12.
22. In 1940, Leonards spent $110,975 or 2.18 percent of total sales on newspaper adverting and an additional $23,910 on other types of ads. Advertising expenses remained 1.5 percent to 2.5 percent of total sales until the 1950s. See "Leonards Operating Statements, 1940–1959," LP.
23. E. B. Weiss, *How to Sell to and through Department Stores*, p. 84; McDaniel, "Amazing Leonard Brothers," 24. Also see Whitmore, "Miracle Merchants," 36. For promotion tactics see Weiss, *How to Sell to and through Department Stores*, pp. 68–82.
24. *Shopper*, Dec. 3, 1939, p. 6; Vachule, "Brother Act," p. 72; *Star-Telegram*, Nov. 30, 1940; Yale Youngblood, "Christmas Past: Leonards Once Was a Christmas Tradition—or Was It the Other Way Around?" *Fort Worth Magazine*, Nov., 1987, pp. 35–36.
25. Clark, "Brother Act," p. 14; McDaniel, "Amazing Leonard Brothers," 24, 48.
26. Newsome interview.
27. Each Sunday, the *Shopper* published a one- or two-section newspaper featuring local entertainment opportunities and retail ads. The ads trumpet one promotion after another. Also see Whitmore, "Miracle Merchants," 36; McMurray interview; Blair interview; Webber interview; McBrayer interview.
28. *Shopper*, 1930–50; *Star-Telegram*, June 10, 1948; Powell and Leonard interview.
29. Jack Hester interview by WB, May 4, 1995; McDaniel, "Amazing Leonard Brothers," 48. A memorandum from Carl Bruner to Marvin Leonard, May 6, 1946, LP, states "You are now in violation of the Robinson Patman Act—but in my judgment the violation can be easily cured. If you incorporate the wholesale and retail separately and continue to sell to your own retail stores at prices much lower than you sell to others (as you are now doing) you will be in continuous violation."
30. *Star-Telegram*, May 12, 1938, "Leonards Section," p. 20.
31. Moates interview; Cook and Moates interview; Leach interview. Also see Clark, "Brother Act."
32. The description of product lines in the past two paragraphs is drawn from *Star-Telegram*, May 12, 1938, "Leonards Section," pp. 1–22.
33. Vachule, "Brother Act," pp. 59–60.
34. Powell and Leonard interview; Bob Johnson interview by WB, Aug. 24, 1994; Woody Graham interview.
35. Vachule, "Brother Act," pp. 59–60.
36. Rubin interview.
37. Ibid.
38. Whitmore, "Miracle Merchants," 38.
39. Janie Witcher, "FEQ, #383," June, 1995.
40. *Star-Telegram*, May 12, 1938, "Leonards Section," p. 17; Cook and Moates interview; Blair, "FEQ."
41. Cook and Moates interview; Vachule, "Brother Act," pp. 81–82.

42. Weiss, *How to Sell to and through Department Stores*, pp. 16–17.
43. Leach interview; Hester interview; Blair interview. Also see *Star-Telegram*, May 12, 1938, "Leonards Section," pp. 5, 7; Julian S. "Jim" Leach, "FEQ, #399," June 9, 1995.
44. Marvin Leonard to Elam Henderson, Apr. 21, 1939, LP; Marvin Leonard to Waldo A. Smith, July 5, 1939, LP; "Beloved General Manager, Mr. E. J. Henderson, Dies," *Hi, Neighbor*, Jan./Feb., 1959, p. 1; Maurice Langford interview by WB, June 28, 1995.
45. *Star-Telegram*, May 12, 1938, "Leonards Section," p. 20. According to the *Shopper*, July 9, 1939, Leonards installed air conditioning in the summer of 1939.
46. Branham interview.
47. "Leonard Brothers Statement of Operations, 1936," LP; Blair interview.
48. Weiss, *How to Sell to and through Department Stores*, pp. 5–6; "Leonards Operating Statements, 1938–1959," LP; Blair interview; Blair, "FEQ."
49. Weiss, *How to Sell to and through Department Stores*, pp. 7, 24, 145–50; Cook and Moates interview; "Financial Records, 1920s–1960s," LP.
50. JG interview, May 12–13, 1997; "Leonards Operating Statement, 1943," LP.
51. Burl Barnes, "FEQ, #013," May, 1995; "Leonards Operating Statement, 1943," LP.
52. Knight, *Fort Worth*, p. 207.
53. Leach interview; Leach, "FEQ."
54. *Shopper*, Sept. 29, 1940, p. 7.
55. Vachule, "Brother Act," pp. 88–89; "Leonards Income Statements, 1939–1941," LP.
56. *Star-Telegram*, Aug. 8, 1940; JG interview, May 12–13, 1997.
57. C. L. Ettelson to Gaylord Chizum, Sept. 1, 1937, LP; Collie Ettelson to Marvin Leonard, Oct. 27, 1937, LP.
58. E. H. Scull (hereafter EHS) to JML, Dec. 6, 1939, LP. Also see Durwood McDonald to Edward Mitchell, Feb. 28, 1938, LP; Durwood McDonald to Edward Mitchell, Mar. 12, 1938, LP.
59. JML to EHS, Dec. 11, 1939, LP.
60. EHS to JML, Dec. 19, 1939, LP.
61. Rubin interview.
62. Blair interview; Knight, *Fort Worth*, pp. 212–13.
63. Hester interview; McMurray interview; Newsome interview; Homer Stewart interview by WB, Jan. 11, 1995; Shockley interview, June 28, 1995; Powell and Leonard interview. On Helen Love, see Cook and Moates interview; Helen Love interview by WB, June 30, 1994; Woody Graham interview. On hiring patterns from 1928 to 1970, see the 86 responses to the "Former Employee Questionnaire," 1995. In particular see Belle Toney, "FEQ, #356," May, 1995; Zelma Partain, "FEQ, #267," June, 1995; Crumby, "FEQ"; Jim Winters, "FEQ, #363," May, 1995.
64. Newsome interview; Blair interview; Zachery interview; "Leonards Financial Statements, 1938–1943."
65. JML to EHS, Aug. 18, 1944, LP; "Financial Records, 1940s."
66. Marvin investigated numerous alternatives to reduce his tax obligation, for himself and for the store. In 1941, the store had reached the top corporate bracket of 55 percent. The brothers dissolved the corporation that held Leonards that year and returned to a partnership arrangement to reduce taxes. Marvin also had Carl Bruner investigate the possibility of seeking tax relief under Section 722 of the Federal tax law, which provided for adjustment of the Excess Profits Tax Credit under certain

circumstances. Bruner reported that Marvin might convince the tax department that the addition to the store's facilities and its product lines between 1936 and 1939 rendered using an average earnings basis for that time period unfair. See Carl Bruner to Marvin Leonard, June 3, 1944, LP.

67. Zachery interview; "J. M. Leonard Financial Statement, Dec. 31, 1943," LP.
68. Zachery interview; JG interviews, Feb. 8, 1994; Apr. 14, 1994; Apr. 21, 1994; Feb. 15, 1996.
69. *Star-Telegram*, Jan 2, 1942; Carl Bruner to Marvin Leonard, "Re: Virginia Company," July 2, 1940, LP; Carl Bruner to Marvin Leonard, "Re: Harold Wilson Matter," July 4, 1940, LP; JML, "Financial Statement, December 31, 1943," LP.
70. Carl Bruner to Marvin Leonard, Jan. 15, 1941, LP. Also see The Fort Worth National Bank, Statement of Condition at the Close of Business, Dec. 31, 1940, LP; JG, Leonard, and Bradshaw interview; Maddux interview.
71. "J. M. Leonard Financial Position, August 31, 1951," LP; "J. M. Leonard Financial Position, March 31, 1957," LP; "Historical Records, Directors and Officers, Fort Worth National Bank from February 28, 1884 through June 26, 1952," in Sass, "Since 1873: The Story of the Fort Worth National Bank." By the 1960s, ownership of the largest Texas banks was increasingly dispersed, making 2 percent a relatively large stockholding. See Buenger and Pratt, *But Also Good Business*, pp. 177–261.
72. *Oklahoma City Daily Oklahoman*, Apr. 6, 1941; Bradshaw interview, Dec. 9, 1994.
73. Jim Trinkle, "Pockets Full of Empty," *Star-Telegram*, May 26, 1966. Also see Jim Browder, "Million Dollar Golf Business," *Press*, May 12, 1964, p. 26; Jim Trinkle, "Colonial—20 Years of Great Tournaments," *Star-Telegram*, May 2, 1965; Ben Hogan interview by Robert A. Calvert and Larry D. Hill, Feb. 8, 1994; Ben Hogan, foreword to *Colonial Country Club*, by Pate, p. 1; Tyler, Barnett, and Barkley, *New HOT*, vol. 3, pp. 204–205.
74. Moncrief interview.
75. *Oklahoma City Daily Oklahoman*, Apr. 6, 1941.
76. Bourland interview.
77. *Star-Telegram*, May 25, 1940.
78. Cano interview; *Star-Telegram*, Mar. 9, 1938; United Press Association Press Release, May 23, 1940, LP; Charles Cline, "Colonial CC is 50 Years Old Today and Bent in its Ways," *Star-Telegram*, Jan. 29, 1986; Pate, *Colonial Country Club*, pp. 12–17.
79. Pate, *Colonial Country Club*, pp. 34–41; C. F. Kelley interview by WB, June 29, 1994; Woody Graham interview.
80. Bourland interview; Pate, *Colonial Country Club*, p. 31.
81. "Statement of J. M. Leonard regarding Shady Oaks," 1965, LP. Also see Pate, *Colonial Country Club*, pp. 24–25.
82. Leach interview. Also see Bourland interview; *This is Colonial*; Pate, *Colonial Country Club*, pp. 51–52.
83. *Star-Telegram*, May 19, 1932; July 17, 1933; July 22, 1937; July 26, 27, Aug. 31, 1939. On O'Daniel, see Tyler, Barnett, and Barkley, *New HOT*, vol. 4, pp. 1107–1108.
84. Paul Leonard interview by VB and WB, Oct. 14, 1994; Clark, "Brother Act," p. 63.
85. Carl Bruner to R. E. Harding, July 19, 1945, LP; Bruner to Marvin Leonard, June 3, 1944, LP; Charles P. Swindler to Marvin Leonard, May 12, 1944, LP.
86. EHS to JML, June 8, 1944, LP. On the relationship between Marvin and Scull and the attempted sale to Macy's, see JML to EHS, May 25, 1944, LP; Durwood

McDonald to H. L. Churchill, Jan. 13, 1944, LP; EHS to JML, May 13, 1944, LP; EHS to JML, June 1, 1944, LP.
87. EHS to JML, June 27, 1944, LP. Hearn and Goldblatt were New York's deep discounters.
88. JML to EHS, June 12, 1944, LP. Also see JML to EHS, July 3, 1944, LP.
89. EHS to JML, June 27, 1944, LP; EHS to JML, Aug. 10, 1944, LP. Also see EHS to JML, Aug. 3, 17, 1944, LP.
90. EHS to JML, Aug. 21, 1944, LP.
91. EHS to JML, Sept. 15, 1944, LP.
92. JML to EHS, Oct. 2, 1944, LP. On the Gamble-Skogmo negotiation, see EHS to JML, Dec. 4, 1944, LP; JML to EHS, Dec. 19, 1944, LP; EHS to JML, Dec. 26, 1944, LP.
93. Bruner to Harding, July 19, 1945; B. Earl Puckett to Carl Bruner, no date, LP; Harold B. Weiss to Carl Bruner, Oct. 24, 1945, LP; Carl Bruner to Marvin Leonard, Oct. 26, 1945, LP; Option Agreement between JML and O. P. Leonard and Tarrant Realty Co. and Allen & Company and Dallas Rupe & Son, Dec., 1945, LP; Carl Bruner to Martin Fruhman, Jan. 25, Mar. 7, 1946, LP; Raymond Rosoff to JML, Sept. 4, 1946, LP.
94. JML to EHS, Oct. 2, 1944; Bruner to Harding, July 19, 1945.
95. Irv Farman interview by WB, July 1, 1994.
96. Knight, *Fort Worth*, pp. 213–14.
97. JG interviews, Apr. 21, 1994; Feb. 15, 1996. Also see Knight, *Fort Worth*, pp. 225–27.
98. JG interviews, Feb. 8, 1994; Apr. 14, 1994; Apr. 21, 1994; Feb. 15, 1996; JG interview by WB, Nov. 21, 1996.
99. Carter interview; Blair interview.

CHAPTER 5

1. For versions of this quote, see Leach interview; Woody Graham interview; Elizabeth Dixon Nisbet interview by WB, June 29, 1995; Cook and Moates interview; Miranda Leonard interview. Also see Adell Chandler, "FEQ, #067," Apr., 1995; Jim Ed Smith, "FEQ, #332," May, 1995.
2. *Star-Telegram*, Sept. 30, 1928; *Time*, Sept. 6, 1948, p. 84.
3. Shea interview; Ringler interviews, Apr. 14, 1994; Feb. 16, 1995; Miranda Leonard interview.
4. *Star-Telegram*, Oct. 5, 1955; Apr. 13, 1956, Dec. 15, 1957. Also see Bradshaw interview, Dec. 9, 1994; Marty Leonard interview, July 14, 1994.
5. See the aerial view of Leonards in *Star-Telegram*, Aug. 31, 1948, "Leonards Section," p. 29.
6. *Hi, Neighbor*, 50th Anniversary Edition, 1968; "Sales and Profit Figures for 1940–60," Expansion Folder, LP.
7. JG interview by VB and WB, Mar. 7, 1997; Knight, *Fort Worth*, pp. 213–14; *Star-Telegram*, July 11, 1960; Leach, *Land of Desire*, pp. 153–90.
8. David G. McComb, *Houston: A History* (Austin: University of Texas Press, 1981), pp. 132–33.
9. *Star-Telegram*, Jan. 9, 1947; Mar. 9, 10, June 2, Aug. 31, 1948; Woody Graham interview; Shockley interviews, June 1, 1994; June 28, 1995; Shea interview.
10. Owens interview; Oscar Tallman interview by WB, June 29, 1994. Also see *Star-Telegram*, Aug. 31, 1948.
11. *Star-Telegram*, Mar. 9, Aug. 31, 1948.

12. Ibid.
13. Clover Riley, "FEQ, #299," May, 1995; *Star-Telegram*, Aug. 31, 1948, "Leonards Section," p. 51; Vachule, "Brother Act," pp. 93–94.
14. *Star-Telegram*, Aug. 31, 1948.
15. Paul Leonard interview; Love interview.
16. *Star-Telegram*, Feb. 9, 1943, p. 7; *Star-Telegram*, Aug. 31, 1948, "Leonards Section," p. 35. Also see John R. James interview by WB, Aug. 26, 1994; Leach, *Land of Desire*, pp. 64–70.
17. *Star-Telegram*, Aug. 31, 1948, "Leonards Section," p. 49.
18. JG interviews, Feb. 8, 1994; Apr. 14, 1994; Apr. 21, 1994; Feb. 15, 1996.
19. Margery Leonard interview; James interview; Woody Oliver interview by WB, June 30, 1995.
20. *Star-Telegram*, Aug. 31, 1948, "Leonards Section," p. 30; Margery Leonard interview; James interview; Oliver interview; JG interview, May 12–13, 1997.
21. JG interview, Apr. 14, 1994; Tyree interview. Also see Vachule, "Brother Act," pp. 92–93; Leach, *Land of Desire*, pp. 72–75.
22. Woody Graham interview; Shea interview; James interview.
23. Moates interview; Leach interview; JG interviews, Feb. 8, 1994; Apr. 14, 1994; Apr. 21, 1994.
24. Vachule, "Brother Act," pp. 30–31; JG interview, Apr. 21, 1994.
25. Love interview; James interview; Blair interview.
26. *Star-Telegram*, Aug. 31, 1948, "Leonards Section," p. 60. Also see James interview.
27. *Star-Telegram*, Aug. 31, 1948, "Leonards Section," p. 60.
28. Mary Barton, "FEQ, #015," May, 1995. Also see Doris Jones Richeson, "FEQ, #407," June, 1995.
29. Bob Bolen interview by WB, Feb. 17, 1995; Christopher S. Davies, "Life at the Edge: Urban and Industrial Evolution of Texas, Frontier Wilderness—Frontier Space, 1836–1986," *SHQ* 89 (Apr., 1986): 443–554.
30. On changes in the type of customers in the 1950s, see Mildred Quattlebaum, "FEQ, #292," May, 1995.
31. *Star-Telegram*, May 2, 1947.
32. *Star-Telegram*, Jan. 5, 1952; *Hi, Neighbor*, Dec., 1959, p. 3; Ringler interviews, Apr. 14, 1994; Feb. 16, 1995.
33. Ringler interviews, Apr. 14, 1994; Feb. 16, 1995.
34. Ringler interview, Apr. 14, 1994; *Star-Telegram*, May 16, Nov. 5, 1948; Apr. 30, 1949; Feb. 20, 1951; June 14, July 4, 1953; Feb. 11, 1954; July 8, 1955.
35. "Sales and Profit Figures, 1940–60," Expansion Folder, LP.
36. *Hi, Neighbor*, June, 1958, p. 5; James interview.
37. Cook and Moates interview; Shea interview.
38. Shea interview.
39. Kelley interview.
40. Shea interview. Also see Kelley interview; *Hi, Neighbor*, Jan./Feb., 1959, pp. 1–2; *You Name It*, 1958, p. 10.
41. Shea interview; Raucher, "Dime Store Chains," 130–33. For the insights of another Montgomery Wards veteran whom Shea hired in hardware, see Burl Barnes interview by WB, May 4, 1995.

42. Shea interview.
43. Ibid.; "Sales and Profit Figures, 1940–60," Expansion 1960 Folder, LP.
44. JG interviews, Apr. 14, 1994; Apr. 21, 1994.
45. Bureau of the Census, *Seventeenth Census: 1950, Population,* General Characteristics, Texas (Washington, D.C., 1952), pp. 43–82; Bureau of the Census, *Eighteenth Census: 1960, Population,* Fort Worth, Texas, Census Tracts (Washington, D.C., 1961), p. 15; memorandum from Paul Leonard to JML, O. P. Leonard, and Bob Leonard, Sept. 14, 1960, Expansion Folder, LP; Cook and Moates interview; Shea interiew; JG interview, Feb. 15, 1996.
46. F. W. Laughbaum interview by VB and WB, Apr. 21, 1994; Cook and Moates interview; Paul Leonard interview.
47. Ringler interview, Feb. 16, 1995. Also see "Leonards Account Books, 1957," p. 9; "Leonards Account Book, 1959," p. 8; "Leonards Account Book, 1960," p. 8, LP.
48. Cook and Moates interview.
49. Cook and Moates interview; JG interviews, Apr. 14, 1994; Apr. 21, 1994.
50. JG interview, Feb. 15, 1996; "Leonards Financial Records, 1957," p. 205; *Shopper,* 1955–57.
51. *United States of America v. Safeway Stores, Incorporated,* Civil No. 3173, Fort Worth Division (1956); JG interview, Feb. 15, 1996.
52. "Leonards Financial Records, 1957," p. 205; "Leonards Financial Records, 1961," p. 246; "Statement of Operations," 1944, LP.
53. *Star-Telegram,* Dec. 4, 1953; June 6, 1955; Ringler interview, Feb. 16, 1995. For a good description of retailing in the 1950s, see David Luskey interview by WB, Jan. 10, 1995.
54. JG interviews, Apr. 14, 1994; May 12–13, 1997. Also see Alice Mills Walden, "FEQ, #365," May, 1995; Nelda Herod, "FEQ, #149," May, 1995.
55. *Star-Telegram,* June 10, 11, 1948; Maddux interview.
56. The quote was used on Everybody's letterhead. See M. S. Leveridge file, LP. Also see Maddux interview.
57. *Star-Telegram,* June 10, 1948. Also see Powell and Leonard interview; Maddux interview.
58. Leonards and Everybody's Consolidated Balance Sheet, Dec. 31, 1955, LP; Third Party Sale of Store, 1940s, LP; 1960 Reorganization Folder, LP; Barrel of Money, Everybody's Folder, LP. For the comments of an Everybody's manager see Frank A. Carriher, "FEQ, #061," June, 1995.
59. Branham interview; Cook and Moates interview; Paul Leonard interview; Powell and Leonard interview.
60. Vachule, "Brother Act," pp. 162–68; Paul Leonard interview; Fred L. Graham interview by WB, Nov. 16, 1995; Langford interview.
61. Vachule, "Brother Act," pp. 167–70; Margery Leonard interview; Tyree interview; Paul Leonard interview.
62. Vachule, "Brother Act," pp. 173–79; *Press,* May 13, 29, 1966; *Star-Telegram,* May 26, 1966.
63. Vachule, "Brother Act," pp. 64–65.
64. Vachule, "Brother Act," pp. 95–96; Shea interview.
65. *Star-Telegram,* Aug. 31, 1948, "Leonards Section," p. 29; Vachule, "Brother Act," pp. 182–83; Paul Leonard interview; Margery Leonard interview.
66. Marvin Leonard to Elam Henderson, Apr. 21, 1939, LP; Marvin Leonard to Waldo A. Smith, July 5, 1939, LP; *Hi, Neighbor,* Jan./Feb., 1959, pp. 1–2; *Star-Telegram,* Sept. 30,

1928; *The Whisper,* 1929, p. 9; Margery Leonard interview; JG interview, Feb. 15, 1996; Cook and Moates interview; Kelley interview; Nisbet interview.
67. "Minutes of the meetings of Oct. 3, 1960, and Oct. 5, 1960," Expansion 1960 Folder, LP; Fred Graham interview; Harvey Russell interview by WB, Aug. 24, 1994; Langford interview.
68. One indication of the importance of Garrett, Henderson, and Haberer was the bonuses paid to the three men. In 1958, the three received higher bonuses than any other employees. See "1958 Bonuses," LP.
69. JG interviews, Feb. 8, 1994; Apr. 14, 1994; Apr. 21, 1994; Feb. 15, 1996. Also see *Hi, Neighbor,* July, 1958, p. 3.
70. Branham interview; Langford interview; JG interviews, Apr. 14, 1994; Apr. 21, 1994; May 12–13, 1997. Also see *The Whisper,* Nov., 1929, p. 10.
71. Shea interview; Kelley interview.
72. Bolen interview.
73. *Lenco News,* Jan. 11, 1956, p. 2; *You Name It,* Mar., 1958, p. 1; *Hi, Neighbor,* May, 1958, p. 1; Edith Loughlin Carter, "FEQ, #063," June, 1995.
74. Moates interview; JG interview, Apr. 21, 1994. Also see Carlos Green, "FEQ, #136," May, 1995.
75. "Hann Still Helps Out With Sales and Prescriptions," *Hi, Neighbor,* Nov., 1958, p. 3; JG interview, Feb. 15, 1996; Langford interview.
76. JG interview, Feb. 15, 1996; Langford interview; Leach interview.
77. *Hi, Neighbor,* Jan./Feb., 1959, p. 1; Shea interview; Kelley interview.
78. *Hi, Neighbor,* Jan./Feb., 1959, p. 1; July, 1959, p. 5; *Star-Telegram,* Dec. 20, 1959. For the differences between Henderson and Overcash and on the managerial difficulties Leonards faced, see Kelley interview; Shea interview; Bolen interview.
79. Clif Overcash, "Objective Report," Oct. 1, 1960, Expansion 1960 Folder, LP. Also see *Hi, Neighbor,* July, 1959, p. 5.
80. "Minutes of the meetings of Oct. 3, 5, 1960," LP.
81. This was a common national trend; see Lizabeth Cohen, "From Town Center to Shopping Center: The Reconfiguration of Community Marketplaces in Postwar America," *American Historical Review (AHR)* 101 (Oct., 1996): 1082–91; Jon C. Teaford, *The Rough Road to Renaissance: Urban Revitalization in America, 1940–1985* (Baltimore: Johns Hopkins University Press, 1990).
82. Bureau of the Census, *Sixteenth Census: 1940, Population,* vol. 2, part 6 (Washington, D.C., 1943), p. 1036; *Seventeenth Census: 1950, Population,* Fort Worth, Texas Census Tracts, pp. 7–10; *Eighteenth Census: 1960, Population,* Fort Worth, Texas Census Tracts, pp. 15–21; *Star-Telegram,* Feb. 19, Dec. 4, 1946; "Big Jump Indicated in City Negro Population," Sept. 30, 1950.
83. *Star-Telegram,* Mar. 22, 1945; Oct. 25, 1949; Sept. 30, 1950; Jan. 7, 1951; Jan. 31, 1953; Aug. 30, Sept. 3, 1956; June 12, 1957.
84. *Press,* Sept. 5, 12, 1956; *Star-Telegram,* Sept. 3, 1956.
85. *Press,* June 23, 1963. Also see *Press,* July 14, 1961; Oct. 17, 1962; Barr interview; McBrayer interview; Bayard Friedman interview by WB, June 21, 1994; Webber interview; Marion J. Brooks interview by WB, May 29, 1996; St. James Baptist Prayer Group interview. To put Fort Worth in perspective, see Numan V. Bartley, *The New South, 1945–1980* (Baton Rouge: Louisiana State University Press, 1995).

86. *Press,* Jan. 16, 18, 1950; *Star-Telegram,* Jan. 16, 18, 1950.
87. *Press,* June 23, 1963. Also see *Press,* Sept. 5, 12, 1956; Apr. 8, 1960; Oct. 17, 1962; Brooks interview; Webber interview; Barr interview.
88. *Star-Telegram,* May 26, 27, 1954; Sept. 30, 1955.
89. *Star-Telegram,* Oct. 7, 1940; May 21, 1941; May 26, 27, 1954; Sept. 30, 1955; *This is Colonial,* p. 2; Pope, *Hand on My Shoulder,* pp. 113–18.
90. Ben Proctor, "Jim Wright," in *Profiles in Power: Twentieth Century Texans in Washington,* ed. Kenneth E. Hendrickson, Jr. and Michael L. Collins (Arlington Heights, Illinois: Harlan Davidson, 1993), p. 243; JG interviews, Feb. 8, 1994; Apr. 14, 1994; Apr. 21, 1994.
91. Statement of Kerven W. Carter, Jr., May 29, 1996, at St. James Baptist Church. Also see Sanders, "Toyland Offered Children Warmth"; Owens interview.
92. *Star-Telegram,* May 7, 1965; John Maddux and Madelon Leonard Bradshaw interview by WB, Sept. 17, 1997; Ringler interviews, Apr. 14, 1994; Feb. 16, 1995; Webber interview; Barr interview.
93. Miranda Leonard interview.
94. In 1965, Art Hall, the head golf professional at Shady Oaks Country Club, reported to fellow managers that "Mr. Leonard objects to colored employees calling him (Art) by his first name." Minutes of Department Heads Meeting, Feb. 2, 1965, Shady Oaks Country Club, LP.
95. This was a point made by another of his daughters. See Marty Leonard interview, July 14, 1994.
96. JG interviews, Apr. 14, 1994; Feb. 15, 1996.
97. *Star-Telegram,* Sept. 20, 1950; Jan. 11, 1956; Sept. 5, 1957; JG interviews, Feb. 8, 1994; Feb. 15, 1996; McBrayer interview; Barr interview.
98. Owens interview; JG interviews, Feb. 8, 1994; Apr. 14, 1994. John Maddux confirmed that Everybody's was desegregated by 1958 when he stopped work. See Maddux and Bradshaw interview.
99. Ringler interview, Feb. 16, 1995. Also see JG interviews, Feb. 8, 1994; Feb. 15, 1996.
100. Ringler interview, Feb. 16, 1995.
101. Ibid.
102. Statement of JML re Shady Oaks, 1965, LP.
103. *Star-Telegram,* July 31, 1952; Sept. 27, 1953; Aug. 30, 1954; July 17, Oct. 5, 1955; July 1, 3, 1956. Also see Marty Leonard interview, Aug. 18, 1997.
104. JG interviews, Feb. 15, 1996; Nov. 21, 1996; *Star-Telegram,* Oct. 5, 1955; JG, "Shady Oaks," typescript, 1994, Leonard Collection.
105. JG interview, Nov. 21, 1996; Marty Leonard interviews, July 14, 1994; Aug. 18, 1997; *Star-Telegram,* Oct. 5, 1955; Jim Trinkle, "Magnanimous Skinflint," 50.
106. *Star-Telegram,* Oct. 5, 1955; Trinkle, "Magnanimous Skinflint," 50.
107. Trinkle, "Magnanimous Skinflint," 70.
108. Statement of JML re Shady Oaks; Jay Y. Crum, "Shady Oaks Golf Club Tops of All," *Fort Worth,* Aug., 1959, pp. 14–15, 38, 61; *Press,* Jan. 1, 1959, pp. 1–2.
109. Crum, "Shady Oaks Golf Club," 15. Also see Friedman interview.
110. *Press,* Aug. 12, 1962. Also see *Star-Telegram,* June 8, 1958; Aug. 9, 1959; Trinkle, "Magnanimous Skinflint," 70; "An Invitation From Shady Oaks Country Club," 1967.
111. "An Invitation From Shady Oaks Country Club," 1967; statement of JML re Shady

Oaks; "Membership Roster, Shady Oaks," Dec. 11, 1962, LP; Statement of JG re Shady Oaks, 1965, LP; Shady Oaks, "Balance Sheet," Oct. 31, 1959, LP; Shady Oaks, "Balance Sheet," Dec., 1960, LP; Shady Oaks, "Recap of All Operations," Sept. 30, 1963, LP; Richard L. Crook to the Board of Governors, Shady Oaks Country Club, Aug. 12, 1964, LP.

112. "Membership Roster, Shady Oaks," Dec. 11, 1962; Marty Leonard interview, Aug. 18, 1997; Miranda Leonard interview; T. F. "Fred" Hodge interview by WB, May 5, 1994; JG interview, Apr. 14, 1994. For an introduction to a topic largely ignored by academics, see Peter Levine, "The American Hebrew Looks at 'Our Crowd': The Jewish Country Club in the 1920s," *American Jewish History* 83 (Mar., 1995): 27–49. On the continued pattern of segregation in Country Clubs, see "The Last Bastions of Bigotry," *Time*, July 22, 1991, pp. 66–67; "What has Changed Since '28? Nothing," *Forbes*, Oct. 27, 1986, pp. 74–76.

113. "Ridgmar and Westover Hills Sales Records," Office of John Maddux; *Star-Telegram*, May 20, 1956; Dec. 15, 1957; Aug. 23, 1963; May 23, 29, 1964; *Fort Worth*, June, 1964, p. 20; *Press*, Mar. 4, 1962; June 24, 1964; Hodge interview; JG interview, Nov. 21, 1996; Maddux interview.

114. *Star-Telegram*, June 22, 1955; Apr. 13, Nov. 22, 23, 1956; JG interview, Feb. 15, 1996.

115. JML Financial Position, Mar. 31, 1957; JML, Financial Statement, May 31, 1956; JML Statement of Financial Position, Aug. 31, 1951; DeGolyer and MacNaughton to JML, Jan. 22, 1957, Oil Folder, LP; Wirt N. Norris to JML, June 11, 1950, Oil Folder, LP; Ben Hogan to Marvin Leonard, Mar. 8, 1948, Golf Folder, LP; Zachery interview; Hodge interview; JG interview, Feb. 15, 1996.

116. JML Financial Position, Mar. 31, 1957, LP; JG, Leonard, and Bradshaw interview; John Barry Hubbard interview by WB, Jan. 11, 1995; Friedman interview; *Century One: 1873–1973, A City and the Bank That Bears Its Name* (Fort Worth: Fort Worth National Bank, 1973).

117. Financial Statements, 1956, 1957, LP.

118. Ringler interviews, Apr. 14, 1994; Feb. 16, 1996; *Star-Telegram*, Feb. 4, Aug. 6, 1941.

119. JG interview, Feb. 8, 1994; Ringler interview, Feb. 16, 1996; Marty Leonard interview, Aug. 18, 1997.

120. Vachule, "Brother Act," p. 98. Also see *Star-Telegram*, Mar. 27, 1949; Louis Luskey interview by WB, June 30, 1994; Transcript of interview with Charles Ringler by KERA/KDTN TV, Feb. 16, 1995, Leonard Collection.

121. Tallman interview; Powell and Leonard interview.

122. JG interviews, Feb. 8, 1994; Apr. 14, 1994; Nisbet interview; Ringler interviews, Apr. 14, 1994; Feb. 16, 1995.

123. JG interview, Feb. 15, 1996; Ringler interview, Feb. 16, 1995.

124. On the trusts for Marvin Leonard's children and his intention in creating them, see JG interviews, Feb. 8, 1994; Apr., 14, 1994; Marty Leonard interview, July 14, 1994; Financial Position, 1957, LP; Request for Ruling from IRS regarded sale of assets by JML Family to O. P. Leonard family, Family Sale Folder, LP. Also see Miranda Leonard interview; Bradshaw interview, Dec. 9, 1994; Marty Leonard interview, Feb. 14, 1996.

125. Margery Leonard interview; Miranda Leonard interview; Marty Leonard interviews, July 14, 1994; Feb. 14, 1996; Bradshaw interview, Dec. 9, 1994.

126. Hodge interview; Margery Leonard interview; Miranda Leonard interview; Marty Leonard interviews, July 14, 1994; Feb. 14, 1996; Bradshaw interview, Dec. 9, 1994; JG interview, May 12–13, 1997. Also see Madelon to Daddy, May 22, 1967, LP.
127. Miranda Leonard interview; Bradshaw interview, Dec. 9, 1994; JG, Leonard, and Bradshaw interview; Marty Leonard to VB and WB, Jan. 10, 1998, authors' possession.
128. JG, Leonard, and Bradshaw interview; Pope, *Hand on My Shoulder*, pp. 116–18.
129. Memorandum from JG to VB and WB, Jan. 16, 1998, p. 6, authors' possession.
130. Vachule, "Brother Act," pp. 51–52. Also see Marty Leonard interviews, July 14, 1994; Feb. 14, 1996; Vaughan interview; McClure interview; JG interview by WB, Sept. 19, 1997.
131. Marty Leonard interviews, July 14, 1994, Feb. 14, 1996; Bradshaw interview, Dec. 9, 1994; Bird interview; McClure interview.
132. Marty V. Leonard to WB, Aug. 27, 1997, authors' possession.
133. Vera Pyle, "FEQ, #291," May, 1995.

Chapter 6

1. *Hi, Neighbor,* Jan., 1965, pp. 2–3; Nov., 1967, pp. 2–3.
2. *Press,* Jan. 1, 1967, p. 4A.
3. Marty Leonard interview, July 14, 1994; Miranda Leonard interview; Bradshaw interview, Dec. 9, 1994.
4. Cissy Lale, "Corporations and Culture," in Knight, *Fort Worth,* pp. 225–60; Leonard Sloane, "Ft. Worth Store and Friendship," *New York Times,* Dec. 14, 1966; "A Private Subway," *Time,* Feb. 22, 1963, p. 44.
5. As an example of what kind of bosses Marvin and Obie were, Elba Crumby commented that they "employed men and women with qualities that saved them having to do the bossing." Crumby, "FEQ."
6. Tallman interview; Moates interview.
7. Edith Loughlin Carter, Leonards Training Director, started the original newsletter, *Lenco News,* in 1955. It consisted of a single sheet of paper mimeographed on one side. After a few years, it became a professionally printed "house organ" called *Hi, Neighbor.* The inaugural issue published in Mar., 1958 in honor of Leonards fortieth anniversary was called *You Name It.* Carter, "FEQ"; *You Name It,* Mar., 1958.
8. C. O. Overcash, "Basic Personnel Concepts," Intracompany Report, Aug. 22, 1959, p. 1.
9. Ibid., p. 2.
10. Ibid.
11. Hollander, "Retailing: Cause or Effect," pp. 228–29; Hollander, *Restraints upon Retail Competition,* p. 85; Louis H. Grossman, *Department Store Merchandising in Changing Environments,* pp. 1–16.
12. "Fort Worth Business Survey," *Press,* Jan. 1, 1959, p. 2; Laughbaum interview.
13. O. Paul Leonard, "Fort Worth Market: Prosperity, Opportunity, Culture, and Unlimited Fun," *Markets of America* 26 (1962): 71–72.
14. Bureau of the Census, *Nineteenth Census: 1970, Population,* vol. 1, part 45 (Washington, D.C., 1972), p. 50; *Eighteenth Census: 1960, Population,* Census Tracts, Fort Worth Texas, pp. 15–90; Bureau of the Census, *Nineteenth Census: 1970, Population,* Census Tracts, Fort Worth Texas (Washington, D.C., 1972), pp. P-1 through P-86.

15. *Eighteenth Census: 1960, Population,* Census Tracts, Fort Worth Texas, pp. 15–90; *Nineteenth Census: 1970, Population,* Census Tracts, Fort Worth Texas, pp. P-1 through P-86; Laughbaum interview; Bolen interview.
16. Profit equals sales minus cost of sales, expenses including salaries, and bonuses. It was before income tax and before other income or losses were figured in. This minimizes the impact on these figures of bookkeeping changes and changes in tax code. Minutes of the Executive Committee, Oct. 3, 1960.
17. Account Books, 1957–1965. Even Doc St. Clair admitted that because of problems with expenses Leonards no longer thoroughly dominated the area from a competitive standpoint. See Minutes, Oct. 3, 5, 1960; Cook and Moates interview.
18. Cook and Moates interview; Clif Overcash, Internal Document, Oct. 1, 1960.
19. Minutes, Oct. 3, 1960; memorandum from Paul Leonard to JML, O. P. Leonard, and Bob Leonard, Sept. 14, 1960.
20. Memorandum from Paul Leonard, Sept. 14, 1960.
21. Ibid.
22. Ibid.
23. Ibid.
24. Minutes, Oct. 3, 1960; Minutes from the Executive Committee, Oct. 5, 1960; Vachule, "Brother Act," p. 104.
25. Vachule, "Brother Act," p. 107.
26. "Sales and Profit Figures," LP.
27. "A Private Subway," *Time,* Feb. 22, 1963, p. 44. Also see JG interview, Sept. 19, 1997.
28. C. J. Lietwiler, "Tramway Revival at Fort Worth, Texas," *Modern Tramway and Light Rail Review,* Oct., 1962; Knight, *Fort Worth,* p. 227. One example of the Downtown Fort Worth Association's promotional efforts was its sponsorship of a courtesy contest. The contest awarded a $100 Savings Bond and a plaque to the person selected as the most courteous, friendly, and helpful person working in the downtown area. *Hi, Neighbor,* Nov., 1961, p. 6.
29. Ringler interview, Feb. 16, 1995.
30. For Marvin's concerns over construction safety, see Oliver interview. Also see "A Private Subway," *Time,* Feb. 22, 1963, p. 44; C. J. Lietwiler, "Tramway Revival at Fort Worth, *Modern Tramway and Light Railway Review,* Oct., 1962; "Fort Worth Trolley Subway under Construction," *Headlights* 24, 1962, no. 7; "Firm Has Its Own Subway," *New York Times,* Dec. 17, 1962; "Dealer of the Month ... Leonards Department Store," *Western Merchandiser,* Aug., 1962; "Downtown Improvement by the 'Do-It-Yourself' Method," *Stores,* June, 1962; "Leonards Builds Private Subway to Prove Downtown Isn't Dead," *Furniture Retailer* 118 (July, 1962); "Leonards Builds Own Subway," *West Texas Today* (1963); "Leonards Backs Downtown with $2 Million Expansion," *Home Furnishings Daily* (Jan. 3, 1963); O. P. Leonard, Jr., "Why We Chose to Expand," *Merchant Trade Journal* (Apr., 1962); Joseph A Navarro and Elizabeth A. Parker, "The M & O Subway, Fort Worth, Texas," (Unpublished Research Paper P-582, Urban Mass Transportation Project, Dec., 1969), pp. 3–5, Leonard Collecton.
31. While Obie did begin other projects without a permit, on such a large project, involving so many professional companies and the use of dynamite excavation, he probably secured the proper permits up front. See Oliver interview; Friedman

interview; Ken Garrett interview by WB, Nov. 16, 1995. Also see JG interview, Apr.14, 1994; Navarro and Parker, "The M & O Subway," pp. 1–3.
32. Oliver interview. See also *Star-Telegram*, Oct. 21, 1962, sec. 4, p. 1.
33. *Star-Telegram*, May 27, 1962; *Press*, May 27, 1962; *Hi, Neighbor*, May, 1962, p. 1; Feb., 1963, pp. 9–10.
34. *Press*, July 7, 1962; *Star-Telegram*, July 7, Oct. 21, 1962.
35. *Press*, July 7, 1962; *Star-Telegram*, July 7, Oct. 21, 1962; Oliver interview; Vachule, "Brother Act," p. 122.
36. *Star-Telegram*, Oct. 21, 1962, sec. 4, p. 1.
37. Imogene Montgomery, "FEQ, #246," June, 1995. Also see *Star-Telegram*, Oct. 21, 1962; *Hi, Neighbor*, Oct., 1962, p. 1; Crumby, "FEQ."
38. "A Private Subway," *Time*, Feb. 22, 1963, p. 44; Charles A. Ringler, *Fact Sheet–Leonard Subway System*, press release Feb. 12, 1963, pp. 8–12, Leonard Collection; Lietwiler, "Tramway Revival"; "All Aboard! Leonards Electrical Subway Will Be in Operation Soon," *Fort Worther* (Dec., 1962): 14; *Star-Telegram*, Jan. 23, 27, Feb. 14, 1963; *Press*, Jan. 27, 1963.
39. Oliver interview; Branham interview.
40. "A Private Subway," *Time*, Feb. 22, 1963, p. 44.
41. Kelley interview; Lietwiler, "Tramway Revival."
42. Vachule, "Brother Act," pp. 115–16; Lale interview; *Hi, Neighbor*, Feb., 1963, pp. 6–8; *Star-Telegram*, Feb. 11, 12, 14, 1963; *Press*, Feb. 11, 12, 1963.
43. Vachule, "Brother Act," p. 116. Ringler, *Fact Sheet—Leonard Subway System*; *Star-Telegram*, Feb. 12, 15, 16, 1963.
44. Ringler, *Fact Sheet—Leonard Subway System*; Vachule, "Brother Act," p. 117.
45. Vachule, "Brother Act," p. 108; Johnson interview; *Star-Telegram*, Special Leonards edition, Feb. 14, 1963, pp. 9–10.
46. *Star-Telegram*, Special Leonards edition, Feb. 14, 1963, p. 9.
47. Cook and Moates interview; Bill Belz interview by WB, June 29, 1995. Also see Bill Belz, "FEQ, #023," June, 1995; *Hi, Neighbor*, Sept., 1970, p. 7.
48. Ringler, *Fact Sheet—Leonard Subway System*.
49. Ringler, *Fact Sheet—Leonard Subway System*; *Star-Telegram*, Special Leonards edition, Feb. 14, 1963, p. 9.
50. *Star-Telegram*, Special Leonards edition, Feb. 14, 1963, p. 7. Also see Montgomery, "FEQ."
51. *Star-Telegram*, Special Leonards edition, Feb. 14, 1963, p. 9.
52. Ringler, *Fact Sheet—Leonard Subway System*.
53. Vachule, "Brother Act," p. 108; *Star-Telegram*, Special Leonards edition, Feb. 14, 1963, pp. 1–24.
54. Maddux interview; Powell and Leonard interview.
55. Cook and Moates interview; Paul Leonard interview.
56. Oliver interview; Cook and Moates interview.
57. Memorandum from Clif Overcash re "Consolidation of Warehouse—TV & Appliance Repair Shops," July 2, 1962, LP; Cook and Moates interview.
58. Cook and Moates interview.
59. *Hi Neighbor*, Nov., 1961, p. 2; Jan., 1962, p. 5; Feb., 1962, p. 3; June, 1962, p. 2; July, 1962, p. 2; Sept., 1962, p. 2; Oct., 1962, p. 2; Jan., 1963, p. 2; July, 1963, p. 2; Jan.,

1964, p. 4; Feb., 1964, p. 2 and 4; Feb., 1965, p. 4; Nov., 1964, p. 6; June, 1965, p. 5; Nov., 1965, p. 5; Feb., 1966, p. 7; Mar., 1966, p. 5.

60. Navarro and Parker, "The M & O Subway," pp. 1–7; *Star-Telegram*, Apr. 23, 1965.
61. Financial Statements, 1960–1965, LP.
62. Marvin first established trusts for his daughters in Sept., 1938. Over the years, Marvin and Mary made gifts of stock and other assets to their daughters, and the girls purchased stock and real estate from their parents. See "Report and Agenda," JML Family Meeting, Apr. 3, 1963, LP. Draft of a letter from Frank B. Appleman to the Commissioner of Internal Revenue, seeking a ruling on the tax ramifications of various stock and real estate transactions between the JML family and the O. P. Leonard family, May, 1964, LP. Maddux interview.
63. "Leonards Passing to Younger Men," *Star-Telegram*, Jan. 6, 1965, p. 1.
64. "OPL Family Purchase Plan," LP.
65. Marty Leonard interview, Feb. 14, 1996.
66. "Appointment Cards," Oschner Clinic, New Orleans, La., May 16–19, 1961, LP. Marty Leonard interview, Feb. 14, 1996; Miranda Leonard interview. Fax from Marty V. Leonard to WB, Aug. 27, 1997, authors' possession.
67. During a 1945 bond drive Marvin purchased $16,000 in U.S. Government Series E bonds in his daughters' names and gave credit for the sale of the bonds to the schools they attended. See E. J. Henderson to Lewell Lafferty, Fort Worth National Bank, Dec. 7, 1945, LP; Marty Leonard interview, Feb. 14, 1996; Bradshaw interview, Dec. 9, 1994; Miranda Leonard interview.
68. "Golf Pros Honor Marvin Leonard," *Fort Worth*, June, 1960; C. L. Richhart, "600 Pay Tribute to Leonard Brothers," *Star-Telegram*, Apr. 28, 1962, pp. 1, 4.
69. Program from the 33rd Annual Golden Deeds Banquet, Exchange Club of Fort Worth, 1962.
70. Program from "Carswell Appreciation Day Honoring the Leonard Brothers," June 14, 1963; "Remarks by Marvin Leonard," Leonards clipping book, Leonard Collection.
71. Sandi Major, "The New Look at the Old Schoolhouse," *Press*, Jan. 1, 1967, p. 4A.
72. Maddux and Bradshaw interview; Jake B. Schrum to WB, Sept. 30, 1997.
73. Tony Slaughter, "Arts Council Will Honor Its Donors," *Star-Telegram*, Sept. 12, 1966, p. 4A; "13 Residents Cited for Animal Aid," *Star-Telegram*, Nov. 20, 1963.
74. Maddux interview; *Star-Telegram*, Oct. 5, 1955. On earnings, see Tom A. Whitley to JML, Oct. 17, 1962, LP; Consolidated Profit and Loss Statement, 1962.
75. JG interview, Sept. 19, 1997; *Press*, Mar. 4, 1962; June 24, 1964; "Westover Hills Home Sites," Feb. 1, 1963, Office of John Maddux; "Ridgmar and Westover Hills Sales Records," 1956–71, Office of John Maddux.
76. *Press*, Mar. 4, 1962; June 24, 1964; *Star-Telegram*, May 20, 1956; Dec. 15, 1957; Mar. 13, 1959; Aug. 23, 1963; May 23, 29, 1964. Also see Maddux interview; Hodge interview; JG interview, Nov. 21, 1996; "Ridgmar East Lot Prices," Office of John Maddux.
77. Maddux and Bradshaw interview; Ridgmar aerial photos, Office of John Maddux; Sales Figures, Office of John Maddux.
78. Maddux interview; *Press*, Mar. 2, 1962; "That Ridgmar Addition Growth Breath-Taking Thing to Behold," *Fort Worth* (June, 1964): 20.
79. Maddux interview.

80. Ibid.; *Morning News,* June 30, 1963.
81. Maddux interview; "Map of Ridgmar Addition, 1958," Office of John Maddux.
82. *Star-Telegram,* Mar. 13, 14, 1959; *Press,* Mar. 27, 1959.
83. Maddux interview.
84. On the creation of urban interstates, see David J. St. Clair, *The Motorization of American Cities* (New York: Praeger, 1986), pp. 120–70. Also see aerial photos, 1963–65, Office of John Maddux; Maddux and Bradshaw interview.
85. *Star-Telegram,* Aug. 23, 1963; *Press,* Mar. 4, 1962; *Fort Worth* (June, 1964): 20; "Ridgmar and Westover Hills Sales Records," 1966.
86. *Fort Worth* (June, 1964), 20; *Star-Telegram,* Aug. 23, 1963; Maddux and Bradshaw interview.
87. *Star-Telegram,* Aug. 23, 1963; May 29, 1964; *Press,* May 29, 1964; *Morning News,* May 29, 1964; "Ridgmar and Westover Hills Sales Records," 1964–67. Also see Ford, *Cities and Buildings,* pp. 214–20.
88. "Ridgmar and Westover Hills Sales Records," 1967–70; Maddux and Bradshaw interview.
89. *Press,* June 24, 1964; Nov. 21, 1965; *Star-Telegram,* Mar. 31, Dec. 19, 1965.
90. Maddux interview; Maddux and Bradshaw interview.
91. JG interview, Nov. 21, 1996; Maddux interview. Also see *Fort Worth* (June, 1964): 20; *Press,* Mar. 4, 1962; June 24, 1964.
92. Melvin Simon to Sid Uberman, July 18, 1966, LP; William E. Harris to Bruce Petty, Apr. 8, 1969, LP; Maddux and Bradshaw interview; "Ridgmar and Westover Hills Sales Records," 1969; *Star-Telegram,* Apr. 27, June 28, 1969; *Press,* Mar. 4, 1962; Apr. 27, 1969.
93. *Press,* Apr. 27, 1969; *Star-Telegram,* May 19, June 28, 1969; Maddux interview.
94. For insights into both reasons for selling Shady Oaks, see Trinkle, "Magnanimous Skinflint," 70–71; "Statement of J. M. Leonard regarding Shady Oaks," 1965; "Statement of Jenkins Garrett regarding Shady Oaks," 1965. Also see H. E. Chiles to Shady Oaks Members, Feb. 9, 1970, LP.
95. On what it took to run a club, see minutes of Shady Oaks Department Meetings, 1963–65, LP.
96. Richard L. Crook to the Board of Governors, Shady Oaks Country Club, Aug. 12, 1964, LP; R. L. Crook to Marvin Leonard, Nov. 3, 1964, LP.
97. "Plans for Sale of Shady Oaks, 1958–1968," LP; "Statement of J. M. Leonard regarding Shady Oaks," 1965; "Statement of Jenkins Garrett regarding Shady Oaks," 1965; "Statement of Fred Hodge regarding Shady Oaks," 1965.
98. "Agreement between JML and Shady Oaks Country Club, Inc.," Nov. 1, 1962, LP; "Shady Oaks Financial Statements," 1959–64, LP.
99. "Plans for Sale of Shady Oaks, 1958–1968," LP; "Statement of J. M. Leonard regarding Shady Oaks," 1965; "Statement of Jenkins Garrett regarding Shady Oaks," 1965; "Statement of Fred Hodge regarding Shady Oaks," 1965. Also see Moncrief interview.
100. Chiles to Members, Feb. 9, 1970; JG interviews, Apr. 14, 1994; Feb. 15, 1996; Hodge interview.
101. Chiles to Members, Feb. 9, 1970; JG interviews, Apr. 14, 1994; Feb. 15, 1996; Hodge interview; "Shady Oaks Financial Statements," 1964–68, LP.

102. On the club and the course, see "An Invitation From Shady Oaks Country Club," 1968, Leonard Collection.
103. Barr interview.
104. *Hi, Neighbor*, Mar., 1965, p. 2; June, 1966, p. 2; "Imaginative M & O Remains a Smash Success," *Star-Telegram*, Apr. 23, 1965.
105. "Tandy Buys Leonards," *Star-Telegram*, Aug. 17, 1967.
106. "Leonards Joins Hands with Tandy," *Hi, Neighbor*, Nov., 1967, p. 3.

Epilogue

1. Trinkle, "Magnanimous Skinflint," 72; Maddux interview.
2. John Marvin Leonard, "Certificate of Death," Aug. 26, 1970, #2847; *Star-Telegram*, Aug. 27, 1970; *Press*, Aug. 27, 1970; *Hi, Neighbor*, Sept., 1970, pp. 1, 4–5. Also see Marty Leonard interviews, July 14, 1994; Feb. 14, 1996; Maddux and Bradshaw interview.
3. *Star-Telegram*, Aug. 28, 1970, p. 18A; *Press*, Sept. 13, 1970, p. 26A.
4. JG to WB, handwritten note on *The 1997 Wal-Mart Annual Report*, pp. 18–19. Also see Bolen interview; Langford interview; Woody Graham interview; David Luskey interview. On Wal-Mart, see James Morgan, "Adventures in the Food Chain," *The Atlantic* 269 (June, 1962): 30–40; Sam Walton, *Sam Walton: Made in America, My Story* (New York: Doubleday, 1992); Bill Saporito, "What Sam Walton Taught America," *Forbes*, May 4, 1992, p. 105; Arthur A. Thompson, Jr., et al., "Wal-Mart Stores, Inc.," in *Strategic Management: Concepts & Cases*, ed. Arthur A. Thompson and A. J. Strickland, II (Chicago: Irwin Press, 1995), pp. 852–84; Sandra S. Vance and Roy V. Scott, *Wal-Mart: A History of Sam Walton's Retail Phenomenon*.
5. *Discount Store News*, Dec. 18, 1989, p. 162; Walton, *Made in America*, pp. 11–33.
6. Irvin Farman, *Tandy's Money Machine*, pp. 230–52.
7. Morgan, "Adventures in the Food Chain," 34.
8. Elizabeth Dixon Nisbet, "FEQ, #106," June, 1995. Also see JG interviews, Feb. 8, 1994; Apr. 14, 1994; Apr. 21, 1994; Feb. 15, 1996; Nov. 21, 1996. Mildred Burns, "FEQ, #053," May, 1995, started to work as a sixteen-year-old student in 1948 on Saturdays selling hand bags. She later worked as a bookkeeper. She recalled that in 1948, "I remember the crowds. That's where everyone met." She stopped working in 1975 when "it had lost the family touch of being Leonards."
9. Crumby, "FEQ." Also see Morgan, "Adventures in the Food Chain"; Leach, *Land of Desire*, pp. 263–390; Weiss, *How to Sell to and through Department Stores*, pp. 16–17.
10. Sarah Elizabeth Calloway, "FEQ, #059," June, 1995. "Winning the Grocery Game," *Consumer Reports*, Aug., 1997, pp. 10–17; "Tomorrow's Success Stores: Supercenters Lead the Way to the Future of Retailing," *1997 Wal-Mart Annual Report*, pp. 16–19.
11. See Target, "5% of Our Pre-Tax Profits Go Back to the Communities We Serve," http://www.targetstores.com.
12. Herod, "FEQ."
13. Marty Leonard to WB and VB, Oct. 24, 1997, authors' possession.
14. Margery Nordin, "FEQ, #255," June, 1995. Also see Robert Lundquist, "FEQ, #214," May, 1995, question 85. When he went to work at Leonards in 1954 in men's clothing, he was impressed with Leonards' size, sales volume, and the loyalty and commitment customers felt for the store.

15. *Press,* Sept. 13, 1970; Vera Pyle, "FEQ"; Crumby, "FEQ." Also see Zee Carter, "FEQ, #064," Apr., 1995 who wrote "Mr. Marvin was wonderful. I was never treated like an employee, but as a friend." Adrine L. Nida, "FEQ, #253," wrote, "Mr. Marvin always called me by name and was very friendly."
16. EHS to JML, Dec. 6, 1939, LP. Also see JML to EHS, Dec. 11, 1939; EHS to JML, Dec. 19, 1939, LP.
17. J. Marvin Leonard, "Last Will and Testament, Sept. 27, 1965," LP.
18. Leach interview.
19. Ibid.; JG interview, Sept. 19, 1997.
20. Leach interview; Marty Leonard interviews, July 14, 1994; Feb. 14, 1996.
21. Mary Leonard Porter to Papa, Apr. 21, 1969, LP. Also see JG interview, Sept. 19, 1997.

BIBLIOGRAPHIC ESSAY

Research begins with an act of faith, a belief that enough sources of new information will turn up to justify a book. Starting this project required more faith than usual, for we began with only a few inches of manuscript sources on Marvin Leonard and Leonards. The once substantial collection of business papers had disappeared in the sale of Leonards to Tandy and then to Dillards. Part of the challenge and the fun of writing this book then was discovering enough evidence to build our own archival collection.

Because many of those closely connected to the store and Marvin were getting old we started by doing as many oral interviews as possible. People interviewed included both store employees and those familiar with Marvin and the store. Working through two local churches we taped two group interviews, one with about twenty white former customers and the other with about twenty black former customers. Taken together the interviews helped us gauge how the store changed over time and understand Marvin's management style and business activities outside the store. They gave us the best insights into his character and personality. Some interviews also offered evidence on race relations and business conditions in Fort Worth from 1918 to 1970. Other interviews provided details available nowhere else.

Memories of fifty and more years ago must be carefully scrutinized, and the accuracy of the interviews depends heavily on the interview process and environment. We tried to overcome some of the problems associated with oral histories by using memory prompts, establishing a time line, and asking a standard set of questions. We held many interviews in individual's homes or in other settings in which they felt most comfortable. In our opening remarks we attempted to get them to relax and impressed on them the importance of their contribution to our work. Fortunately most of our conclusions could be verified by more than one interview. Each interview was indexed, and all quotes from the interviews were taken from the tapes.

As we did the interviews many of the people we interviewed kindly gave us letters, memos, and clippings regarding the store. J. B. Moates brought a gleam to our eyes when he gave us complete financial records for the 1950s and early 1960s. Still, we needed more. We looked at the local bank where Marvin had served as a director and came up empty. Visits to the Texas State Library and to the American History Center at the University of Texas added newspapers and county voting records to our store of information. At the University of Texas at Arlington Library we found a useful set of clippings and photographs on Marvin and the store. We also found the papers of other Fort Worth businessmen. The local history collections at the Fort Worth Public Library contained a few more papers of local businessmen and a good selection of city maps and Chamber of Commerce publications. Their "WPA Guide to Fort Worth" was among our most useful sources on the city from 1910 to 1940. They also had excellent clippings files on race relations and other important topics. Unearthing these varied sources helped us form better questions, but they did not always answer them. Marvin remained a distant, godlike figure.

Finally about midway through the project we hit the jackpot. Two large cardboard boxes of letters, memos, financial records from the 1920s to the 1960s, and other papers related to Marvin Leonard and Leonards were found in the basement of his home. They waited for us in a cabinet in the corner for twenty-five years or more until the house was being cleaned after his widow's death. The contents of these boxes offered the best understanding of his personality and motivation. These papers, referred to in the notes as the Leonard Papers, together with other primary source material given to us by those connected to Leonards form the Leonard Collection. Also part of the collection are the photographs, in-store publications, and other material assembled by Marty Leonard for the Leonards Museum.

Incorporated with the Leonard Collection were two unpublished manuscripts: Jo Ann Vachule, "The Brother Act," (typescript, 1988) and John David Scott, "Obie," (typescript, 1983). Both manuscripts included extensive quotes from interviews conducted with now-deceased members of the family and store managers. The Vachule manuscript also contained a useful family tree.

Despite finding a substantial cache of primary source material and doing more than sixty oral interviews, an obvious gap in our records remained. We had very little information on the average employee below the department manager level and very few female perspectives. Taking advantage of a mailing list assembled in 1995 by Marty Leonard when she began soliciting memorabilia for the Leonards Museum, we mailed out questionnaires to 412 former employees. After sending a follow up letter and then telephoning those who had not responded, we collected a total of 86 completed questionnaires—about 25 percent of the sample after accounting for invalid addresses and deaths that occurred since the list was compiled.

Like oral history, using questionnaires brings a list of well-known problems. Many former employees were long dead so our sample could never be representative of the total population of former employees. Those who were most estranged from the store were probably not on the list of 412 or may not have responded. Memory varies from reality when you write as well as when you speak. To compensate for these problems we followed the procedures laid out in Arlene Fink, *How to Conduct Surveys: A Step by Step Guide* (Beverly Hills, Calif.: Sage, 1985) and Seymour Sudman and Norman M. Bradburn, *Improving Interview Method and Questionnaire Design* (San Francisco: Jossey-Bass, 1979).

The questionnaire used both forced-choice and open-ended questions. Some questions required that the respondents recall factual information—for example, when the employee began work, what department he or she worked in, and what tasks would make up a regular work day. Others tapped perceptual dimensions of working for Leonards. Several of the dimensions we were interested in have well-tested measures. For these questions, which focused on employees attitudes about their supervisors, their identification with Leonards, and their satisfaction with various aspects of working at the store, we relied on John P. Robinson, Robert Athanasion, and Kendra B. Heads's *Measures of Occupational Attitudes and Occupational Characteristics* (Ann Arbor, Mich.: Institute of Social Research, 1969) for specific questions and scales.

We took several precautions to make the questionnaire as reliable, valid, and useful as possible. The close-ended questions all used a 5-point Likert scale, and as noted above, we used scaled measures for attitudinal questions. We customized the remaining questions as much as possible to the unique circumstances at Leonards to serve as a memory prompt and to increase the validity of our measures. Because the sample we surveyed was composed primarily of older adults, we used a large, easy-to-read typeface on the survey instrument and allowed ample space for respondents to reply, clarify, and elaborate on each question. We pre-tested the questionnaire on a small group of non-Leonards employees of a similar age to make sure that the questionnaire was readable and not overly taxing in length or difficulty. We pre-tested whether respondents could understand each question and without too much difficulty recall the information requested. As in the case of oral interviews, we also compared the questionnaire responses with other sources.

While they have limitations, the questionnaires offered a one-of-a-kind glimpse of the store and Marvin Leonard from the bottom up. The former employees that responded held a variety of jobs in departments across the store and began working for the store as early as 1928 and as late as 1970. An almost equal number of men and women filled out questionnaires. In addition to answering questions about attitudes and work life at Leonards, respondents filled in details about job training, compensation, customers, and major competitors. They also told us their fondest memories and recounted events that still rankled after all these years. Their biographical information allowed us to make tentative observations on the demographic makeup of store employees. These questionnaires are cited in the notes as: "Former Employee Questionnaire (FEQ)." Eventually the questionnaires and the Leonard Collection will be donated to the University of Texas at Arlington Library.

We filled some remaining gaps in our information by carefully reading local newspapers. Northeast Texas papers offered much on what it was like to grow up in the region at the turn of the century. The Fort Worth newspapers were particularly useful in rounding out our picture of competitive conditions in the 1920s. They answered the compelling questions of why and how Leonards was successful when so many other similar stores failed. Our great regret was that we found no surviving collections of the numerous newspapers published for the Fort Worth black community.

What the newspapers could not tell us we often found by consulting published sources. Over the years several articles were written about Marvin, his brother Obie, and the store. We also used the U.S. Census, *The Texas Almanac,* government publications about Cass County, memoirs, autobiographies, and contemporary studies of retailing. Again, some of these sources have defects. Those who write an autobiography or memoir bring their own biases and distorted memories to their work. Studies of current business conditions in the 1920s may be just as nearsighted as studies of current business conditions in the 1990s. As often as possible we balanced these sources against others.

In the end our detective work paid off. This book is based on the large body of primary source material that is summarized below.

Our notes indicate when we have also relied upon secondary sources. In addition, those interested in the field should consult the list of store histories included after the summary of primary sources. These are books and articles that helped us understand the unique features of this industry.

ARCHIVAL COLLECTIONS

Leonard Collection/Leonard Museum
Marvin Leonard Papers
Business Records
Photographs
In-store Publications: *The Whisper* (1920s); *Lenco News* (1950s); *Hi, Neighbor* (1950s & 1960s)
Leonard Family, "Certificates of Death"
Cass County Property Tax Receipts

Jo Ann Vachule, "The Brother Act," (typescript, 1988)
John David Scott, "Obie," (typescript, 1983)

Local History Division, Fort Worth Public Library
Works Progress Administration Guide to Fort Worth (unpublished manuscript compiled between 1938 and 1941). In particular see Department Stores, "WPA Guide to Fort Worth," page 16556.
Chamber of Commerce Publications
Publications by Fort Worth Businesses
Fort Worth Maps
Mary Daggett Lake Papers
Clippings files
Business History, Miscellaneous Manuscripts

Jenkins Garrett Library, University of Texas at Arlington
William Jary Collection
WPA Guide to Fort Worth (manuscript)
Star-Telegram Photographs & Special Editions
George Washington Armstrong Collection
Herbert Breedlove Fuqua Papers

Texas State Library
Election Returns, 1887, 1911, Secretary of State Papers

NEWSPAPERS
Atlanta (Tex.) Citizens Journal, 1904–1908
Atlanta (Tex.) News, 1910–11
Cass County Sun, 1906–10
Dallas Morning News, 1921–68
Fort Worth Star-Telegram, 1918–70
Fort Worth Press, 1922–70
Fort Worth Shopper, 1930–60
Jefferson Jimplecute, 1900–15
New York Times, 1962–70
Oklahoma City Daily Oklahoman, 1941
Omaha (Tex.) Breeze, 1908–14
Pittsburg (Tex.) Gazette, 1895–1915
Sulphur Springs Gazette, 1911–14

ORAL INTERVIEWS
(VB = Victoria Buenger; WB = Walter Buenger)
Barnes, Burl, by WB, May 4, 1995.
Barr, Willard, by WB, April 14, 1994.
Belz, Bill, by WB, June 29, 1995.
Bird, Francis, by WB, August 26, 1994.
Blair, James, by WB, July 6, 1995.

Bolen, Bob, by WB, February 17, 1995.
Bourland, Vergal, by WB, February 19, 1994.
Bradshaw, Madelon Leonard, by VB & WB, December 9, 1994; by VB, June 8, 1997.
Branham, Juanita, by VB, February 19, 1994.
Brooks, Marion J., by WB, May 29, 1996.
Cano, Joe, by WB, February 8, 1994.
Carter, Lillie Bell, by WB, January 9, 1995.
Cook, Ralph (and J. B. Moates), by VB & WB, August 8, 1994.
Farman, Irv, by WB, July 1, 1994.
Friedman, Bayard, by WB, June 21, 1994.
Garrett, Jenkins, by WB, February 8, 1994; by WB, April 14, 1994; by VB & WB, April 21, 1994; by WB, February 15, 1996; by WB, November 21, 1996; by VB & WB, March 7, 1997; by VB & WB, May 8, 9, 1997; by VB & WB, May 12, 13, 1997; by WB, September 19, 1997.
Garrett, Jenkins, Marty Leonard, and Madelon Bradshaw, by WB, September 17, 1997.
Garrett, Ken, by WB, November 16, 1995.
Graham, Fred L., by WB, November 16, 1995.
Graham, Woody, by WB, May 6, 1994.
Hester, J. B. "Jack," by WB, May 4, 1995.
Hodge, T. F. "Fred," by WB, May 5, 1994.
Hogan, Ben, by Robert A. Calvert & Larry D. Hill, February 8, 1994.
Hubbard, John Barry, by WB, January 11, 1995.
Hudson, Charles, by WB, February 16, 1995.
James, John R., by WB, August 26, 1994.
Johnson, Bob, by WB, August 24, 1994.
Kelley, C. F., by WB, June 29, 1994.
Lale, Max, and Cissy Stewart Lale, by WB, May 15, 1996.
Langford, Maurice, by WB, June 28, 1995.
Laughbaum, F. W., by VB & WB, April 21, 1994.
Leach, Jim, by WB, February 8, 1994.
Leonard, Gayle (and Connie Powell), by WB, August 25, 1994.
Leonard, Marty, by VB & WB, July 14, 1994; by WB, February 14, 1996; by VB & WB, May 20, 1997; by WB, August 18, 1997.
Leonard, Margery, by WB, January 9, 1995.
Leonard, Miranda, by VB & WB, October 27–28, 1996.
Leonard, Paul, by VB & WB, October 14, 1994.
Love, Helen, by WB, June 30, 1994.
Luskey, David, by WB, January 10, 1995.
Luskey, Louis, by WB, June 30, 1994.
McBrayer, Stayley, by WB, June 20, 1994.
McClure, Cricket, by VB & WB, October 16, 1994.
McMurray, Jack, by VB & WB, June 11, 1994.
Maddux, John, by VB & WB, June 10, 1994.
Maddux, John, and Madelon Leonard Bradshaw, by WB, September 17, 1997.
Moates, J. B., by Robert A. Calvert & Larry D. Hill, February 8, 1994; Moates (and Ralph Cook), by VB & WB, August 8, 1994.

Moncrief, Tex, by WB, June 20, 1994.
Neely, M. J., by WB, June 21, 1994.
Newsome, Wilbur, by VB & Tom Born, June 1, 1994.
Nisbet, Elizabeth Dixon, by WB, June 29, 1995.
Oliver, Woody, by WB, June 30, 1995.
Owens, Darlene, by WB, August 16, 1995.
Powell, Connie (and Gayle Leonard), by WB, August 25, 1994.
Ringler, Charles, by WB, April 14, 1994; by WB, February 16, 1995.
Rosen Heights Baptist Group Video by VB & WB, March 23, 1995.
Rubin, Benny, by VB & WB, April 21, 1994.
Russell, Harvey, by WB, August 24, 1994.
St. James Baptist Prayer Group by WB, May 29, 1996.
Shea, Ray, by VB & WB, June 11, 1994.
Shockley, Lloyd and Ruth, by VB & Born, June 1, 1994; by WB, June 28, 1995.
Stewart, Homer, by WB, January 11, 1995.
Tallman, Oscar, by WB, June 29, 1994.
Tyree, Hugh and Laura Mae, by WB, July 1, 1994.
Vaughan, Libbie, by WB, January 10, 1995.
Webber, Bobby, by WB, August 18, 1995.
Zachery, Mack, by WB, May 6, 1994.

PUBLISHED SOURCES

Barton, L. M. *A Study of 81 Principal American Markets*. Chicago: 100,000 Group of American Cities, 1925.
Clark, Neil M. "Brother Act." *Saturday Evening Post* (June 24, 1944): 14–15, 59–63.
Emmet, Boris. *Department Stores: Recent Policies, Costs, and Profits*. Stanford, Calif.: Stanford University Press, 1930.
Entenberg, Robert David. *The Changing Competitive Position of Department Stores in the United States by Merchandise Lines*. Pittsburgh, Pa.: University of Pittsburgh Press, 1957.
Grossman, Louis H. *Department Store Merchandising in Changing Environments*. East Lansing: Michigan State University Business Studies, 1970.
Hollander, Stanley C. *Restraints upon Retail Competition*. East Lansing: Bureau of Business and Economic Research, Michigan State University, 1965.
Hollander, Stanley C. "Retailing: Cause or Effect." In *Emerging Concepts in Marketing*, edited by William S. Decker. Chicago: American Marketing Association, 1963.
Humphrey, William. *Farther Off from Heaven*. New York: Alfred A. Knopf, 1977.
Johnston, John Wallis. *The Department Store Buyer*. Austin, Tex.: Bureau of Business Research, 1969.
Kuznets, Simon S. *Cyclical Fluctuations: Retail and Wholesale Trade United States, 1919–1925*. Westport, Conn.: Hyperion Press, 1926.
Leonard v. Small, County Judge, et al., No. 12277, *South Western Reporter*, second series, 826–30.
McDaniel, Ruel. "How Those Amazing Leonard Brothers Gross $8,000,000 a Year." *American Business* 8 (October, 1938): 22–24, 48–49.
Owens, William A. *A Season of Weathering*. New York: Scribner's, 1973.
Owens, William A. *This Stubborn Soil*. New York: Scribner's, 1966.

Pope, Lena. *Hand on My Shoulder: The Story of Lena Pope and the Home that Evolved from Her Dreams*. Fort Worth: Branch-Smith, 1966.
Texas Almanac and State Industrial Guide, 1904. Galveston: A. H. Belo, 1904.
Texas Almanac and State Industrial Guide, 1914. Galveston: A. H. Belo, 1914.
Texas Almanac and State Industrial Guide, 1925. Dallas: A. H. Belo, 1925.
Texas Almanac and State Industrial Guide, 1929. Dallas: A. H. Belo, 1929.
Texas Almanac and State Industrial Guide, 1931. Dallas: A. H. Belo, 1931.
Time. September 6, 1948, p. 84; February 22, 1963, p. 44.
Trinkle, Jim. "Golf's Magnanimous Skinflint." *Golf Digest* 22 (May, 1970): 48–50, 70–71.
United States of America v. Safeway Stores, Incorporated. Civil No. 3173, Fort Worth Division, 1956.
Weiss, E. B. *How to Sell to and through Department Stores*. New York: McGraw-Hill Book Company, 1936.
Whitmore, Eugene. "The Miracle Merchants of Ft. Worth." *American Business* 19 (April, 1949): 8–9, 36–38.

STORE HISTORIES

Baker, Henry Givens. *Rich's of Atlanta: The Story of a Store Since 1867*. Athens: School of Business Analysis, University of Georgia, 1953.
Benson, John, and Gareth Shaw, eds. *The Evolution of Retail Systems, 1800–1914*. New York: Leicester University Press, 1992.
Benson, Susan Porter. *Counter Cultures: Saleswomen, Managers, and Customers in American Department Stores, 1890–1940*. Chicago: University of Illinois Press, 1986.
Brough, James. *The Woolworths*. New York: McGraw-Hill, 1982.
Curry, Mary Elizabeth. *Creating an American Institution: The Merchandising Genius of J. C. Penney*. New York: Garland Publishing, 1993.
Farman, Irvin. *Tandy's Money Machine*. Chicago: Mobium Press, 1992.
Greer, William. *America the Bountiful: How the Supermarket Came to Main Street*. Washington, D.C.: Food Marketing Institute, 1986.
Hendrickson, Robert. *The Grand Emporium*. New York: Stein and Day, 1979.
Katz, Donald. *The Big Store: Inside the Crisis and Revolution at Sears*. New York: Viking, 1987.
Klassen, Henry C. "T. C. Power & Bro.: The Rise of a Small Western Department Store, 1870–1902." *Business History Review* 66 (Winter, 1992): 671–722.
Leach, William. *Land of Desire: Merchants, Power, and the Rise of a New American Culture*. New York: Pantheon Books, 1993.
Lebhar, Godfrey. *Chain Stores in America, 1859–1950*. New York: Chain Store Publishing, 1950.
Marcus, Stanley. *Minding the Store*. Boston: Little, Brown, and Co., 1974.
Raucher, Alan R. "Dime Store Chains: The Making of Organization Men, 1880–1940." *Business History Review* 65 (Spring, 1991): 130–63.
Rosenberg, Leon Joseph. *Dillard's: The First Fifty Years*. Fayetteville: University of Arkansas Press, 1988.
Rosenberg, Leon Joseph. *Sangers': Pioneer Texas Merchants*. Austin: Texas State Historical Association, 1978.

Samson, Peter. "The Department Store, Its Past and Its Future: A Review Article." *Business History Review* 55 (Spring, 1981): 26–34.

Santick, Joy L. *Timothy Eaton and the Rise of His Department Store.* Toronto: University of Toronto Press, 1990.

Sibley, Celestine. *Dear Store: An Affectionate Portrait of Rich's.* Garden City, N.Y.: Doubleday, 1967.

Strasser, Susan. *Satisfaction Guaranteed: The Making of the American Mass Market.* New York: Pantheon Books, 1989.

Sumner, G. Lynn. *The Story of W. T. Grant and the Early Days of the Business He Founded.* New York: Prentice-Hall, 1954.

Tedlow, Richard. *New and Improved: The Story of Mass Marketing in America.* New York: Basic Books, 1990.

Traub, Marvin, and Tom Teicholz. *Like No Other Store: The Bloomingdale's Legend and the Revolution in American Marketing.* New York: Time Books, 1993.

Twyman, Robert W. *History of Marshall Field and Co.* Philadelphia: University of Pennsylvania Press, 1954.

Wendt, Lloyd, and Herman Kogan. *Give the Lady What She Wants! The Story of Marshall Field and Company.* Chicago: Rand McNally and Co., 1952.

White, John R., and Kevin D. Gray. *Shopping Centers and Other Retail Properties: Investment, Development, Financing, and Management.* New York: John Wiley & Sons, 1996.

Vance, Sandra S., and Roy V. Scott. *Wal-Mart: A History of Sam Walton's Retail Phenomenon.* New York: Twayne Publishers, 1994.

INDEX

Pages containing illustrations appear in bold.

A. and L. August, 52
A&P (Great Atlantic and Pacific Tea Company), 38; strategy in Fort Worth, 46–49
Allen & Company, 116
Allied Stores Corporation, 114–16

Banks, W. A. (employee), 92
Barksdale, M. B. (employee), 101
Barr, Willard, 144, 188
Barton, Mary (employee), 127
Belz, Bill (employee), 171
Bigby, Cliff (employee), 91
blacks: and Leonards, 76–77, 118, 141–46
Blair, James (employee), 85, 107, 126
Bledsoe, Roy (employee), 91
Bohrer, J. E. (employee), 59
Bomar, W. P., 143
Bourland, Vergal, 111–12
Brachman, Solomon, 151
Bradshaw, Madelon Leonard (daughter of Marvin), 83, 84, **147,** 178
Branham, Juanita (employee), 101–102
Breacher's, 52
Bredemus, John, 79
Brooks, Marion J., 143, 145
Bruner, Carl: background, 70–71, 128; as a consultant, 109, 113, 114, 116–18, 121; diverse roles at Leonards, 66, 86, 101, 102, 138, 158

Cano, Joe, 4, 112
Carr, O. E., 64
Carswell Air Force Base, 117, 180

Carter, Amon, 78, 112, 136, 143, 179; and Johnson Ranch, 147–49
Carter, Kerven, 144
Carter, Lillie Bell, 118
Carter & Burgess, 182
cash-only stores, 26–27, 38, 192. *See also* Piggly Wiggly
Cass, A. B., Jr., 184–85
Cass County, Texas, 16. *See also* Linden, Texas; Northeast Texas
chain stores, 41, 46, 47, 49, 52, 54–55, 114–17, 127, 132. *See also* grocery industry; retailing industry
Chicago Mail Order Co., 116
Chizum, Gaylord, 152
Churchill, H. L., 114
Civil Service Board. *See* Leonard, Marvin: community service
Clark, Sterling, 63
Cockrell, E. R., 63
Coffee, Alden, 4, 112
Cohn, Saul, 115
Colonial Country Club: design and location, 79–80; and fire, 113; map, 80; Marvin and management, 110–12, 194; membership, 66, 81, 112; National Invitational, 110–12; opening, 61, 79; sale to members, 112–13
Colton's, 52
Cook, Ralph (employee), 174
cotton: in Cass County, 16, 19; and debt, 21; and Fort Worth, 33, 48, 75; and Marvin's move to Dallas, 27–28
Cox's, 117, 161

Cravens, Travis, 151
Crook, R. L., 186
Crumby, Elba (employee), 77, 195
Culps, Carl (employee), 138–39

Dallas, Texas, 25, 28–29
Dallas Rupe & Son, 116
Deal, I. C., 184
DeBakey, Michael, 177
Dillard's, 185
Dobson and Co., 37
Drennan, Lois "Steve" (employee), 91, 145
Dyer, Ed (employee), 91

Ellison's, 117
Empress Fashion Shop, 50
Erwin, Morris E. (employee), 69
Ettelson, C. L. "Collie," 105–106
Everybody's, 95, **96,** 164, 176–77; birth, 85; customers, 135; financial performance, 86, 135, 175; merchandise and product lines, 86, 95, 135; merger with Leonards, 165, 173–75; promotions, 94, 135–36; renovation, 135; strategy, 86, 95, 135–36
Exchange Club of Fort Worth, 178

Fair, The, 52, 74, 117, 161
Fakes Furniture, 57, 117
Federated Stores, 122
Ferguson, C. R. (employee), 89–90
1st Street Grocery, 45
Foley's, 122
Fort Worth, Texas: downtown, 117–18, 134, 157, 160–61, 188–89; Downtown Fort Worth Association, 161, 166, 175, 188; Flood of 1949, 153; and the Great Depression, 78–79; maps, 36, 120, 176, 181; population and economy, 1910–1930, 25, 33–35, 39, 45–48, 56, 72–74; population and economy, 1930–1960, 104, 117, 121, 127, 131–32, 141–42, 150, 161; population and economy after 1960, 180–81; race relations, 141–43; suburbs, 117, 157, 161, 183, 188–89; Town Hall movement, 188; trade area, 29, 34, 47, 55, 73, 127; and World War II, 106–107

Fort Worth Good Government League, 185
Fort Worth Merchandise Co. *See* Leonards: wholesale operations
Fort Worth National Bank, 74, 143, 175, 179, 185; and Leonards, 37, 44, 124, 167; and Marvin, 109–10, 152; merger with Farmers and Mechanics National Bank, 47
Fort Worth Wholesale Grocery. *See* Leonards: wholesale operations
Fort Worth Wholesale Produce. *See* Leonards: wholesale operations
Four State Salvage, 37
Friedman, H. E., 150
Frigidaire, 55
Fruhman, Martin, 116
Fuqua, H. B. "Babe," 143, 152
furnishing merchants, 26–27
F. W. Woolworth & Co., 54, 195

Gamble-Skogmo, 116
Gan's, 52–53
Garrett, Jenkins (employee): and Bluff Park case, 66–67; diverse roles, 138, 153, 159, 163; as Leonards' attorney, 133–34, 151, 177, 183, 185; and Marvin, 144–45; pre-1945, 82, 118; post-1945, 131, 139, 146–47, **149,** 152, 188, 196
Garrett, Virginia, 131
Genung, J. H., 46
Gimbels, 115, 140
Glen Garden Country Club, 79, 178
Golden Deeds Award, 178
golf: and bent grass, 79–80, 112; U.S. Open Golf Tournament of 1941, 112. *See also* Colonial Country Club; Glen Garden Country Club; River Crest Country Club; Shady Oaks Country Club; Starr Hollow Ranch
Graham, Woody (employee), 139, 174
Great Atlantic and Pacific Tea Company. *See* A&P
Green, H. S., 185
Green, William T., 185
Griffith, John (son-in-law of Marvin), 150, 152

grocery industry: and credit, 38; independents, 38, 41–42, 49; national chains, 38–49, 68, 133–34, 192; Neighborhood Grocers Association, 42; rivalry and trends, 38–39, 41–42, 46–49, 133–34. *See also* individual stores
G. T. Leonard Grocery, 41, 86, 95

Haberer, B. V. "Bill" (employee), 101, 138–39, 163, 174
Hamrick, Claude (employee), 90
Hanger, William A. "Bill," 63–64
Hann, Armour (employee), 90, 140, 163
Harding, Robert Ellison, 109, 114, 116–17; and Marvin Leonard, 37–38, 44. *See also* Fort Worth National Bank
Harry J. Adams, 42, 45
Haws and Garrett, 167
Helpy-Selfy Grocery, 49
Henderson, Elam (employee), 101, **102**, 129–30, 140–41, 150; background, 137–38
Henderson, Jessie May, 150
Hester, Jack (employee), 101, 133, 158
H. H. Pittman, 42
Hodge, Fred, 187
Hogan, Ben, 110, **111**, 151–52
Houtchens, S. F., 66
Hughes, Lawrence, 149
Hurdleston, Charles H., 64

Jackson's, 52
J. C. Penney, 52, 54, 55, 127; and Ridgmar Mall, 185; strategy, 132
John Leonard, Dealer in General Merchandise, 18–19
Johnson, Bob (employee), 171
Jones, Robert Trent, 149
Joske's, 130

Kee, John A., 104
Kelley, C. F. (employee), 129–31, 141
Kinney's Shoes, 55
Ku Klux Klan: in Fort Worth, 63–66; and Marvin, 64–66

Lattimore, Hal, Sr., 64

Laughbaum, F. W., 132, 188
Leach, J. S. "Jim" (employee), 101, 104, 113, 158, 196
Lederman's Cigar Store, 50
Lena Pope Home, **5**, 78, 82, 113, 143, 152, 155, 179, 194
Leonard, Bob (Robert Woolridge, son of Obie), 62, 136–37, 163, 188
Leonard, Byrdie Clementine (sister of Marvin), 17
Leonard, Cora Suvalia (sister of Marvin), 17
Leonard, Emma Clementine "Tiny" Hill (mother of Marvin), 17, 21; death, 29
Leonard, Enola (Emma Enola, Mrs. J. C. Moulton, sister of Marvin), 20, 36–37, 49, 62, 79, 84; birth, 19; marriage and family, 82; and Marvin, 29; ownership of Leonards stock, 41
Leonard, John (Obadiah John Thomas, father of Marvin), 16, 21, 37; death, 62; family, **18**; family farm, 20–21. *See also* John Leonard Dealer in General Merchandise
Leonard, Laura Maranda (sister of Marvin), 17
Leonard, Mabel (wife of Tom), 36
Leonard, Margery (Margery Fay Woolridge, wife of Obie), 50–51, 62, 124, 154
Leonard, Margery Ann (Mrs. Leland Hodges, daughter of Obie), 62
Leonard, Martha Ann (sister of Marvin), 17, 19
Leonard, Martha Jane (Mrs. James Anthony, daughter of Obie), 62
Leonard, Marty (Martha Vaughan, daughter of Marvin), 83, 84, 146, **147**, 150, 177
Leonard, Marvin (John Marvin), **5, 9, 18, 26, 81, 84, 102, 111, 147, 149, 149**; analytical abilities, 22, 196; birth, 15; childhood, 15, 19–31; community service, 82–83, 113, 179, 193–94; contrasted with Obie, 50, 113, 146, 169; in Dallas, 28; death, 15, 190; diverse investments, 152; and downtown, 161, 166, 188, 192; education, 21; education in

Leonard, Marvin *(cont.)*
storekeeping, 25–28; family life, 82–85, 146; golf, 71, 79–82, 110, 146, 152, 194; health, 79, 154, 177, 192; honors, 178–79, 190; and Leonards, 4, 136, 157, 190; management style, 7, 50, 69–72, 76, 95, 99, 100, 103, 130, 134, 158, 197; marketing touch, 6, 77, 92, 124, 185; marriage, 82, 155; "Mr. Marvin," 4; personality, 4, 62, 75–76, 84–85, 106, 116, 144, 178, 197; philanthropy, 78–79, 113, 152–53, 179, 194; and race, 24, 144; and security, 30, 114, 153–54, 177, 186, 188, 195; and social life, 51, 110, 154, 188; status in Fort Worth, 15, 67, 78, 87, 121–22, 157, 178–79; and taxes, 108–109, 113, 116, 151, 176; and World War I, 27–28. *See also* Fort Worth, Texas; Fort Worth National Bank; Ku Klux Klan; prohibition

Leonard, Marvin, oil and gas, 108–109, 118, 151–52, 176; with Neville Penrose, 108–109

Leonard, Marvin, real estate and insurance interests: Bellaire estates, 108; Bluff Park, 66–67, 121; Colonial Hills, 82, 109; David Crockett Life Insurance, 151; residential development, 50, 73, 82, 151, 176–77; Seventh Street Realty, 109; State Reserve Life, 151, 176–77; Tarrant Realty, 109. *See also* Ridgmar

Leonard, Mary (Mary Elinor Vaughan, wife of Marvin), 82–85, **84, 147,** 150, 154–55, 196

Leonard, Mary (Mary Elinor Leonard Porter, daughter of Marvin), 82, 83, **147,** 178

Leonard, Miranda (daughter of Marvin), 65, 83, 84, 146, **147,** 178

Leonard, Nancy Alice Powell (wife of Paul), 137

Leonard, Obie (Obadiah Paul, brother of Marvin), 20, 43, 45, **48,** 49, 97, **102,** 113; birth, 19; community service, 136–37; education, 22–23, 29; and insurance, 151; and investments, 113–14, 136–37, 189; marriage and family, 50–51, 62; "Mr. Obie," 4; and new construction and renovation at Leonards, 75, 104, 123–24; partnership with Marvin, 41, 146; and pecans, 62, 66, 114, 136; purchase of Leonards, 176–77; and race relations, 145–46; role at Leonards, 6, 36, 50, 123, 126, 158; and subway, 167–70. *See also* Leonards, 1948–1962: escalators

Leonard, Paul (Obie Paul, son of Obie), 51, 113, 130, 136–38; and management, 140–41, 159, 162–65, 188–89

Leonard, Tom (Green Thomas, brother of Marvin), 17, 35–37, 95, 155. *See also* G. T. Leonard Grocery

Leonard, Virginia McGinley (wife of Bob), 137

Leonards, **9–14, 44, 76, 121, 125, 147;** customer loyalty, 3–4, 194–95; drugs, 68–69, 87, 90, 140; Farm Store, 104–105, 122, 134; groceries, 35, 39–41, 43, 68, 86–87, 89–90, 96, 101, 108, 120, 126, 133–34; hard lines, 43–45, 71, 87, 91, 97, 100, 120, 122, 171; identity and basic characteristics, 3–8, 27, 60, 68, 77–78, 87, 105–106, 153, 158–59, 171, 192–95; management succession, 114, 136–38, 140, 177; and mannequins, 6, 118, 123, 124; name, 3, 41, 45, 120–24, 131; possible sale of, 77–78, 105–106, 114–17; soft lines, 90, 97, 101, 120, 122, 123, 164; wholesale operations, 49, 68, 95–96, 176–77; and women employees, 91, 102, 107; workroom operations, 75, 86, 96, 104, 122

Leonards, 1918–1929: advertising, 40, 58–59; birth, 32, 35–38; and chain store competition, 39, 43, 46–47, 55, 58–60; competitors, 37–39, 46, 49, 58 (*see also* under individual store names); credit for expansion, *see* Fort Worth National Bank; customers, 47, 59–60, 69; decor, 47, 72; employees, 50, 69 (*see also* under individual employee names); financial performance, 32, 37, 67, 74; layout, 35, 43, 44, 59; and Leonard family, 37, 49–

50; location and size, 32; merchandise and product lines, 35, 40–41, 43–45, 50, 68, 72; operations, 68–72; parking, 66; and railroads, 40; service, 59; sources of merchandise, 35, 37, 39–40, 43–44, 50, 58, 59; strategy, 33, 39, 49, 52, 55, 58–60, 68–69; structure, 50, 71–72

Leonards, 1930–1947: administration, 101; advertising, 89; air conditioning, **11**, 101, 122; atmosphere, 77, 87; and blacks, 118; check cashing, 92; compensation, 102–103; competitors, 94–95 (*see also* under individual store names); customers, 76–77, 89, 105; decor, 89, 115; employees, 84 (*see also* under individual employee names); and Fair Trade Laws, 97–98; financial performance, 85, 103, 108, 115; graph, 163; and the Great Depression, 74, 78–79, 85; layout, 75, 89–92; location and size, 75, 95, 100; merchandise and product lines, 89–92, 97–99, 104, 114; new construction and renovation, 74–76, 87, 104; parking, 105; promotions, 77, 93–95; and scrip, 78; service, 92, 93, 99–100; sources of merchandise, 95, 96–99, 107–108; strategy, 86, 89, 95, 97; structure, 91, 98, 99–103, 117; and World War II, 106–108

Leonards, 1948–1962: administration, 126, 129; advertising, 132–33; atmosphere, 124; bureaucracy, 139–40, 159, 160; chain store controls, 129–31, 141; compensation, 125; competitors, 132–35, 164 (*see also* under individual store names); credit for expansion, *see* Fort Worth National Bank; customer credit, 134, 153, 164–65; customers, 127, 140, 142; decor, 122; and desegregation, 141–46; escalators, 124, **125;** Executive Committee, 163–65; Fair Trade Laws, 133; fashion, 122, 123, 128; financial performance, 121, 129, 130–31, 134, 135, 162; graph, 163; layout, 120–26; location and size, 120, 122, 139; merchandise and product lines, 126, 129, 130, 159; parking, 134; personnel policy, 159–60; promotions, 124, 126, 128, 152; and Safeway, 133–34; sources of merchandise, 125, 130, 133; strategy, 119, 122–23, 127, 164–66; structure, 125–27, 129

Leonards, after 1962: administration, 173–74; advertising, 172; automation, 188; bureaucracy, 175, 193; credit for expansion, *see* Fort Worth National Bank; customers, 170; Executive Committee, 175; financial performance, 175–76; layout, 170–73; location and size, 170–71; merchandise and product lines, 174; new construction and renovation, 165–66, 169, 172–73; promotions, 171; sale to Dillard's, 192–93; sale to O. P. Leonard family, 157, 176–77; sale to Tandy Corporation, 157, 189, 193; and suburbs, 192; subway, *see* M & O Subway; subway aisle, 171; warehouse operations, 174

Leveridge, Ted (employee), 86, 135
L. G. Gilbert, 35, 51, 54
Lillianthal, Felix, 101
Linden, Texas, 16, 23–25; schools, 22
Lit Brothers, 141
Lockridge, Robert F., 124
Long, Jack, 48–49
Love, Helen (employee), 107, 126
Lupton, Charles, 83
Luskey's, 117

M & O Subway, **13, 168,** 175, 189; construction, 166–70; opening, 170; symbolism of, 8, 157, 179
McBrayer, Stayley, 152
McDonald, Durwood, 106, 114, 116
McDonald, William M., 63
Mack, Hobson (employee), 69
Mack, Robert (employee), 69
Macy's, 114–16
Maddux, John, 144, 190; and Ridgmar, 182–85
Marcus, Stanley, 151. *See also* Neiman Marcus
Marvin & Obie Leonard Junior High School, 179

INDEX   243

Massingham, F. T. (employee), 69
Maxwell, Perry, 79
May Department Store, 115
Meacham, Henry, 64
Meacham's, 51, 54, 117
Mistletoe Heights (Fort Worth), 82
Moates, J. B. (employee), 90, 100, 107, 139–40
Model Grocer, 45
Moncrief, W. A., 62
Monnig, William, 78, 83, 143
Monnig's, 51–53, 57–58, 117, 132, 133; drugs, 68–69; wholesale, 52–53
Montgomery, Imogene (employee), 169
Montgomery Wards, 52, 74, 94, 127, 130, 164, 192; strategy, 55–56
Morgan, James (employee), 45, 66
Morse, H. H., 147
Mrs. Baird's, 48
M-System, 42

Nash Hardware Company, 71
National Clothing Co., 54–55
National Department Stores, 115
Neiman Marcus, 185
Newsome, Wilbur (employee), 94
Nisbet, Elizabeth Dixon (employee), 193
Nordin, Margery (employee), 195
Norris, J. Frank, **102**, 153
Northeast Texas: cities, 19; economy and railroads, 16, 18–21; and Leonards's employees, 69; map, 17; race relations, 24, 142, 144. *See also* cotton; Linden, Texas

O'Daniel, W. Lee "Pappy," 113
Oliver, Woody (employee), 167
Overcash, Clifton "Clif" (employee), 159–60, 162–63, 165, 174, 188; background, 140–41

Packing House Market, 45
Penney's. *See* J. C. Penney
Pierce, Harold, 112
Piggly Wiggly: in Fort Worth, 42, 47; strategy, 56, 41, 49, 126
Plummer, Ralph, 149

Pope, Lena, 78, 82. *See also* Lena Pope Home
Powell, Connie (employee), 107
Preston Geren (architecture firm), 167
prohibition: in Northeast Texas, 24–25; and Marvin, 25, 63, 65
Puckett, Earl B., 114–15
Pyle, Vera (employee), 156, 195

R. E. Cox. *See* Cox's
retailing industry: and chain stores, 54–58, 132, 164, 192; continuous adaptation, 4–5, 51–58, 93, 94–95, 132, 160–61; and department stores, 103; and discount stores, 164; and fashion, 52–53, 118, 132, 160; in Fort Worth, 32–33, 37; in Northeast Texas, 25–27; rivalry and market positioning, 52–58, 132, 160; and salvage, 37; and suburban shopping malls, 185, 195; and World War I, 38. *See also* individual stores; cash-only stores; chain stores; furnishing merchants; grocery industry
Richardson, Sid, 143
Richeson, Doris, 127
Ridgmar: commercial property, 183–84; development and Marvin, 180–86; location, 179; map, 181; and Westover Hills, 151
Ringler, Charles, 129, 144, 145; background, 128; contribution to Leonards, 128, 138, 153
River Crest Country Club, 79, 83
Robertson, Alma Bennett (employee), 88–89
Rooke, Harry (employee), 129
Rosenthal's Furniture, 87
Ross, Fred J., 126
Rossoff, Raymond, 116
Rouer, R. E., 67
Rubin, Benny, 98–99, 107

Safeway, 127, 133–34
St. Clair, R. D. T. "Doc" (employee), 75, 93–94, 98, 125–26, 130, 140, 158, 163; background, 71; and the Farm Store,

104–105; as merchandise manager, 100–101
Saint James Baptist Church, 63
Sandegard's, 38, 41. *See also* Harry J. Adams
Sanger Brothers, 51, 54, 57
Saunders, 46–49
Schnadig, Edgar, 116
Scull, E. H., 106, 114–17
Sears, 127, 164, 185, 192
Seventh Street Gang, 143, 185
Shady Oaks Country Club: design and location, 149–50; map, 148, 188; Marvin and management, 186–87, 194; membership, 150–51; and Ridgmar, 180; sale to members, 150, 185–87
Shea, Ray (employee), 130–31, 139, 140–41, 159
S. H. Kress, 54, 74, 129
Shockley, Lee Roy (employee), 69
Shockley, Lloyd (employee), 69
Small, Hugh, 63
Small, P. J., 67
Smith, Al (employee), 90
Southern Wholesale Grocery Company, 49. *See also* Leonards: wholesale operations
S. S. Kresge, 54, 141
Stahala, Bob, 151, 182
Starr Hollow Ranch, 188, 190, 196–97
Star-Telegram, 52–53
State Welfare Board. *See* Leonard, Marvin: community service
Stocks, C. L. (employee), 99–100
Stripling, W. K., 143
Stripling's, 51, 57, 99, 117, 132, 143, 185, 189; wholesale, 52
Style Shop, The, 52
Symington, Catherine, 76

Target, 194
Texas Co-operative Supply Co., 43

Thomas, J. B., 143
Tolar, Texas. *See* Starr Hollow Ranch
Toyland, **10,** 93–94, 144, 194
Trav Daniels Sporting Goods Company, 71
Turner and Dingee, 38–39, 41. *See also* H. H. Pittman
Tyree, Laura Mae (Moulton, daughter of Enola), 82

Uberman, Sid, 185
Union Clothing Company, 55

Vaughan, Annie May (mother of Mary Vaughan Leonard), 82
Vaughan, Frank O. (Father of Mary Vaughan Leonard), 82
Vogue, The, 52

Waggoner, W. T., 78
Wal-Mart, 94, 127; comparison to Leonards, 190–94
Walton, Sam, 94, 190, 192, 195
Wards. *See* Montgomery Wards
Washer Brothers, 52–53, 117
Webber, Bobby, 144
Wess, Harold B., 115
Western Auto, 55
Whitley, Tom (employee), 182
Wingate, Lucas, 143
Winters, Jim (employee), 107
Witcher, Janie (employee), 99
Wood, Craig, 112
Woolworth's. *See* F. W. Woolworth & Co.
Wright, Jim, 143
W. T. Farley, 54
W. T. Grant, 54–55, 74

Young, Travis P. (employee), 127–28

Zachery, Mack, 108

**KENNETH E. MONTAGUE
SERIES IN OIL AND BUSINESS HISTORY**

Hyman, Harold M. *Oleander Odyssey: The Kempners of Galveston, Texas, 1854–1980s.* 1990.

McDaniel, Robert W., with Henry C. Dethloff. *Pattillo Higgins and the Search for Texas Oil.* 1989.

Malavis, Nicholas G. *Bless the Pure and Humble: Texas Lawyers and Oil Regulation, 1919–1936.* 1996.

Margavio, Anthony V., and Craig J. Forsyth. *Caught in the Net: The Conflict between Shrimpers and Conservationists.* 1996.

Miles, Ray. *"King of the Wildcatters": The Life and Times of Tom Slick, 1883–1930.* 1996.

Pratt, Joseph A., and Christopher J. Castaneda. *Builders: Herman and George R. Brown.* 1999.